AF806969

CORE TAX ANNUALS

Income Tax 2010/11

CORE TAX ANNUALS

Income Tax 2010/11

Sarah Laing CTA

Series General Editor: Mark McLaughlin CTA (Fellow) ATT TEP

Bloomsbury Professional

Bloomsbury Professional Ltd, Maxwelton House, 41–43 Boltro Road, Haywards Heath, West Sussex, RH16 1BJ

A CIP Catalogue record for this book is available from the British Library.

ISBN: 978 1 84766 513 3

Typeset by Phoenix Photosetting, Chatham, Kent

Printed in the UK by CPI William Clowes Beccles NR34 7TL

Preface

Income Tax 2010/11 is the fifth edition of this publication and is part of the Core Tax Annual series now published by Bloomsbury Professional. The book is designed to provide a clear, concise reference to all aspects of income tax law and practice, with cross-references to legislation, case law, and other source material.

Changes implemented by the *Finance Act 2010*, which received Royal Assent on 8 April 2010, and *Finance (No 2) Act 2010*, which received Royal Assent on 27 July 2010, are fully reflected throughout. This edition also makes reference to various proposed changes that were announced in the new government's emergency Budget on 22 June 2010, but which will be legislated for in a third 2010 Finance Bill, currently planned for the autumn of 2010.

Although *Income Tax 2010/11* is part of Bloomsbury Professional's Core Tax Annuals series (see back cover for further details), it is also a useful stand-alone guide to the UK's income tax system. Readers will hopefully find it easy to navigate and more digestible than other reference material. The objective of the book is to provide an easy-to-use, straightforward solution to many common income tax issues, with an emphasis on practical rather than theoretical points. Bullet points, checklists, summaries, worked examples and tables have been used throughout to aid comprehension.

I hope that you find this book useful. We always welcome any comments or suggestions for future editions.

Sarah Laing CTA

August 2010

Contents

Table of statutes

[*All references are to paragraph numbers*]

Table of statutory instruments

[All references are to paragraph numbers]

Table of cases

[All references are to paragraph numbers]

List of abbreviations

AIA	annual investment allowance
ASP	alternatively secured pension
CA	Court of Appeal
CAA 2001	Capital Allowances Act 2001
CDFI	Community Development Finance Institution
CGT	capital gains tax
CIS	Construction Industry Scheme
CPA 2004	Civil Partnership Act 2004
CTA 2009	Corporation Tax Act 2009
CTA 2010	Corporation Tax Act 2010
CTC	child tax credit
CTF	child trust fund
CTT	capital transfer tax
DTA	double taxation agreement
EIS	Enterprise Investment Scheme
FA	Finance Act
FOTRA	free of tax to residents abroad
FYA	first-year allowance
HMRC	Her Majesty's Revenue and Customs
ICTA 1988	Income and Corporation Taxes Act 1988
IHT	inheritance tax
IHTA 1984	Inheritance Tax Act 1984
IHTM	Inheritance Tax Manual
IRC	Inland Revenue Commissioners
ITA 2007	Income Tax Act 2007
ITEPA 2003	Income Tax (Earnings and Pensions) Act 2003
ITTOIA 2005	Income Tax (Trading and Other Income) Act 2005
NIC	National Insurance contributions
NICA 2006	National Insurance Contributions Act 2006
PACE 1984	Police and Criminal Evidence Act 1984
PAYE	Pay As You Earn
PIBS	permanent interest-bearing shares
PILON	payment in lieu of notice
POAT	pre-owned asset tax
RBC	remittance basis charge
reg	regulation
RQE	residue of qualifying expenditure
s	section
SAYE	Save As You Earn
Sch	Schedule
SCO	Special Compliance Office

SDLT	Stamp Duty Land Tax
SERPS	State Earnings Related Pensions Scheme
SI	Statutory Instrument
SLD	student loan deductions
SAP	statutory adoption pay
SMP	statutory maternity pay
SP	HMRC Statement of Practice
SPP	statutory paternity pay
SSCBA 1992	Social Security Contributions and Benefits Act 1992
SSP	statutory sick pay
STIU	Special Trades Investigation Unit
TA 1925	Taxes Act 1925
TCEA 2007	Tribunals, Courts and Enforcement Act 2007
TCGA 1992	Taxation of Chargeable Gains Act 1992
TIOPA 2010	Taxation (International and Other Provisions) Act 2010
TMA 1970	Taxes Management Act 1970
TME	trustees' management expenses
VATA 1994	Value Added Tax Act 1994
VCT	venture capital trust
WDA	writing down allowance
WTC	working tax credit

Chapter 1

The UK tax system

INTRODUCTION

Who is liable?

1.1 The following are liable to income tax:

- individuals (including children, although the child's income may be treated as the parent's income, where the capital which gave rise to the income was provided by the parent, if the income exceeds £100 per parent in any tax year (*ITTOIA 2005, s 629(3)*; *R v Newmarket Income Tax Commrs, ex parte Huxley* 7 TC 49);
- trustees; and
- personal representatives of a deceased individual.

Companies pay corporation tax on profits and gains (see *Corporation Tax 2010/11* Bloomsbury Professional), but may suffer income tax (eg on investment income) and may be required to account for income tax on certain payments.

What is chargeable?

1.2 Income tax is charged broadly on the worldwide income of UK residents, subject to certain exceptions for individuals who are not ordinarily resident or not domiciled in the UK. A non-resident is generally only liable to income tax on UK income (see **Chapter 9**). Where the same income is liable to both UK and foreign tax, double taxation relief is generally available (HMRC Booklet HMRC6: *Residence, domicile and the remittance basis*).

If a receipt is classified as a capital receipt, it will generally be taxable in accordance with the capital gains tax rules (see *Capital Gains Tax 2010/11* Bloomsbury Professional).

Before 6 April 2005, the tax legislation classified categories of income under separate headings called 'Schedules', sometimes subdivided into 'Cases', each with a different set of income tax rules. These rules were replaced for income tax purposes, following a rewrite of the tax legislation, to make the tax law clearer and easier to use. Schedules A, D, F and D Case VI under the old rules are referred to as property income, trading income, investment income and miscellaneous income respectively under the rewritten legislation (*ITTOIA 2005, ss 1, 629*).

The tax year

1.3 The tax year runs from 6 April to 5 April in the following year. The tax year 2010/11 runs from 6 April 2010 to 5 April 2011.

Notification of sources of income

1.4 An individual who is:

- chargeable to income tax (or capital gains tax) for a tax year; and
- has not received a notice from HMRC requiring the completion of a tax return,

must notify HMRC that he is chargeable to tax by 5 October following the end of the relevant tax year in which his income (or gains) arose.

However, notification is not required where the income comes from certain sources (eg employment income dealt with under PAYE, or investment income taxed at source) and the individual is not a higher or additional rate taxpayer, and where there are no chargeable gains (*TMA 1970, s 7*).

Acts of Parliament

1.5 Tax law is published primarily through statutes. The major statutes are as follows:

- the *Income and Corporation Taxes Act 1988 (ICTA 1988)*, although much of the legislation contained in this Act has now been rewritten into *ITEPA 2003*, *ITTOIA 2005* and *ITA 2007* for income tax purposes, and into *CTA 2009*, *CTA 2010* and *TIOPA 2010* for corporation tax purposes;
- the *Corporation Tax Act 2009 (CTA 2009)*;
- the *Corporation Tax Act 2010 (CTA 2010)*;
- the *Taxation (International and Other Provisions) Act 2010 (TIOPA 2010)*;
- the *Taxation of Chargeable Gains Act 1992 (TCGA 1992)*;
- the *Income Tax (Earnings and Pensions) Act 2003 (ITEPA 2003)*;

- the *Income Tax (Trading and Other Income) Act 2005 (ITTOIA 2005)*;
- the *Income Tax Act 2007 (ITA 2007)*;
- the *Inheritance Tax Act 1984 (IHTA 1984)* (previously known as the *Capital Transfer Tax Act 1984*);
- the *Value Added Tax Act 1994 (VATA 1994)*; and
- the *Social Security Contributions and Benefits Act 1992 (SSCBA 1992).*

The *Taxes Management Act 1970 (TMA 1970)*, the *Customs and Excise Management Act 1979*, and the *Social Security Administration Act 1992* regulate the institutions involved in the imposing and collecting of the main taxes, and the *Capital Allowances Act 2001 (CAA 2001)* the granting of capital allowances.

The *Commissioners for Revenue and Customs Act 2005* provides the legal basis for the integrated department, Her Majesty's Revenue and Customs (HMRC), and the independent prosecutions office, Revenue and Customs Prosecutions Office.

Income tax is imposed each year by way of a Finance Act (though the legislation authorises the continuity of the operation of the administrative machinery). The Finance Acts also make amendment to the other main statutes and provide additional rules to implement government policy changes or to target avoidance. Social security changes are made by statutes other than the annual Finance Act.

Introduction of income tax

1.6 Income tax was first introduced as a temporary measure by William Pitt in order to help finance the Napoleonic wars. Unfortunately, a tax on income meant that it became necessary for an individual to declare his income. This was most unpopular and when the then prime minister, Henry Addington, reintroduced income tax in 1803 he chose a method of classifying income by its source and charged each source of income separately under a Schedule. Using this method, a taxpayer's total income could not be ascertained without assessing and computing his income under each source or Schedule.

Income tax was last introduced by Sir Robert Peel in 1842 as a three-year temporary measure, but it has been with us ever since. There have been four consolidations since 1842, in the *Income Tax Acts 1918* and *1952* and in the *Income and Corporation Taxes Acts 1970* and *1988.*

The Tax Law Rewrite Project has been rewriting existing tax legislation into a more logical and 'user-friendly' format. The publication of the *Income*

Tax (Earnings and Pensions) Act 2003 (ITEPA 2003) covers income from employments, pensions and social security benefits and replaces the former Schedule E. The *Income Tax (Trading and Other Income) Act 2005 (ITTOIA 2005)* covers income from trades, professions and vocations, savings income and investments. It replaced the six cases of former Schedule D and Schedule F. The *Income Tax Act 2007 (ITA 2007)*, which took effect from 6 April 2007, covers basic provisions about the charge to income tax, income tax rates, the calculation of income tax liability and personal reliefs; various specific reliefs (including relief for losses, the enterprise investment scheme, venture capital trusts, community investment tax relief, interest paid, Gift Aid and gifts of assets to charities); specific rules about trusts, deduction of tax at source, manufactured payments and repos, the accrued income scheme and tax avoidance; and general income tax definitions.

Liability to income tax

1.7 Income tax is a tax on income, but also on some capital receipts.

The taxation of employment income is generally charged under the provisions of *ITEPA 2003* from 6 April 2003.

The *Income Tax (Trading and Other Income) Act 2005 (ITTOIA 2005)* took effect from 6 April 2005. The Act covers the taxation of trading, property, savings and investment, and miscellaneous income.

Certain persons are exempt from all taxes on income and gains, while some are specifically exempt from income tax. Certain income is also exempt from income tax.

Provision for charge

1.8

Property income	Formerly Schedule A. Rents (and other receipts) from UK land and buildings; see **Chapter 7**, Property business profits and losses
Trading income	Formerly Schedule D, Case I and II; see **Chapter 6**, Starting a business
Savings and investment income	Formerly Schedule D, Case III, IV and V; see **Chapter 3**, Savings and investments
Miscellaneous income	Formerly Schedule D, Case VI
Employment income	Formerly Schedule E; see **Chapter 5**, Employment, including:

	Earnings of an employee resident and ordinarily resident in the UK (other than 'foreign emoluments' (ie earnings of non-UK domiciled employees from non-UK resident employers) earned wholly abroad)
	Earnings of an employee not resident (or resident but not ordinarily resident) in the UK
	'Foreign emoluments' of an employee resident in the UK, which are remitted to the UK
Investment income	Formerly Schedule F. Dividends and distributions of UK resident companies

Note that there is no longer a Schedule B (abolished from 1988) or Schedule C (abolished from 1996).

Basis of charge

1.9 An individual's taxable income is broadly calculated by (*ITA 2007, s 23*):

- adding together the amounts under the various categories of income for that tax year;
- reducing this amount by certain allowable deductions and personal allowances to arrive at total taxable income;
- applying the tax rates in force for the tax year to the total taxable income; and
- reducing the tax calculated by certain other deductions and allowances (if available).

See **1.48**, How income tax is calculated, generally for further details.

Exempt income

1.10 Certain types of income are exempt from income tax, including the following:

- compensation for loss of office (up to £30,000) (see **Chapter 5**, Termination payments);
- income from certain investments (see **Chapter 3**, Taxable and exempt income);
- premium bond prizes;
- casual winnings from competitions and betting;

- maintenance payments;
- statutory redundancy payments (see **Chapter 5**, Termination payments);
- certain social security benefits (eg income support) are not taxable; however, various other state benefits (eg jobseeker's allowance) are taxable;
- scholarship income;
- repayment supplement in respect of tax overpayments (including most VAT repayments);
- benefits payable under certain sickness and unemployment insurance policies;
- certain types of pension (eg to war widows, wound and disability pensions to members of the armed forces, and pensions awarded to employees disabled at work);
- damages and compensation for personal injury (including annuities or periodical payments received as damages);
- compensation for certain mis-sold personal pensions;
- housing grants;
- compensation paid by banks on unclaimed accounts opened by Holocaust victims and frozen during World War II;
- the first £70 interest on a National Savings Bank ordinary account (new accounts no longer available) and interest on National Savings Certificates; and
- interest on damages for personal injuries.

Basis of charge – example

1.11

Example 1.1

In 2010/11 a single person aged under 65 receives income from employment of £15,000, net rental income of £3,650, income from writing occasional articles of £650 and net building society interest of £352. His income tax liability for 2010/11 is as follows:

	£	£
Income		
Income from employment (tax deducted under PAYE £1,705.00)		15,000.00
Income from UK land and property		3,650.00

	£	£
Other income		650.00
UK interest	352.00	
Tax deducted at source	88.00	
		440.00
Total income		19,740.00
Less personal allowance		6,475.00
Taxable income		£13,265.00
Income tax due		
£13,265 at 20%		2,653.00
Less tax deducted at source		
PAYE	1,705.00	
Building society interest	88.00	1,793.00
Total tax due		£860.00

Taxation of spouses

1.12 A husband and wife, and civil partners, are treated as independent taxpayers. This applies for income tax, CGT and inheritance tax. This independent treatment affects a number of reliefs but principally the 'personal allowances' (see **1.18**) and the capital gains tax annual exemption.

If, after 1989/90, a husband and his wife who is 'living with' him are beneficially entitled to income from property held in their names, they will be treated as entitled to it in equal shares unless they make a joint declaration (on form 17) to the contrary (*ITA 2007, s 836*). The declaration has effect in relation to income arising on or after its date; however, a declaration made before 6 June 1990 also had retrospective effect. The declaration is ineffective if (*ITA 2007, s 836(3)*):

- notice of it is not given to the inspector (on form 17) within 60 days of its making; or
- the spouses' interests in the property do not correspond to their interests in the income.

Once validly made, the declaration continues in effect unless and until the spouses' interests in either the income or capital cease to accord with the declaration.

From 6 April 2004, distributions (usually dividends) from jointly-owned shares in close companies are no longer automatically split 50/50 between husband

and wife but are taxed according to the actual proportions of ownership and entitlement to the income (*ITA 2007, s 837*).

Taxation of minors

1.13 There is a statutory duty on 'every person ... who is chargeable' (*TMA 1970, s 7(1)*) to income tax or CGT for a particular tax year and who has not received a notice to make a return of his total income and gains to give notice of his chargeability to HMRC not later than six months after the end of that year. 'Every person ... chargeable' includes a child under the age of 18: in effect the obligation to make a return in respect of non-settled property will fall upon the child's parent or guardian. Such a parent, etc may also be held responsible for any tax chargeable on the child (*TMA 1970, s 73*; see also *R v Newmarket Income Tax Commrs, ex parte Huxley* (1916) 7 TC 49).

Same-sex couples

1.14 The *Civil Partnership Act 2004 (CPA 2004)*, which gave legal recognition to same-sex couples, came into force on 5 December 2005. Broadly, the Act allows same-sex couples to make a formal legal commitment to each other by entering into a civil partnership through a registration process. A range of important rights and responsibilities flows from this, including legal rights and protections. For tax purposes, civil partners are now treated the same as husband and wife couples. For example, where one of the partners was born before 6 April 1935, the partners are entitled to an allowance equivalent to the married couple's allowance (*SI 2005/3229, SI 2005/3230*) (see **1.19**).

INCOME OR CAPITAL

Distinction

1.15 Tax legislation generally makes a distinction between income and capital items when analysing receipts and expenditure.

Revenue receipts must be distinguished from capital receipts, because it is normally only revenue receipts which are chargeable to income tax.

In general, a sum which is derived from the sale of a capital item will not give rise to an income receipt, but it does not follow that what is a capital expense to one party is necessarily a capital receipt to the other party.

What is income and what is capital is a question of law, rather than of fact. However, all of the circumstances surrounding a transaction must be taken into account, and the weight to be given to a particular circumstance depends on common sense, rather than any single legal principle.

The basic principle in determining whether or not a grant was an income or capital receipt was set out in *Glenboig Union Fireclay Co Ltd v IR Commrs* (1921) 12 TC 427 by Lord Wrenbury:

> 'was that compensation profit? The answer may be supplied, I think, by the answer to the following question. Is a sum profit which is paid to an owner of property on the terms that he shall not use his property so as to make a profit? The answer must be in the negative. The whole point is that he is not to make a profit and is paid for abstaining from seeking to make a profit … it was the price paid for sterilising the asset from which otherwise profit might have been obtained.'

The test is, therefore, whether the thing in respect of which the taxpayer has received compensation is either:

- a mere restriction of his trading opportunities; or
- the depreciation of one of the capital assets of his business (*Burmah Steam Ship Co Ltd v IR Commrs* (1931) 16 TC 67).

The following two well-known tests are used for distinguishing a revenue receipt from a capital one, although both are of limited value:

(1) The first test is to distinguish receipts which relate to assets which form part of the permanent structure of the business. An example of this would be machinery, the sale of which would give rise to a capital receipt.

(2) The second test is to distinguish between circulating and fixed capital. A fixed capital asset is retained in the business with the object of making profits. An example of this would again be machinery. Circulating capital, on the other hand, is acquired to be used or sold. An example would be the raw materials used in the business (*ITTOIA 2005, ss 105, 207*).

Capital	**Revenue**
Receipts from sale of business assets	Payments *in lieu* of trading receipts, including:
Sale of fixed assets is a capital receipt although a profit on the sale of trading stock constitutes an income receipt	• agreed damages for loss of profits arising from delay in repairs
Receipts for the sale or destruction of the taxpayer's profit-making apparatus	• damages in excess of repair costs to cover lost profits

Receipts in return for restrictive covenants	• compensation for increased revenue expenditure
Payments received in return for the sterilisation of assets are capital receipts, although treatment of lump sums for 'exclusivity agreements' depends on purpose of payment	• damages for negligence of agents resulting in a trading loss
One-off receipts	• rebates against price due for goods supplied
A one-off receipt strongly, but not conclusively, suggests a capital receipt	Recurring receipts are more likely to be revenue receipts

RELIEFS, ALLOWANCES AND DEDUCTIONS

Introduction

1.16 All UK-resident individuals are entitled to personal allowances (*ITA 2007, s 56*). Personal allowances are given by deduction from total income (*ITA 2007, Pt 3*), but all other allowances are given by way of a credit against an individual's tax liability.

Allowances are normally reflected in a PAYE tax coding, but self-employed taxpayers generally claim personal reliefs and allowances through their self-assessment tax returns.

Certain non-residents are also entitled to personal allowances (see **Chapter 9**). An individual who leaves the UK to take up permanent residence abroad is entitled to full personal allowances for the tax year of departure and an individual who comes to the UK permanently is eligible to full personal allowances from the tax year of arrival (*ITA 2007, s 56*).

Income tax allowances

1.17

	2008/09	2009/10	2010/11
	£	£	£
Personal allowance	6,035	6,475	6,475
Income limit for personal allowance	N/A	N/A	£100,000
Age allowances – persons over 65 (note (a))			

	2008/09	2009/10	2010/11
	£	£	£
Personal allowance – persons 65 to 74	9,030	9,490	9,490
– persons 75 and over	9,180	9,640	9,640
Married couple's allowance: (10%) (note (b))			
– either spouse born before 6.4.1935	6,535	N/A	N/A
– elder spouse 75 and over	6,625	6,965	6,965
Effective maximum income for claims			
Income limit (allowance reduced by 1/2 excess)	21,800	22,900	22,900
Personal allowance – persons 65 to 74	27,790	28,930	28,930
Personal allowance – persons 75 and over	28,090	29,230	29,230
Married couple's allowance – elder spouse born before 6.4.1935			
– income of husband aged 65 to 74	35,780	37,320	37,320
Married couple's allowance – born before 6.4.1935			
– age 75 and over	36,260	37,820	37,820
Married couple's allowance – minimum where income exceeds limits	2,540	2,670	2,670
Blind person's allowance	1,800	1,890	1,890

Notes:

(a) Age-related allowances apply in the first tax year in which the age threshold is reached (*ITA 2007, s 36*).

(b) The married couple's allowance is available only where one party reached the age of 65 by 5 April 2000. Relief is given at 10% of the allowance.

The personal allowance for those aged under 65 will be increased to £7,475 for 2011/12. However, the basic rate band will be reduced from April 2011 so that higher rate taxpayers do not benefit from the increase.

Personal allowance

1.18 The personal allowance is currently available to each individual taxpayer, whether single or married, and is deducted from total income for the tax year (*ITA 2007, s 35*). However, from 2010/11, the basic personal allowance is subject to a single income limit of £100,000. Where an individual's 'adjusted net income' is below or equal to the £100,000 limit, they continue to be entitled to the full amount of the basic personal allowance. If 'adjusted net income' exceeds the £100,000 limit, the personal allowance is reduced by £1 for every £2 above the income limit. The personal allowance may be reduced to nil from this income limit (*FA 2009, s 4*). 'Adjusted net income' is the measure of an individual's income that is used for the calculation of the existing income-related reductions to personal allowances for those aged between 65 and 74, and for those aged 75 and over (see **1.20**).The allowance is increased in the tax year in which the individual reaches the age of 65 and is further increased at the age of 75. However, the higher allowances are reduced if the taxpayer's income exceeds the specified income limit, by half the income in excess of the limit until it reaches the normal personal allowance limit (*ITA 2007, s 36*).

Example 1.2

Susan has 'adjusted net income' in 2010/11 of £107,000, so her income exceeds the £100,000 limit by £7,000. The personal allowance is therefore reduced by half the amount that exceeds £100,000, ie £3,500. Susan is entitled to a personal allowance of £2,975 for 2010/11 (£6,475 – £3,500).

Married couple's allowance

1.19 The married couple's allowance may only be claimed (from 2000/01) if at least one of the parties to the marriage was born before 6 April 1935 (*ITA 2007, s 45(2)(c)*).

Where the marriage or civil partnership was entered into on or after 5 December 2005, the claimant is to be the spouse or civil partner with the highest income for the tax year concerned (*ITA 2007, s 46*). Where the parties to the marriage or civil partnership have the same total income for the year, they are to specify by an election who is to be the claimant for that year (*ITA 2007, s 47*). The allowance will be restricted if the claimant's income for the year exceeds the specified amount. The allowance is given for the year in which the 65th or 75th birthday (as appropriate) falls, or would have fallen but for earlier death in that year.

Unlike the personal allowance, the married couple's allowance is not given as a deduction from total income. Instead, relief is allowed at the rate of 10% of the amount of the allowance by means of a reduction in the claimant's income tax liability (*ITA 2007, s 45*).

Age allowances – income limit

1.20 The higher rate personal allowance and married couple's allowance are restricted to the extent that total income (after allowable deductions but before deducting allowances) exceeds a specified limit (£22,900 for 2009/10 and 2010/11) (*ITA 2007, ss 36(2)* and *37(2)*). In the case of a married couple or civil partnership, the limit applies to each of the spouses or partners (*ITA 2007, ss 45(4)* and *46(4)*).

The allowances are reduced by half of the excess of income over the limit. The reduction in the higher rate personal allowance cannot go beyond that of the amount of the basic personal allowance so that individuals will never receive less than £6,475 for 2009/10 and 2010/11 (*ITA 2007, ss 45(5)* and *46(5)*).

It is always the claimant's income that determines the level of abatement (if any). This is so even if it is the other spouse or civil partner's age that has given entitlement to the higher level of relief. However, the married couple's allowance is only subject to restriction once the claimant's personal allowance has first been reduced to the standard level.

The abatement process cannot reduce the married couple's allowance below the standard amount of that allowance for 1999/2000 and earlier years, or below an equivalent amount for subsequent tax years based on indexation of the 1999/2000 figure of £1,970. For 2009/10 and 2010/11, that indexed figure is £2,670. Any abatement utilised in reducing the claimant's personal allowance cannot also be used to reduce age-related married couple's allowance.

Age allowances – examples

1.21

Example 1.3

Sally, aged 70, has income of £12,000 for 2010/11. She is not married and has no other income. Her income and taxable income for the year will be:

	£
Income	12,000
Less: Allowance	9,490
Taxable income	2,510

Example 1.4

Ruth is 69 and her husband, Stephen, is 76. In 2010/11 Ruth receives a pension of £7,750 and Stephen receives a pension of £25,850. Interest on their joint bank account is £500 (gross). No claim is made to transfer the married couple's allowance.

Their tax position for 2010/11 is as follows:

	Ruth	Stephen
	£	£
Pensions income	7,750	25,850
Personal allowance: basic	(9,490)	(9,640)
Restriction by ½ of £2,950 (down to £6,475)		1,475
	Nil	17,685
Tax thereon:		
£17,685 × 20%		3,537.00
Married couple's allowance £6,965 @ 10%		(696.50)
	Nil	£2,840.50

Both Ruth and Stephen receive higher rate personal age allowances. Stephen's allowance is restricted by half of his excess income over the income limit of £22,900, but not to the extent it would reduce it below the basic allowance of £6,475.

Blind person's allowance

1.22 An allowance (£1,890 for 2009/10 and 2010/11) may be claimed by a blind person, which is given in addition to the personal allowance, and reduces the taxpayer's total income. A married blind person who cannot use all the relief may transfer the unused part to the other spouse (or civil partner), whether the other spouse is blind or not (*ITA 2007, s 39*). A married couple, or civil partners, both of whom qualify for relief, can each claim the allowance.

The allowance can only be claimed by someone who is registered as blind (but not partially sighted). A person may register as blind even if they are not totally without sight. HMRC will, by concession, allow the relief in the previous year if evidence of blindness had already been obtained by the end of it (*ITA 2007, s 38*).

Tax credits

1.23 Working tax credit (WTC) and child tax credit (CTC) are social security benefits, and do not have to be covered by a comparable tax liability. They are not set against an income tax liability, but are paid out directly by HMRC. Prior to 6 April 2006, tax credits could be paid to employees via their wage packets.

Working tax credit – basic element

1.24 Claimants with children or a disability are eligible for WTC provided they work at least 16 hours a week and are aged 16 or over, or qualify for the 50-plus element (see below).

Workers with neither children nor a disability are eligible provided they work at least 30 hours a week and are aged 25 or over. Gaps between jobs of up to seven days are ignored.

Working tax credit – other elements

1.25 Provided they are eligible for the basic element of WTC, claimants to WTC may be entitled to various other elements, based on their circumstances:

- *A second adult element.* This is automatic where a joint claim to WTC is made, unless one of the claimants is over 50 and the 50 plus element is payable (see below).
- *A lone-parent element.* Where a single claim is made and the claimant is responsible for a child or children.
- *A 30-hour element.* This is designed to encourage those with a disability, or families with children, to move to full-time work. Couples with children will be entitled to it if one of the couple works at least 30 hours a week, or if they jointly work 30 hours a week, provided that one of them works at least 16 hours. Note that, for the purposes of claiming the childcare element of WTC, both partners in a couple must work for at least 16 hours a week.
- *A disability element.* Joint claimants may each claim this if they both qualify.
- *A severe disability element.* Joint claimants may each claim this if they both qualify.
- *A 50-plus element.* This is available to those aged 50 or over who are returning to work after 6 April 2003 following a period of at least six months out of the labour market. It is divided into two rates – one for those working at least 16 hours, and one for those working at least 30 hours. Joint claimants may each claim the 50-plus element if they both qualify for it.
- *Childcare element.* Families are eligible for the childcare element where a lone parent or both partners in a couple work at least 16 hours a week. It is paid directly to the main carer by HMRC, either weekly or four-weekly at the claimant's choice. It is worth up to 80% of qualifying childcare costs, although a maximum limit to those costs is set. Childcare costs are calculated on the basis of the average weekly cost, either using

the four weeks immediately prior to the claim, or, in the case of monthly payments, multiplying by 12 and dividing by 52.

- Any 'relevant' change in childcare costs must be reported to HMRC. A relevant change occurs where there is any change in the childcare provided; or there is an increase or decrease in childcare costs of £10 a week or more for a four-week period.
- When a relevant change occurs, the childcare element of WTC must be recalculated. It is important to note that where childcare costs decrease, and, therefore, less WTC is due, the recalculation will be made from the week following the four-week period of the change. Where costs increase, so that more WTC is due, the recalculation is made from the later of:
  - the first day of the week in which the change occurred; and
  - the first day of the week in which falls the date three months prior to the change being notified to HMRC.

Child tax credit

1.26 Child tax credit can be claimed by people who are responsible for one or more children or qualifying young persons (*TCA 2002, s 8(1)*). It is immaterial whether the claimant is in work. In that respect CTC differs from the child elements of the former working families' tax credit (WFTC) which were only available where the claimant, or claimant's partner, was in work (*SI 2002/2007, SI 2003/738*).

Payments are made by HMRC directly to the main carer. Children are eligible up to 1 September following their 16th birthday. The credit remains payable after that date for those in full-time, non-advanced, education up to the age of 19. The usual test to be applied is that the child is 'normally living with' the claimant(s). Where there are competing claims, the test is who has the 'main responsibility' for the child. This is subject to a joint election as to who has the main responsibility but, in the absence of such an election, HMRC will decide on the information available. Child tax credit remains payable for up to eight weeks following the death of a child.

Child tax credit – elements

1.27

- *Family element*. This is the basic element, paid to all families eligible for CTC and taking the place of the children's tax credit. A higher family element is available for the year following the birth of a child.
- *Child element*. A child element for each child in the family.

- *Disabled child element.* Paid where disability living allowance is payable or the child is registered blind.
- *Enhanced disabled child element.* This is payable to families caring for a child with severe disability, where the highest rate of the care component of disability living allowance is payable.

Working tax credit

1.28

Element	2008/09 £	2009/10 £	2010/11 £
Basic element	1,800	1,890	1,920
Disability element (see note below)	2,405	2,530	2,570
30-hour element	735	775	790
Second adult element	1,770	1,860	1,890
Lone-parent element	1,770	1,860	1,890
50-plus element:			
(a) working over 16 but less than 30 hours per week	1,235	1,300	1,320
(b) working over 30 hours per week (see note below)	1,840	1,935	1,965
Childcare element:			
percentage of eligible costs up to weekly maximum of:	80%	80%	80%
(a) for one child	£175	£175	£175
(b) for two or more	£300	£300	£300

From 2012, the 50-plus element will be removed from the working tax credit.

Child tax credit

1.29

Element	**Circumstance**	2008/09 £	2009/10 £	2010/11 £
Family	Family element	545	545	545
	Family element, baby addition	545	545	545

Element	Circumstance	2008/09 £	2009/10 £	2010/11 £
Individual	Each child or young person	2,085	2,235	2,300
	Each disabled child or young person	2,540	2,670	2,715
	Each severely disabled child or young person	1,020	1,075	1,095

The baby addition will be abolished from April 2011.

Income thresholds and withdrawal rates

1.30

	2008/09	2009/10	2010/11
First income threshold	£6,420	£6,420	£6,420
First withdrawal rate	39%	39%	39%
Second income threshold	£50,000	£50,000	£50,000
Second withdrawal rate	6.67%	6.67%	6.67%
First threshold for those entitled to:			
child tax credit only	£15,575	£16,040	£16,190
Income disregard	£25,000	£25,000	£25,000

From April 2011, the income threshold for the withdrawal of the family element of child tax credit will be reduced from £50,000 to £40,000, and the withdrawal rate will be increased from 6.67% to 41%.

The withdrawal rate for the other tax credits will rise to 41% (from 39%), and the income disregard will drop from £25,000 to £10,000, both from April 2011.

HMRC guidance on tax credits

1.31 The following leaflets are available to download, in Portable Document Format (PDF), from www.hmrc.gov.uk/taxcredits/forms-and-leaflets/leaflets.htm:

Tax credits: How HMRC handle tax credit overpayments (December 2009)

WTC1: Child Tax Credit and Working Tax Credit. An introduction (April 2010)

WTC2: A guide to Child Tax Credit and Working Tax Credit (April 2010)

WTC5: Working Tax Credit – Help with the costs of childcare (June 2010)

WTC5/CP: Working Tax Credit – The childcare element – Information for childcare providers (August 2010)

WTC6: Child Tax Credit and Working Tax Credit. Other types of help you could get (April 2010)

WTC7: Tax Credits penalties. What happens at the end of a check (April 2010)

WTC8: Child Tax Credit and Working Tax Credit – How do overpayments happen? (June 2009)

WTC9: Could you get help with your everyday costs? (April 2010)

WTC10: Tax Credits – Help us to help you get it right (July 2009)

WTC/AP: Child Tax Credit and Working Tax Credit: how to appeal against a tax credit decision or award. This leaflet explains in detail how to make an appeal against a Child Tax Credit or Working Tax Credit notice. (April 2009)

WTC/FS1: Tax credits enquiry (April 2010)

WTC/FS2: Tax credits examinations (April 2010)

WTC/FS3: Tax credits formal request for information (July 2010)

WTC/FS4: Tax credits meetings (May 2006)

WTC/FS5: Tax credits – coming to the UK (December 2008)

WTC/FS6: Tax credits – leaving the UK (December 2008)

COP26: What happens if we've paid you too much tax credit? (July 2010) is a code of practice setting out how HMRC will deal with overpayments of tax credit. A form TC846 'Recovery of overpaid tax credits disputed (Request to reconsider)' is also available (January 2010).

Foster carers' relief

Relief

1.32 A relief for foster carers was introduced with effect from 6 April 2003 (*ITTOIA 2005, s 803 et seq*). The relief applies to individuals who provide foster care services to local authorities, either directly or indirectly (*ITTOIA 2005, s 804*).

The relief replaced the previous treatment of income from fostering. It consists of two elements:

- foster carers whose gross receipts from foster care do not exceed an individual limit (see below) in a year will be exempt from tax on their income from foster care; and

- foster carers whose gross receipts from foster care exceed the individual limit may choose between:
  - computing their business profits using the normal rules; or
  - treating as their profit the amount by which their gross receipts from foster care exceed their individual limit.

The individual limit is made up of two elements (*ITTOIA 2005 s 808*):

- a fixed amount per residence of £10,000 for a full year; and
- an additional amount per child for each week, or part-week, that the individual provides foster care. The amounts are £200 a week for a child aged under 11 and £250 a week for a child aged 11 or older (see **Example 1.6**).

Exemption

1.33 Where an individual's total foster care receipts do not exceed his limit, those receipts will be exempt from tax altogether for that year. The mechanism for granting exemption is to treat the profits or losses of the trade as nil. The mechanism for relief is not optional in these circumstances – if the receipts are less than the income limit then it is not possible to claim relief for any loss actually incurred.

The method of calculation varies according to whether or not accounts are drawn up to 5 April. Where the accounting year end is 5 April, or where the profits are calculated simply by reference to the tax year, an individual's foster care receipts will be exempt from tax if his total foster care receipts do not exceed his limit. His limit for the tax year in question is calculated as his share of the fixed amount, plus each amount per child.

Example 1.5

Anne and Carol live together. Anne has fostered children for many years and Carol now starts to act as a foster parent too. Carol's basis period for the year in question is 270 days.

Anne's share of the fixed amount is £5,000. Carol's share for the first period of her trade is £3,699 ((£10,000/2) × 270/365).

Example 1.6

Angela is a foster carer throughout the tax year. She fosters a ten-year-old boy for 30 weeks and a 14-year-old girl for 40 weeks during the year. Nobody else provides foster care from her home.

Angela's fixed amount is £10,000.

The 'amount per child' for the boy is £6,000 (30 weeks at £200 per week) and for the girl £10,000 (40 weeks at £250 per week).

Angela's limit is therefore calculated as £16,000.

If Angela draws accounts up to 5 April, and her total receipts are under £16,000, the foster income is exempt from tax.

Community investment tax relief

1.34 Community investment tax relief applies to investments made on or after 17 January 2002 (*ITA 2007, ss 333–382*).

The scheme borrows much from the Enterprise Investment Scheme (EIS) (see **Chapter 3**) with the position of the SME company in that scheme being taken by an accredited Community Development Finance Institution (CDFI). The investment in the CDFI may be in the form of a loan, shares or securities held for a five-year period.

The investor, which may be a company or an individual, can claim tax relief of up to 25% of the amount invested once a tax relief certificate has been issued by the CDFI, but the tax relief must be spread over the five-year term of the investment giving only 5% tax relief per year. The tax relief reduces the investor's tax liability, and is limited by the amount of that liability. If the investor receives any significant value from the CDFI within a six-year period starting one year before the date of the investment, the tax relief is withdrawn.

Tax relief under this scheme must be claimed on an annual basis at the rate of 5% of the 'invested amount' for the tax year (or accounting period for a corporate investor) in which the investment date falls and the four subsequent tax years (or accounting periods). If the investment was by way of a loan, the 'invested amount' will not necessarily be the amount of the loan made available at the beginning of the five-year investment period. The tax relief due under this scheme is a tax reducer rather than an allowance, so it cannot reduce the taxpayer's tax liability below zero.

The investor must receive a tax relief certificate from the CDFI before claiming any tax relief in respect of the investment.

1.35 For shares and securities the invested amount will normally be the amount subscribed for in cash. However, where the investor has received a significant receipt of value (see below) which does not exceed the permitted levels, the invested amount is treated as being reduced by the amount of value received.

Since an investment made as a loan may be drawn down over an 18-month period and repaid in stages (see conditions of investment below), the 'invested amount' for the tax years or accounting periods corresponding to the five-year investment period is determined according to the average balance of the loan in the relevant 12-month investment period as follows:

- nothing repayable in the first two years after investment;
- in the third year, up to 25% of the capital outstanding after two years;
- in the fourth year, up to 50% of the outstanding loan; and
- in the fifth year, up to 75% of the outstanding loan.

Example 1.7

Alfie makes a loan of £100,000 to P Ltd, an accredited CDFI. The loan is repayable at the rate of £10,000 per year the beginning of year 3. In year 5 the loan is increased to £150,000. The tax relief due is calculated as follows:

Year	Average capital balance of loan in the relevant investment period	Tax relief due at 5% of capital balance in the relevant investment period
1	£100,000	£5,000
2	£100,000	£5,000
3	£90,000	£4,500
4	£80,000	£4,000
5	*see below	£5,000

*Relief in year 5 is the lower of average capital balance for:

– the year that falls in this tax year – £150,000; and

– the six months beginning 18 months after the investment date – £100,000.

Interest relief

1.36 Income tax relief (at various effective rates) is available for an interest payment if it relates to one of the specified categories of loan (see **1.37** below) (*ITA 2007, s 383*).

Relief is not granted in the following circumstances (*ITA 2007, s 384*):

- where interest is paid on an overdraft or under credit card arrangements;
- where interest is paid at a rate greater than a reasonable commercial rate (in which case the excess is ineligible for relief);
- where the main benefit of the arrangement is the reduction of tax; or
- where relief is sought by a company within the charge to corporation tax.

Interest paid as a revenue rather than capital item on money borrowed wholly and exclusively for the purposes of a trade, profession or vocation is not subject to the foregoing restrictions.

There are provisions intended to prevent any double deductions for interest.

Where only part of a loan satisfies the conditions for interest relief, only a proportion of the interest will be eligible for relief. That proportion is one which is equal to the proportion of the loan fulfilling those conditions at the time the money is applied.

Full interest relief is generally available on a joint loan to a husband and wife (or civil partner) where only one of them satisfies the qualifying conditions as respects investment in a close company or partnership and that spouse makes the payments or they are made out of a joint account.

Relief generally takes the form of a deduction from or offset against total income in respect of the interest paid. However, as with mortgage interest, if relief is not available at source, relief for interest on a loan to purchase a life annuity is given by way of a reduction in the income tax otherwise payable, though the rate of relief in this case remains the basic rate; an effective order of offset of reliefs is provided. Any necessary apportionment of the interest where a loan is used for the purpose of purchasing such an annuity and for other qualifying purposes is made on a specified basis.

Categories of qualifying loan

1.37 Interest relief is available on loans applied for the following purposes:

- to purchase machinery and plant (*ITA 2007, s 388*);
- in acquiring an interest in a close company (*ITA 2007, s 392*);
- in acquiring an interest in a co-operative (*ITA 2007, s 401*);
- in acquiring shares in an employee-controlled company (*ITA 2007, s 402*);
- in acquiring an interest in a partnership (*ITA 2007, s 398*); or
- to pay inheritance tax (*ITA 2007, s 403*).

The giving of credit to a purchaser under any sale is treated as the making of a loan to defray money applied by him in making the purchase.

Interest on loan to invest in an employee-controlled company – conditions

1.38 Interest may be eligible for income tax relief if it is paid on a loan made to an individual to acquire ordinary shares in an employee-controlled company or to pay off another loan which would have qualified for interest relief. Relief will only be given if the following conditions are satisfied:

(1) the company must be (from the date on which the shares are acquired to the date on which interest is paid) (*ITA 2007, s 397(2)*):

   (a) an unquoted company resident only in the UK; and

   (b) a trading company or the holding company of a trading company;

(2) the shares must be acquired before, or not later than 12 months after, the date on which the company first becomes an employee-controlled company;

(3) during the tax year in which the interest is paid, the company must either (*ITA 2007, s 397(3)*):

   (a) first become an employee-controlled company, or

   (b) be employee-controlled throughout a period of at least nine months;

(4) the individual must be a full-time employee of the company from the date of buying the shares to the date on which the interest is paid. Relief will continue to be given for interest paid up to 12 months after the taxpayer has ceased to be a full-time employee (*ITA 2007, s 397(4)*);

(5) the taxpayer must not have recovered any capital from the company unless that amount is treated as a repayment of the loan in whole or in part (*ITA 2007, s 406*).

Relief for gains on life policies and investment bonds

1.39 Gains on certain life assurance policies, life annuity contracts and capital redemption policies (including 'investment bonds') are subject to higher rate tax as income of an individual.

Relief is afforded to such gains by way of top-slicing relief. The gain which is charged is averaged over the years the investment has been held and it is only then added to the individual's other income for the tax year in point to determine whether higher rate tax is payable. Any higher rate tax so calculated is then multiplied by the number of years the investment has been held (*ITTOIA 2005, Pt 4, Ch 9*).

Payments to a trade union, police organisations or friendly society for death benefits

1.40 Relief is available of 50% of that part of a payment of a member's contribution to a trade union or police organisation allocated to superannuation, funeral expenses or life assurance benefits (*ITA 2007, ss 457* and *458*). The maximum amount of relief to which an individual is entitled for a tax year is £100.

Maintenance payments

1.41 Tax relief for maintenance payments was generally withdrawn from 6 April 2000. However, relief is still available if one or both of the parties to the marriage was aged 65 or over at 5 April 2000. Where the relief still applies, the payer is entitled to tax relief in 2010/11 at 10% for qualifying maintenance payments up to the first £2,670. The maximum tax reduction in 2010/11 is therefore £267. All maintenance received after 5 April 2000 is non-taxable income (*ITA 2007, s 453*).

Post-cessation expenses

1.42 Relief for expenses related to a business incurred within seven years after trading has ceased, is given against income and capital gains of the year in which the expense is paid (*ITTOIA 2005, s 250*). Any expenses which cannot be relieved in this way can only be set against any post-cessation receipts arising from the business.

The expenses allowed are those amounts spent:

- in remedying, or as damages for, defective work done, goods supplied or services rendered in the course of the former business activity;
- for legal or professional services in connection with any claim that the work, goods or services were defective;
- for insurance against expenses described above;
- recovering debts which have been included in business profits before cessation; and
- debts which have been included in business profits before cessation but which have subsequently (within seven years of cessation) become bad debts or have been released under a formal voluntary arrangement.

Claims must be made through the self-assessment return form within 12 months of the filing date (ie for expenditure in 2010/11, the claim should be made in the 2010/11 return due on 31 January 2012, or notified by way of amendment of the return by 31 January 2013).

Pre-incorporation losses

1.43 Where a claim has been made to carry forward losses from self-employment against future profits but the business has been transferred to a company before all the losses have been used, relief for those losses may be given against income received from the company.

The conditions for relief are that:

- the business must have been transferred to the company wholly or mainly in return for shares in the company (at least 80% of which are retained); and
- the trader continues to be the beneficial owner of the shares and the company must continue trading at least to 5 April following the date of transfer.
- The losses are set:
- first against income from the company which is paid without deduction of tax at source, for example, a salary paid by the company; and
- then against investment income such as dividends, interest or deemed distributions.

Claims must be made through the tax return for the year in which the income is received in the same way as for post-cessation expenses above.

Charitable donations

Payroll giving

1.44 Payroll giving schemes enable full tax relief to be given on donations to charity by employees who authorise their participating employers to deduct the payments from their pay before tax. There is no upper limit for tax relief on donations; employees may give as much as they like under the scheme. Payments by the employer towards the scheme agent's expenses are an allowable deduction for the employer (*ITEPA 2003, ss 713–715*; *ITTOIA 2005, s 72*; *FA 2000, s 38*; *SI 2000/2074*).

The agreed deductions the employer makes from the employee's pay are done before tax is deducted, which means that the employee obtains tax relief included in the donation at his or her top rate of tax. This is illustrated as follows:

Employee's pledge to charity (gross)	Actual cost to employee @ 20% tax	Actual cost to employee@ 40% tax
£5.00	£4.00	£3.00
£10.00	£8.00	£6.00

For example, if an employee pays tax at the basic rate, it will only cost £4.00 to donate £5.00 to the charity of choice as shown in the table above.

The main benefit of payroll giving is to create a regular flow of funds for the benefit of the charity or charities of the employee's.

An individual will be eligible to make donations under a payroll giving scheme provided that they are an employee or pensioner and the employer deducts PAYE tax from their pay or pension.

Most payroll giving agencies make a small charge which they deduct from employee donations before distributing them to charity. The charge is normally no more than 4% of the donation, or 25p per donation, whichever is the greater. Some employers pay the agency's charges so that the full amount of employee donations can go to charity.

'Gift Aid' payments made by individuals

1.45 Individuals can make one-off or regular gifts to charity under the Gift Aid scheme. There is no lower or upper limit on donations upon which tax relief may be claimed. The payment is treated as paid 'net' (ie as if basic rate income tax had been deducted at source). The basic rate tax deemed to have been deducted by the donor is clawed back by HMRC if the donor's income tax and capital gains tax liability for the year is insufficient to match the tax retained. A higher rate taxpayer may claim additional relief against income tax or capital gains tax, as appropriate. Donors may join the Gift Aid scheme by telephone or Internet, and can complete a single declaration to cover a series of donations (*ITA 2007, Pt 8, Ch 2*).

Individual donors making Gift Aid donations can elect for the donation to be treated as paid in the previous tax year. The election must be made to HMRC by the date on which the donor's tax return was submitted for the previous tax year and, in any event, no later than 31 January following that tax year. An election can only be made if the gift could be paid out of taxed income or gains of the previous tax year (*ITA 2007, s 426*).

Individuals may donate tax repayments arising from self-assessment returns to a chosen charity. The charity must be included in a list maintained by HMRC for this purpose, which can be accessed on the HMRC website (www.hmrc.gov.uk). Qualifying donations are treated as eligible for tax relief under the

Gift Aid scheme. Donations do not qualify for tax relief if the donor receives a benefit from the gift in excess of prescribed limits (*ITA 2007, s 429*).

Covenants

1.46 A charitable deed of covenant is a legally binding agreement to transfer income to a charity, which is capable of exceeding three years. Covenants were previously a separate form of charitable gift, but tax relief for donations by deed of covenant is given under the Gift Aid rules from 6 April 2000. However, deeds of covenant set up before that date continue to operate. Covenants are treated as Gift Aid donations.

Other charitable donations

1.47 Income tax relief is available for gifts of stock by businesses, and for gifts of quoted shares and securities. Relief is also available for gifts of land and buildings to charity from 6 April 2002, if certain conditions are satisfied. The relief for donations of shares and securities or land and buildings is given by deduction from total income, rather than by extending the basic rate band (*ITTOIA 2005, ss 107–110*).

Example 1.8

Olivia makes a Gift Aid payment of £1,000 in 2010/11. Her tax position if she is (a) a basic rate taxpayer, and (b) a higher rate taxpayer, is as follows:

	(a) liable at 20%	(b) liable at 40%
	£	£
Payment made to charity	1,000	1,000
20% treated as deducted by taxpayer (paid to the charity by HMRC)	250	250
Total received by charity	1,250	1,250
Tax relief @ 20%/40%	250	500
Net cost to Olivia	1,000	750

If Olivia is a higher rate taxpayer and wishes to pass on the benefit of the higher rate relief to the charity, she should make a payment of £1,334. In that case:

- the total received by the charity would be £1,667 (1,334 × 100/80 (ie 100 – 20));

- Olivia would receive tax relief of £667 (1,667 × 40%);
- leaving a net cost to Olivia of £1,000.

If Olivia is an employee and pays all her tax through the PAYE system, the higher rate relief could be given by a coding adjustment.

Otherwise, she would need to claim relief through the self-assessment return. The gross amount (amount paid plus the basic rate tax credit, ie £1,250 in the above example) is added to the basic rate limit, so that income of £1,250, which would otherwise be taxable at the higher rate, is taxed only at the basic rate. The effect of this (assuming all income is earned income) is to reduce the tax liability by £250, giving total relief on the donation of £250 + £250 = £500 (ie 40% of £1,250).

To compensate for the reduction in the basic rate of tax from 22% to 20% from 6 April 2008 (see **1.51**), charities making Gift Aid repayment claims can claim transitional relief (paid by the government) of 2% on donations between 2008/09 and 2010/11.

HOW INCOME TAX IS CALCULATED

Introduction

1.48 For tax years up to and including 2006/07, taxpayers who submitted their tax returns by 30 September after the tax year could ask HMRC to calculate their tax liability. If their tax return was submitted later than that date, they would usually have to calculate the tax themselves.

Tax returns for 2007/08 onwards made on paper have to be filed by 31 October. So a 2010/11 paper return, for example, will have to be filed by 31 October 2011. The date will be the same for taxpayers who want HMRC to calculate their tax liability (previously 30 September). The filing date of 31 January remains for returns filed online (see **Chapter 2** for further details).

Calculating the tax payable

1.49 Broadly, the tax liability is calculated by:

- working out 'total income' by adding together all the income under the various categories of income, allowing in each case, for any eligible deductions and expenses as well as any taxable benefits and gains;
- deducting from that amount any reliefs (including any Gift Aid donations) to arrive at total income (for the purpose of the age allowance restriction);

- deducting the personal allowance (and blind person's allowance where applicable) to arrive at 'taxable income';
- applying the relevant tax rates to the taxable income to arrive at the tax due;
- deducting from that amount any relief or allowance given as a tax reduction such as Enterprise Investment Scheme relief to arrive at the total tax liability; and
- adding to that amount any notional tax deducted from payments made by the taxpayer, such as on Gift Aid payments, and deducting tax already paid through PAYE, tax deducted at source and foreign taxes paid where applicable.

Student loans

1.50 HMRC is responsible for collecting repayments of student loans taken out by new borrowers after August 1998. An employer must collect student loan repayments through the PAYE system by making deductions of 9% from an employee's pay to the extent that earnings exceed the equivalent of £15,000 a year. This equates to £1,250 a month or £288 a week.

The repayments are otherwise dealt with through the self-assessment system (eg for the self-employed), in which case the repayments broadly equal 9% of total income (excluding unearned income, if it is £2,000 or less) in excess of the £15,000 per annum threshold.

As each pay day is looked at separately, and repayments may vary according to how much the employee has been paid in that week or month. If income falls below the starting limit for that week/month, the employer should not make a deduction.

There are also provisions for paying off the loan more quickly. Voluntary repayments of £5 or more may be made direct to the Student Loans Company, at any time, even if the employee does not earn above the threshold.

Example 1.9

Charles leaves university in June 2009 and starts working in August 2009 earning £1,500 a month (£18,000 a year).

His repayments will commence in April 2010.

Income in April 2010: £1,500 – £1,250 (starting limit) = £250

£250 × 9% = £22 repaid in April.

Rates of tax

1.51 The tax system is a progressive one, the tax rates increasing as income increases, from a basic rate of 20%, a higher rate of 40% and, from 6 April 2010, an additional rate of 50% (*ITA 2007, s 6*; *FA 2009, s 6*). (Note that, prior to 2008/09, a starting rate of 10% applied to all income. For 2008/09 onwards, the 10% starting rate only applies to savings income below the starting rate threshold (£2,440 in 2009/10 and 2010/11) and, if savings income exceeds this limit, the rate band does not apply.)

FA 2008 abolished the 10% starting rate and introduced a new 10% starting rate for savings and starting rate limit for savings (*FA 2008, s 5*). For 2008/09, the starting rate limit for savings was £2,320, increasing to £2,440 in 2009/10 and remaining unchanged at £2,440 for 2010/11. *ITA 2007* sets out different types of income and the order in which they are taxed. The first slice is non-savings income, which is not separately defined in *ITA 2007*, but broadly covers earnings, pensions, taxable social security benefits, trading profits and income from property. The next slice is savings income (broadly, bank and building society interest). Dividend income is the top slice.

The 10% starting rate is for savings income only. If non-savings income is above this limit, the 10% starting rate for savings does not apply. This means that the individual's savings income will be charged to tax at the 20% basic rate up to the basic rate limit (£37,400 for 2009/10 and 2010/11).

Income tax rates

1.52

	2008/09	2009/10	2010/11
Starting rate for savings: 10%*	£0–£2,320	£0–£2,440	£0–£2,440
Basic rate: 20%	£0–£34,800	£0–£37,400	£0–£37,400
Higher rate: 40%	Over £34,800	Over £37,400	£37,401–£150,000
Additional rate: 50%	Not applicable	Not applicable	Over £150,000

* From 2008/09 the 10% starting rate applies for savings income only. If non-savings income is above this limit, the 10% starting rate for savings will not apply.

Special income tax rates

1.53

	2008/09	2009/10	2010/11
Savings income:			
Starting rate	10%	10%	10%
Basic rate	20%	20%	20%
Higher rate	40%	40%	40%
Additional rate	N/A	N/A	50%
Dividend income:			
Ordinary rate	10%	10%	10%
Upper rate	32.5%	32.5%	32.5%
Additional rate	N/A	N/A	42.5%

From 2010/11, there are three rates of tax for dividends (*FA 2009, s 6*):

- dividends otherwise taxable at the 20% basic rate continue to be taxable at the 10% dividend ordinary rate;
- dividends otherwise taxable at the 40% higher rate continue to be taxable at the 32.5% dividend upper rate; and
- dividends otherwise taxable at the new 50% additional rate (see **1.52**) are taxable at a new 42.5% dividend additional rate.

Order of allocation of income to tax bands

1.54 Sources of income are treated as the top slice of income in the following order (*ITA 2007, Pt 2, Ch 3*):

(1) capital gains;

(2) life insurance policy gains;

(3) lump sum termination payments from employment;

(4) dividend income;

(5) other savings income; and

(6) all other income and profits.

Repayment claims

1.55 Claims can be made for repayment of tax paid through deduction at source (mainly savings interest) where an individual's income does not exceed personal allowances or where reliefs and allowance can be set against income on which tax has been paid (*ITA 2007, s 17*). However, the tax credit on dividends is not repayable.

HMRC will deal with repayment claims by issuing a repayment claim form outside the self-assessment system. Where payments on account exceed the final tax liability, a claim for repayment can be made through the tax return or earlier where the taxpayer believes tax has been overpaid. But, if the repayment subsequently proves to be excessive, interest is chargeable on the shortfall.

Income tax computation

1.56 The amount of a person's income to which the income tax rates are to be applied is generally known as 'taxable income' (*ITA 2007, s 23*).

Taxable income is statutory 'total income' less amounts deductible from total income.

To find a person's ('the taxpayer') liability to income tax for a tax year, the following steps are applied:

Step 1

Identify the amounts of income on which the taxpayer is charged to income tax for the tax year.

The sum of those amounts is 'total income'.

Each of those amounts is a 'component' of total income.

Step 2

Deduct from the components the amount of any relief (under a provision listed at **1.57** below) to which the taxpayer is entitled for the tax year.

The sum of the amounts of the components left after this step is 'net income'.

Step 3

Deduct from the amounts of the components left after Step 2 any allowances to which the taxpayer is entitled for the tax year (under *ITA 2007, Pt 3, Ch 2* (individuals: personal allowance and blind person's allowance)).

At Steps 2 and 3, the reliefs and allowances are deducted in the way which will result in the greatest reduction in the taxpayer's liability to income tax (*ITA 2007, s 25(2)*).

Step 4

Calculate tax at each applicable rate on the amounts of the components left after Step 3 (see **1.51** for rates).

Step 5

Add together the amounts of tax calculated at Step 4.

Step 6

Deduct from the amount of tax calculated at Step 5 any tax reductions to which the taxpayer is entitled for the tax year (under a provision listed in **1.58** below).

Step 7

Add to the amount of tax left after Step 6 any amounts of tax for which the taxpayer is liable for the tax year under any provision listed in **1.59** below).

The result is the taxpayer's liability to income tax for the tax year.

Reliefs

1.57 If the taxpayer is an individual, the provisions referred to at Step 2 in **1.56** above are broadly as follows (*ITA 2007, ss 24* and *25*):

(a) early trade losses relief (*ITA 2007, s 72*);

(b) share loss relief (*ITA 2007, Pt 4, Ch 6*);

(c) gifts of shares, securities and real property to charities, etc (*ITA 2007, Pt 8, Ch 3*);

(d) payments to trade unions or police organisations (*ITA 2007, ss 457* and *458*);

(e) pension schemes: relief under net pay arrangement: excess relief (*FA 2004, s 193(4)*);

(f) pension schemes: relief on making the claim (*FA 2004, s 194(1)*);

(g) trade loss reliefs: against general income (*ITA 2007, s 64*); carry-forward loss relief (*ITA 2007, s 83*); terminal loss relief (*ITA 2007, s 89*); and post-cessation relief (*ITA 2007, s 96*);

(h) property reliefs: carry-forward (*ITA 2007, s 118*); against general income (*ITA 2007, s 120*); and post-cessation (*ITA 2007, s 125*);

(i) employment loss relief against general income (*ITA 2007, s 128*);

(j) loss relief against miscellaneous income (*ITA 2007, s 152*);

(k) interest payments (*ITA 2007, Pt 8, Ch 1*); annual payments and patent royalties (*ITA 2007, Pt 8, Ch 4*);

(l) manufactured dividends on UK shares: payments by non-companies (*ITA 2007, s 574*); manufactured interest on UK securities: payments not otherwise deductible (*ITA 2007, s 579*);

(m) plant and machinery allowances in a case where the allowance is to be given effect under *CAA 2001, s 258* (special leasing of plant and machinery) (*CAA 2001, Pt 2*);

(n) industrial buildings allowances, in a case where the allowance is to be given effect under *CAA 2001, s 355* (buildings for miners, etc: carry-back of balancing allowances) (*CAA 2001, Pt 3*);

(o) patent allowances in a case where the allowance is to be given effect under *CAA 2001, s 479* (persons having qualifying non-trade expenditure) (*CAA 2001, Pt 8*);

(p) deduction for liabilities related to former employment (*ITEPA 2003, s 555*);

(q) strips of government securities: relief for losses (*ITTOIA 2005, s 446*);

(r) listed securities held since 26 March 2003: relief for losses: persons other than trustees (*ITTOIA 2005, s 454(4)*); and

(s) relief for patent expenses (*ITTOIA 2005, s 600*).

Tax reductions

1.58 If the taxpayer is an individual, the provisions referred to at Step 6 in **1.56** above are broadly as follows (*ITA 2007, s 26*):

(a) tax reductions for married couples and civil partners (*ITA 2007, Pt 3 Ch 3*);

(b) EIS relief (*ITA 2007, Pt 5, Ch 1*);

(c) VCT relief (*ITA 2007, Pt 6, Ch 2*);

(d) community investment tax relief (*ITA 2007, Pt 7, Ch 1*);

(e) qualifying maintenance payments (*ITA 2007, s 453*);

(f) payments for benefit of family members (*ITA 2007, s 459*);

(g) spreading of patent royalty receipts (*ITA 2007, s 461*);

(h) relief for interest on loan to buy life annuity (*ICTA 1988, s 353(1A)*);

(i) top slicing relief (*ITTOIA 2005, s 535*);

(j) relief for deficiencies (*ITTOIA 2005, s 539*);

(k) double taxation relief (*TIOPA 2010, Pt 2*);

(l) relief for foreign tax where no double taxation arrangements (*TIOPA 2010, s 18(1), (3)*);

(m) relief: qualifying distribution after linked non-qualifying distribution (*ITTOIA 2005, s 401*), and

(n) relief where foreign estates have borne UK income tax (*ITTOIA 2005, ss 677* and *678*).

Tax reductions are deducted in the order which will result in the greatest reduction in the taxpayer's liability to income tax for the tax year (*ITA 2007, s 27(2)*).

1.59 If the taxpayer is an individual, the provisions referred to at Step 7 in **1.56** above are broadly as follows (*ITA 2007, s 30*):

(a) Gift Aid: charge to tax (*ITA 2007, s 424*);

(b) pension schemes: the short service refund lump sum charge (*FA 2004, s 205*);

(c) pension schemes: the special lump sum death benefits charge (*FA 2004, s 206*);

(d) pension schemes: the unauthorised payments charge (*FA 2004, s 208(2)(a)*);

(e) pension schemes: the unauthorised payments surcharge (*FA 2004, s 209(3)(a)*);

(f) pension schemes: the lifetime allowance charge (*FA 2004, s 214*);

(g) pension schemes: the annual allowance charge (*FA 2004, s 227*); and

(h) social security pension lump sum (*F(No 2)A 2005, s 7*).

Allocation of income to tax bands

1.60 To ensure that certain classes of income do not escape charge to tax at the higher and additional rates for higher and additional rate taxpayers, the rules provide for these classes of income to be treated as the 'top slice' of income as follows (*ITA 2007, s 16*):

- savings income is treated as the top slice of taxable income; and
- dividend income is treated as the top slice of savings income.

If a person has savings income but no dividend income, the savings income is treated as the highest part of the person's total income (*ITA 2007, s 16(3)*). If a person has dividend income but no savings income, the dividend income is treated as the highest part of the person's total income (*ITA 2007, s 16(4)*). If a person has both savings income and dividend income:

(a) the savings income and dividend income are together treated as the highest part of total income, and

(b) the dividend income is treated as the higher part of that part of total income (*ITA 2007, s 16(5)(a)* and *(b)*).

This is subject to two exceptions. Where a taxpayer receives certain gains from a life insurance policy (*ITTOIA 2005, ss 535–537*) or a taxable lump sum on termination of employment, the income from these sources are generally treated as the highest part of taxable income, with life insurance gains at the top (*ITA 2007, s 16(2)*).

However, capital gains in excess of the exemption limit are treated as the very highest part of taxable income and gains.

Deductions and reliefs

1.61 Since the rate at which income (and gains) is taxed depends on the tax band in which it falls, the way in which deductions and reliefs are given is important. Reliefs deductible from total taxable income allow for tax savings at the top rate (*ITA 2007, s 16*).

The taxpayer can set deductions against different classes of income in the order resulting in the greatest reduction in the tax liability (eg against earned income taxed at 20% before dividend income taxed at 10%) (*ITA 2007, ss 25* and *27*).

The personal and blind person's allowances are deducted from income after all other deductions have been made and 'total income' for the purpose of the personal and married couple's age allowance restriction is the income before those deductions. These allowances can be offset against income in the most beneficial way to produce the lowest tax liability.

Double tax relief

1.62 A UK resident taxpayer is normally subject to UK tax on foreign income and a non-resident individual is generally subject to UK tax on income from a UK source. In both cases, the income is liable to tax in the UK and overseas. To prevent a UK resident individual being taxed twice on the same income, relief from double taxation on foreign income is normally available.

If the income arises in a country with which the UK has a double taxation agreement, there may be complete exemption from UK tax on that income.

Where there is no double taxation agreement, relief may be claimed against the UK tax liability for the lower of the UK tax or the foreign tax. Otherwise, the income net of any foreign tax paid would be charged to UK tax, but this is not usually beneficial (*ITA 2007, s 28(4)*). See **Chapter 9** for more on double tax relief.

Chapter 2

Income tax compliance

INCOME TAX SELF-ASSESSMENT

Introduction

2.1 Under the system of self-assessment, tax returns are generally required to be filed by 31 January after the end of the tax year to which the return relates (*TMA 1970, s 8, 8A* or *12AA*).

Tax returns for 2007/08 onwards made on paper must be filed by 31 October (*FA 2007, s 88*). This means that a 2009/10 paper return, for example, will have to be filed by 31 October 2010. The date will be the same for taxpayers who want HMRC to calculate their tax liability. The present filing date of 31 January will remain for returns filed online. See the Carter Report (at **2.3** below) for further details.

Where a notice to file a return has been issued, but no return is filed by the prescribed date, HMRC may serve a determination, to the best of their information and belief, of the amount of the tax due. This then serves as a self-assessment in prescribing how much tax is due, and when, but can be superseded by a self-assessment by HMRC or the taxpayer.

From 1 April 2010, neither determinations nor superseding self-assessments can be made more than four years from the prescribed filing date or, in the case of a superseding self-assessment, more than 12 months after the determination (*FA 2008, Sch 39, para 48*; *SI 2009/403, art 2*).

Electronic filing

2.2 HMRC's internet service allows taxpayers to send their tax returns over the Internet. This service also allows agents to send tax returns on behalf of their clients. Taxpayers may register to use the internet filing service online via the HMRC website. A user identity is displayed on the screen when the taxpayer has chosen a password and successfully registered online. Confirmation of the user identity is sent by post within seven working days of registering. Before sending the tax return over the Internet, the sender will be asked for a user identity and password. Upon receipt, HMRC immediately forward either an online acknowledgement or a notice of rejection.

For 2007/08 tax returns and those for subsequent years, there are two separate filing dates. For paper returns, there is a new date of 31 October (for tax year 2009/10, therefore, that is 31 October 2010). For returns filed online, the date remains at 31 January (for tax year 2009/10, therefore, that is 31 January 2011). A calculation of tax liability is automatically provided when a return is filed online.

HMRC have also introduced a new online filing facility. It is now possible for taxpayers and their agents to file self-assessment returns online for earlier tax years. The 2007/08 return is the first 'earlier year' return available online.

The Carter Report

2.3 In July 2005, the Paymaster General asked Lord Carter of Coles to undertake a review of HMRC online services. He was asked to advise on measures which would help increase the use of key online services, including self-assessment, VAT and corporation tax, with a view to improving the lot of the taxpayer whilst at the same time maintaining compliance standards.

The aim of the review was to help get to a point where businesses and individual taxpayers will be able to file online more quickly, accurately and efficiently. Emphasis is placed on 'certainty' so that taxpayers can be confident that they have complied fully.

The subsequent *Review of HMRC Online Services* ('The Carter Report') recommendations were published at Budget 2006 and aim to implement universal electronic delivery of tax returns from businesses and 'IT-literate individuals' by 2012. Lord Carter subsequently reviewed the responses to the Partial Regulatory Impact Assessment (RIA) published with his original report, considered further representations from tax practitioners and revised his recommendation. In a Written Ministerial Statement in July 2006, Paymaster General, Dawn Primarolo, said that the government would accept Lord Carter's revised recommendations for self-assessment filing deadlines for 2007/08 and subsequent returns, namely 31 October for paper returns and 31 January for online returns.

There is a tiny minority of self-assessment tax return filers (including registered pension schemes set up under trust) for whom facilities to file online are not yet available. HMRC will allow extra time (until the 31 January deadline) for those taxpayers to file paper returns.

Filing the return – relevant dates

2.4 The tax return (form SA100) is usually issued by HMRC during April, shortly after the end of the tax year.

Taxpayers who have previously filed online are no longer issued with a paper return in April, but are sent a letter requiring them to file a return.

Key Dates	*What happens/Why is this date important?*
6 April 2010	The new tax year starts. A 2009/10 tax return or Notice to Complete a Tax Return (SA316) will be sent out to all people who receive a tax return each year.
31 July 2010	Taxpayers will be charged a second automatic penalty of £100 if their 2008/09 tax return was due back by 31 January 2010 but it has not been sent in.
31 October 2010	If the taxpayer is completing a paper tax return for 2009/10, he must send it back by this date if he wants HMRC to: ● calculate the tax due; ● tell the taxpayer what to pay by 31 January 2011; ● collect tax through your tax code, if possible, where the taxpayer owes less than £2,000.
30 December 2010	If the taxpayer submits returns electronically, it must be sent by this date if he wishes HMRC to collect tax through his tax code, if possible, where he owes less than £2,000.
31 January 2011	If the taxpayer was sent a tax return by 31 October 2010, this is the deadline for sending back the completed 2009/10 tax return.
1 February 2011	If the taxpayer was sent a tax return by 31 October 2010, he will be charged a penalty of £100 if HMRC have not received the return by this date.
6 April 2011	The new tax year starts. A tax return or Notice to Complete a Tax Return (SA316) will be sent out to all people who meet the criteria to receive a tax return each year.

Information notices

2.5 HMRC may require certain information from persons generally or from taxpayers in particular (*FA 2008, Sch 36, paras 1* and *2*; *ITA 2007, s 748*).

An officer of HMRC may, by notice in writing, require a taxpayer to provide information or to produce a document if the information or document is reasonably required for the purpose of checking the taxpayer's tax position (*FA 2008, Sch 36, para 1*).

HMRC also have the power to obtain information and documents from third parties if they are reasonably required to check a taxpayer's tax position (*FA 2008, Sch 36, para 2*). However, HMRC may not issue a third party notice without the agreement of the taxpayer or the approval of the tribunal (*FA 2008, Sch 36, para 3*). There is also a requirement that HMRC must provide the taxpayer concerned with a copy of the third party notice, unless the tribunal has disapplied this requirement (*FA 2008, Sch 36, para 4*). HMRC are empowered to obtain, from a third party, information about a taxpayer whose identity is not known (*FA 2008, Sch 36, para 5*). Such notices require first-tier tribunal approval.

The information requested in an 'information notice' may be specified or 'described' by HMRC, which means that HMRC are not restricted to asking for documents that they can specifically identify (*FA 2008, Sch 36, para 6*). If a tribunal has approved the giving of an information notice, the notice must say so, as there are different rules for the penalties for failure to comply with the notice depending on whether it was issued by HMRC or by the tribunal. For further information on HMRC powers, see the HMRC Compliance Handbook (www.hmrc.gov.uk/manuals/chmanual/Index.htm).

2.6 In *R (on the application of Cooke) v HMRC* [2007] EWHC 167 (Admin), the court examined whether a notice given under former *TMA 1970, s 20(3)* to the taxpayer's solicitor (and, therefore, given by a senior officer on behalf of the Commissioners, by virtue of *s 20B(3)*) was subject to the various procedural safeguards to which other notices given under *s 20(3)* (to persons other than lawyers) are subject.

HMRC generally use orders in place of search warrants. HMRC officers, or officers of other government departments who carry out duties under the *National Minimum Wage Act 1998*, can use the information obtained for the assessment and collection of tax and the payment of tax credits.

It is a criminal offence intentionally to falsify or destroy documents called for by HMRC.

TAX RETURNS

Tax returns

2.7 The basic tax return (SA100) for the year ended 5 April 2010 consists of six pages. There are, in addition, supplementary pages to cover employment, share schemes, self-employment, partnerships, land and property, foreign income, trusts and estates, capital gains and non-residence. The return comes with a tax return guide with notes on how to complete the return.

Additional tax return supplementary pages and helpsheets can be obtained from HMRC using their Orderline: 0845 9000 404 (fax: 0845 9000 604). A tax calculation guide is available to those who wish to calculate their own tax. Taxpayers can obtain advice from their local tax offices and HMRC operate a Helpline (open during evenings and weekends) on 0845 9000 444 for general advice.

Those with straightforward tax affairs, whose tax liability can be met through PAYE deductions, will not normally be required to complete tax returns, although it is the taxpayer's responsibility to notify HMRC if a return is needed, generally within six months following the end of the tax year. A short tax return is available for those with relatively simple tax affairs (eg employees with a modest amount of property income), consisting of four pages plus accompanying guidance. There are no supplementary pages, except for capital gains. There is no need to calculate the tax on the return, although there is a two-page indicative calculation for those who wish to do so.

Disclosure rules relating to tax avoidance schemes apply from 1 August 2004. Taxpayers using certain tax avoidance schemes and arrangements are required to make a disclosure to that effect on their self-assessment returns. HMRC maintain a register of known schemes, each of which has a reference number. Taxpayers are required to enter the reference number on their self-assessment return if appropriate (*TMA 1970, ss 7–9, Sch 3A*; *FA 2004, ss 306–319*; SP 1/97). See **2.108** for further commentary on disclosure of tax avoidance schemes.

Tax returns and guides

Individuals

2.8

Tax return – SA100

Tax return guide – SA150

Short tax return – SA200

Your guide to the short tax return – SA210

Helpsheets

2.9

HS237: Community Investment Tax Relief

HS320: Gains on UK life insurance policies

HS325: Other taxable income

HS340: Interest and alternative finance payments eligible for relief on qualifying loans and alternative finance arrangements

HS341: Enterprise Investment Scheme – Income Tax Relief

HS342: Charitable giving

Employment

2.10

Employment Pages – SA101

Notes on Employment – SA101 (Notes)

Helpsheets

2.11

HS201: Vouchers, credit cards and tokens

HS202: Living accommodation

HS203: Car benefits and car fuel benefits

HS205: Seafarers' Earnings Deduction

HS207: Non-taxable payments or benefits for employees

HS208: Payslips and coding notices

HS210: Assets provided for private use

HS211: Employment – residence and domicile issues

HS212: Tax equalisation

HS213: Payments in kind

Self-employment

2.12

Self-employment Pages – SA103

Notes on Self-employment – SA103 (Notes)

Helpsheets

2.13

HS220: More than one business

HS222: How to calculate your taxable profits

HS224: Farmers and market gardeners

HS227: Losses

HS229: Information from your accounts

HS231: Doctors' expenses

HS232: Farm stock valuation

HS234: Averaging for creators of literary or artistic works

HS236: Foster carers & adult placement carers

HS238: Revenue recognition in service contracts – UITF 40

HS252: Capital allowances and balancing charges

Partnership

2.14

Partnership Pages (Short Version) – SA104

Notes on Partnership (Short) – SA104 (Notes)

Partnership Pages (Full Version) – SA104F

Notes on Partnership (Full) – SA104F (Notes)

UK property

2.15

UK Property Pages – SA105

Notes on UK Property – SA105 (Notes)

Helpsheets

2.16

HS251: Agricultural land

Trusts

2.17

Trusts etc Pages – SA107

Notes on Trusts etc – SA107 (Notes)

Helpsheets

2.18

HS270: Trusts and settlements – income treated as the settlor's

HS390: Trusts and estates of deceased persons: foreign tax credit relief for capital gains

HS392: Trust management expenses (TMEs)

Corrections and amendments – relevant dates

2.19 In conjunction with the changes to the tax return filing dates for 2007/08 onwards (see **2.1** above), consequential changes were also made to revise the period during which a return can be amended.

For the years up to and including 2006/07, the latest possible date was linked to the first anniversary of the filing date. This meant that HMRC had nine months from receiving the return in which to correct obvious errors. The correction did not take effect if the taxpayer gave notice to HMRC rejecting it within 30 days. A taxpayer could also make amendments to the return by notifying HMRC within a year from the filing date. However, a penalty could still be imposed if there was evidence that the original return was made fraudulently or negligently.

For 2007/08 onwards, the introduction of differential filing dates for different methods of filing a return advanced the date for those filing by paper. To avoid disadvantaging those who file early, the amendment window date is now therefore linked to the 31 January anniversary date for all paper and online returns.

Where the notice to make a return is issued after 31 October following the tax year, for the years up to and including 2006/07, a period of three months is allowed for completion of that return, and the period during which a return can subsequently be amended runs from this later date. A number of consequential changes have been made to retain this minimum period of three months and the amendment window links.

Time limits for HMRC assessment or determination

2.20 *FA 2008* introduced legislation, effective from 1 April 2010, to reduce the time limit for the making of assessments by HMRC to four years from the end of the year of assessment (*FA 2008, Sch 39, para 7*; *SI 2009/403, art 2*). Prior to 1 April 2010 the time limit was five years (*TMA 1970, s 34(1)(a)*).

In the case of fraudulent or negligent conduct, prior to 1 April 2010, the time limit was 20 years from 31 January following the end of the year of assessment for income tax and CGT (*TMA 1970, s 36(1)*). However, *FA 2008* amended *TMA 1970, s 36(1)* from 1 April 2010, so that an assessment on a person in a case involving a loss of income tax or capital gains tax brought about carelessly or deliberately by the person can now be made at any time not more than six years after the end of the year of assessment to which it relates (subject to *subsection (1A)* and any other provision of the *Taxes Acts* allowing a longer period) (*FA 2008, Sch 39, para 9*; *SI 2009/403, arts 3–10*).

For a Special Commissioners' case relating to the validity of an assessment made by HMRC within the prescribed time limits see *Mashood v Whitehead* [2002] STC (SCD) 166.

2.21 In the case of assessments on personal representatives, prior to 1 April 2010, the time limit was three years from 31 January following the end of the year of assessment in which the deceased died (*TMA 1970, s 40(1)*). However, *FA 2008* introduced provisions to reduce the time limit, with effect from 1 April 2010, for making assessments to four years from the end of the year of assessment (*FA 2008, Sch 39, para 11*; *SI 2009/403, art 2(2)*).

Prior to 1 April 2010, where there has been fraud or neglect on the part of the deceased, the six years of assessment before the deceased's death could be reopened, again within three years after 31 January following the end of the year of assessment in which he died (*TMA 1970, s 40(2)*). However, the wording in *s 40(2)* was changed with effect from 1 April 2010 so that it relates to careless or deliberate behaviour by the person who has died (*FA 2008, Sch 30, para 11(3)(a)*; *SI 2009/403, arts 3–10*). The time limit for making the assessment has also been reduced so that, from 1 April 2010, it is not more than four years after the end of the year of assessment (*FA 2008, Sch 30, para 11(3)(a)*).

2.22 From 1 April 2010, where no tax return has been delivered, so that HMRC are empowered to make a determination of the tax liability, there is a time limit of three years from the filing date (*SI 2009/403, arts 3–10*). Prior to 1 April 2010, the time limit was five years from the filing date. Moreover, no self-assessment can supersede such a determination unless made within 12 months of it (*TMA 1970, s 28C(5)*).

Partnership and trustee returns

2.23 *Partnership returns.* In addition to the tax returns for individuals, a separate partnership return (form SA800) must be filed for partnerships, including a 'partnership statement', containing the names, addresses and tax references of each partner, together with their share of profits, losses, charges on income, tax deducted at source, etc.

Trustee returns. A separate trust and estate tax return (form SA900) must be filed by trustees to establish the tax liabilities on any income and gains chargeable on them and on certain settlors and beneficiaries.

Record keeping

2.24 Individuals, trustees and partners are required to keep all records relevant to a tax return, normally until the end of the following periods (*TMA 1970, s 12B, Sch 1A, para 2A*):

- sole traders and partners carrying on a business (including letting property) – five years and ten months from the end of the tax year;
- in any other case – 22 months from the end of the tax year.

However, if HMRC make an enquiry into a return, the records must be kept until that enquiry is completed, if later than those dates.

In addition, where a claim is made other than in a return, supporting records must be kept until any HMRC enquiry into a return is complete, or until HMRC are no longer able to start an enquiry.

Penalties may be charged for a failure to comply (see **2.45**) although, in practice, penalties are usually imposed only in more serious cases of record-keeping failure. Details of HMRC's approach to penalties for failure to preserve records can be found in their Enquiry Manual at EM4650.

Primary legislation requires records to be kept which enable a taxpayer to make an accurate return. Further detail of the required records is then set out in secondary and tertiary legislation. Previously, record-keeping requirements differed from tax to tax, but Budget 2008 announced measures to pave the way for an aligned approach to record-keeping requirements. The revised rules took effect from 1 April 2009 (*TMA 1970, s 12B*, as amended by *FA 2008, s 115* and *Sch 37*; *SI 2009/402, art 2*).

Records to be kept

Taxpayers in business

2.25 *TMA 1970, s 12B* requires that a taxpayer must 'keep all such records as may be requisite for the purposes of enabling him to make and deliver a correct and complete return for the year or period'.

The information to be retained includes records of:

- all receipts and expenditure;
- all goods bought and sold; and

- all supporting documents relating to business transactions, including accounts, books, deeds, contracts, vouchers and receipts.

Examples include bank statements, stock and work-in-progress records, details of money introduced into the business, and records of goods or money taken from the business for personal use. Where a car or other asset is used for both business and private purposes, the records should enable an apportionment to be made.

Employers are also required to preserve certain PAYE records for three years following the tax year to which they relate (*SI 2003/2682, reg 97*).

All taxpayers

2.26 The following should be kept by all taxpayers (if applicable):

- employment details supplied by the employer about pay, tax deducted, benefits and expenses payments (eg forms P60, P45, P11D and P9D);
- records of tips, benefits or other receipts connected with an employment but not provided by the employer;
- a record of state pension and other taxable social security benefits;
- bank and building society records of interest received;
- dividend vouchers; and
- details of purchases, sales and gifts of assets giving rise to chargeable gains.

Original documents may generally be retained as copies and computerised records may be kept if they can be reproduced in legible form, but certain tax certificates, statements and vouchers must be retained in their original form.

Some useful HMRC guides

2.27 Note: HMRC are gradually phasing out print versions of some of their leaflets. Where information is now only available electronically, the relevant web address is shown.

General

2.28 Your tax return: the basics (www.hmrc.gov.uk/sa/your-tax-return.htm).

Savings and investments

2.29 Letting a room in your home (www.hmrc.gov.uk/individuals/tmaletting-my-home.shtml)

2.30 *Income tax compliance*

Rent a room scheme (www.hmrc.gov.uk/individuals/tmarent-a-room-scheme.shtml)

Tax back (www.hmrc.gov.uk/taxback/index.htm)

Enterprise Investment Scheme (www.hmrc.gov.uk/eis/eis-index.htm)

Venture capital trusts (www.hmrc.gov.uk/guidance/vct.htm)

Property Income Manual (www.hmrc.gov.uk/manuals/pimmanual/index.htm)

CVS guidance (www.hmrc.gov.uk/guidance/cvs.htm)

Business

2.30 Employed or self-employed for tax and National Insurance Contributions (www.hmrc.gov.uk/leaflets/es-fs1.pdf)

Are your workers employed or self-employed for tax and National Insurance Contributions (www.hmrc.gov.uk/leaflets/es-fs2.pdf)

Employers and contractors – reviewing your records (www.hmrc.gov.uk/leaflets/ecfs1.pdf)

Compliance checks – what happens during and at the end of a check (www.hmrc.gov.uk/leaflets/ecfs3.pdf)

Compliance checks – types of penalty (www.hmrc.gov.uk/leaflets/ecfs4.pdf)

IR160: Enquiries under Self-Assessment (August 2009) (www.hmrc.gov.uk/pdfs/ir160.pdf)

Booklet 480: Expenses and benefits: a tax guide (December 2009) (www.hmrc.gov.uk/guidance/480.pdf)

Booklet 490: Employee travel: a tax and NICs guide for employers (November 2009) (www.hmrc.gov.uk/helpsheets/490.pdf)

CIS340: Construction Industry Scheme (www.hmrc.gov.uk/forms/cis340.pdf)

Employment

2.31 Employed or self-employed for tax and National Insurance Contributions (www.hmrc.gov.uk/leaflets/es-fs1.pdf)

Compliance checks – what happens during and at the end of a check (www.hmrc.gov.uk/leaflets/ecfs3.pdf)

Compliance checks – types of penalty (www.hmrc.gov.uk/leaflets/ecfs4.pdf)

Using Your Own Vehicle for Work – a fact sheet for employees (www.hmrc.gov.uk/mileage/employee-factsheet.htm)

PAYE Settlement Agreements (www.hmrc.gov.uk/guidance/paye-settlements.htm)

Company cars (www.hmrc.gov.uk/cars/index.htm)

Booklet 480: Expenses and benefits: a tax guide (December 2009) (www.hmrc.gov.uk/guidance/480.pdf)

Booklet 490: Employee travel: a tax and NICs guide for employers (November 2009) (www.hmrc.gov.uk/helpsheets/490.pdf)

CWG2: Employer Further Guide to PAYE and NICs (December 2009) (www.hmrc.gov.uk/guidance/cwg2.pdf)

Overseas issues

2.32 HMRC6: Residence, domicile and the remittance basis (February 2010) (www.hmrc.gov.uk/cnr/hmrc6.pdf)

The Non-resident Landlords Scheme (www.hmrc.gov.uk/cnr/nr_landlords.htm)

TAX PAYMENTS

How tax is collected

2.33 Most taxpayers pay their tax without need for direct contact with HMRC as tax is either collected through the PAYE system or by deduction of tax at source from savings income. Some taxpayers who receive income gross of tax, or who have to pay tax at the higher rate on investment income, or who have capital gains above the annual exempt limit, and all self-employed people, have to pay some or all their income tax directly to HMRC.

Tax paid directly to HMRC

2.34 Taxpayers are generally required to make two equal payments of their income tax liabilities (including any Class 4 NIC liability) on account:

- by 31 January in the tax year; and
- by 31 July following the tax year,

based on the total income tax payable directly in the previous tax year.

The balance, together with any capital gains tax, is normally payable (or repayable) by 31 January after the tax year. If an HMRC notice requiring a tax return was received after 31 October following the tax year, the balancing payment is due three months from the date of the notice (*TMA 1970, ss 59A, 59B, 86*; *Income Tax (Payments on Account) Regulations 1996 (SI 1996/1654)*).

Payments on account are not required where (*SI 1996/1654*):

- more than 80% of the previous year's tax liability was covered by tax deducted at source and dividend tax credits; or
- the previous year's net tax and Class 4 NIC liability was less than £1,000 (£500 prior to 2009/10; *SI 2008/838*).

In addition to this test, there is a power for an officer of the Board to direct that interim payments are not required for a tax year, and make any consequent adjustment. The time limit for making this direction is 31 January following the tax year (*TMA 1970, s 59A(9)*).

HMRC will accept payment of tax by credit card (see the HMRC website at www.billpayment.co.uk/hmrc/scripts/help1.asp for further details).

Example 2.1

Paula's self-assessment for 2009/10 shows profits of £50,000 (with no tax deducted) and interest (gross) of £3,000 (tax deducted, £600).

Once calculations for the year have been finalised, her total tax and NIC liability is actually £15,822 (tax £12,934, NIC £2,888). Her due payment for 2009/10 is, therefore, £15,222.

The £1,000 test does not relieve Paula of the need to make interim payments, so she has to consider the percentage test.

Paula has to make interim payments for 2010/11 because her tax deducted at source (£600) is not more than 80% of her total liability (£15,822).

Each payment on account for 2010/11 will be half the payment due for 2009/10, ie £7,611.

Reducing payments on account

2.35 A taxpayer may claim to reduce the payments on account for any tax year, if he believes that the liability for that year will be less than his liability for the preceding year. The claim may be made at any time before 31 January following the end of the tax year. The reasons for the claim must be given (*TMA 1970, s 59A(3)*).

The claim may be in a standard format (on form SA303), or can be made as part of the tax return, although a letter to HMRC will suffice. Interest is charged where payments on account prove to be inadequate following the claim. In addition, a penalty may be imposed if the claim is made fraudulently or negligently.

Collecting additional tax due through the PAYE code

2.36 Employees and pensioners who submit their tax returns by 31 October following the tax year may have tax underpayments of less than £2,000 collected through their PAYE tax codes in a later tax year, if preferred. Tax due for 2009/10 would normally be collected through the PAYE code in 2011/12 (*SI 2003/2682, reg 186*).

Business Payment Support Service

2.37 The HMRC Business Payment Support Service (BPSS) provides a fast-track service that offers support to businesses needing more time to pay their tax bills. The taxes covered include corporation tax, VAT, PAYE, income tax and national insurance contributions, and applicants can quickly agree terms they can afford with HMRC over the phone. The majority of businesses applying under the scheme have agreed repayment timetables spread across three to six months. Construction firms account for a quarter of those benefiting from these new arrangements, with many retailers and manufacturers also agreeing payment schedules they can afford. The BPSS can be contacted on 0845 302 1435 from 8am to 8pm Monday to Friday and from 8am to 4pm at weekends. Further information is available at www.hmrc.gov.uk/pbr2008/business-payment.htm.

Important dates for income tax

2.38

31 January 2011	Return to be filed for 2009/10 (online filing); balancing payment or repayment due for 2009/10; 1st payment on account due for 2010/11
April 2011	Return issued for 2010/11
31 July 2011	2nd payment on account due for 2010/11
31 October 2011	All paper returns for 2010/11 to be filed: HMRC to calculate tax, or if the direct tax liability of under £2,000 to be collected through PAYE
31 January 2012	Online returns to be filed for 2010/11; paper returns to be filed for 2010/11 for certain taxpayers (including registered pension schemes set up under trust) for whom no online facilities exist. Balancing payment or repayment due for 2010/11; 1st payment on account due for 2011/12
April 2012	Return issued for 2011/12

31 July 2012	2nd payment on account due for 2011/12
31 October 2012	All paper returns for 2011/12 to be filed: HMRC to calculate tax, or if the direct tax liability of under £2,000 to be collected through PAYE
31 January 2013	Return to be filed for 2011/12; balancing payment or repayment due for 2011/12; 1st payment on account due for 2012/13

INTEREST AND PENALTIES

Interest

Interest on unpaid tax

2.39 Interest is normally charged on late payments on account and balancing payments (*TMA 1970, s 86*):

- from the due date of payment,
- to the date the tax (and Class 4 NICs) is actually paid.

Interest charges also apply to late payment of penalties and surcharges, and in respect of tax return amendments and discovery assessments.

Interest is payable gross and is not deductible for tax purposes.

Interest on overpaid tax

2.40 Interest paid by HMRC on tax overpaid is known as a repayment supplement. The supplement normally runs (*ICTA 1988, s 824*):

- from the date of payment (or in the case of income tax deducted at source, from 31 January following the relevant tax year);
- to the date the repayment order is issued.

Tax deducted at source includes PAYE, but excludes amounts relating to previous years. If a penalty or surcharge is repaid, a repayment supplement is also added to that repayment.

The repayment supplement is tax free (*ITTOIA 2005, s 749*).

Surcharges

2.41 In addition to late payment interest charges, where the balancing payment of tax (or Class 4 NICs) for a year of assessment remains unpaid after the due date, surcharges are imposed as follows (*TMA 1970, ss 59C, 86*):

- if the tax due is unpaid after 28 days following the due date (ie normally by 28 February) – 5% of the unpaid amount; and
- if the tax is still unpaid after six months following the due date – a further 5% of the tax unpaid.

A surcharge is due for payment within 30 days after the date on which it is imposed, and attracts interest if paid late. An appeal can be made within 30 days of the date on which the surcharge was imposed, if appropriate. A surcharge is not imposed if a penalty has been incurred based on the same tax (ie a tax-geared penalty for failure to notify chargeability to tax, or failure to submit a return, or making an incorrect return), or if agreement has been reached with HMRC in advance to pay the tax by instalments, where those instalments are duly paid in accordance with the agreement (*ITTOIA 2005, s 749*; *SI 1989/1297*).

Rates of interest on unpaid tax

2.42

From	*To*	*% Rate*
6.9.04	5.9.05	7.5
6.9.05	5.9.06	6.5
6.9.06	5.8.07	7.5
6.8.07	5.1.08	8.5
6.1.08	5.11.08	7.5
6.11.08	5.12.08	6.5
6.12.08	5.1.09	5.5
6.1.09	26.1.09	4.5
27.1.09	23.3.09	3.5
24.3.09	28.9.09	2.5
29.9.09		3.0

Rates of interest on overpaid tax: repayment supplement

2.43

From	*To*	*% Rate*
6.9.04	5.9.05	3.5
6.9.05	5.9.06	2.25
6.9.06	5.8.07	3.0

From	*To*	*% Rate*
6.8.07	5.1.08	4.0
6.1.08	5.11.08	3.0
6.11.08	5.12.08	2.25
6.12.08	5.1.09	1.5
6.1.09	26.1.09	0.75
27.1.09	23.3.09	0
24.3.09	28.9.09	0
29.9.09		0.5

Relevant dates for unpaid tax

2.44 The relevant dates from which interest on unpaid amounts runs are as follows:

IT, Class 4 NIC	– payments on account (*TMA 1970, s 59A*)	due date for payment (31 January and 31 July)
	– any other case (and CGT)	31 January after year of assessment or (where taxpayer gave notice of chargeability before 5 October following the tax year and the return was not issued until after 31 October) three months after notice to deliver the return, if later.
		Where a return is submitted by 31 October for calculation by HMRC of the tax due, interest runs from 30 days after the notification of the liability if after 30 December.
PAYE and Class 1 NIC		14 days after end of relevant tax year
Class 1A NIC		19 July after end of tax year in which contributions were payable
Class 1B NIC		19 October after end of relevant tax year
PAYE settlement agreement		19 October after end of relevant tax year

Penalties

Late returns

2.45 The following automatic penalties are charged for late returns (*TMA 1970, s 93*):

- £100 if the return is not made by 31 January following the tax year (or the filing date for the return, if later);
- a further £60 per day where HMRC obtain a direction from the tribunal to charge the daily penalty;
- a further £100 (where the daily penalty is not imposed) if the return is not made by 31 July (or six months from the filing date, if later);
- a tax-related penalty (in addition to the fixed penalties) if the return is not made by next 31 January (or one year from the filing date, if later), of an amount equal to the tax that would have been payable under the return.

However, the fixed penalties cannot exceed the amount of tax outstanding at the return due date, and will be refunded if a tax repayment is due. In addition, fixed penalties can be set aside by the tribunal if the taxpayer had a reasonable excuse for not delivering the return. Each member of a partnership is separately liable to the £100 fixed penalties and £60 daily penalties for a late partnership return, except that the fixed penalties may not be reduced. However, there is no tax-related penalty for late partnership returns.

As a result of the decision in *Steeden v Carver* (1999) SpC 212, in which possible late delivery of a return was examined, HMRC published the following policy:

- Returns found in the tax office post box before 7.30am on 1 February will be treated as having been delivered on 31 January and, therefore, filed on time.
- Returns placed in the tax office post box on 1 February, but after 7.30am, will be opened before 7.30am on 2 February and treated as filed on 1 February; accordingly, these returns will have been filed late. However, although the deadline for opening an enquiry into a return is extended, it is HMRC practice not to impose the automatic penalty. The automatic penalty will not be imposed if there was a reasonable excuse before the deadline has passed. In the *Steeden* case, it was held that a reasonable excuse exists throughout 31 January because the return is not late at any time on that day. It is HMRC practice not to charge the automatic penalty for late filing if the return is actually, or is deemed to have been, received at any time on 1 February.
- For returns delivered by other means (eg by hand, courier or electronically), HMRC can determine more precisely when they have

actually been delivered. In such cases, if a return is delivered on 1 February, but before midnight, then again the deadline for opening an enquiry is extended but it is HMRC practice not to impose the automatic penalty. Returns filed at any time on 2 February will result in the automatic penalty being imposed.

Incorrect returns

2.46 *FA 2007* contained provisions for a single penalty regime for incorrect returns for income tax, corporation tax, PAYE, NIC and VAT. Penalties are now determined by the amount of tax understated, the nature of the behaviour giving rise to the understatement and the extent of disclosure by the taxpayer. The rules apply for errors made during 2008/09 and later years (*FA 2007, s 97* and *Sch 24*; *SI 2008/568, art 2*).

FA 2008 extended the new penalties regime for incorrect returns across most taxes, levies and duties, for incorrect returns for periods commencing from 1 April 2009 where the return is due to be filed from 1 April 2010 (*FA 2008, s 122*).

The provisions contained in *FA 2007* are highly significant because they represent a new regime for tax-based penalties and a major change in the way those penalties are applied by HMRC. They create a single penalty framework for the submission of inaccurate documents and failure to advise HMRC of an understatement of tax due. They also make clear that the penalties are behaviour-related and new terms are used to describe such behaviour. The main concepts in the revised provisions are as follows:

- A single penalty regime for incorrect returns replaces all existing penalty systems for incorrect returns for income tax, corporation tax, PAYE, the construction industry scheme, and VAT, as well as underpayments of NIC as a result of an error in one of those returns.
- The level of penalty will depend on the underlying behaviour of the taxpayer giving rise to the incorrect return, with a stepped and differentiated approach leading to a penalty from nil to 100%. There will be statutory maximum and minimum penalties for each behaviour.
- All penalties are mitigable for disclosure, within a range. There is no provision for mitigation based on either co-operation or the seriousness of the offence.
- There is a new concept of 'suspended penalties' where the taxpayer can demonstrate that his compliance has improved over a specified period.
- All penalties will be subject to the right of appeal.

The rules do not deal with the fixed and tax-geared penalties and surcharges that are imposed for non-compliance, eg for failure to submit a return on time.

For further information on penalties relating to inaccuracies, see the HMRC Compliance Handbook at www.hmrc.gov.uk/manuals/chmanual/CH80000.htm.

2.47 *FA 2007, Sch 24, para 3* makes it clear that a penalty will be behaviour-related and defines the key terms. Three categories are identified:

- careless (defined as failure to take reasonable care);
- deliberate, but not concealed; and
- deliberate and concealed.

The penalties have been designed so that people who take reasonable care when completing their returns will not be penalised. If they do not take reasonable care, errors will be penalised, and the penalties will be higher if the error is deliberate. Disclosing errors to HMRC early will substantially reduce any penalty due.

'Reasonable care' varies according to the person, the particular circumstances and their abilities. Every person is expected to make and keep sufficient records for them to provide a complete and accurate return. A person with simple, straightforward tax affairs needs only to keep a simple system of records, and these must be regularly and carefully updated. A person with larger and more complex financial tax affairs will need to put in place more sophisticated systems and maintain them equally carefully. HMRC believe it is reasonable to expect a person who encounters a transaction or other event with which he is not familiar, to take care to check the correct tax treatment, or to seek suitable advice. HMRC expect people to take their tax seriously.

2.48 *FA 2007, Sch 24, para 4* sets out the maximum penalty payable for each type of behaviour, expressed as a percentage of the potential lost revenue. For the most serious category of 'deliberate understatement with concealment' the maximum penalty is in line with the current rate of 100%. Penalties for the two less serious categories are lower – for behaviour which is deliberate but not concealed, the maximum is 70%, and for 'careless' behaviour, the maximum is 30%.

FA 2007, Sch 24, paras 9 and *10* deal with the maximum reductions that may be obtained. These are summarised as follows:

Behaviour	*Maximum penalty*	*Minimum penalty with unprompted disclosure*	*Minimum penalty with prompted disclosure*
Careless	30%	0%	15%
Deliberate but not concealed	70%	20%	35%
Deliberate and concealed	100%	30%	50%

2.49 *FA 2007, Sch 24, para 8* sets out provisions where an inaccuracy is one of timing rather than absolute tax loss. Where the payment has been delayed, eg as the result of an inaccurate accounting adjustment, resulting in tax being paid in a later period, 5% of the delayed tax is treated as lost revenue and is liable to the penalty. This is charged on an annual basis and pro-rated for part years.

Failure to notify liability to tax by 5 October after tax year

2.50 The law requires a person to tell HMRC when certain events happen. These events include:

- where a person has income tax, capital gains tax or corporation tax to pay but has not been given notice to make a return for the period;
- when a person starts a new taxable activity;
- when the turnover from an existing activity has reached a certain level; or
- when the nature of the activity changes.

The amount of the penalty which may be charged for failing to notify HMRC about such events is a percentage of the tax:

- that is unpaid at a specified date, or
- to which the person is liable for the relevant period.

This tax is known as the 'potential lost revenue'. The percentage is determined by the behaviour that led to the failure to notify – higher penalties are payable if the failure was deliberate (*FA 2008, Sch 41*).

For further information on failure to notify penalties, see the HMRC Compliance Handbook at www.hmrc.gov.uk/manuals/chmanual/CH70000.htm.

Failure to maintain records

2.51 A penalty of up to £3,000 per tax year may be charged for a failure to keep and preserve appropriate records supporting personal, trustees' or partnership returns (*TMA 1970, s 12B(5)*).

Self-employed individuals: failure to notify liability to pay Class 2 NICs

2.52 Self-employed individuals are required to notify their liability to pay Class 2 National Insurance contributions to HMRC in the same way as liability to income tax must be notified. The penalties set out at **2.50** apply equally to NICs as they do for income tax. The penalty may be reduced at HMRC's discretion, or can be avoided if there is a 'reasonable excuse' for the late notification, or if HMRC are satisfied that the individual's profits were below the small earnings exception threshold for national insurance purposes.

Offence of fraudulent evasion

2.53

Where a person commits an offence of fraudulent evasion of income tax, he or she is liable to a prison term not exceeding six months on a summary conviction or not exceeding seven years on conviction on indictment. In either case, a fine may be levied instead of or in addition to the prison term (*TMA 1970, ss 20BB, 93–107*; *FA 2000, s 144*).

Other penalties

2.54

Negligently or fraudulently making or submitting incorrect returns, accounts, claims for allowances, relief or to reduce or cancel payments on account, etc	Up to the difference between the amount payable under the return, etc and the amount which would have been payable if the return, etc had been correct
Other returns, etc – failure to comply with a notice to deliver any return or other document, to furnish any particulars, to produce any document or record, to make anything available for inspection or give any certificate listed in *TMA 1970, s 98*	(a) An initial penalty up to £300 (b) If the failure continues after the above penalty is imposed, a further penalty up to £60 per day
Negligently or fraudulently delivering any return, incorrect information, etc within the above provisions	Up to £3,000
Assisting in the preparation of incorrect returns, accounts and other documents	Up to £3,000
Fraudulently or negligently giving a **certificate of non-liability to income tax** in connection with receiving bank or building society interest gross or failing to comply with an undertaking in the certificate	Up to £3,000

Refusal to allow deduction of income tax at source	£50
Falsification of documents – intentionally falsifying, concealing or destroying documents in connection with back duty investigations	On summary conviction, a penalty not exceeding the statutory maximum (currently £5,000). On conviction on indictment, imprisonment for up to two years or a fine or both
Witnesses before tribunal – neglect or refusal to appear before tribunal or refusal to be sworn in or answer questions	Up to £1,000
Failure to disclose tax avoidance scheme under *FA 2004* provisions by promoter, etc	(a) An initial penalty up to £5,000 (b) If the failure continues after the above penalty is imposed, a further penalty up to £600 per day
Interest on penalties	Penalties carry interest from the date on which they become due and payable.

HMRC ENQUIRIES

Enquiries into returns

2.55 Budget 2007 announced certain changes to the HMRC enquiry windows that affect individuals, trustees and partnerships which complete income tax self-assessment tax returns. Broadly, the changes link the period during which HMRC can enquire into returns to the date the return is received by HMRC.

Returns for 2007/08 onwards

2.56 The enquiry window closes one year after delivery of the return (*TMA 1970, s 9A(2)*; *FA 2007, s 96*). So, where a return is received before the filing deadline, the enquiry window will close earlier than under previous legislation.

A return may be selected at random, although the majority of returns will be selected for a particular reason. HMRC are not required to state whether the enquiry is random or otherwise. They may send a written notice requiring the taxpayer (and third parties) to produce documents, accounts and other information in order to check the accuracy of a tax return or amendment (*FA 2008, Sch 36, Pt 1*).

HMRC will issue a 'closure notice' notifying the taxpayer when the enquiry is complete, and make any amendments required to the return (or claim). The taxpayer has 30 days in which to appeal against HMRC's amendments, conclusions or decisions. This is also the period by which any tax payable (or repayable) as a result of the amendment must be paid (or repaid). Alternatively, the taxpayer may apply to the tax tribunal for HMRC to issue a closure notice in appropriate cases.

HMRC's enquiry powers equally apply to claims made separately from the return. A return or amendment may not be enquired into more than once (*TMA 1970, ss 28A, 28C*).

Discovery assessments

2.57 The return and self-assessment of tax can usually be regarded as final once the enquiry time limit has expired. However, HMRC may make a 'discovery assessment' to make good a loss of tax due to non-disclosure, if:

- the loss of tax is due to the taxpayer's fraudulent or negligent conduct; or
- HMRC could not reasonably be expected to identify the loss of tax from the information made available.

Put simply, the term 'discovers' means 'finds out' but there must be sufficient evidence to support a genuine discovery by HMRC (see, for example, *Scott (t/a Farthings Steak House) v McDonald (HMIT)* (1996) SpC 91, where an inspector was found to have acted unreasonably, and in bad faith, in making discovery assessments during an investigation case).

In *R v Kensington Income Tax Commrs, ex parte Aramayo* (1913) 6 TC 279, Bray J said at p 283:

> '… it seems to me to be quite clear that the word "discover" cannot mean ascertain by legal evidence; it means, in my opinion, simply "comes to the conclusion" from the examination he makes, and, if he likes, from any information he receives.'

The risk of a discovery assessment by HMRC is reduced if all relevant information is disclosed on the tax return and in any accompanying documents if their relevance is explained, and if any contentious issues are brought to HMRC's attention in the additional information space on the tax return. The time limit for making an assessment involving fraud or neglect is 20 years after 31 January following the end of the tax year (*TMA 1970, s 29*).

Determination of tax

2.58 If a return is not submitted, HMRC may make a 'determination' of the amount of tax considered to be due, within five years after the normal filing date for the return. This determination is treated as a self-assessment, until it is superseded by an actual self-assessment, which must be submitted within the same time limit (or 12 months after the determination, if later) (*TMA 1970, ss 31, 36, Sch 1A*).

Enquiry procedures

2.59 When HMRC start an enquiry, it does not necessarily mean that they think something is wrong. Further information is sometimes required to ensure that a return is correct. Returns are also selected at random for enquiry to ensure the system is operating fairly.

The enquiry might be concerned with one or more particular aspects of a tax return or the whole of it. If nothing is wrong, HMRC will not make any amendments to the return. If the enquiry reveals that an innocent mistake has been made, HMRC will:

- tell the taxpayer in writing that they have completed their enquiries; and
- amend the self-assessment to the correct figures.

The taxpayer will not be liable to a penalty, but HMRC will charge interest on any additional tax that may be due. A surcharge penalty may also be incurred if payment is made late.

Where tax credits are claimed and an enquiry shows that an award may have been wrong they will review that award.

The extent to which a taxpayer co-operates with HMRC and provides information is entirely a personal choice. However, in calculating the amount of any penalty, HMRC take into account the extent to which the taxpayer has been helpful and freely and fully volunteered any information about income or gains, which were omitted or understated.

The HMRC Charter (entitled *Your Charter*) sets out the standards of service that taxpayers can expect to receive from HMRC, and the roles and responsibilities of both HMRC and taxpayers in general. The Charter can be accessed on the HMRC website at www.hmrc.gov.uk/charter/.

What happens first?

2.60 When HMRC are ready to close their enquiries, they will normally ask the taxpayer and their professional adviser, if they have one, to attend a meeting.

HMRC will tell the taxpayer:

- what they have found;
- the amount of tax HMRC believe is owed; and
- how far they believe the late payment or underpayment of tax is due to fraudulent or negligent conduct on the taxpayer's part.

HMRC will listen to any explanations the taxpayer wishes to give. HMRC will then advise the maximum amount of penalties they believe could be determined under formal procedures, and the amount of interest and possibly surcharge that the taxpayer could pay.

Finally, HMRC will explain that it is normal to ask someone in the taxpayer's position to offer to pay one sum for tax, interest, and penalties or surcharge. HMRC will then ask if the taxpayer is prepared to make such an offer. If the taxpayer asks, HMRC will suggest an amount.

HMRC calculate an offer by adding together the tax, the interest on that tax, any surcharge and an amount for penalties. Interest is calculated from the date the tax should have been paid up to the date it was actually paid or will be paid.

The penalty figure will be a percentage of the tax underpaid or paid late. In law, it could be 100% of that amount, but in practice it is always less than that in a negotiated settlement.

HMRC start with a penalty figure of 100% and reduce it by an amount which depends on:

- whether the taxpayer disclosed all the details of his tax affairs;
- how well the taxpayer co-operated over the whole period of the enquiry; and
- the seriousness of the offence.

Disclosure – a reduction of up to 20% (30% for full voluntary disclosure where there was no fear of early discovery by HMRC)

2.61 If a full disclosure was made at the time HMRC first opened the enquiry, the taxpayer will receive a considerable reduction in the amount of the penalty.

If the taxpayer denies until the last possible moment that anything is wrong, he will receive little or no reduction for disclosure.

Between these two extremes, a wide variety of circumstances is possible. HMRC will consider how much information the taxpayer gave, how quickly, and how that contributed towards settling the enquiry.

Co-operation – a reduction of up to 40%

2.62 If the taxpayer supplied information quickly, attended interviews, answered questions honestly and accurately, gave all the relevant facts and paid tax on account when it became possible to estimate the amount due, he will then receive the maximum reduction for co-operation.

If the taxpayer put off supplying information, gave misleading answers to questions, did nothing until HMRC took formal action and generally obstructed the progress of the enquiry, he will not receive any reduction at all.

Between these extremes, there is a wide range of possible circumstances, and HMRC will look at how well the taxpayer has co-operated with the enquiry.

Seriousness – a reduction of up to 40%

2.63 The taxpayer's actions may amount to a pre-meditated and well-organised fraud or something much less serious. HMRC will take into account what he did, how he did it, how long it went on and the amounts of money involved. The less serious the offence, the bigger the reduction in the penalty.

Example 2.2

If HMRC think that the reduction for disclosure is 15%, for co-operation 30% and for seriousness 20%, the total reduction will be 65%, making the expected penalty 35% (100% – 65%).

The calculation of what HMRC consider to be a suitable offer may be as follows:

Tax underpaid	£10,337
Interest, say	£4,165
Penalty at 35%	£3,618
Total	£18,120

Negotiations

2.64 HMRC will have already agreed the figures for tax, interest and, where appropriate, surcharge leaving only the penalty to be negotiated.

The taxpayer will have the opportunity to draw HMRC's attention to any matters affecting the penalty figure, which the taxpayer thinks they have not given enough weight to. HMRC will consider the effect of these on the figure they had in mind, and will comment on any figure the taxpayer might suggest. As a result, HMRC might be able to reach an agreement either straightaway or after a few days' consideration.

If the taxpayer agrees to make an offer, he has to sign a formal letter offering to pay the agreed sum within a stated period and give or send that letter to HMRC. If HMRC are happy with it, they will then issue a letter of acceptance.

The exchange of letters amounts to a legal contract between HMRC and the taxpayer, and both parties are bound by its terms. If the taxpayer pays under the terms of the contract, HMRC cannot use formal proceedings to recover the tax, interest, surcharge or penalties. For this reason, they make sure that the terms of the letter are precise.

When HMRC send the acceptance letter, they will include a payslip showing the Accounts Office Network Unit to which payment should be sent. When the taxpayer pays the amount under the terms of the contract, the matter will be at an end. If the taxpayer does not keep to the terms of the contract, HMRC will charge interest for late payment and may take court action to recover the amount due.

HMRC will not take advantage of the fact that a formal closure notice has not been issued. If any additional liabilities, relating to the years covered by the enquiry, come to light at any time after they have accepted an offer, they will not under any circumstances seek to amend the assessment. But they will arrange to recover any such liabilities.

Where a taxpayer agrees a settlement, but cannot pay the full amount straightaway, it may be possible to arrange payment by instalments. HMRC will expect as large a down payment as possible, and agreement to pay the rest, including an amount for extra interest, by instalments over as short a period as possible. HMRC will suggest payment by direct debit.

If the taxpayer does not want to make an offer, or an offer transpires to be unacceptable to HMRC, HMRC will regard this as the end of negotiations (unless the taxpayer seeks to reopen them). HMRC will then proceed as follows.

HMRC will issue a notice of closure for each self-assessment year that has an open enquiry, which will explain:

- that their enquiries have finished;
- what their conclusions are;

- the amendments being made; and
- that for other years involved they will issue assessments.

The tax due will be shown on the taxpayer's next Statement of Account.

Interest

2.65 When the further tax appears on a Statement of Account, interest will automatically be charged and will run from the date that the tax should have been paid until the date it is actually paid.

Surcharges

2.66 These will, where appropriate, be imposed automatically when the additional tax liabilities appear on the Statement of Account. However, HMRC do not impose surcharges on any tax on which tax-geared penalties are also being charged.

Careless and deliberate behaviour

Time limits

2.67 Assessments on an individual, involving a loss of income tax or capital gains tax brought about *carelessly* by the person, can generally be made at any time not more than six years after the end of the year of assessment to which it relates (*TMA 1970, s 36(1)*).

Assessments on an individual in a case involving a loss of income tax or capital gains tax:

(a) brought about *deliberately* by the person,

(b) attributable to failure to comply with an obligation to notify HMRC of a liability to tax (under *TMA 1970, s 7*); or

(c) attributable to arrangements in respect of which the person has failed to comply with an obligation under *FA 2004, s 309, 310* or *313* (obligation of parties to tax avoidance schemes to provide information to HMRC),

can be made at any time not more than 20 years after the end of the year of assessment to which it relates (*TMA 1970, s 36(1A)*).

Fraud

2.68 There is no definition of 'fraud' in the Taxes Acts, so resort must be made to relevant decided cases.

In *Barclay's Bank Ltd v Cole* [1967] 2 QB 738, at 743–744, Lord Denning MR said:

> '"Fraud" in ordinary speech means the using of false representations to obtain an unjust advantage: see the definition in the Shorter Oxford English Dictionary. Likewise in law "fraud" is proved when it is shown that a false representation has been made knowingly, or without belief in its truth, or recklessly, careless whether it be true or false: see *Derry v Peek* (1889) 14 App. Cas. 337 *per* Lord Herschell.'

Willis J in *Ex parte Watson* (1888) 21 QBD 301 stated at 309:

> '"Fraud" in my opinion is a term that should be reserved for something which is dishonest and morally wrong and much mischief is, I think, done, as well as much unnecessary pain inflicted, by its use where "illegality" and "illegal" are really appropriate expressions.'

In *Amis v Colls* 39TC at 163, Cross J remarked:

> 'Mr Karmel argued that, as the conduct alleged (that is, fraud) might have formed the subject of criminal proceedings, the proper standard is not satisfaction on the balance of probabilities, as is the normal test in civil proceedings, but satisfaction beyond reasonable doubt, the test in criminal cases. I should have thought that, as these are civil proceedings, the civil standard was the proper one to adopt.'

Nevertheless, in *Les Croupiers Casino Club v Pattison* 60 TC1 196, Nourse J, in the Court of Appeal, commented:

> '… the standard of proof in civil proceedings, while it is always proof on the balance of probabilities, is nevertheless flexible, being higher or lower according to the nature and gravity of that which has to be proved … Another, and I think preferable, way of stating this principle is to say that the more grave the act or omission to be proved, the more convincing must be the evidence which is required to tip the balance of probabilities.'

In *Hudson v Humbles* 42 TC 380, Pennycuick J said at 386:

> 'There is nothing in the proviso (to ITA 52/S47(1) – now TMA 70/S36) which in any way restricts the nature of the evidence which the Revenue must give in order to establish prima facie a case of fraud or wilful default … I do not think it is necessary for the Revenue, in order to raise a prima facie case, to show the particular quality or source of the receipts which had not been accounted for.'

In an attempt to clarify the meaning of fraud and negligence, the heading of *TMA 1970, s 36* (currently entitled 'Fraudulent or negligent conduct') is to be renamed 'Loss of tax brought about carelessly or deliberately etc' from 1 April 2010 (*FA 2008, s 118* and *Sch 39, para 9(6)*).

HMRC have wide-ranging statutory powers to call for documents or to search premises in cases of suspected fraud or negligence. However, unless they are considering a prosecution, they will normally invite the taxpayer to co-operate and negotiate a settlement without recourse to these powers. Furthermore, the fact that a settlement has been negotiated will not preclude a prosecution in all cases.

FA 2007 contained measures to extend the *Police and Criminal Evidence Act 1984 (PACE 1984)* to all HMRC's criminal investigations in England and Wales (*FA 2007, s 82*), and the *Police and Criminal Evidence Act 1984 (Application to Revenue and Customs) Order 2007 (SI 2007/3175)* brought these new powers into play with effect from 1 December 2007. In particular, the regulations give HMRC a wide range of powers to search, seize and retain items during a criminal investigation into a taxpayer's affairs.

Appeals

2.69 The appeals system was completely reformed from 1 April 2009. The way in which appeals against HMRC decisions were handled up to 1 April 2009 was inherited from the two predecessor departments (namely the Inland Revenue and HM Customs and Excise). The system reflected both developments over a period of time and the different approaches of those two former departments. Appeals were made to different tribunals, and different appeal and review processes operated in different areas depending on the particular tax or scheme involved. Since the merger of the two departments, HMRC had been considering the alignment and modernisation of the administration of appeals, particularly in the context of the Review of Powers that was looking at taxpayer safeguards and the reform of the tribunal system being developed by the Ministry of Justice. A consultation document entitled *HM Revenue and Customs and the Taxpayer: Tax Appeals against decisions by HMRC* was published in October 2007 and a *Summary of Responses and Future Direction* was published in March 2008.

2.70 The *Tribunals, Courts and Enforcement Act 2007 (TCEA 2007)*, which received Royal Assent on 19 July 2007, is the initial legislation governing the new regime and it provides for a new two-tier tribunal structure subdivided into chambers (see below). *TCEA 2007* is supported by *FA 2008, s 124*, which gave the Treasury power, by secondary legislation, to make provisions for reviews of HMRC decisions, and changes to appeals administration procedures, and details the matters that such an Order might cover.

2.71 The subsequent *Transfer of Tribunal Functions and Revenue and Customs Appeals Order 2009 (SI 2009/56)* provides for the actual transfer of the functions of former tax tribunals to the new tribunals established under *TCEA 2007* (broadly effective from 1 April 2009). The Order also makes consequential amendments to legislation relating to tax tribunals and the appeals they consider. In addition, the Order makes changes to HMRC appeals and review processes and related administrative changes.

2.72 The new tribunal does not affect just tax cases. It incorporates a wide range of previously independent tribunals, from the Meat Hygiene Appeals Tribunal and the Antarctic Act Tribunal to the Information Tribunal and the Special Educational Needs and Disability Tribunal, through to the Social Security Tribunal, the Social Security Commissioner and the Lands Tribunal.

Right of appeal

2.73 The taxpayer generally has a right of appeal against any formal decision by an officer of HMRC, the majority of appeals made being against assessments.

For a detailed guide to the new appeals system, see *Hamilton on Tax Appeals* (Bloomsbury Professional).

Time limits

2.74 Appeals must normally be made within 30 days after the date of the issue of the assessment (or the amendment to the self-assessment), although HMRC may accept a late appeal where there is a reasonable excuse for the delay. The appeal must state the grounds on which the appeal is being made (eg that HMRC's amendment is incorrect).

Procedures

2.75 Where an appeal is not settled between a taxpayer and an HMRC officer, it is listed for hearing by the tax tribunal.

Tax tribunal

2.76 One of the most important changes brought about by the new system is the fact that two different tribunals are introduced into the tax litigation process. These two new tribunals are known as:

- the First-tier Tribunal (*TCEA 2007, s 3(1)*); and
- the Upper Tribunal (*TCEA 2007, s 3(2)*).

The persons hearing cases in the tribunals are referred to as judges or other members (collectively, referred to as 'members'), depending on their qualifications.

2.77 The vast majority of cases will be first heard by the First-tier Tribunal, which should therefore be considered as the successor to the General and Special Commissioners.

Under the old system, appeals from the Commissioners or the VAT and Duties Tribunal would (in England and Wales) almost invariably be heard by the Chancery Division of the High Court – some cases occasionally being able to 'leapfrog' this stage to be heard by the Court of Appeal.

Under the new system, appeals from the First-tier Tribunal will invariably be heard by the Upper Tribunal. The Upper Tribunal is a superior court of record and will, therefore, have the same status as the High Court itself. Indeed, it is expected that the Upper Tribunal will often be presided over by High Court judges or (in Scotland) judges of the Court of Session. Furthermore, the Upper Tribunal may exercise the same authority, powers and privileges and rights as those higher courts in relation to:

- the attendance and examination of witnesses;
- the production and inspection of documents; and
- all other matters incidental to the Upper Tribunal's functions.

Appeals from the Upper Tribunal will be heard by the Court of Appeal (in England and Wales and in Northern Ireland) or the Court of Session (in Scotland).

First-tier Tribunal

2.78 Tax matters are handled by a specialist tax chamber of the First-tier Tribunal (the 'Tax Chamber'). However, it should be noted that tax credit appeals are dealt with in the Social Entitlement Chamber.

Upper Tribunal

2.79 In the Upper Tribunal, there will be fewer chambers. Appeals from the Social Entitlement Chamber of the First-tier Tribunal will all be dealt with by the Administrative Appeals Chamber of the Upper Tribunal. Again, tax matters are heard by a specialist finance and tax chamber of the Upper Tribunal.

Bringing cases to the tribunal

2.80 One of the changes that is introduced under the new system is that taxpayers are given greater control over the listing of a hearing before a tribunal, particularly in direct tax cases. Historically, the request for a hearing was generally made by the tax office when negotiations reached an impasse. Whilst this definitely simplified matters for taxpayers (as it removed one level of bureaucracy from them), there was often a perceived 'closeness' between the tax authorities and the independent appeal Commissioners. Once a taxpayer appeals against a decision by HMRC (in writing to HMRC), there are now three possible courses of action. Either:

- the taxpayer can make a formal request that HMRC review the matter in question; or
- HMRC may offer a review of the matter to the taxpayer; or
- the taxpayer may notify the appeal directly to the First-tier Tribunal.

Whichever approach is taken, it does not prevent the parties from settling the dispute by mutual agreement.

2.81 If a taxpayer requires HMRC to review the matter, HMRC must set out their initial view of the matter within 30 days of their receipt of the request for the review, or such longer period as is reasonable.

A request may not be made (and HMRC may not be required to conduct a review) if either:

- the taxpayer has already requested a review in relation to the matter; or
- HMRC have already offered a review in relation to the matter; or
- the taxpayer has already notified the First-tier Tribunal of the appeal.

2.82 When HMRC offer a review to the taxpayer, the offer must include HMRC's view of the matter in question. The taxpayer then has 30 days (starting with the date stated on HMRC's offer of a review) to request that HMRC conduct a review. It is imperative that taxpayers note this time limit carefully, because failure to accept the offer of a review means that the dispute will be treated as settled (in accordance with HMRC's views of the matter). Furthermore, the taxpayer may not withdraw from any agreement under *TMA 1970, s 54(2)* (requests to repudiate or resile from agreement). However, the matter may still be taken to the First-tier Tribunal (see below).

2.83 HMRC may not offer a review (and HMRC may not be required to conduct a review) if either:

- the taxpayer has already requested a review in relation to the matter; or

- HMRC have already offered a review in relation to the matter; or
- the taxpayer has already notified the First-tier Tribunal of the appeal.

HMRC REVIEW

2.84 There are three outcomes of a review: the original HMRC view will be either upheld, varied or cancelled. The nature and extent of the review will depend on what appears to be appropriate to HMRC in the particular circumstances. However, HMRC must bear in mind the steps taken by HMRC in first deciding the matter and any steps taken by any person seeking to resolve the disagreement.

2.85 The review must also take into account any representations made by the taxpayer, provided that they are made sufficiently early to give HMRC a reasonable opportunity to consider them. To avoid difficulties with this hurdle, it is therefore suggested that the representations be included in the request for a review (or the acceptance of the offer of the review).

Timescale for review

2.86 HMRC must notify the taxpayer of their conclusions of the review and their reasoning within a 45-day period (unless the parties agree a different timescale). That 45-day period runs:

- in a case where the taxpayer requested the review, from the day on which HMRC notified the taxpayer of their initial view of the matter; and
- in a case where the taxpayer accepted HMRC's offer of a review, from the day on which HMRC received the acceptance of the offer.

The conclusions reached by the review are then deemed to stand (as a *TMA 1970, s 54(1)* agreement) and the taxpayer is unable to withdraw from this deemed agreement under *s 54(2)* (requests to repudiate or resile from agreement).

2.87 If HMRC fail to give their conclusions within the 45-day period (or such other period as agreed), then the initial HMRC view is deemed to stand (as a *s 54(1)* agreement) and the taxpayer is unable to withdraw from this deemed agreement under *s 54(2)* (requests to repudiate or resile from agreement). HMRC are required to notify the taxpayer of the conclusion that is deemed to have been reached.

This provision begs the question: what is the point of asking HMRC for a review? Not only are there concerns about the effectiveness of a review, especially if HMRC reviewers will not be able to diverge from HMRC policy;

however, if HMRC fail to meet their own 45-day time limit, then the parties are deemed to have agreed to the original HMRC position that was subject to the review in the first place. If taxpayers wish to avoid this 'Catch 22' situation, then they should try to agree with HMRC for an extension of the 45-day period so that HMRC cannot argue that they have run out of time. In either case, however, the matter may still be taken on appeal to the First-tier Tribunal.

Notifying an appeal

2.88 Once HMRC have been notified that their decision is to be appealed against, the taxpayer may notify the First-tier Tribunal of the appeal. Once this is done, it will be for the tribunal to decide the matter. However, different procedures apply depending on whether HMRC have given their view of the matter:

- following a review under *TMA 1970, s 49B* (where the appellant requires a review by HMRC); or
- when offering a review under *TMA 1970, s 49C* (ie HMRC offer the review).

2.89 Once a review has been concluded (or once the period for the review expires without HMRC notifying the taxpayer of their conclusion), the taxpayer may notify the First-tier Tribunal of the appeal. This should generally be done within a 30-day period.

If the taxpayer is late in notifying the First-tier Tribunal of the appeal, then the appeal may not proceed unless the tribunal gives permission.

2.90 Once the tribunal has been notified of the appeal, the tribunal will decide the matter in question.

The operation of the period for notifying the tribunal depends on the circumstances of the case:

- If HMRC have notified the taxpayer of their conclusions following the review, the period to appeal runs for 30 days starting with the date of the notice on which HMRC state their conclusions of the review.
- If HMRC have failed to conclude the review in time (usually within 45 days), the taxpayer may notify the tribunal of the appeal at any time between:
  - the conclusion of the review period (usually 45 days); and
  - the 30th day following HMRC giving the document under *TMA 1970, s 45E(9)* – the deemed conclusion of the review (being in accordance with the original decision).

Notifying an appeal to the tribunal (after review offered but not accepted)

2.91 Although the review procedures are likely to catch out many taxpayers, the option of not accepting an offer of a review could be even more troublesome for taxpayers. As previously noted, an offer of a review must be accompanied by a statement of HMRC's position (*TMA 1970, s 49C(2)*). Furthermore, a taxpayer's failure to accept the offer of the review within 30 days means that the HMRC view will be deemed to have been accepted by both parties as their settled position from which the taxpayer cannot withdraw.

2.92 The taxpayer will, however, have the opportunity to notify the First-tier Tribunal of the appeal in such circumstances and the tribunal will decide the matter. Nevertheless, the timing will be critical. If the notification to the tribunal is within the 30-day period (ie within the 30 days after the date of the document by which HMRC sends the offer of a review), then the matter can be heard by the tribunal without any additional hurdle. However, if the tribunal is notified later (for example, because the taxpayer is unaware of the consequences of not accepting the offer of a review), then the appeal may not proceed to the tribunal unless the tribunal gives permission.

Procedure if no review offered or requested

2.93 In direct tax cases, the taxpayer will usually have the opportunity to request a review at the same time as notifying HMRC of the appeal against the decision. However, the taxpayer may not necessarily do this and there is no obligation on HMRC to offer one. In such circumstances, the parties will be able to continue to discuss matters until such time as the taxpayer either requests a review or applies directly to the tribunal, or HMRC formally offers a review. Then, the procedures discussed above will be triggered.

2.94 HMRC produce comprehensive guidance on appealing against decisions: *How to appeal against an HMRC decision – direct tax* (www.hmrc.gov.uk/dealingwith/appeals/directtax.htm).

PUBLISHING DETAILS OF DELIBERATE TAX DEFAULTERS

2.95 From 1 April 2010, HMRC may publish a person's name and other information to identify that person as a deliberate tax defaulter. Personal details will be published where the following three conditions are met (*FA 2009, s 94*):

- As a result of an investigation, it is found that the person has incurred one or more relevant penalties. A relevant penalty is a penalty for a deliberate, or a deliberate and concealed,

  - inaccuracy in a return or other document,
  - failure to comply with certain obligations, or
  - VAT or Excise Duty wrongdoing.
- The potential lost revenue for the relevant penalty or total relevant penalties exceeds £25,000.
- The penalty reduction for quality of disclosure for any of the relevant penalties is less than the maximum.

HMRC are obliged to notify the person that they are going to publish their information and give them time to make representations about why they should not do so. No information may be published until the relevant penalty becomes final. If there is more than one relevant penalty, HMRC may not publish until the last relevant penalty becomes final.

There are two time limits:

- HMRC must publish the details within 12 months of the relevant penalty becoming final. Where there is more than one relevant penalty, the period of 12 months starts on the date when the last of these penalties becomes final.
- HMRC can only continue to publish this information for 12 months.

PAYE COMPLIANCE

Introduction

2.96 Income tax and national insurance contributions collected through the PAYE system on salaries and benefits constitute the Exchequer's largest single item of cash flow and additional liabilities as a result of employer compliance reviews completed by local offices contribute in excess of £215.8 million annually.

A PAYE compliance check, apart from covering income tax and NICs due on payments of salaries and wages, will also cover many other employer-related issues, including other relevant aspects of the NIC legislation, student loan deductions (SLDs), the national minimum wage, statutory sick pay (SSP), statutory maternity pay (SMP), statutory paternity pay (SPP) and statutory adoption pay (SAP). Notification of an impending employer compliance visit or investigation should not, therefore, be taken lightly.

The legislation governing PAYE is found in the *Income Tax (Pay As You Earn) Regulations 2003 (SI 2003/2682)*.

2.97 *Income tax compliance*

The March 2010 Budget contained an announcement that proposed new legislation will allow HMRC to require a financial security from employers where amounts of PAYE income tax and NICs are seriously at risk following a history of serious non-compliance in terms of late or non-payment. HMRC will set the amount of the security based on the potential tax liability. There will be a right of appeal against the imposition of the security and the amount. A new criminal offence will be introduced where a person fails to give a security when required to do so. The measure will not have effect until regulations are made, but the operative date is intended to be 6 April 2011 (see HMRC 2010 *Budget Note* BN70: www.hmrc.gov.uk/budget2010/march/bn70.htm).

HMRC guidance 'EC/FC1: Reviewing you records' will be useful to anyone expecting a compliance visit.

Compliance checks

2.97 A new framework for compliance checks took effect from 1 April 2009 which changed the way that HMRC conduct enquiries, visits and inspections. *FA 2008, Schs 36, 37* and *39* contain the legislation for the new regime. In summary, *Sch 36* gives HMRC one set of new powers covering all the taxes concerned. This includes powers to visit businesses (without the right of appeal) and inspect the premises, assets and records, and to ask taxpayers and third parties for more information and documents. *FA 2008, s 114* provides the powers to access premises and inspect any computer used by the business.

Further rules, contained in *Schs 37* and *39*, are designed to provide greater flexibility in setting record-keeping requirements after 1 April 2009, along with new time limits for assessment and claims which did not come into force fully until April 2010 (although there were some transitional arrangements from 1 April 2009).

2.98 Under the new regime, there is a statutory requirement for HMRC to give at least seven days' prior notice of a visit, unless either an unannounced visit is necessary, or a shorter period is agreed. There is also a new requirement that unannounced visits must be approved beforehand by a specially trained HMRC officer.

2.99 The legislation, Codes of Practice and guidance governing the new regime contain certain safeguards for businesses and taxpayers. Broadly, in carrying out compliance checks:

- HMRC's powers must be used reasonably and proportionately;
- taxpayers should be clear about when a compliance check begins and ends;

- HMRC officers do not have the right to enter any parts of premises that are used solely as a dwelling, whether to carry out an inspection or to examine documents produced under an information notice. They can, however, enter if invited; and
- unannounced visits will be made where agreement has been given by an authorised HMRC officer.

2.100 In addition to examining statutory records (such as PAYE deduction working sheets and expenses payments records), HMRC often ask for supplementary information to enable them to ascertain and quantify a tax position. Examples of supplementary information may include appointment diaries, notes of board meetings, correspondence, commercial employment contracts, explanations and schedules. Under the new framework, an information notice for supplementary information must be reasonable, proportionate, and reasonably required to check the tax position. There is a right of appeal against an information notice unless the First-tier Tribunal has approved the issue of the notice. Agreement is required from an authorised HMRC officer before asking for tribunal approval.

2.101 There may be occasions where HMRC cannot obtain information and documents from the taxpayer, or wish to check the accuracy of information and documents provided. Where HMRC think it is necessary to gather information by using a third party notice, they must have the approval of the person whose tax position is being checked and the independent First-tier Tribunal before the notice can be issued. Agreement of an authorised officer within HMRC is required before the request is referred to the First-tier Tribunal. Officers cannot inspect or require auditors or tax advisers to produce documents which ask for or give advice to a client about their tax affairs.

Safeguards

2.102 There are certain things that HMRC are not allowed to request. Such items include information relating to the conduct of appeals against HMRC decisions, legally privileged information, information about a person's medical or spiritual welfare, and journalistic material.

There are also some time constraints relating to information that may be requested. This includes information over six years old, which can only be included in a notice issued by or with the approval of an authorised HMRC officer. In addition, HMRC cannot give a notice in respect of the tax position of a dead person more than four years after the person's death.

Powers can be exercised before a return is received in certain circumstances. This could include a situation where there is a reason to believe that a taxpayer did not notify chargeability to tax, did not register for VAT if required, or is operating in the informal economy.

Settlements

2.103 The majority of compliance visits result in some discrepancies being uncovered, and HMRC will usually calculate the 'lost' tax and national insurance over a period of six years plus the current year. This period may be extended if they suspect that deductions have been withheld deliberately. HMRC may also seek penalties (see below), although these will normally depend on the gravity of the discrepancy and the degree of co-operation and disclosure from the employer.

Often the audit investigator will be looking only for tax and possibly national insurance on the 'income' not taxed, instead of effecting a gross position. Amounts treated as benefits would not be grossed up or included in the assessment of national insurance under-deduction.

Penalties

2.104 HMRC may seek to impose a penalty where a taxpayer:

- fails to comply with an information notice;
- conceals, destroys or otherwise disposes of documents required by an information notice;
- conceals, destroys or otherwise disposes of documents that they have been notified are, or likely to be, required by an information notice; or
- deliberately obstructs an inspection that has been approved by the First-tier Tribunal.

There are three types and amounts of penalty:

- a standard penalty of £300;
- a daily penalty of up to £60 for every day that the failure or obstruction continues after the date the standard penalty is assessed; and
- a tax-related penalty.

Daily or tax-related penalties cannot be considered unless a standard penalty, in respect of the failure or obstruction, has been assessed. Moreover, they can only be assessed by, or applied with, the agreement of an authorised HMRC officer.

A tax-related penalty is in addition to the standard penalty and any daily penalties. The amount of the penalty is decided by the Upper Tribunal, based on the amount of tax at risk.

A person is not liable to a penalty if they have a reasonable excuse for:

- failing to comply with an information notice; or
- obstructing an inspection;

and they remedy that as soon as the excuse ends. The excuse will then be treated as continuing until the correction is made.

Normally, daily penalties will not be assessed after the failure has been remedied.

Special Civil Investigations Section

2.105 The Special Civil Investigations Section (SCI) investigates the tax affairs of individuals, partnerships, companies and particular transactions, and also situations where substantial amounts of tax may be at risk. Investigations are sometimes started in local offices and subsequently handed over to SCI, whilst others are handled by SCI from the outset.

The Special Trades Investigations Unit (STIU) is a subsidiary unit of SCI with offices located both in London and Leicester. It deals almost exclusively with the CMT ('cut, make and trim') sector of the clothing industry in Leicester, Birmingham and the east end of London. Whilst this is a small section it is very active in its particular sphere and has had a significant impact in raising PAYE/National Insurance contributions compliance levels in this sector. A significant proportion of businesses in the CMT sector of the clothing industry are run by Asian immigrants, or second generation UK domiciles of Asian origin. STIU receives a great deal of information (often anonymous in origin) concerning the use of illegal immigrants as direct labour or out-workers by bona fide UK businesses. The employment of illegal immigrants significantly increases the risk that PAYE will not be operated on wages paid to the worker. Whilst there appears to be no provision for information to be swapped between the Home Office and HMRC concerning the use of illegal immigrants by employers, nevertheless STIU is likely to be in the forefront of government agencies with an interest in the provisions of the *Asylum and Immigration Act 1996*.

The Agricultural Compliance Unit is also a subsidiary unit of SCI based in Leeds and deals with self-employed gang masters in order to ensure that they operate the PAYE rules on gangs of casual workers utilised by farmers at peak times during harvesting. There has been an increased tendency in recent years for casual workers in the agricultural sector to be recruited from unemployed peasant workers from Eastern Europe. There is a significant risk that these workers may contravene immigration control regulations and that wages will be paid in cash without deduction of tax under the PAYE regulations.

It is important to establish whether the SCI is involved in an investigation at the outset, because these HMRC staff will usually be more experienced and aware of technical aspects. They may also be more rigorous in the way in which they conduct the investigation.

It is generally perceived that the remit of the SCI is to seek quick and effective settlements, which will promote a speedy cash flow to the Exchequer. In practice, SCI inspectors are often more ready to come to ad hoc arrangements than their counterparts in local tax districts.

Dispensations

2.106 A dispensation is a notice from HMRC which relieves an employer from reporting expenses payments and benefits in kind on forms P11D because HMRC are satisfied that no tax is payable on them. Dispensations generally cover 'qualifying travelling expenses' (other than business mileage payments) or amounts incurred wholly, exclusively and necessarily in the performance of the duties of the employment. HMRC normally accept that expenses payments which are covered by a dispensation do not count as earnings for NIC purposes. Where an employer has a dispensation the items listed will not be treated as a benefit in kind and liable to Class 1A NICs.

The following conditions must be satisfied before a dispensation is granted:

- no tax would be payable by employees on expenses paid or benefits provided; and
- expenses claims are independently checked and authorised within the firm and, where possible, are supported by receipts.

A dispensation may be considered for controlling directors who decide their own expenses provided that there is independent documentation to vouch for the expenditure.

Complaints

2.107 Most PAYE compliance reviews are settled by agreement. However, if an amount cannot be agreed upon, HMRC may make a formal determination for the tax underpaid, student loan deductions, and penalties. A notice of decision will be issued for outstanding NICs and statutory payments.

An employer can appeal to the tribunal against any determination or notice of decision within 30 days of issue.

There is a set procedure for dealing with complaints concerning the way an investigation has been conducted. Full details are set out in the HMRC

Factsheet entitled *Complaints and putting things right* (www.hmrc.gov.uk/factsheets/complaints-factsheet.pdf. Broadly, the steps are as follows:

(1) The HMRC officer dealing with the investigation should be contacted in the first instance, or their line manager or the person in charge of the HMRC office.

(2) If the matter cannot be settled, contact the Director with overall responsibility for the office dealing with the investigation. The Director will review the complaint objectively.

(3) Where matters are still not resolved, contact the Adjudicator. The Adjudicator acts as an unbiased and independent referee. The Adjudicator can be contacted at:

The Adjudicator's Office,
Haymarket House,
28 Haymarket,
London,
SW1Y 4SP.
Telephone: 020 7930 2292
E-mail: adjudicators@gtnet.gov.uk

(4) If at any time a person is not satisfied with the service they are receiving from HMRC or the Adjudicator, they should contact their MP and ask for the case to be referred to the Parliamentary Ombudsman. The Ombudsman accepts referrals from any MP, but the local MP should be contacted in the first instance.

(5) Allegations of very serious misconduct by HMRC staff, such as assault or corruption, are dealt with by the Independent Police Complaints Commission (IPCC) (www.ipcc.gov/uk/index/ complaints.htm).

DISCLOSURE OF TAX AVOIDANCE SCHEMES

Background

2.108 *FA 2004, s 319(1)* requires promoters and, in some cases, users to provide HMRC with information ('disclosure') about certain direct tax schemes that might be expected to obtain a tax advantage as one of the main benefits.

The disclosure regime was extended from 1 August 2006 to include the whole of income tax, corporation tax and capital gains tax. From that date, the schemes required to be disclosed are those that fall within certain hallmarks. In addition, the time limit for disclosure of schemes devised in-house has been reduced to 30 days from the date that the scheme is implemented (*SI 2006/1544*) and a *de minimis* provision added so that neither individuals nor businesses that are

SMEs have to disclose in-house schemes. The three key changes are:

- For income tax, corporation tax and capital gains tax purposes, the range of disclosable tax arrangements is no longer limited to employment or financial products. Under the revised rules, they potentially include any tax arrangement relating to any aspect of those taxes (*SI 2006/1543* as amended by *SI 2007/785* and *SI 2007/2484*).
- For income tax, corporation tax and capital gains tax purposes, the range of disclosable tax arrangements is no longer limited by a series of filters. Instead a tax arrangement becomes disclosable if any one of a series of 'hallmarks' applies.
- Disclosure of newly implemented 'in-house' tax arrangements relating to income tax, corporation tax and capital gains is now due within 30 days of implementation, rather than by the filing date for the return period in which the first transaction of the tax arrangement was implemented.

Promoters of schemes, or the taxpayers themselves, are now obliged to make disclosure of specific information within five days of the scheme being made available by the promoter, or implemented by the taxpayer (*SI 2006/1543* as amended by *SI 2007/785* and *SI 2007/2484*).

This means that HMRC will be aware of the scheme before it has been put to any widespread use.

Hallmark schemes from 1 August 2006

2.109 In the 2006 Budget, the Chancellor announced that the disclosure regime was to be extended to include the whole of income tax, corporation tax and capital gains tax. From 1 August 2006, the schemes required to be disclosed are those that fall within certain hallmarks as prescribed by the *Tax Avoidance Schemes (Prescribed Descriptions of Arrangements) Regulations 2006 (SI 2006/1543).*

From 1 August 2006, the *Tax Avoidance Schemes (Prescribed Descriptions of Arrangements) Regulations 2004 (SI 2004/1863)* were revoked, and the 2006 regulations apply to the whole of income tax, corporation tax and capital gains tax. The regulations contain hallmarks (ie descriptions of arrangements in line with the system used for value added tax). If a scheme falls within any one hallmark, it will be notifiable.

The hallmarks fall into three groups:

- three generic hallmarks that target new and innovative schemes;
- a hallmark that targets mass marketed tax products; and
- hallmarks that target areas of particular risk.

The three generic hallmarks are derived from the existing 'filters' of confidentiality, premium fee and off-market terms.

Two specific hallmarks concern:

- schemes intended to create tax losses to offset income or capital gains tax; and
- certain leasing schemes.

Full details regarding the hallmarks are set out in the HMRC guidance (June 2006), which is available online at www.hmrc.gov.uk/ria/disclosure-guidance.pdf.

The forms to complete

2.110 There are four different forms available for use in the following circumstances:

- AAG1 – Disclosure of avoidance scheme (Notification by scheme promoter);
- AAG2 – Disclosure of avoidance scheme (Notification by scheme user where offshore promoter does not notify);
- AAG3 – Disclosure of avoidance scheme (Notification by scheme user where no promoter, or promoted by lawyer unable to make full notification);
- AAG5 – Disclosure of avoidance scheme (Continuation sheet).

On receipt of the above forms, the HMRC Anti-Avoidance Group issues a unique scheme reference number for each disclosure of a hallmarked scheme it receives. The number is issued within 30 days of the Anti-Avoidance Group receiving the disclosure.

The reference numbers are eight digits in length and are issued to either scheme promoters or, where they have the liability to make disclosure, the scheme user.

Scheme reference numbers will be issued where the scheme has been designed for use 'in-house'.

Promoters are required to provide the reference numbers allocated by the Anti-Avoidance Group to clients who use their schemes. Promoters may find it more convenient to issue the number to their clients when it is received, although the strict statutory requirement does not require this. Promoters should ensure that they inform their clients of their obligation to include the reference number on their tax return or form AAG4.

2.111 *Income tax compliance*

Following the announcement in the Pre-Budget Report 2008 (PBRN22), two sets of regulations (*SI 2009/611* and *SI 2009/612*) were made, operative from 1 April 2009, that aim principally to simplify and improve the way that scheme users report a scheme reference number back to HMRC. A document containing updates to HMRC's guidance on tax avoidance disclosure is available on the HMRC website (at www.hmrc.gov.uk/avoidance/guidance-march.htm). The updates reflect the changes introduced by these two statutory instruments.

Penalties

2.111 Failure by promoters or scheme users to comply with their obligations to notify prescribed information in respect of notifiable proposals and arrangements or failure by promoters to inform clients of the scheme reference number renders them liable to (*TMA 1970, s 98C(1), (2)*):

- an initial penalty of up to £5,000; and
- a further penalty of up to £600 for each day the failure continues after the imposition of the initial penalty.

Scheme users who fail to supply the prescribed information required in their returns are liable to a penalty of (*TMA 1970, s 98C(3), (4)*):

- £100 for the first failure;
- £500 for a second failure; and
- £1,000 for every failure thereafter.

A failure of this nature will not incur the scheme user a further penalty for the submission of an incomplete return (*FA 2004, s 313(4)*).

Penalties will be determined by an officer of the Board of HM Revenue & Customs, but a right of appeal lies to the First-tier Tribunal (*TMA 1970, ss 100, 100C*).

DISCLOSURE OF NIC AVOIDANCE SCHEMES

Background

2.112 The Tax Avoidance Disclosure (TAD) regime applies to NIC avoidance schemes from 1 May 2007 (*SSAA 1992, s 132A* inserted by *National Insurance Contributions Act 2006 (NICA 2006), s 7*). Prior to 1 May 2007, a person who had to disclose a scheme for both tax and NICs could make a single disclosure. The only change after 1 May 2007 is that they must explicitly explain how the scheme works for NICs. The main impact of the extension will, therefore, be upon schemes that are notifiable for NICs only.

TAD applies only to schemes which fall within certain criteria. First, there must actually be a scheme and that scheme must be expected to provide an advantage for NIC purposes – this might be a reduction or deferral of payment of an NI liability. That advantage must be one of the main benefits of using the scheme.

Secondly, a scheme that passes through the above tests is notifiable only if it falls within one of several descriptions ('hallmarks').

Hallmarks

2.113 The hallmarks most likely to trigger a NICs disclosure are (*SI 2007/785*):

- Confidentiality from other promoters. This applies to promoters only. The test focuses on any element within the scheme that delivers the expected NICs advantage. It is a hypothetical test: would any promoter want to keep that element confidential from other promoters in order to facilitate continued or repeated use of that element?
- Confidentiality from HMRC. Again focuses on any element within the scheme that delivers the expected NICs advantage. The test is, would the promoter want to keep the element confidential from HMRC in order to facilitate continued or repeated use of that element:
- Premium fee. This is another hypothetical test which focuses on whether it is likely that any promoter would expect to receive a premium fee for the element (or similar) that delivers the NICs advantage.
- Standardised NICs Products. This hallmark is aimed at so-called 'plug and play' schemes that use standardised documentation and transactions and whose main purpose is to obtain a NICs advantage. There are exceptions for schemes that consist of certain statutory reliefs and for schemes made available (by any promoter) before 1 August 2006.

Reporting

2.114 The obligation to disclose an NIC scheme normally falls upon the promoter, that is to say someone who either makes the scheme available for implementation or is to any extent involved in the design of the scheme. In practice, promoters are often accountants, lawyers or banks, but may include payroll consultants and service providers.

A promoter disclosure does not identify clients. HMRC issues a scheme reference number that a promoter must pass on to clients. Clients who use a scheme for which they have a scheme reference number must notify HMRC. For NICs schemes, the client will normally be the employer, who, if they use the scheme, must notify HMRC on form AAG4 by the filing date of the PAYE return affected.

A tough penalty regime exists alongside TAD. Failure to disclose a scheme may lead to an initial penalty of up to £5,000, and an additional £600 a day for each day that the failure continues. Failure to notify a scheme reference number may incur an initial penalty of £100, rising to a maximum of £1,000 for subsequent failures.

Chapter 3

Savings and investments

TAXABLE AND EXEMPT INCOME

Introduction

3.1 Certain types of income are exempt from tax, as are certain types of people. This chapter looks at various categories of savings and investments that are either classed as 'tax efficient' or have various tax exemptions attaching to them. Where any tax-efficient investment is being considered, it is always important to weigh up possible future changes to the tax system. In addition, the possibility of investment transactions being treated as trading by HMRC should also be borne in mind, as once a trade has been established, the more beneficial capital gains treatment (eg use of the annual exemption, special reliefs and use of capital losses) does not apply.

This chapter deals mainly with the position of investors resident and domiciled in the UK. It does not consider the position of the British expatriate.

Income received without deduction of tax – examples

3.2

- National Savings Bank interest;
- interest on 3.5% War Loan;
- interest on government stocks (unless application is made for net payment).

Exempt investment income

3.3 Income from certain investments is exempt from tax, including the following:

- income from Individual Savings Accounts (ISAs);
- accumulated interest on National Savings (including index-linked) Certificates;

- interest and terminal bonuses under Save As You Earn (SAYE) schemes;
- interest awarded as part of an award of damages for personal injury or death;
- dividends on ordinary shares in a venture capital trust.

Joint savings and income

3.4 Where savings or investments are held in joint names, each taxpayer is taxable only on their share of the income. Income from savings or investments held jointly by husband and wife is usually split equally (*ITA 2007, s 836*). Where the savings and investments, and the income from them, are owned in unequal shares, an election can be made for the income to be split on that unequal basis (*ITA 2007, s 837*). The election cannot be backdated. The election does not apply to life insurance policies, life annuities or capital redemption policies. For 2004/05 onwards, income consisting of a distribution from a close company is not split equally in this way, but is taxed in accordance with each spouse's actual share in the income.

Tax rates

3.5 Special rates of tax apply to dividends and other savings income. Savings income is taxed at the top slice of an individual's income (except for employment termination payments and life policy gains) and dividend income is treated as the top slice of savings income (*ITA 2007, s 1012*).

For the years up to and including 2007/08, savings income other than dividends was taxed at:

- 10% up to the 'starting rate' limit;
- the 'lower rate' (savings rate) of 20% up to the basic rate limit; and
- the 40% higher rate above that.

From 2008/09 onwards, the 'starting rate' only applies to savings income. If an individual's non-savings taxable income exceeds the starting rate (£2,440 for 2009/10 and 2010/11), the starting rate band will be unavailable. The basic rate of income tax has been reduced from 22% to 20% and the savings rate has been merged with it. Banks and building societies now automatically deduct tax at a rate of 20% from interest earned. Individuals who are entitled to have any of their savings income taxed at the 10% rate will be able to claim some tax back from HMRC.

For 2008/09 and 2009/10, dividend income is taxed at:

- 10% up to the basic rate limit; and
- 32.5% thereafter.

From 2010/11, there are three rates of tax for dividends (*FA 2009, s 6*):

- dividends otherwise taxable at the 20% basic rate continue to be taxable at the 10% dividend ordinary rate;
- dividends otherwise taxable at the 40% higher rate continue to be taxable at the 32.5% dividend upper rate; and
- dividends otherwise taxable at the new 50% additional rate (see **1.52**) are taxable at a new 42.5% dividend additional rate.

Interest and other savings income

3.6 Savings income includes interest from banks and building societies, interest distributions from authorised unit trusts, interest on gilts and other securities including corporate bonds, purchased life annuities and discounts (*ITTOIA 2005, ss 369, 422, 547*).

This income is taxed in the tax year of receipt with no relief for expenses. For 2005/06 onwards, most of the classes of income formerly charged under Schedule D Case III have been brought together in *ITTOIA 2005, Pt 4* (Savings and Investment income).

In most cases, tax at the 20% basic rate is deducted at source from bank and building society interest (*ITA 2007, Pt 15*) and basic rate taxpayers will have no further tax to pay. Higher rate taxpayers will have additional tax to pay, to the extent that savings income exceeds the basic rate tax limit. Non-taxpayers, or taxpayers only subject to tax at the starting rate of 10%, may claim repayment of the excess tax deducted at source.

An individual may register with banks and building societies (on a form R85) to receive interest gross (ie without tax deduction at source), if taxable income is expected to be below his available allowances for the tax year (*SI 1990/2231*). A penalty of up to £3,000 may be imposed for fraudulent or negligent self-certification (*TMA 1970, s 99A*).

Dividends

3.7 Special rates of income tax apply to dividend income. These rates are known as the dividend ordinary, the dividend upper rate and (since 6 April 2010) the dividend additional rate (*ITA 2007, s 13*).

Dividend income includes (*ITA 2007, s 19*):

- dividends and distributions from UK companies;
- dividends and 'relevant foreign distributions' from non-UK resident companies. A relevant foreign distribution is a distribution (other than a dividend) corresponding to taxable distributions from UK companies;
- stock dividends from UK-resident companies; and
- the release of a loan to a participator in a close company.

UK dividends (and certain other distributions) paid by companies carry a tax credit of 1/9th of the amount distributed (equal to 10% of the dividend plus the tax credit). An individual shareholder whose income does not exceed the basic rate limit has no further tax to pay on the dividend.

Higher rate 40% taxpayers pay an additional 22.5% (ie 32.5% less the 10% tax credit), equivalent to 25% of the cash amount received.

From 6 April 2010, individuals are liable to income tax at the dividend additional rate on dividend income which would otherwise be chargeable at the additional rate of income tax (*ITA 2007, s 13(2)*). For 2010/11, the dividend additional rate is set at 42.5% (*ITA 2007, s 8(3)*). The tax credit attaching to dividends and distributions from UK companies is set against the tax charged at the dividend additional rate.

The tax credits on dividends cannot be refunded to non-taxpayers.

Taxation of savings income – examples

3.8

Example 3.1

For 2010/11, John has earnings of £20,000 and interest from savings accounts of £5,000. His personal allowance for the year is £6,475. John's taxable income for 2010/11 is £18,525 (£20,000 + £5,000 – £6,475).

After deducting the personal allowance from his earnings, the amount of earnings that is taxable is more than £2,440 (£20,000 – £6,475 = £13,525), so none of his savings income is taxed at 10%. His other income is taxed at 20% and he cannot claim any tax back from HM Revenue & Customs.

Example 3.2

In 2010/11, Christine has earnings of £6,800 and savings income of £4,000. She is entitled to personal allowances of £6,475. Christine's taxable income for the year is £4,325 (£6,800 + £4,000 – £6,475).

Christine's personal allowance is used against her earnings of £6,800, so only £325 (£6,800 – £6,475) is taxable. The rest of the starting rate limit (£2,440 – £325 = £2,155) can be used against savings income. Earnings are charged to tax before savings income, as follows:

Earnings £325 × 20% = £65

Savings £2,155 × 10% = £215.50

Savings £1,845 (£4,000 – £2,155) × 20% = £369

Total tax due = £649.50

Other savings income

Relevant discounted securities

3.9 These are certain securities where the investor's return consists mainly of a discount or premium payable on redemption rather than interest payable and involves, or may involve, a deep gain. The discount is the difference between issue price and the amount payable on redemption and it is normally taxable at the date of redemption or disposal. The payment is made gross without deduction of tax. A 'deep gain' arises if the discount or premium is capable of being more than 15% of the redemption price, or if smaller, 0.5% of the redemption price for each year between issue and redemption (eg the discount on a ten-year bond must be at least 5%) (*ITTOIA 2005, ss 427–432*).

Strips of government securities

3.10 These are relevant discounted securities, but tax is chargeable on the discount each year even if no disposal is made. The discount is the difference between the market value on 5 April at the end of the tax year and the market value on 6 April at the beginning of the tax year.

Losses

3.11 Losses on disposals of relevant discounted securities before 27 March 2003 may be set against taxable income in the same tax year but cannot be carried forward or back. Relief may generally be claimed for losses on strips of government securities from 27 March 2003, including losses on strips of overseas government securities acquired from that date (*ITTOIA 2005, ss 427–460*).

Accrued income scheme – government stock, loan stock, etc

3.12 Accrued interest securities include interest-bearing marketable securities, such as government loan stock, company loan stock, permanent interest-bearing shares (PIBS) in a building society but not shares in a company, National Savings Certificates or relevant discounted securities (*ITA 2007, Pt 12).*

The scheme does not apply to companies (*ITA 2007, s 618*). Nor does it apply where the nominal value of all accrued income securities held does not exceed £5,000 at any time either in the tax year in which the next interest payment falls or in the previous tax year. For example, if the next interest payment after a purchase or sale falls between 6 April 2010 and 5 April 2011, the relevant years will be 2010/11 and 2009/10. In addition, the scheme does not apply on death.

A charge arises where the securities are purchased without a right to the next payment of interest (ex-dividend) or sold without a right to the next payment of interest (cum-dividend). The amount taxable on an ex-dividend purchase is the interest accrued on a daily basis from the date of purchase to the next interest date, and on a cum-dividend sale, the amount accrued from the last interest date to the date of sale. This is generally the amount by which the purchase price is reduced or the sale price increased.

Similarly, relief is available for cum-dividend purchases for interest accrued from the last interest date to the date of purchase and, for ex-dividend sales, for interest accrued from the date of sale to the next interest date. The relief is deductible from the gross interest receivable.

If the overall result is an amount chargeable to tax, it is taxed as income received at the end of the interest period.

TAX ON INVESTMENTS

Alternative finance arrangements

3.13 Certain alternative finance arrangements have been developed to cater for investors who require access to products that do not involve the receipt or payment of interest (because for example, it is important to them to adhere to *Shari'a* law, which prohibits receipt or payment of interest). For tax purposes, any profit element attributable to the following financial arrangements entered into on or after 6 April 2005, will be taxed as interest on the payer and recipient (although for financing purposes, the profit element will continue to be treated as a finance return, not interest) (*FA 2005, ss 46–57*):

(a) Purchase and resale arrangements – where an asset is bought for onward sale at a profit and all or part of the sale price is deferred. At least one party to the arrangements must be a financial institution; and

(b) Profit-share return arrangements – where a person deposits money with a financial institution who invests it as they see fit and shares any profit made with the investor.

FA 2007 contained new rules governing the taxation of certain types of investment bonds, known as '*sukuk*', which satisfy the *Shari'a* law prohibition on paying or receiving interest. These products replicate the economic effect of debt securities on which interest is payable, and the measure will ensure that they are taxed on a par with equivalent conventional securities (*FA 2007, s 53*).

Bank and building society accounts

3.14 Income from savings, including interest arising to a UK-resident individual on an account with a UK bank or building society, is normally paid with tax deducted at the basic rate of tax (for 2007/08 and earlier years tax was deducted at the lower rate of tax (20%)). Basic rate taxpayers do not have to pay additional tax, but taxpayers liable at the higher and (from 2010/11 the additional) rate will have a further liability arising on the gross interest (*ITA 2007, s 16*).

For 2008/09 onwards, individuals whose only taxable income is savings income are entitled to have the first slice of income (£2,440 for 2009/10 and 2010/11) above the personal allowance taxed at 10%. Any savings income above this annual threshold will be taxed at 20%. Since the bank or building society will normally deduct tax at 20% from interest earned, individuals who are entitled to have any of their savings income taxed at the 10% rate will be able to claim a repayment from HMRC.

Non-taxpayers are able to receive their interest gross by filling in form R85 (available from banks, building societies, post and tax offices, or see the HMRC Tax back pages online at www.hmrc.gov.uk/taxback/index.htm.

Where interest is paid without deduction of tax at source (eg on interest credited to ordinary and investment accounts with the National Savings Bank), it is taxed on a current-year basis.

A certificate of deposit or time deposit of over £50,000 made for at least seven days will be credited with gross interest. Companies, clubs, etc and foreign residents with UK bank accounts continue to receive interest gross. Deposits with overseas banks, etc and overseas branches of UK banks (including Channel Islands and Isle of Man) continue to have interest paid gross.

Capital gains tax can apply if currency accounts are operated other than for personal expenditure. Every withdrawal is then treated as a disposal for CGT purposes.

Building societies can offer permanent interest-bearing shares (PIBS). PIBS are a kind of hybrid between shares and a deposit. The main characteristics of PIBS are that they are only repayable on the winding up of the society, or with the prior consent of the Building Societies Commission, and that they rank behind the claims of ordinary shareholders and creditors in a winding up. They are treated as interest-bearing securities. Building societies must deduct income tax at the basic rate of tax. They fall within the accrued income scheme, and are treated as qualifying corporate bonds and so are exempt from capital gains tax for individuals.

Normally, a bank account in a foreign currency can be opened at a UK bank as well as in a foreign country. The interest is chargeable to UK income tax if received by a UK resident.

If the account is held abroad, interest will be paid according to local rules and taxed on receipt in the UK. If the interest is paid from abroad with a local withholding tax deducted, this can usually be offset against the UK tax liability.

If an exchange gain is made by converting foreign currency to sterling, this is normally chargeable to capital gains tax for individuals resident or ordinarily resident in the UK. Losses are allowable. CGT does not apply if the currency was acquired to meet personal expenditure outside the UK, or the gain was made by a non-UK domiciled individual on an account held overseas (it is taxed if remitted to the UK, but with no relief for losses).

Betting

3.15 Winnings from betting (including pool betting or lotteries or games with prizes) are normally paid free of tax and are not subject either to income tax or capital gains tax. Rights to winnings obtained by participating in any pool betting or lottery or game with prizes are not chargeable assets. For example, a gain or loss realised on the purchase of a share in the winnings of a ticket which has drawn a horse in a sweepstake is outside the scope of the tax.

Where the prize takes the form of an asset, it should be regarded as having been acquired by the 'winner' at its market value at the time of acquisition (*TCGA 1992, s 51(1)*).

Enterprise Investment Scheme (EIS)

3.16 Under the EIS, qualifying individuals can claim tax relief at the 'EIS rate' of tax (currently 20%) on new equity capital of up to £500,000 per tax year from 2008/09 (*ITA 2007, s 158*; *FA 2008, s 31(1)*). Prior to 2008/09 the limit was £400,000. EIS shares must be held for a minimum of three years. They are exempt from capital gains tax on profits after the three-year retention period. And capital losses (reduced by EIS relief not withdrawn) can be set against income tax or capital gains tax (*ITA 2007, Pt 5*).

EIS investments can shelter capital gains. Gains on any asset can be deferred by subscribing for qualifying EIS shares and issued in the period within one year before and three years after the disposal. As 28% CGT can be deferred (from 23 June 2010), and 20% income tax relief claimed, a maximum tax relief of 48% may be available. Any deferred gain becomes chargeable on the happening of certain events, eg on disposal of the EIS shares at any time.

The EIS scheme is covered in further detail in **3.37**.

Venture capital trusts

3.17 Various tax reliefs are available to individuals aged 18 or over who invest in shares in venture capital trusts (VCTs). These are quoted companies that invest in qualifying unquoted companies trading wholly or mainly in the UK (*ITA 2007, Pt 6*).

As a tax shelter, the net of tax return from this investment can be excellent. If an investor can sell out merely at par after five years after a tax refund of £30,000 on a £100,000 investment, he has done tolerably well. If, instead, he is selling his shares at a profit rather than at par plus indexation, the net return could be spectacular given that any profit on that disposal is free of CGT. Much is dependent on the investor being able to make his exit easily and at a good price, which makes this a high-risk investment.

VCTs are covered in further detail in **3.49**.

Chattels, collectables, etc

3.18 Investment into antiques, jewellery, stamps, coins, paintings, works of art, etc can create a liability to capital gains tax if there is a gain at the time of sale, which is not covered by the annual CGT personal exemption.

There is, however, a helpful CGT exemption for chattels (currently £6,000) (*TCGA 1992, s 262(2)*), but a corresponding restriction on loss relief.

The obligation and onus of proof of eligibility are on the taxpayer (see, for example, *Neely v Ward (HMIT)* [1993] BTC 110).

If a set is broken down to try to avoid CGT (eg a pair of candlesticks sold individually), HMRC can invoke anti-avoidance rules to treat two or more transactions as one where parties are acting in concert. Tangible moveable property which is a wasting asset (ie one which has a predictable useful life not exceeding 50 years) is outside CGT, provided it is not used for the purposes of a trade.

The above comments cover collecting only if it remains an investment activity. If HMRC successfully maintain that a trade has developed, then profits will be subject to income tax.

Child trust fund (CTF)

3.19 All children born since September 2002 have received an initial voucher worth at least £250, with those from low-income families receiving an additional £250 paid directly into their accounts, making £500 in total. However, as announced on 24 May 2010, government contributions to CTFs will be reduced to a basic £50 from August 2010. Contributions will cease completely from 1 January 2011.

Since April 2010, the government have been contributing £100 every year to the CTF accounts of all disabled children, with severely disabled children receiving £200 per year. The payments started in April 2010 for children in receipt of Disability Living Allowance at any point during the 2009/10 tax year. As noted above, all government contributions to CTFs will cease from 1 January 2011.

Family and friends may contribute up to £1,200 a year to each account. It should, however, be noted that, before parents or carers can receive the voucher, they must first claim and be awarded Child Benefit. Child Benefit is paid regardless of family income and it goes to parents or carers of all children living in the UK, until the child reaches the age of 16.

A further universal payment of £250 has formerly been made to the child at age seven, with children from low-income families receiving £500. However, as announced on 24 May 2010, such contributions ceased with effect from August 2010.

There will be no tax to pay on the income or gains arising on the monies in the account, provided the person entitled to the fund is a UK resident at the time the fund is paid out.

There are three types of Child Trust Fund (CTF) account to choose from:

(1) savings accounts;

(2) accounts that invest in shares; and

(3) stakeholder CTF accounts.

Stakeholder accounts are the government's preferred way of saving. The following table shows the key differences between the two:

Stakeholder	*Non-stakeholder*
Must have exposure to shares	Need not be exposed to shares
Some investments are prohibited (see below)	Almost unrestricted investment choice
Maximum provider charge is 1.5% of the account's value per year	No maximum provider charge
Minimum contribution not exceeding £10	Minimum contribution may be more or less than £10
The account must provide a 'lifestyling' facility (see below)	'Lifestyling' is not compulsory

Both types of account have the following features in common:

- only children born on or after 1 September 2002 are eligible;
- all payments are a gift to the child and cannot be reclaimed;
- the money can only be paid out to the child and is locked in until they are 18;
- tax-efficient growth; and
- up to £1,200 per year may be paid into each account.

3.20 A stakeholder account must meet certain requirements, in particular:

- the account must include at least some exposure to equities;
- the underlying investments must represent a mixture of assets which is both appropriate and suitable for long-term savings for a child;
- any underlying investments held directly (rather than indirectly – for example, through a collective investment scheme) for the CTF account must not be, or include:
  - investment trust shares or securities;
  - collective investment scheme shares, if these are dual priced;
  - with-profits endowment policies or rights in contracts of insurance whose value is linked to shares in a dual-priced fund;

- company shares;
- company securities whose value could fall below 80% of their purchase price;
- cash in bank or building society deposit or share accounts whose interest rate is more than 1% below the Bank of England base rate; and
- depositary interests in any of the above;

- it must be possible, starting no later than the child's 13th birthday, to gradually move the underlying investments into lower risk assets (such as cash and government bonds) to reduce the chance of losses. This is commonly referred to as 'lifestyling';
- the minimum payment amount which the CTF account manager will accept must not be more than £10; and
- the total regular charges which can be made by the CTF account manager must not be more than 1.5% a year.

The registered contact, ie the person who opens a CTF account for a child, will be responsible for managing the account for the child. From 6 April 2009, CTF providers no longer require the CTF voucher from parents in order to open an account. The registered contact, and the child, when he or she has turned 16, can change account or CTF provider at any time. The account stops being a CTF account on the child's 18th birthday. The young adult then has full access to the money in the account and can use it how he or she thinks best.

Commodities and financial futures

3.21 Transactions in commodities may take the following forms:

- actual purchases and sales of a commodity ('physicals');
- 'futures' contracts, where there is frequently no intention of supplying or taking delivery of the commodity on maturity of the contract; or
- a combination of both.

If an investor buys physicals and makes his own trading decisions, the profit is likely to be taxable as trading income (*TCGA 1992, s 143*). HMRC will consider on the facts in every case whether, in their view, a trade is carried on. With futures, a contract is made to buy or sell a quantity at a fixed price. Where the contract is to buy, a price rise meanwhile gives a profit as the investor can buy at the fixed price and sell at the higher market price. If the contract is to sell, a price fall also means a profit for the investor. By buying and selling, traders expecting physical delivery of the commodity can hedge against the risk that unsold goods will depreciate due to a fall in the underlying commodity, or that pre-booked forward sales will show a loss if the price rises. Futures also avoid the difficulties of dealing with the commodity itself, such as storage, perishables, insurance, etc. Statement of Practice 3/02 sets out HMRC's views on the tax treatment of transactions in financial futures and options.

3.22 Gains on disposal of unit trusts specialising in commodities are subject to CGT unless the trust is based abroad. This is inevitable as overseas trusts cannot be 'authorised'. Then, unless the trust or fund has 'distributor' status, the profit will be subject to income tax. The unit trust does not pay tax on capital gains.

Gains (or losses) arising in the course of dealing in commodity or financial futures or options, which do not fall to be treated as trading profits or losses, come within CGT. An outstanding obligation under a futures contract is treated as an asset for CGT and the closing out of it constitutes the disposal of it. If money is received it will be fully taxable as gain and if it is paid out it will constitute a loss (ie the actual price of the underlying physicals is ignored and only the 'differences' on the futures contract are taken into account). Exceptionally, if delivery is taken or made, the full price of the physical will be taken into account.

Investors mainly use financial futures and options to hedge potential losses if the markets or currencies move unfavourably, and resulting profits or losses will be of a capital, not a revenue, nature. Similarly, buying and selling options or futures as an incidental and temporary part of a change in investment strategy will probably result in capital gains or losses. Other transactions accepted by HMRC as capital include where a taxpayer sells gilts and futures to protect the value of his gilts holdings; where a currency future is bought before buying an asset denominated in that currency; where index futures are bought (or put options sold) to protect the value of a taxpayer's portfolio from market falls.

However, the tax treatment of transactions in financial futures or options clearly related to an underlying asset will follow the tax treatment of any underlying asset.

A manufacturer's profits or losses through financial futures to hedge the price of his raw materials are treated as part of the profits or losses of the trade.

Enterprise zones

3.23 Wider availability and a special rate of industrial buildings allowances (IBAs) for buildings constructed in an enterprise zone (EZAs) were introduced by *FA 1980*. The legislation was intended to stimulate new building in certain areas of physical and economic decay such as London Docklands. However, on 17 December 2007, it was announced that EZAs will be withdrawn completely from April 2011. There will be no phasing-out period (*FA 2008, s 86*).

Under the current provisions, once an area has been designated an enterprise zone the designation lasts for ten years.

Construction expenditure on a site in an enterprise zone incurred:

- within ten years of the designation of the zone; or
- under a contract entered into within ten years of the designation of the zone and incurred within 20 years of the designation of the zone,

qualifies for a higher rate of IBA.

Under the enterprise zone legislation, the range of buildings qualifying for IBA is extended (*CAA 2001, s 271(1)(b)*).

There is a higher rate of initial allowance and a higher rate of writing down allowance (WDA) where those allowances are claimed by the person who incurred, or is deemed to have incurred, expenditure on constructing the building.

These allowances are sometimes referred to as enterprise zone allowances, but in reality they are normal IBA at a higher rate.

The normal IBA rules apply to buildings in enterprise zones with one or two exceptions. The legislation about qualifying hotels, which require a deemed sale after two years in which the hotel is not a qualifying hotel, does not apply to buildings in enterprise zones. This means that, where a qualifying hotel has qualified for enterprise zone allowances, there is not a deemed sale after two years in which it is not a qualifying hotel.

3.24 The cost of constructing a new building of any size which is to be used for industrial or commercial (but not residential) purposes qualifies in full for tax relief (*CAA 2001, s 281*). The capital cost of the land on which the building stands does not attract any form of relief and so it is often advisable to convert the non-tax deductible capital sum into a tax deductible annual sum. This is achieved by acquiring the land under a long lease, say 125 years, with no premium payable and with a full ground rent (probably reviewable at intervals of five years).

The allowances are available to the person who erects a building or to the person who buys a building from a developer (but not to both). In the case of a purchase from a developer, it is important to ensure that the building is unused at the date of sale, otherwise the tax relief is considerably less attractive. In the case of an investor this means that the building must not have been occupied by the tenant prior to the sale, although it can be the subject of a lease. In addition a joint election must be made whereby the developer concedes his allowances and the investor is deemed to have erected the building.

For an individual the allowances are available to set against any form of income of the year of purchase or the following year (*CAA 2001, s 306*). Since expenditure is deemed to be incurred on the date on which it becomes payable it is often possible to ensure that the year of purchase is in fact two years, by providing that the purchase price is paid partly in one tax year and partly in the next, although anti-avoidance measures exist to prevent abuse. There is also anti-avoidance to ensure that where there is an 'arrangement' affecting value, the disposal value is increased to what it would have been but for the 'arrangement' (see *R v IR Commrs, ex parte Matrix Securities Ltd* [1994] STC 272 regarding arrangements having an artificial effect on pricing).

Annual writing down allowances of 25% are also available (*CAA 2001, s 310*).

Enterprise zone property trusts are collective schemes whereby individuals buy an interest in a portfolio of properties in enterprise zones for from £5,000 with no upper limit, with full income tax relief except on the portion representing the cost of land (typically between 4% and 8% of the investment).

Gilts (British government stock)

3.25 Stocks are issued by the government as a way of raising funds. For most stock issues there will be a guaranteed price and date for redemption. Interest is paid during the lifetime of the stock.

'Gilt-edged securities' means the securities specified in *TCGA 1992, Pt 2, Sch 2*.

The interest is subject to income tax and may be linked to inflation. The tax deducted, which can be reclaimed by non-taxpayers, is treated as satisfying the investor's liability at the basic rate. Taxpayers liable at the higher rate of 40% have a further tax bill of 20% to pay, and those liable at the additional rate of 50% will have a further tax bill of 30% to pay.

Gilts are not chargeable assets for capital gains tax – even if sold in the first year of ownership. There is a charge to income tax on holders of certain securities who realise profits on their sale (or gift) or redemption (including conversion into shares or other securities). This replaces tax under the rules for deep discount and deep gain securities and qualifying convertible securities, abolished from 1996/97 when new tax rules for corporate and government debt were introduced. The securities concerned are, broadly, securities issued at a discount to their redemption value of greater than half of one per cent for each year of their projected lives.

The proceeds of transfer or redemption, less acquisition and certain incidental costs, are charged to income tax. Losses may be set against other income (subject to certain restrictions for trusts and tax-exempt bodies). Death is an occasion of charge, as is the transfer of securities from personal representatives to legatees.

Special rules apply for gilt strips and securities issued at different times under the same prospectus. Shares, unstripped gilts, life assurance and capital redemption policies, and securities linked to the value of assets dealt with under capital gains tax, are specifically excluded from these rules.

Individual Savings Accounts

3.26 From 6 April 2010, individuals can subscribe to an individual savings account (ISA), up to an overall limit of £10,200. Up to one-half of the allowance can be saved in cash with one provider. The remainder can be invested in stocks and shares with either the same or a different provider. For investors aged 50 and over, the increase in the subscription limit to £10,200 from £7,200 took effect from 6 October 2009.

From 6 April 2011, the annual ISA limits will increase annually in line with inflation, measured by reference to the Retail Prices Index at September of the previous year, and rounded up to the nearest multiple of £120. In the event that inflation is zero, the previous limits would be unchanged. The limit for a cash ISA will remain at one-half of the overall limit.

Husbands and wives each have their own subscription limits. Income and gains are exempt from tax).

Withdrawals may be made at any time without loss of tax relief, but once a withdrawal is made a further deposit cannot be made to make up for it once deposits have already been made up to the allowed limits.

The general conditions for accounts and subscriptions to accounts are laid out in the *Individual Savings Account Regulations 1998 (SI 1998/1870), reg 4.*

HMRC produce comprehensive guidance on ISAs on their website at www.hmrc.gov.uk/isa/index.htm.

Example 3.3

Bill (aged 35) invests £6,000 in an ISA on 1 June 2010. In September 2010 he withdraws £500. In December 2010 he wishes to make a further investment. The maximum further investment he can make is £4,200 (£10,200 – £6,000). The amount withdrawn is not taken into account.

Investment trusts

3.27 The investor buys shares in public companies, usually via a stockbroker. The portfolio of shares is referred to as an investment trust.

Approved (as opposed to unapproved) investment trusts are now exempt from corporation tax on chargeable gains but the gains must not be distributed to shareholders as dividends.

Unapproved trusts are not exempt from tax on gains and, on a liquidation, a double charge can arise – one in the hands of the trust and another in the hands of shareholders. The trust must pay corporation tax on any unfranked income received.

When the shares are sold, any gain is subject to CGT. There is a scheme to ease the calculation of indexation allowance for those making monthly contributions to these trusts (SP 2/97).

National Savings

3.28 The various National Savings schemes offering gross returns have become more attractive now that tax at 20% is deducted at source from most forms of saving income, provided the return is competitive. The forms of National Savings are varied. Current products include:

- *National Savings Certificates* – These may be index-linked or fixed interest accounts. Typically, there is a minimum investment of £100 and a maximum of £15,000 (£30,000 if a husband and wife separately hold £15,000). Purchases and sales do not need to be shown on income tax returns. All returns are tax free.

- *Guaranteed Equity Bonds* – These offer growth potential linked to the FTSE 100 Index while keeping capital secure. Bonds are held for five years and no withdrawals are made during the term of the investment. The minimum purchase is £1,000, and the maximum investment is £1 million (or £2 million joint). Interest is paid gross and is taxable.

- *National Savings Income Bonds* – The minimum investment is £500 and the maximum is £1 million in total. There is no fixed investment term. Interest rates are variable, with tiered rates. They give investors a regular monthly income at a competitive (variable) interest rate. The interest is paid gross but is taxable.

- *National Savings Investment Account* – This is a deposit account run through the post office. Minimum investment is £20, maximum £1 million plus accumulated interest. Notice of one month is needed for withdrawals. Interest is variable. The interest is paid gross but is subject to income tax.

- *National Savings Easy Access Savings Account* – This is a fairly low interest-earning account run through post offices. Anyone over the age of 11 can hold an account. The minimum opening deposit is £100 and the maximum investment is £2 million (£4 million for joint investors). Interest is paid gross but is taxable.
- *National Savings Premium Bonds* – Premium Bonds cannot really be called an investment. They are a gamble that the interest forgone on the capital will result in a substantial win in a prize draw. The minimum investment is £100 (or £50 if bought monthly on standing order) and the maximum holding is £30,000. Winnings are tax free. The odds against a £1 bond winning in a particular month are approximately 24,000:1. The size of each month's prize fund is set by allocating the equivalent of one month's interest on the total value of eligible Bonds. The annual rate was 1.5% at May 2010. For current rates, see the National Savings and Investments website at www.nsandi.com/products/pb/rates.
- *National Savings Children's Bonus Bonds* – Individuals can invest on behalf of children under 16 a minimum of £25, up to a maximum of £3,000 per child. A bonus is added on the fifth anniversary of purchase, and all returns are totally exempt from UK income tax, even if funded by a parent.
- *National Savings Pensioners Guaranteed Income Bonds* – Those aged 60 or over can invest in this product. The minimum purchase is £500, and £1 million may be invested in total. Interest rates are guaranteed for the length of the Bond's term. Interest is paid gross but is taxable.

Racehorses

3.29 Profits arising from this type of investment will arise from prize money and from the sale of the horse during or after its racing career.

Under current regulations, not more than 12 people may share in a syndicated ownership with each shareholder contributing to the purchase, training, maintenance and running costs.

Shares can be sold to other shareholders (first offer) or to outsiders.

Investment may also be made into syndicated stallions – the income comes from stud fees – but the rules are not as strict as for racehorse syndication. Frequently, there are up to 40 shareholders, and the syndicate is run by a committee.

Stud fees have been held by a court to be receipt of annual income chargeable under former Schedule D, Case VI, but not trading receipts under former Case I (*Benson v Counsell* (1942) 24 TC 178; *Lord Glanely v Wightman* (1933) 17 TC 634).

Stallions acquired for stud purposes are ineligible for capital allowances. In *Earl of Derby v Aylmer* (1915) 6 TC 665 the taxpayer owned two stallions at stud and was assessed in respect of profits derived from stud fees. He contended that he was entitled to a deduction under the then legislation to take account of the diminished value of the stallions year by year. Both the special commissioners and Rowlatt J rejected the taxpayer's claim.

No charge to capital gains tax will arise on the sale of a horse because of the exemption which covers tangible moveable property and a wasting asset (with a predictable life not exceeding 50 years). This is so provided it has not been used for business purposes – so it may be unwise to seek a deduction for costs of purchasing and keeping horses (eg for advertising and promotional purposes) if they are likely to make a fortune either racing or at stud.

Shares

3.30 Successful investors on the stock market will benefit from the capital growth of the share, dividends paid (usually half-yearly by quoted companies) and perhaps 'perks' (eg a discount on company goods).

Due to the risk of investment in unquoted companies, various tax reliefs are available (eg enterprise investment scheme, venture capital trusts: see **3.49**).

Investors receive cash dividends to which a tax credit attaches. They are liable to income tax on the cash plus tax credit. There is a higher rate liability at 32.5% for taxpayers so liable, and, from 2010/11, a rate of 42.5% for those liable to income tax at the additional rate of 50%. Those liable to tax at the basic rate, however, have no further tax liability.

Capital gains tax is chargeable on the capital growth of the shares on disposal. The cost or value of the shares could be index-linked for inflation up to April 1998. Thereafter, until its abolition on 5 April 2008, taper relief was available. Between 6 April 2008 and 22 June 2010, capital gains tax was charged at a flat rate of 18%. For disposals on or after 23 June 2010, a higher rate of capital gains tax of 28% applies to gains (or part of gains) exceeding the basic rate of income tax. Gains within the basic rate tax band continue to be charged at the 18% rate (*F(No 2)A 2010, s 2* and *Sch 1*). Capital losses on a disposal can be set off against gains realised in the same year – if there is an excess of losses, this can be carried forward for use in future years against future gains.

Unit trusts

3.31 Under this type of investment, the investor (the unit holder) purchases units in a unit trust. The trust would normally consist of a portfolio of shares specialising in certain markets (eg Japan, world technology, American smaller companies, etc). This can spread the risk for the investor, but reduces the opportunity for speculative gain. Some trusts offer a regular income, others capital growth, and some a mixture of both. The units are easily marketable in normal conditions and prices for buying and selling (the spread) are quoted daily. Several unit trust groups also offer savings plans.

Authorised unit trusts are exempt from capital gains tax on gains made within the trust.

Depending on the type of income some unit trusts may prefer to be unauthorised and taxed as trusts (authorised trusts are severely restricted in their types of investment and cannot currently invest, for example, in commodity futures or property).

Dividends paid to unit holders carry a tax credit and higher rate taxpayers will be liable to pay additional tax at the higher rate where applicable. Any gain made by the investor on disposal of the units is subject to capital gains tax at the appropriate rate.

FOREIGN SAVINGS AND INVESTMENTS

Offshore funds

3.32 Offshore funds are popular with UK residents not domiciled in the UK because UK tax is usually payable only on income and gains remitted to the UK (*ITTOIA 2005, s 832*).

Investors in funds resident overseas have the opportunity to benefit from the advantages of the tax havens where most of them are based. Such funds take the form of open-ended investment companies, or unit trusts. The return can be high, but dangers may lurk in exchange rates when funds are converted into sterling and in the fact that the traditional City safeguards for investors may not apply. On the other hand, currency movement may well be in the investor's favour.

A fund can apply to HMRC for 'distributor' status, the main test being that it distributes 85% of its income which would have been subject to corporation tax if resident in the UK. If the status is awarded, investors will still be subject to capital gains tax on the profit on disposal of the shares or units, but without indexation relief if the fund is 90% or more invested in CGT-exempt assets.

Gains made by investors in non-distributor funds (sometimes called roll-up funds because the income is rolled up into the settlement) are subject to income tax. However, if the interest was acquired before 1984, the part of any gain accruing before 1984 attracts CGT.

Dividends from the funds are paid gross to investors, with income tax payable at basic, higher and, from 6 April 2010, additional rates if applicable.

The funds with non-distributor status may still have strong appeal for some taxpayers.

The advantages are:

- The effective rate of return is much higher because no tax liability arises until the investor sells shares or units in the fund. The tax charge can be reduced to a minimum by selling the shares in a low tax year (perhaps after retirement) or may be eliminated completely by selling during a year of non-residence when the investor is outside the UK tax net altogether.
- Another attractive way to use the funds would be for parents to invest money for their minor children. Income arising during their minority would normally be charged as that of the parent(s). If the money were invested in a sterling fund there would be no taxable income until the shares were sold – and this could be done once the children reached 18, when the income would be treated as their own and not the parents.
- The method of actually taxing an offshore fund also has substantial advantages. The computation of the gain chargeable as income broadly follows the capital gains tax rules which allow a proportionate part of the original purchase price to be deducted as acquisition cost (which may be an advantage over the 5% per annum tax-free 'withdrawal' facility for an insurance bond). One tax disadvantage is that there is a charge to income tax on death.

Foreign securities

3.33 If equities are bought in foreign countries, it will be important to establish the residence of the company, which will decide if the dividends received are franked or unfranked for the UK corporate investor.

It is usual for shares on an overseas company register to be in the name of a nominee – 'marking name' – and this is arranged by a bank or broker. UK stamp duty is not charged when foreign shares are purchased, but other costs (including an equivalent duty in the foreign country) can more than equal this saving.

Dividends and interest may also be received subject to a withholding tax. This cannot be reclaimed from HMRC by non- or lower-rate taxpayers.

Unless the income is assessed on a remittance arising basis, foreign dividends should be regarded as arising when the dividend is payable by the foreign company and not the date of receipt in the UK (*ITTOIA 2005, s 832*). These dates can sometimes straddle the end of a tax year and may need careful attention from the point of view of cash flow.

The UK capital gains tax rules apply to disposals and other capital transactions in overseas shares. The UK gain is calculated by converting both the acquisition costs and disposal proceeds to sterling – not by converting the gain in foreign currency to sterling.

LIFE ASSURANCE GAINS

Gains deemed as income

3.34 Gains may arise on the following policies:

- UK life assurance policies;
- life annuities; or
- capital redemption policies.

Not all policies give rise to chargeable event gains.

Under the provisions of *ITTOIA 2005, s 461*, chargeable event gains are deemed to be income for tax purposes.

Taxable person

3.35 Any such gains of a bare or simple trust are treated as income of the beneficiary.

If the rights of a policy are held in trust, any gain resulting from a chargeable event is usually chargeable on the settlor. If it is the death of the settlor that gives rise to the gain, it is attributable to him. However, the gain is chargeable on the trustee if any of the following apply:

- the individual who created the trust is not resident in the UK at the time of the chargeable event;
- the individual who created the trust is dead at the time of the chargeable event;
- a company or other entity created the trust, and is not resident in the UK at the time of the chargeable event;
- a company or other entity created the trust, and has come to an end at the time of the chargeable event.

Gains that are deemed to be trustees' income are always chargeable at the rate applicable to trusts (RAT rate).

HMRC helpsheet 'HS320: Gains on UK life insurance policies' contains more information.

TAX-EFFICIENT INVESTMENTS

Introduction

3.36 What qualifies as a tax-efficient investment depends on the circumstances of a particular individual. An exemption from capital gains tax will be of no benefit to an individual who can confidently expect to have the full annual exempt amount available each year. Similarly, tax relief will not be important to non-taxpayers. Obviously, it would be impossible to cover every aspect in a work of this size, but the more popular vehicles offering various tax breaks are covered in the following paragraphs.

Enterprise Investment Scheme

3.37 The Enterprise Investment Scheme (EIS) aims to promote the raising of equity finance for new and small companies.

The EIS offers a series of potential reliefs for the investor:

- income tax relief at 20% of the amount invested is available up to a maximum of £500,000 per year, as long as the investor has less than 30% of the shares of the company and certain other conditions are satisfied (*ITA 2007, s 158*; *FA 2008, s 31*; *SI 2008/3165*). For 2006/07 and 2007/08, the maximum subscription limit was £400,000. It is not possible to carry forward unused relief, but there is a limited carry-back facility;
- a gain made by the investor prior to investment can be deferred by rolling into the EIS shares for which the investor subscribes. This relief is available even if the investor has more than 30% of the company share capital. It is even possible for the investor to create the company himself;
- any gain made on the ultimate disposal of EIS shares is exempt from CGT, if income tax relief was given on the subscription for these shares (ie the investor owned less than 30%, subscribed less than £500,000 and other relevant conditions were satisfied);
- even though a gain is exempt, the loss arising on the ultimate disposal of shares can be relieved against any capital gains and an election can be made when the loss is suffered to relieve the loss against income;
- if EIS shares that did not qualify for income tax relief are sold, the gain triggered can be rolled into a second EIS investment.

An individual is eligible for EIS income tax relief for cash subscribed for new shares issued to him or her. The shares must be issued in order to raise money for a business activity that qualifies under the EIS scheme (most trades qualify). The company must use the money raised for the trading activity and, prior to 22 April 2009, 80% of the cash raised by the EIS subscriptions had to be used within 12 months of the issue of shares, with the remaining 20% used within 24 months (*ITA 2007, Pt 5, Ch 3*). From 22 April 2009, however, the '80% within 12 months' rule was relaxed so that all money raised by the issue of shares must be wholly employed in a qualifying activity within two years of the EIS share issue, or (if later) within two years of the qualifying activity commencing (*FA 2009, s 27* and *Sch 8, paras 1–3*).

Prior to 22 April 2009, the investee company was required to use money raised from the issue of other shares on the same day and of the same class as the EIS shares within the same time limits. This link has now been removed and there will be no restriction on the use of money raised by the issue of non-EIS shares (*FA 2009, s 27* and *Sch 8, paras 1–3*).

The subscription must be entirely for cash. In *Thompson v Hart* [2000] STC 381, EIS relief was denied as the shares were issued in exchange for the transfer of properties.

3.38 Relief is available to an individual for a minimum subscription of £500 (*ITA 2007, s 157(2)*) and a maximum of £500,000 in a fiscal year (*ITA 2007, s 158*). These limits are applied separately to husband and wife and so can provide a reduction of tax for a married couple of up to £200,000 (2 × 500,000 × 20%). The investment can be direct into a company, or can be through an investment fund approved for EIS purposes.

Prior to 2009/10, where shares were issued before 6 October, the individual could elect that relief was given in the previous fiscal year for a sum specified by the taxpayer that was up to the lower of: (a) one half of the sum subscribed; and (b) £50,000 (£25,000 prior to 2006/07). This claim could be made in the self-assessment tax return for the preceding year, or could be an independent claim. The facility to relate back a subscription required rules for the attribution of relief to shares.

For 2009/10 onwards, the £50,000 limit on carry back is removed. However, the total investment that can be taken into account for the purposes of calculating income tax relief for any particular year will remain subject to a limit, currently £500,000 subscribed.

Example 3.4—Carry back limit prior to 2009/10

Charles subscribes for shares in Duke Ltd at a cost of £80,000 in 2008/09 and the shares are issued in September 2008. He acquires further EIS shares in Eggs Ltd in January 2009 for £110,000. In 2007/08, Charles had claimed EIS relief in respect of an investment of £230,000.

If he so wished, Charles could make an election to treat part of the shares as being issued in the previous year. The maximum which could be carried back in this way is the lower of:

One half of the amount subscribed (for shares issued on or before 5 October): £40,000

Overall maximum: £50,000

Remaining relief for previous year: £400,000 – £230,000 = £170,000

Maximum available to carry back: £40,000

Previously, it was possible that a charge to capital gains tax could occur on a 'share for share' exchange where such a gain would not normally be charged. *FA 2009* removed the rules that prevent the normal 'share for share' exchange capital gains tax rules from applying to the gain on the disposal of shares when all deferral relief has been recovered. From 22 April 2009, on the occasion of a qualifying 'share for share' exchange (under *TCGA 1992, ss 135* and *136*), any deferral relief given will be recovered as before, but no gain or loss will be brought into charge in respect of the disposal of the shares that form the subject of the exchange.

Investor connected with the company

3.39 For EIS income tax relief (but not for the CGT deferral relief), the individual must not be connected with the company into which the individual makes the investment at any time during a period that begins two years before the issue of shares and normally ends three years after that issue (*ITA 2007, s 163*). Where the company has raised funds through the subscription to carry on a trade which has not yet commenced, the three-year period during which the investor must not be connected with the company starts with the date of commencement of the company's trade.

An individual is connected with a company, for the purpose of EIS relief, in any of the following circumstances:

- the individual controls the company;
- the individual owns shares that give him or her more than 30% of the votes;
- the individual's shares plus his loan capital exceed 30% of the company's share capital (measured at par value) plus its loan capital;
- the individual trades in partnership with the company;

- the individual is an employee of the company;
- the individual is a director of the company, unless exempted by the rule below;
- the individual subscribes for shares as part of an arrangement under which another individual subscribes for shares in another company to which the first individual is connected.

3.40 A director is not treated as connected with the company if he or she is unpaid. 'Unpaid' is given a wide definition as including becoming entitled to any payments either from the company or from a related person at any time during the three-year exclusion period.

However, for this purpose, the following payments are ignored:

- reimbursement of expenses wholly, exclusively and necessarily incurred in performance of duties of the director;
- a reasonable return by way of interest on funds lent to the company;
- a 'reasonable' dividend on the investment of the company;
- a market rent on property let to the company;
- 'reasonable' charges for services provided to the company.

These exclusions are applied from the period of subscription onwards. The EIS income tax relief is not available where the individual has served as a director of the company before the share subscription; the individual is then treated as connected with the company. Where the target company has taken over a trade from another company, a directorship in the predecessor company would also deny relief.

Capital gains tax exemption

3.41 Where shares are issued on which income tax relief has been given, any gain made on the ultimate disposal of those shares by the individual investor is exempt from CGT. In order for this CGT exemption to apply, income tax relief must have been given and not withdrawn, otherwise the exemption is lost. Income tax relief can be withdrawn in two alternative scenarios:

(1) There can be a clawback of relief by a failure of the conditions that are necessary for the three years following the subscription. This could be a result of an action by the company or by the individual becoming connected with the company, such as taking paid employment or directorship.

(2) The individual's liability to income tax for the year's subscription could be reduced to £nil. This could arise through relief given for trading

losses under *ITA 2007, s 72*. Hence, any decision as to the way in which trading losses are to be relieved must take account of the possibility of the withdrawal of EIS relief and its effect on a potential exposure to CGT at a later date.

Capital gains tax deferral relief

3.42 Unlike EIS income tax relief, CGT deferral relief, when there is investment in shares that fulfil the EIS requirements, can be claimed by trustees as well as individuals.

Where a capital gain arises to an individual or to trustees, deferral relief can be claimed if the taxpayer subscribes for shares that fulfil the EIS requirements at any time during a period that begins 12 months before the disposal that caused the gain and ends 36 months after the date of disposal. Deferral relief operates so that the gain that would have been charged is frozen and brought into charge when there is ultimately a disposal of the 'EIS shares'. If the conditions for EIS relief are contravened at any time during the three years following the investment, such as by value being received from the company, the deferred gain is treated as arising on the date that the contravention occurs. It should be noted that the mechanism for the operation of deferral relief is not reduction in the base cost of the shares acquired by subscription; instead, the disposal of those shares causes the original gain to be brought into charge, as well as any gain on the shares themselves.

Unlike the provisions for EIS income tax relief, CGT deferral relief is available to individuals who are 'connected with the company'. This means that a company can be set up to carry on a new trade with the entire shareholding spread around members of the family, whilst still allowing a gain that has accrued to be deferred by reference to the investment made in the company. In contrast to the position for income tax, deferral relief for investment into EIS eligible shares requires the investor to be either resident or ordinarily resident in the UK and not to be exempt from CGT by virtue of a double tax agreement. There is no maximum to the size of the gain that can be deferred. Virtually any gain that arises on an individual or on trustees can be deferred (other than a gain imputed by *TCGA 1992, s 86* or *87* on a settlor or a beneficiary of a non-resident settlement or the gain arising under *TCGA 1992, s 161* where a capital asset is appropriated for trading stock).

Until 6 April 2008, shares that qualified under EIS rules would fulfil the requirements to be treated as a 'business asset' for CGT taper relief purposes. Hence, if the shares were kept for more than two years, only 25% of the gain arising was charged to CGT. However, the gain that was deferred was not afforded any additional taper relief. Thus, the gain, after any taper relief, was computed at the time of the disposal and this sum was then frozen and brought into charge when the shares into which the gain has been deferred were sold. From 2008/09, taper relief ceases to be an issue as it has been abolished and replaced with entrepreneurs' relief. Entrepreneurs' relief may be available in a limit amount of cases. Between 6 April 2008 and 5 April 2010, the first £1 million of chargeable gains made should qualify for relief. Between 6 April 2010 and 22 June 2010, the lifetime limit for entrepreneurs' relief was £2 million (*FA 2010, s 4*). From 23 June 2010, this limit has been raised again to £5 million.

A taxpayer obtains deferral relief by making a claim. The taxpayer is free to claim part of a gain. This means that a gain equal to the annual exempt amount can be left in charge, without any actual tax cost. If the investor has capital losses available, a larger part of the gain can be left in charge to be put against the losses. The use of deferral relief is, thereby, very flexible and it can be a valuable planning device.

Criteria for the company

3.43 The restrictions on the relationship between the individual investor and the company apply for a period of three years only. This starts on the date of subscription, unless the company is then not carrying on the trade for which the funds are being raised, in which case the period starts on the later date that trade commences.

The company issuing the shares must, throughout the three-year period, be an unquoted company which exists 'wholly for the purpose of carrying on one or more qualifying trades' (subject to a *de minimis* exemption), or is the parent company of a trading group (*ITA 2007, Pt 5, Ch 4*).

Qualifying trades are all trades other than (*ITA 2007, ss 192–199*):

- dealing in land, commodities, shares, etc;
- dealing in goods other than as a wholesaler or retailer;
- banking, insurance or other financial activities;
- oil extraction;
- leasing;
- providing legal or accountancy services;
- property development;
- farming or market gardening, forestry, etc;
- managing hotels;
- managing nursing homes, etc;

- providing services for any of the foregoing trades, where the service providing company and the company to which the services are provided are under common ownership; and
- shipbuilding and coal and steel production (for shares issued on or after 6 April 2008) (*FA 2008, s 32* and *Sch 11*).

The emergency Budget on 22 June 2010 contained an announcement that, from a date to be announced, the current legislation requiring there to be a qualifying trade carried on wholly or mainly in the UK will be changed. In future, the requirement will be that the company issuing the shares must simply have a permanent establishment in the UK. 'Permanent establishment' will be defined based on Article 5 of the Organisation for Economic Co-operation and Development (OECD) Model Tax Convention on Income and Capital.

The emergency Budget on 22 June 2010 also announced that new legislation, effective from a date to be announced, will exclude shares in a company from qualifying for the purposes of the EIS or VCT legislation if it is reasonable to assume that the company would be treated as an 'enterprise in difficulty' for the purposes of the European Commission's Rescue and Restructuring Guidelines, published in the Official Journal at OJC 2004/C 244/02, at section 2.1.

3.44 It is, however, possible for a company to qualify as an EIS company when it has a property managing subsidiary. (This is permitted by *FA 2004*, which also relaxed some of the more technical restrictions where the company is the parent of a group of companies.)

The balance sheet total of the company must not exceed £7 million (£15 million prior to 2006/07) before the issue of eligible shares, nor £8 million (£16 million prior to 2006/07) after the issue of eligible shares.

The maximum amount raised must not be more than £2 million in any 12-month period. A company or group of companies must have no more than 50 full-time employees (or their equivalent) at the date on which the relevant shares or securities are issued (*FA 2007, s 51* and *Sch 16*).

The taxpayer must subscribe for 'eligible shares'. These are defined as new ordinary shares which, throughout the period of three years beginning with the date on which they are issued, carry no present or future preferential right to dividends or to a company's assets on its winding up and no present or future right to be redeemed. Ordinary shares are defined as 'shares formerly part of the ordinary share capital of the company'. Shares are treated as never having been eligible if the cash raised by the company on the issue of those shares was used for a purpose other than a qualifying business activity.

Eligible shares are treated as ceasing to be eligible if an event occurs after the date of issue, which causes the company not to be a qualifying company or, in the case of a group of companies, ceases to be the parent company of a trading group.

Procedure

3.45 In order to obtain EIS income tax relief, the company must first apply to HMRC on form EIS1 for permission to grant certificates to its investors. HMRC then issues the company with form EIS2, which is authority to send its investors certificates demonstrating that the company fulfils the EIS requirements (form EIS3). A claim for income tax relief is then made by the investor on receipt of his or her certificate. It is usual for HMRC to ask for certificate EIS3 also in claims for deferral relief. As certificate EIS3 can only be issued after following the procedure of application form EIS1 and authority form EIS2, the effect of HMRC's approach is to force a company to carry through the EIS application procedure even where deferral relief only is being claimed.

Relief can be claimed at any time up to five years after the 31 January following the year in which the shares were issued (*ITA 2007, s 202*).

A company can obtain advance clearance from HMRC that it meets the EIS requirements. Application should be made to:

HMRC
Centre for Research and Intelligence (CRI)
Ty-Glas
Llanishen
Cardiff
CF14 5ZG

This office also provides advance clearance for companies under the venture capital trust (VCT) scheme, and monitors the action of companies that have issued shares under EIS or the VCT scheme.

Clawback of relief

3.46 EIS income tax relief is clawed back and any CGT deferral relief is brought into charge if, at any time during the three-year period from the date of the issue of the shares (or, if later, the date of commencement of the trade financed by the issue), any one of the following events takes place (*ITA 2007, Pt 5, Ch 7*):

- the shares are sold;
- the company ceases to carry on as a qualifying trade;
- value is received by the investor; or

- the individual becomes 'connected with' the company (income tax relief only).

If the qualifying trade ceases before the issue of shares or, more likely, never commences or, alternatively, if value is treated as being received by the investor before the issue of shares, the shares are treated as having never been eligible. If the failure of the conditions takes place at a later date, the shares are treated as ceasing to be eligible at that time. It should be noted that the shares ceasing to be eligible causes any gain that was deferred to be brought into charge. Hence, if £100,000 of gain has been deferred but later, during the three-year period, there is £1 of value received by the EIS investor, the whole £100,000 gain is thereby brought into charge.

3.47 An individual is treated as receiving value from the company if the company:

- repays, redeems or repurchases any of its share capital or securities which belong to the individual or makes any payment to the individual for giving up the individual's right to any of the company's share capital;
- repays any debt owed to the individual (subject to some exemptions) or makes a payment for giving up the individual's right to any debt;
- releases or waives any liability of the individual to a third person;
- makes a loan or advance to the individual;
- provides 'a benefit or facility' to or for the individual;
- transfers an asset to the individual at undervalue; or
- makes 'any other payment' to the individual (unless otherwise exempted).

Payments to an individual investor who is a director are exempted when they are within the categories listed above.

A similar list applies for CGT deferral relief.

If there is reorganisation of the company or there is a 'share for share' exchange, whereby a newly created company issues shares in exchange for 'EIS shares' that are held, the shares acquired on the reorganisation are to be treated as if they were the original shares issued. However, it is necessary for an acquiring company to fulfil the EIS provisions in its own right. The takeover of a company by a quoted company will normally cause clawback and crystallisation of any deferred gain (*ITA 2007, ss 247–249*).

Permitted payments from the company

3.48 *FA 2001* (now dealt with by *ITA 2007, ss 213–223*) introduced complex provisions that omit certain types of payment received from the company without causing clawback of EIS relief. If any of these are in point, careful reading of *ITA 2007, ss 213–223* is essential.

In summary, the following are possible, but all are subject to carefully defined restrictions:

- if a company has been unsuccessful, reorganisation of the company so that trade can continue under the ownership of a new company normally can be achieved without clawback of the EIS relief;
- payments can be made to an investor who sells goods or services to the company as long as the amount paid does not exceed the market value of the supply;
- interest can be paid to the investor on any sum linked to the company, as long as the rate of interest represents reasonable commercial return;
- the investor can sell an asset to the company for its market value;
- rent can be paid to the investor for the company's occupation of property, as long as the payment does not exceed a commercial rent for that property;
- the company can pay off a trade debt owed to the investor;
- the investor can sell other shares to the company, as long as no more than market value is paid;
- other payments totalling not more than £1,000 in aggregate can be made to the investor (described in the legislation as 'receipts of insignificant value') (*ITA 2007, s 215*).

Venture capital trusts

3.49 The venture capital trust scheme started on 6 April 1995. It is designed to encourage individuals to invest indirectly in a range of small, higher-risk trading companies whose shares and securities are not listed on a recognised stock exchange, by investing through venture capital trusts (VCTs).

The emergency Budget on 22 June 2010 contained an announcement that, from a date to be announced, the current legislation requiring shares making up a VCT's ordinary share capital to be included in the official UK list throughout the relevant accounting period will be changed. This requirement will be replaced with a requirement that the shares instead be admitted for trading on any EU regulated market. The effect is that VCTs will be able to be listed on markets throughout the EU/European Economic Area (EEA).

The emergency Budget on 22 June 2010 also announced that new legislation, effective from a date to be announced, will exclude shares in a company from qualifying for the purposes of the EIS or VCT legislation if it is reasonable to assume that the company would be treated as an 'enterprise in difficulty' for the purposes of the European Commission's Rescue and Restructuring Guidelines, published in the Official Journal at OJC 2004/C 244/02, at section 2.1.

VCTs are similar to investment trusts, and are run by fund managers who are usually members of larger investment groups. Investors can subscribe for, or buy, shares in a VCT, which invests in trading companies, providing them with funds to help them develop and grow. VCTs realise their investments and make new ones from time to time.

VCTs must be approved by HMRC for the purpose of the scheme. HMRC give approval if certain conditions are met. Investors in an approved VCT will be entitled to various income tax and capital gains tax reliefs, and VCTs are exempt from corporation tax on any gains arising on the disposal of their investments (*ITA 2007, Pt 6*).

An individual can subscribe up to £200,000 in a tax year and obtain tax relief (*ITA 2007, s 262*). For shares issued on or after 6 April 2006, the rate of tax relief is 30% (*ITA 2007, s 263*).

For shares issued on or after 6 April 2006, individuals must hold VCT shares for a minimum period of five years to qualify for income tax relief (*ITA 2007, s 266*).

Example 3.5

Sylvia subscribes for shares in Dolly Mixture Ltd at a cost of £180,000. Her tax liability for the year is £19,500. VCT investment relief may be claimed as follows:

		£
Income tax due for the year		19,500
Less:		
VCT investment relief		
Lower of: £180,000 @ 30%	£54,000	
Income tax liability	£19,500	(19,500)
Income tax payable		Nil

3.50 A VCT is required to meet the following conditions (*ITA 2007, Pt 6, Ch 4*):

- its income must be derived wholly or mainly from shares or securities;

- its ordinary share capital (and the share capital of each class, if it has more than one) must be quoted on a recognised stock market (but see **3.49** above);
- it must not retain, for any accounting period, more than 15% of the income it derives from shares or securities;
- at least 70% of its investments must be represented throughout its accounting period by 'qualifying holdings' of shares or securities (*ITA 2007, s 280*).

With effect from 6 April 2007, any money that a VCT holds (or is held on its behalf) is treated as an investment for the purpose of the 70% and 15% tests above (*FA 2006, Sch 14, para 8*).

At least 50% by value of those 'qualifying holdings' must be represented by 'eligible shares', that is, ordinary shares carrying no present or future preferential rights to dividends or to assets on a winding up, and no present or future preferential right to be redeemed.

VCTs are required to ensure that at least 10% of the total investment from the VCT in any one company is in ordinary, non-preferential shares. Guaranteed loans and securities do not count towards this fixed proportion of qualifying investments, which a VCT must hold.

The specification for the 'qualifying holdings' into which a VCT is permitted to invest is complex. The company must not hold shares or securities listed on any stock market, either in the UK or abroad, nor on the unlisted securities market. However, a VCT is permitted to hold shares that are dealt with on the Alternative Investment Market (AIM). There are provisions whereby the VCT can receive quoted shares as a result of its exercise of conversion rights.

To be a 'qualifying holding', the shares must be in a company that has gross assets that do not exceed £7,000,000 (£15,000,000 prior to 2006/07) before the subscription by the VCT, nor £8,000,000 (£16,000,000 prior to 2006/07), after that subscription. The maximum amount raised must not be more than £2 million in any 12-month period. A company or group of companies must have no more than 50 full-time employees (or their equivalent) at the date on which the relevant shares or securities are issued (*FA 2007, s 51* and *Sch 16*).

Formerly, the VCT scheme required 80% of the money received by the investee companies to be wholly employed for the purposes of the relevant trade within 12 months and the balance within a further 12 months. *FA 2009* replaced these rules with a single requirement that all the money raised must be wholly employed within two years, or, if later, within two years of the commencement of the qualifying activity (*FA 2009, s 27* and *Sch 8, para 5*).

Each company into which the VCT invests must exist for the purpose of carrying on one or more qualifying trades (*ITA 2007, Pt 6, Ch 4*).

An investor receives tax relief on an investment in a VCT only if the VCT is approved by HMRC. To be approved, the VCT must meet a number of conditions (*ITA 2007, s 274*). The approval process is governed by the *Venture Capital Trust Regulations 1995 (SI 1995/1979,* amended by *SI 1999/819*). The *Venture Capital Trust (Amendment) Regulations 2008 (SI 2008/1893),* which came into force on 1 September 2008, amended the 1995 regulations to introduce greater flexibility to deal with cases where a VCT has breached, or is likely to breach, the conditions for its approval to continue.

Life assurance (qualifying policies)

3.51 A life assurance company is exempt from tax on both the income arising and the capital gains made in the fund it holds for qualifying life assurance policies. Therefore, for the investor the premium paid on such a policy is invested (after management charges) in a fund that is tax free and the tax exemption will increase the sums that can be paid out to the investor. In practice, investment in a qualifying life policy falls into two categories:

(1) providing a fund to pay at death, typically either to fund inheritance tax or to take advantage of the facility to write the policy in trust and, thereby, pass the fund free of inheritance tax to the next generation;

(2) building up a fund, typically over ten years, after which the policy matures and pays out.

Qualifying conditions

3.52 The tax-free fund consists of premiums from 'qualifying policies' only. In order to be a 'qualifying policy', it must satisfy the statutory conditions in *ICTA 1988, s 266*. For whole life or endowment assurances the term must be at least ten years. The premiums must be payable at yearly or shorter intervals for at least ten years or until the event specified, whether death or disability. The total premiums payable under the policy in any period of 12 months must not exceed twice the amount payable in any other 12-month period or one-eighth of the total premiums payable if the policy were to run for the specified term.

The policy must guarantee that the sum payable on death will be at least 75% of the total premiums payable if the policy were to run its term, except that a 2% reduction for every year by which the person exceeds 55 years of age is permitted and when a new policy is issued for an old one the part of the premiums that are attributable to the old policy are ignored. Where a policy includes one or more options, the policy must be tested on each option and will only 'qualify' if it meets the conditions on every such test. A policy may make provision for total or partial surrender without ceasing to qualify, but if an option in a qualifying policy is exercised after 13 March 1984, and either extends the term of the policy or increases the benefits payable under it, the policy ceases to qualify.

A temporary assurance for a period of not more than ten years may be a qualifying policy, but only if the surrender value is not to exceed the total premiums previously paid. A term policy of less than 12 months cannot be a qualifying policy. This provision is likely to make a policy issued for less than ten years unattractive.

Life assurance (single premium bonds)

3.53 Quite apart from life assurance taken out to provide a lump sum on an individual's death, perhaps to pay funeral expenses or an inheritance tax liability, life policies can be used as an investment mechanism. Although usually referred to as either life assurance bonds or investment bonds, these are, technically, single premium whole life insurance policies. Having taken out such a life assurance bond, the investor can withdraw a sum up to 5% of his or her initial purchase consideration in each fiscal year and the withdrawal is treated as a withdrawal of capital, with no income tax consequences. If less than the 5% is taken in one year, the surplus is carried forward to the following year.

A withdrawal greater than the 5% and, indeed, full encashment of the bond, can be made without any charge to tax by a basic rate taxpayer, as long as the 'chargeable event' that arises, when added to the taxpayer's other income, does not exceed the basic rate band.

For a higher rate tax payable, or one for whom the 'chargeable event' takes the taxpayer into higher rates, there is a charge to income tax at higher rate only.

Chargeable event

3.54 For this purpose, a chargeable event is any one of the following (*ITTOIA 2005, s 484*):

- a payment under the policy at death;
- a payment at the maturity of the policy;
- a surrender of the policy rights;
- an assignment of policy rights for money or money's worth; or
- a withdrawal in excess of 5%.

Even if an assignment is taxed as a chargeable event, this does not stop a later assignment giving a second charge to tax by virtue of the second chargeable event. This provision was introduced to cancel the advantages that were enjoyed under the so-called second-hand bond scheme.

On death, maturity or assignment, the gain is the difference between the amount received from the insurance company and the initial premium paid, less any withdrawals that have been made.

If there is a partial, rather than a complete, encashment of the policy, the gain brought into charge is the sum that is paid out of the policy, less 5% of the initial subscription for each year during the life of the policy, insofar as this has not been taken into account in previous gain computations. The 5% is calculated by reference to the policy year, not the tax year. A policy year commences on the day the policy is taken out and on each 365-day anniversary thereafter. Many modern policies allow partial surrenders at frequent intervals and such surrenders gave rise to complex calculations. In an attempt to reduce the work involved, both for life offices and HMRC, a different system of determining both whether there has been a gain and its extent applies.

On assignment, the gain is the excess of the consideration received, except when assignment is between connected persons when market value is substituted, plus the amount or value of any relevant capital payments over the total amount of premiums paid with adjustments for the assignment.

Where the chargeable gain arises on death, the chargeable event is the income of the individual who owns the policy and not of his or her personal representatives.

Top-slicing relief

3.55 The gain is brought into charge after top-slicing relief (*ITA 2007, s 535*). The gain is spread back over a number of years by dividing it by the number of complete years:

- for the first chargeable event – since the start of the policy;
- for any later chargeable event other than final termination – since the previous chargeable event;
- on final termination – the number of whole years from the start of the policy.

The slice of the gain is then added to the taxpayer's other income to discover the amount of extra tax payable by reason of its addition. If the addition of that sum does not give rise to anything but tax at the basic rate, no tax is payable. If the sum gives a liability at higher rate, the charge is computed as if there were a credit for tax at basic rate.

When there is a chargeable event through death or maturity and there is a loss, an individual may deduct that loss from total income so far as it does not exceed gains taxed in earlier partial surrender or assignments. Thus, the tax on gains made earlier may be recovered. The relief does not apply to losses on assignments.

Example 3.6

Gilbert's total income in 2009/10 is £49,295. In March 2010 he receives £30,000 when he cashes in an investment bond. The original sum invested in July 2002 was £10,000. The chargeable event gain is therefore £20,000 and the top-slice element is £2,500 (eight complete years).

	With top slicing	
	£	£
Income		49,295
Chargeable event gain – top-sliced		2,500
		51,795
Less: personal allowance		(6,475)
		45,320
At basic and starting rates	37,400	
At 40%	7,920	
	45,320	

Income tax attributable to top-slice is:

$7{,}920 \times (40\% - 20\%) = £1{,}584$

Tax payable is 8 × £1,584	12,672

Purchased annuities

3.56 A monthly sum paid from a purchased annuity is treated as if it were two separate payments – a capital content which does not attract a charge to income tax (nor to CGT), and an income payment, which attracts a charge to income tax at the basic rate of 20%. However, this treatment is only available where the purchase is made by an annuitant (*ITTOIA 2005, ss 717, 725*).

The apportionment between income and capital is made by dividing the purchase cost into the two elements by reference to government mortality tables. Even where an individual receives special terms from a company as the individual has a lower than average life expectancy, the government tables are automatically applied for tax purposes. The capital element that is computed by reference to the table remains constant, even if the individual lives to such an age that the payments made that have been deemed to be capital, exceed, in aggregate, the initial purchase price. In this respect, the treatment is in contrast to that which applies to insurance bonds.

A purchased annuity can be structured so that the monthly payments increase each year in line with inflation. This does not affect the calculation of the division between the deemed capital element and the income element. The calculation of the division is made as at the date of the first payment. The consequence of this treatment is that inflationary increases in the annuity paid are automatically treated as income attracting a charge to income tax.

Chapter 4

Pensions and benefits

UK PENSIONS

Introduction

4.1 Pensions are generally treated as earned income and most of them are taxed under the *Income Tax (Earnings and Pensions) Act 2003* on entitlement in the tax year. Examples include:

- state retirement pensions;
- voluntary pensions paid by UK employers (or their successors);
- certain foreign pensions for services to the Crown or a government abroad; and
- other pensions (eg occupational pensions), other than tax-exempt pensions and pensions from abroad.

Tax advantages of making pension contributions include:

- contributions or premiums (up to certain limits) attract tax relief at the individual's top rate (but they do not reduce earnings for National Insurance contributions);
- employers can contribute to an employee's occupational or personal pension scheme reducing their taxable business profits and without the contributions being treated as a benefit in kind to the employee;
- a tax-free lump sum (within permitted limits) can be paid on retirement; and
- non-taxpayers can obtain basic rate tax relief on personal pension contributions of up to £3,600 per tax year.

4.2 With regard to state retirement pensions, everyone is likely to be entitled to different amounts depending on how many years they have paid, been treated as having paid, or been credited with National Insurance contributions.

The earliest an individual can receive a state pension is when they reach state pension age. This age is currently different for men and women, although women's state pension age will gradually increase between 2010 and 2020 to become the same as men's. At the moment, state pension age is as follows:

- men – 65 years old;
- women:
  - 60 years old if born on, or before, 5 April 1950;
  - 65 years old if born on, or after, 6 April 1955;
  - for women born on or after 6 April 1950 but on or before 5 April 1955, it is 60 years old plus one month for each month (or part month) that birth date fell on or after 6 April 1950.

In May 2006, the government published the White Paper, entitled *Security in retirement: towards a new pensions system*. The White Paper set out a number of proposals for changing the state pension system for people who reach state pension age on or after 6 April 2010. The first phase of the reforms was completed with the *Pensions Act 2007* becoming law in July 2007. The second phase, the *Pensions Act 2008*, was introduced to Parliament on 5 December 2007 and received Royal Assent on 26 November 2008. The government plans to introduce the reforms from 2012, but information will be made available in advance of this date to ensure that those affected are prepared for the changes before they take effect.

The *Pensions Act 2008* takes forward measures aimed at encouraging greater private saving. These include a duty on employers automatically to enrol their eligible employees, between the ages of 22 and state pension age, into a workplace pension scheme (provided they are not already in such a scheme) and provide a minimum contribution. Employers will be required to contribute a minimum of 3% (on a band of earnings). This will supplement the 4% contribution from the employee and around 1% in the form of tax relief.

The *Pensions Act 2008* also allows for the establishment of the personal accounts scheme from 2012. This is as a new low-cost saving vehicle aimed at employees who do not have access to a good quality work-based pension scheme – in the main, medium to low earners. There will be a contribution limit of £3,600 per year (based on 2005 earning levels) and a general ban on transfers in and out of the scheme, to focus the scheme on the target market. For more information on the *Pensions Act 2008*, see the Department for Work and Pensions website at www.dwp.gov.uk. It is possible to obtain a forecast as to how much state pension (which can be either basic state pension or additional state pension, or both) an individual might expect to receive (reflecting today's position and given in today's values). The older the individual (up until retirement), the more accurate this estimate is likely to be. A forecast can be obtained from the government website (www.direct.gov.uk).

Pensions exempt from tax

4.3 The following pensions are exempt from tax:

- wounds and disability pensions of members of the Armed Forces;
- pensions awarded to employees disabled at work;
- war widow's pension;
- pensions for victims of Nazi persecution; and
- certain pensions paid to non-UK residents (eg colonial and overseas service pensions).

Benefits paid by any of the following Services schemes are exempt from income tax, even where the recipient continues to serve in any capacity (*ITEPA 2003, ss 639, 640A*):

- new armed forces pensions;
- armed forces compensation schemes; and
- early departure payments scheme.

State pensions guidance

4.4 The following leaflets are available from the government website (www.direct.gov.uk):

Guides for those planning ahead

4.5

PTB1: Pensions: the basics. A guide from the Government

PM2: State Pensions – Your guide

PM6: Pensions for women

PM7: Contracted-out pensions – Your guide

SERPSL1: Important information for married people – Inheritance of SERPS

BM01: Backdating membership of an Occupational Pension Scheme

BR19: State Pension forecast

BR19L: Understanding your State Pension forecast

BR33: State Pension – The choices available to you

CPF5: Your pension statement

SPD1: Your guide to State Pension Deferral: Putting off your State Pension to get extra State Pension or a lump-sum payment later

SPD2: How to get extra weekly State Pension or a lump sum payment: Your introduction to State Pension Deferral

Over 50?: Are you over 50?

Guides for pensioners

4.6

PC1L: A Guide to Pension Credit – Do I qualify and how much could I get?

PG2: Pensioners' guide Wales

PG1: Pensioners' guide England

PG3: Pensioners' guide Scotland

GL24DWP: If you think a decision is wrong

WFPL1: Your guide to Winter Fuel PaymentsBRA5: Benefit and pension rates

PSCUST1: The Pension Service Customer Charter

Claim forms

4.7

BR1: State Pension – Use this form to apply for State Pension if less than four months away from State Pension age

BF225: State Pension – Dependants' allowance

PC1: Pension Credit application form

WFP1R: Winter Fuel Payment claim form for UK for past winters 1997/98, 1998/99 and 1999/2000

WFP2: Winter Fuel claim form – EEA and Switzerland for past winters

General information

4.8 Guides and information sheets can be ordered online from the government website at www.direct.gov.uk, or by phone on 0845 731 3233.

Occupational pensions income

4.9 Tax on pensions under occupational schemes is dealt with under the PAYE system. Certain lump sum payments (within permitted limits) received on retirement are not taxable.

From 2003/04 onwards, pension income is charged to tax under *ITEPA 2003, Pt 9*.

The extent of the charge is to all pension income, excluding any exempt income and less any express deductions permitted (ie payroll giving and the 10% deduction for overseas pensions).

'Pension income' includes pensions, annuities and income of 'other types' that are included in the statutory list provided (*ITEPA 2003, s 566(2), (4)*):

- pensions paid by (or on behalf of) any person who is in the UK (*ITEPA 2003, s 569*);
- pensions paid by (or on behalf of) any person who is outside the UK, to a person who is UK resident (*ITEPA 2003, s 573*);
- UK social security pensions (the state pension, graduated retirement pension, industrial death benefit, widowed mother's allowance, widowed parent's allowance and widow's pension) (*ITEPA 2003, s 577*);
- pensions and annuities paid by an approved retirement benefits scheme (including unauthorised payments) (*ITEPA 2003, s 580*);
- annuities paid under formerly approved superannuation schemes (*ITEPA 2003, s 590*);
- annuities from approved personal pension schemes (including income withdrawals) (*ITEPA 2003, s 595*);
- unauthorised personal pension payments (*ITEPA 2003, s 601*);
- annuities under retirement annuity contracts (*ITEPA 2003, s 605*);
- annuities for the benefit of dependants (*ITEPA 2003, s 609*);
- annuities under sponsored superannuation schemes (*ITEPA 2003, s 610*);
- annuities paid in respect of another person's services in any office or employment (*ITEPA 2003, s 611*);
- pensions payable by or on behalf of certain overseas governments to UK-resident persons (and their dependants) who were engaged in service to the overseas government (*ITEPA 2003, s 615*);
- payments made out of the House of Commons Member's Fund (*ITEPA 2003, s 619*);
- payments representing the return of surplus employee additional voluntary contributions (*ITEPA 2003, s 623*);
- pre-1973 pensions paid under the *Overseas Pensions Act 1973* (*ITEPA 2003, s 629*); and
- voluntary annual payments paid to former employees (and their dependants) by or on behalf of a former employer (or their successor) (*ITEPA 2003, s 633*).

The term 'pension' includes a pension that is paid voluntarily or that may be discontinued.

A special or additional pension paid to a person who has retired because he is disabled following an injury at work, or because of a work-related illness, is not taxed (*ITEPA 2003, s 644*).

TAXATION OF PENSIONS

The simplified pensions tax regime

4.10 A single regime for the taxation of pension income applies from 6 April 2006 (A-Day). From that date, a single set of simplified rules came into effect around how pensions are taxed, designed to offer simpler and more flexible retirement arrangements. Under the unified regime, the tax treatment for all types of approved schemes, including occupational schemes, small self-administered schemes (SSASs, personal pensions, self-invested pension plans (SIPPs), and retirement annuity contracts has been amalgamated into the rules for registered pension schemes. In addition, the tax treatment of unapproved schemes has been changed (see **4.27**).

The main points of the unified pensions regime can be summarised as follows:

- The many former sets of rules governing the taxation of pensions were replaced with a single, universal regime.
- It is possible to save in more than one pension scheme at the same time.
- There is no limit on the amount of money that can be invested in pension schemes, although there are limits on the amount of tax relief available.
- Tax relief is available on contributions up to 100% of an individual's annual earnings (up to an annual allowance set at £255,000 for 2010/11 to 2015/16).
- Non-taxpayers are entitled to tax relief on pension contributions. Individuals can invest up to £2,880 in any one tax year and receive tax relief of £720; thus, the total pension savings with tax relief will be £3,600 gross per annum.
- From A-Day, flexible retirement is introduced, allowing people in occupational pension schemes to continue working while drawing their pension, where the scheme rules allow it.
- Where scheme rules allow, up to 25% of a pension fund may be taken as a tax-free lump sum.
- If a pension pot is more than the 'lifetime allowance' when the individual comes to take his or her pension, they may be subject to a tax charge at

that time. But this will only apply if total pension savings are in excess of £1.8 million (standard lifetime allowance applying for 2010/11 to 2015/16).

- The rules on when a pension may be taken have changed. From 6 April 2010, an individual cannot take a pension before he or she is 55. There are two exceptions to this: individuals will still be able to retire early due to poor health; and, if they have the right to retire before 50 at 6 April 2006, that right may be protected.

Legislation

4.11 The legislation governing the unified tax regime applying from 6 April 2006 is found in *FA 2004, Pt 4*. This is supplemented by *FA 2005, Pt 5, FA 2006, Pt 7, FA 2007* and numerous regulations. *FA 2007* received Royal Assent on 19 July 2007. The pension provisions are contained within *ss 68–70* and *Schs 18–20* and *27* (*Pt 3*).

Annual allowance

4.12 Individuals can obtain tax relief on contributions up to an annual maximum amount, which is £255,000 for 2010/11. Under current legislation, the annual allowance will be maintained at this level up to and including 2015/16 (*SI 2010/922*).

Contributions

4.13 Contributions are no longer restricted to a fraction of capped earnings. There is, however, an annual allowance charge of 40% on contributions or increases in excess of the annual allowance, but only where tax relief has been given on those contributions. The *de minimis* limit of £3,600 under the old system is retained.

Contributions may be paid by (*FA 2004, ss 188, 196*):

- the scheme member;
- the member's current or former employer; or
- a third party on behalf of the member.

In addition to cash, contributions may be in the form of shares from a Share Incentive Plan (SIP), or a Save As You Earn Scheme (SAYE) (*FA 2004, s 195*).

An individual's contributions are usually paid net of the basic rate of tax. Employers who previously used the net pay arrangement for occupational schemes may continue to do so under the new regime (*FA 2004, s 192*).

Restricted tax relief

4.14 Under the previous government, legislation was set to take effect from 6 April 2011 to recover tax relief above the basic rate on pension contributions made by or on behalf of individuals with high income. The legislation for the restrictions was contained in *FA 2010*. However, in the emergency Budget on 22 June 2010, the coalition government announced that it would repeal the provisions of *FA 2010* and, consequently, the restrictions on tax relief would not go ahead in April 2011. In line with industry recommendations, the government is considering whether a significant reduction in the annual allowance (provisional analysis by the Treasury suggested a level in the region of £30,000–£45,000) may be a more effective method of achieving at least equal savings in revenue expenditure.

FA 2009 contained anti-forestalling provisions preventing those potentially affected by the new restrictions (outlined in the previous paragraph) on tax relief from seeking to forestall the change by increasing pension savings in excess of their normal regular pattern on or after 22 April 2009. A new special charge (known as the 'special annual allowance charge' (SAAC)) of 40% may apply where pension savings exceed £20,000 per annum. Increases in pension savings within the new provisions will also come within the 'Tax Avoidance Disclosure' legislation (*Budget Note 2009: BN47*; *FA 2009, s 72* and *Sch 35*).

SAAC applies to high earners who 'increase their pension savings on or after 22 April 2009 over and above their normal pattern of regular pension savings', but only if their total pension savings exceed £20,000 in that year. It does not apply to:

- any arrangements for regular pension savings which were in place before 22 April 2009; or
- contributions to certain new arrangements (where 20 or more people accrue benefits in the same way) entered into or set up after 22 April 2009 by employers for the benefit of their staff.

For contributions which have been made less frequently than quarterly over the past three years, the savings limit is increased from £20,000 to the average of those contributions, but capped at £30,000.

The anti-forestalling provisions were modified further by *FA 2010* so that employer contributions are also included in the definition of income for SAAC purposes (*FA 2010, s 23* and *Sch 2*).

Although the tax relief restrictions contained in *FA 2010* will not go ahead from April 2011, in the emergency Budget on 22 June 2010, it was confirmed that the anti-forestalling provisions will be monitored, but will currently remain in place.

Lump sums

4.15 All schemes can pay tax-free lump sums of up to 25% of the value of the pension rights. The maximum permissible lump sum will be 25% of the lifetime allowance. Individuals who, at 6 April 2006, were already entitled to a greater sum can protect their existing benefits.

Lifetime allowance

4.16 There is a single lifetime allowance on the amount of pension savings that can benefit from tax relief. The value of the lifetime allowance was set at £1,500,000 for 2006/07. For 2009/10 was £1,750,000, and for 2010/11 it is £1,800,000. Under current legislation, it will remain at this level for all years up to and including 2015/16 (*SI 2010/922*).

The lifetime allowance applies to everyone irrespective of the type of scheme to which they belong. Different forms of calculation are needed to establish an individual's entitlement. For a defined benefit scheme, the single valuation factor is 20:1. This means that a final salary pension that pays £75,000 per annum is deemed to be worth £1,500,000.

An individual receiving payment of a pension at A-Day-minus-one is treated as having used part of his lifetime allowance if, following A-Day-minus-one, he begins to receive a new benefit. In this event the factor is 25:1.

There is a lifetime allowance charge of 25% on funds in excess of the lifetime allowance which are used to provide a pension. If funds in excess of the lifetime allowance are taken as a lump sum, there is a lifetime allowance charge of 55%.

Pension age

4.17 The minimum pension age has been increased from 50 to 55 with effect from 6 April 2010. Those with certain existing contractual rights to draw a pension earlier may have that right protected. There is special protection for members of those approved schemes in existence before A-Day with low normal retirement ages, such as those for sportsmen and sportswomen.

It is no longer necessary for a member to leave employment in order to access an employer's occupational pension. Members of occupational pension schemes may, where the scheme rules allow it, continue working for the same employer whilst drawing retirement benefits.

Under the unified system, the requirement that pensions were secured by age 75 continued. However, *F(No 2)A 2010* contains provisions to end the existing rules on the effective annuitisation by age 75 requirement from April 2011

(*F(No 2)A 2010, s 6* and *Sch 3*). Transitional protection applies from 22 June 2010 for individuals who will reach 75 before April 2011 and have not yet secured an income. Broadly, the transitional provisions extend the maximum age for annuitisation from 75 to 77 and this will also apply for inheritance tax purposes.

From A-Day pension income could be delivered after age 75 through an alternatively secured pension (ASP). This is an alternative method to provide benefits via an income for life which may be used by those with principled objections to the pooling of mortality risk. The rules for ASPs were amended slightly from 6 April 2007 to require that a minimum income level is drawn. There will also be an unauthorised payment tax charge where ASP funds remaining on a member's death are transferred to the pension funds of another scheme member.

Death benefits

4.18 Death benefits from a scheme can be in the form of either a lump sum, a pension to one or more dependants or a combination of lump sum and pension. This depends on whether any benefit is in payment at the time of the member's death and the age of the member at death.

Non-cash benefits

4.19 Employers may make provision for retired former employees, which takes a form other than cash and these non-cash benefits may be provided together with a pension or entirely separately. Prior to 6 April 2006, these benefits were not taxable if only non-cash benefits were provided but were taxable if provided together with taxable cash benefits. This anomaly was rectified from 6 April 2006 by the new pensions legislation which ensure that most non-cash benefits received by former employees are taxable. This brings more closely into line the taxation on non-cash benefits received by pensioners with those received by employees. A *de minimis* limit exists for benefits which do not exceed £100 in the relevant tax year.

Budget 2007 contained a measure to ensure that the exemptions from tax work as intended, the group of 'excluded benefits' on which there is no tax charge has been expanded to include a number of exemptions similar to those received by employees. Broadly, the additional exclusions relate to continued provision of accommodation and related removal expenses, welfare counselling, recreational benefits, annual parties and similar functions, equipment for disabled former employees, which, with necessary differences to reflect the situation of retired people, mirror exemptions conferred on employees. Exclusions also relate to the writing of wills and benefits which were first provided before 6 April 1998.

Trivial pensions

4.20 Under the old rules, an individual whose pension 'pot' was valued at less than £2,500 could take his entire fund, subject to a small tax charge. From A-Day, the 'trivial pension' allowance is 1% of the lifetime allowance. Thus, for 2010/11[the limit is £18,000, ie a pension of £900 per annum.

Annuities

4.21 From A-Day, it is no longer compulsory to use the pension fund to purchase an annuity at 75. Instead, people can use the 'alternatively secured pension' route, by which pension assets can be passed to members of the family on death.

Transitional arrangements

4.22 Transitional arrangements protect pension rights built up before A-Day, including protection for rights to lump sum payments that existed at A-Day. There are two options for transitional protection from the lifetime allowance charge:

- primary protection which will be given to the value of the pre-A-Day pension rights and benefits valued in excess of £1,500,000; or
- enhanced protection which will be available to individuals who cease active membership of approved pension schemes by A-Day.

Provided that they do not resume active membership in any registered scheme, all benefits coming into payment after A-Day-minus-one will normally be exempt from the lifetime allowance charge.

Personal pension term assurance

4.23 In relation to contributions made after 31 July 2007 under occupational registered pension schemes (unless the insurer received the application for the policy before 29 March 2007 and the policy was taken out as part of the pension scheme before 1 August 2007), individuals cannot obtain tax relief for their contributions to fund pension-related personal term assurance. This change does not affect relief for contributions paid by employers.

For contributions under other registered pension schemes, the change outlined above will take effect for all contributions made after 5 April 2007, unless the insurer received the application for the policy before 14 December 2006 and the policy was taken out as part of the pension scheme before 6 April 2007. The relief may be lost if such a policy is varied.

Deduction for employers

4.24 As before, employers are able to claim a deduction in computing profits chargeable to UK tax for contributions which are paid by them to registered pension schemes (*FA 2004, s 196*). The previous practice of spreading large contributions over two to four years has been brought into legislation (*FA 2004, s 197*).

To be deductible, employer contributions must actually have been paid, not merely provided for in their accounts.

An anti-avoidance rule applies where an employer contributes to a registered scheme, but the related benefits will not be paid (wholly or partly) out of that scheme because some other arrangement has been made (*FA 2004, s 196A*). In this case, tax relief would be limited to the proportion of contributions relating to benefits which could only be paid out of the registered scheme.

Registration

4.25 A simpler process now applies for scheme registration and reporting (*FA 2004, ss 153, 157, 242*). The former limits on what a scheme may invest have been lifted and replaced by a single set of investment rules that applies for all pension schemes.

FA 2004, Sch 36, paras 1–6 contain provisions which treat certain pension schemes, mainly previously approved schemes, which were in existence immediately before A-Day as registered pension schemes under the unified system. Schemes that can become registered pension schemes with effect from A-Day under the unified registered pension schemes tax regime include certain retirement benefit schemes approved under former *ICTA 1988, ss 590–612*, personal pension schemes approved under former *ICTA 1988, ss 630–655*, and a range of other schemes, funds, etc.

Eligibility

4.26 Individuals (aged under 75) who satisfy at least one of the following criteria will be eligible to join a registered pension scheme (*FA 2004, s 189*):

- UK resident at some time during the tax year;
- earnings are chargeable to UK tax; or
- resident in the UK at some time in the previous five years and when they became a member of the pension scheme.

Members who are not resident in the UK, and not in receipt of UK earnings, but used to be UK resident at some time in the last five years can still contribute to a scheme.

Employees seconded overseas can remain members of an occupational scheme, even where the ten-year limit for foreign service is exceeded before 6 April 2006.

Individuals coming to work in the UK who are existing members of overseas pension schemes will be eligible for tax relief on their contributions paid whilst in the UK, so long as the previous country of residence also gave relief (an intervening short stay in another country where no relief was available is ignored for this purpose) (*FA 2004, Sch 33*).

Non-registered schemes

4.27 Unapproved pension schemes are now known as employer-financed retirement benefits schemes. There is no facility for such schemes to be registered with HMRC and none of the tax advantages for registered schemes apply. Rights that existed before 6 April 2006 are protected. Amounts in non-registered pension schemes are not tested against the lifetime allowance or the lifetime allowance charge.

For a funded scheme, the following applies:

- Employer contributions, and the scheme administration costs, will only be deductible when pension benefits are actually paid and taxed on the employee (*FA 2004, s 245*).
- Employer contributions are not taxable on the employee.
- Scheme income and gains will be taxed at the rate applicable to trusts.
- The lump sum will be fully chargeable to income tax.
- The value of the fund (even a discretionary fund) will form part of an individual's death estate for IHT purposes.

Where an employee has made contributions to a registered pension scheme, but the related benefits are reduced because benefits are paid out of an unregistered scheme instead, tax relief will be denied on any expenses associated with providing the benefits. However, if the employer has already been denied relief on the contributions into the registered scheme, he will still obtain relief on the cost of the benefits (*FA 2004, s 246A*).

Where an employer guarantees benefits in an unfunded scheme, the cost of the guarantee will be assessed on the employee as a benefit in kind (*FA 2004, s 248*).

Investment

4.28 Under the unified pensions regime, there is a greater measure of freedom of investment choice (*FA 2004, Sch 36*). Thus, a pension fund can invest in residential property, as well as commercial property, works of art, etc (*FA 2004, s 186*). However, the borrowing rules for pension schemes changed on A-Day. The previous 75% limit on borrowing by self-invested personal pensions was reduced to 50% of the value of the fund. Care needs to be taken in this area – significant penalties may be imposed on self-directed pension schemes investing in residential property.

Although investment in pensions is promoted on the basis of tax breaks, there can be draconian tax charges which would eliminate these tax breaks. Besides, the types of investments being promoted often offer tax breaks anyway. The loss of control of such assets is also a disadvantage.

Loans to members (and connected persons) are prohibited and will be treated as an unauthorised payment (*FA 2004, Sch 30*) (see **4.31**).

4.29 Much has been written or said about the advantages of a Self-Invested Personal Pension (SIPP). Broadly, a SIPP is a type of personal pension where the policyholder has elected to direct the investments of the scheme fund using non-insurance company assets. SIPP investors can build up diversified portfolios through investment in a wide range of allowable asset classes including cash, UK and international equities, gilts, bonds, exchange traded funds, unit trusts, investment trusts, warrants, covered warrants and even contracts for difference. Commercial property is also allowable in some SIPPs.

Careful consideration of all factors should be undertaken before entering into such an arrangement. The possible advantages are:

- income tax relief is available at rates up to 40%;
- no capital gains tax is payable on any increase in value of the investment on an ultimate sale;
- rental profits (less mortgage payments) can accumulate within the SIPP for reinvestment;
- rental profits are not subject to income tax;
- commercial properties acquired for letting can use pension scheme as shelter;
- choice of property is not limited to UK;
- 25% of sale proceeds can be taken as tax-free lump sum;
- the balance of sale proceeds is taxed as earned income; and
- property may not have to be sold on retirement if sufficient other assets built up in pension fund to pay 25% tax-free lump sum and if income generated is sufficient to meet income requirements.

4.30 However, there are some possible disadvantages:

- there may be difficulty in finding suitable tenants: the property may not be a good investment with no income stream;
- will the property be easy to sell at retirement?;
- substantial costs may arise, such as stamp duty land tax, and legal and professional costs on purchase and on sale;
- concentration of pension investment in one or two properties may be unwise (perhaps indirect investment via property funds would be more sensible);
- control of properties is with pension scheme as landlord/freeholder not the person whose pension fund it is in;
- property may have to be sold to take benefits or to meet lifetime limits;
- transfer of own property into pension scheme may give rise to capital gains tax; and
- new limits on borrowing by pension schemes may restrict ability to invest in property via a pension scheme.

Compliance issues

4.31 The legislation governing the new pensions regime specifically requires that all scheme tax payments will need to be made electronically. Online reporting is also now mandatory.

Where unauthorised payments are made (see below), the following tax charges will arise (*FA 2004, s 208*):

- a higher rate tax charge on the payment; and
- an additional surcharge of 15% where the unauthorised payment is 25% or more of the pension fund value.

Furthermore, a higher rate tax charge on the fund value will be payable by the scheme administrator where a scheme makes one or more unauthorised payments in a year or is deregistered.

An unauthorised payment may occur in any of the following situations:

- loans made to a member or connected person;
- payment made after death for the benefit of a connected person;
- reduction in pension payments to increase the lump sum;
- assignment of the benefits of the scheme in order to avoid a lifetime allowance charge; and

- surrender of pension rights in order to avoid a lifetime allowance charge.

Scheme administrators will be required to submit an event report to HMRC in the following circumstances (*FA 2004, s 251*):

- at commencement or cessation of the scheme;
- if the scheme fails to observe any registration requirement;
- on the retirement of a member who is entitled to large benefits, or who has claimed enhanced protection;
- where a member receives benefits early;
- where lump sum payments are made for serious ill health;
- where tax-free lump sums are made under the transitional rules; and
- where benefits are taken before the normal retirement age.

Penalties may be imposed for non-compliance (*FA 2004, ss 257–266*)

FOREIGN PENSIONS

Overseas members

4.32 One feature of the simplified pension regime which came into effect on 6 April 2006 (see **4.10**) is that it allows full membership of a UK-registered pension scheme to any person, whether they are resident in the UK or not. There is no special limit on the period during which an overseas employee can be a member of a UK 'registered pension scheme'.

Foreign pensions

4.33 A foreign pension is defined as being (*ITEPA 2003, s 573(1)*):

- paid by or on behalf of a person who is outside the UK to a person who is resident in the UK; but
- not including any pension subject to *ITEPA 2003, Pt 9, Chs 5–14*.

ITEPA 2003, Pt 9, Chs 5–14 effectively cover all other types of pension apart from those paid by or on behalf of a person who is outside the UK to a person who is resident in the UK.

A UK resident is liable to tax on a foreign pension on an arising basis (*ITTOIA 2005, s 7(4)*) unless the person entitled to the pension:

- is able to satisfy HMRC that he is not domiciled in the UK; or
- is a Commonwealth (including a British) citizen or citizen of the Republic of Ireland and is able to satisfy HMRC that he is not ordinarily resident in the UK.

Such an individual continues to remain chargeable in respect of a foreign pension only on a remittance basis. In all other cases a foreign pension is taxable irrespective of whether it is actually remitted to the UK. However, all such pensions (excluding those taxed only on a remittance basis) are eligible for a 10% deduction.

Republic of Ireland

4.34 Pensions arising in the Republic of Ireland are treated as if they arose in the UK. Such a pension still qualifies for the 10% deduction (*ITTOIA 2005, Pt 8*) (see **4.33**).

Unapproved retirement benefit schemes

4.35 A new charge to tax was imposed on benefits received after 26 July 1989 from unapproved retirement benefit schemes. Individuals in receipt of such benefits are chargeable as employment income taxed under *ITEPA 2003, ss 393* and *394*.

The charge extends, strictly, to lump sums paid to UK residents by schemes established abroad. However, a revised concession gives full or partial exemption from income tax, depending on the exact level of foreign service, where the employment giving rise to the benefits was largely carried on abroad. The text of the revised ESC A10 is as follows:

> 'LUMP SUMS PAID UNDER OVERSEAS PENSION SCHEMES
>
> Income Tax is not charged on lump sum relevant benefits receivable by an employee (or by his personal representatives or any dependant of his) from an Overseas Retirement Benefits Scheme or an Overseas Provident Fund where the employee's overseas service comprises:
>
> (a) not less than 75% of his total service in that employment; or
>
> (b) the whole of the last 10 years of his service in that employment, where total service exceeds 10 years; or
>
> (c) not less than 50 % of his total service in that employment, including any 10 of the last 20 years, where total service exceeds 20 years.
>
> If the employee's overseas service is less than described above, relief from income tax will be given by reducing the amount of the lump sum which

would otherwise be chargeable by the same proportion as the overseas service bears to the employee's total service in that employment.

In addition, income tax is not charged on lump sum relevant benefits receivable by an employee (or by his personal representatives or any dependant of his) from any Superannuation Fund accepted as being within Section 615(6) ICTA 1988.

For the purposes of this concession the term "relevant benefits" has the meaning given in Section 612 ICTA 1988 and the term "overseas service" shall be construed in accordance with the definition of "foreign service" found at paragraph 10 Schedule 11 ICTA 1988.'

Overseas Pensions Act 1973

4.36 Under the provisions of the *Overseas Pensions Act 1973*, the UK government assumed responsibility for certain overseas pensions. Where, immediately before 6 April 1973, a UK resident was entitled to a foreign pension, that pension continues to be regarded as a foreign pension notwithstanding that it is now paid by the UK government. Statutory increases in the pension paid by the UK government are not subject to this provision and are taxed in full (*ITEPA 2003, s 629(1)*). A 'statutory increase' is a sum paid under any provision of the *Pensions (Increase) Act 1971* (*ITEPA 2003, s 630*).

Certain foreign pensions for this type are totally exempt from income tax (*Overseas Pensions Act 1973, s 1*). The recipient of such a pension will incur no charge to tax in respect of that pension, provided he or she is the existing pensioner or the widow/widower of the existing pensioner, and the double taxation relief arrangement under which the exemption applies continues in operation. Once again, statutory increases fall outside this provision (*ITEPA 2003, ss 629, 630* and *643*). These provisions apply to those pensions which were paid by the governments of the following countries and which were exempt from tax under a double taxation agreement (*ITEPA 2003, s 643*):

- Malawi (including those for services to the government of the Federation of Rhodesia and Nyasaland);
- Trinidad and Tobago; and
- Zambia (including those for services to the government of Northern Rhodesia or the government of the Federation of Rhodesia and Nyasaland).

4.37 Relief under *ITEPA 2003, s 629* is extended by ESC A49 to widows' pensions paid to widows of Singapore nationality, who are resident in the UK and whose husbands were UK nationals employed in the service of the government of Singapore. The concession reads as follows:

> 'WIDOW'S PENSION PAID TO WIDOW OF SINGAPORE NATIONALITY, RESIDENT IN THE UNITED KINGDOM, WHOSE HUSBAND WAS A UNITED KINGDOM NATIONAL EMPLOYED AS A PUBLIC OFFICER BY THE GOVERNMENT OF SINGAPORE
>
> Sections 614 and 615, ICTA 1988 exempt from tax certain overseas pensions, including pensions paid by the United Kingdom Government to non-residents in respect of public service with the governments of former colonies (*ITEPA 2003, s 643*) extends this relief to United Kingdom residents, in receipt of pensions transferred to the care of the United Kingdom Government, by the Governments of Zambia, Malawi and Trinidad and Tobago. This sub-section should be extended to exempt from tax widows' pensions paid to widows of Singapore nationality, who are resident in the United Kingdom and whose husbands were United Kingdom nationals employed in the service of the Government of Singapore.'

Note that the provisions of former *ICTA 1988, ss 614* and *615* have been rewritten into the provision of *ITEPA 2003, s 643* for the tax year 2003/04 and subsequent tax years.

Investment of pension funds for overseas employees

4.38 Some superannuation funds are entitled to relief from UK tax on income derived from investments. The relief takes the form of taxing such income to the same extent as it would be taxed if it was the income of a person who is not resident, nor ordinarily resident, nor domiciled in the UK. Such funds are also exempt from capital gains tax.

Armed forces and war pensions

4.39 Benefits paid by any of the following Services schemes are exempt from income tax, even where the recipient continues to serve in any capacity (*ITEPA 2003, ss 639, 640A*):

- new armed forces pensions;
- armed forces compensation schemes; and
- early departure payments scheme.

Wounds and disability pensions

4.40 Income from the following list of wounds and disability pensions is exempt from income tax and will not be reckoned in computing income for any of the purposes of the *Income Tax Acts*. The qualifying pensions are (*ITEPA 2003, s 641(1)*):

- wounds pensions granted to members of the armed forces of the Crown;
- retired pay of disabled officers granted on account of medical unfitness attributable to or aggravated by armed forces service;
- disablement or disability pensions granted to members, other than commissioned officers, of the naval, military or air forces of the Crown on account of medical unfitness attributable to or aggravated by armed forces service;
- disablement pensions granted to persons who have been employed in the nursing services of any of the naval, military or air forces of the Crown on account of medical unfitness attributable to or aggravated by armed forces service;
- injury and disablement pensions payable under any War Risks Compensation Scheme for the Mercantile marine; and
- a benefit under a scheme established by an order under *Armed Forces (Pensions and Compensation) Act 2004, s 1(2)*, payable to a person by reason of his illness or injury by way of a lump sum, or following the termination of the person's service in the armed forces or reserve forces.

Where only part of the retired pay or pensions is attributable to the qualifying pensions (above), then relief will only extend to that part certified by the Secretary of State for Social Services, after consultation with the appropriate government department, to be attributable to disablement or disability (*ITEPA 2003, s 641(2)*).

Victoria Cross and other awards

4.41 No liability to income tax arises on a pension or annuity if it is paid to the holder of an award for bravery in respect of the award. Awards for bravery include (*ITEPA 2003, s 638*):

- the Victoria Cross;
- the George Cross;
- the Albert Medal or the Edward Medal;
- the Military Cross;
- the Distinguished Flying Cross;
- the Distinguished Conduct Medal;
- the Conspicuous Gallantry Medal;
- the Distinguished Service Medal;
- the Military Medal; and
- the Distinguished Flying Medal.

Pensions in respect of death due to war

4.42 The payment of the pensions or allowances set out below is not treated as income for any purposes of the *Income Tax Acts* (*ITEPA 2003, s 639*). The pensions and allowances are:

(1) any pension or allowance payable by or on behalf of the Ministry of Defence as relates to death due to:

  (a) service in the armed forces of the Crown or wartime service in the merchant navy, or

  (b) war injuries;

(2) any pension or allowance at similar rates and subject to similar conditions which is payable by the Ministry of Defence in respect of death due to peacetime service in the armed forces of the Crown before 3 September 1939; and

(3) any pension or allowance which is payable under the law of a country other than the UK and which is of a character substantially similar to a pension or allowance falling within para (1) or (2) above.

If one of the above pensions or allowances is withheld or abated by reason of the receipt of a non-qualifying pension or allowance, then an equal amount of the non-qualifying pension or allowance to the qualifying pension or allowance that is withheld or abated will be treated as falling within the exemption.

NON-TAXABLE STATE BENEFITS

Introduction

4.43 The basic rule is that all benefits payable under *Social Security Contributions and Benefits Act 1992, Pts II–IV* and its Northern Ireland counterpart, the *Social Security Contributions and Benefits (Northern Ireland) Act 1992*, are taxable under the charge on general earnings provisions of the *Income Tax (Earnings and Pensions) Act 2003* (*ITEPA 2003, ss 660* (Taxable benefits: UK benefits – Table A) and *677* (UK social security benefits wholly exempt from tax: Table B)).

Non-taxable benefits

4.44 The following benefits are not taxable (*ITEPA 2003, ss 656–677*):

- attendance allowance;
- bereavement payment;
- child benefit;

- child tax credit;
- council tax benefit;
- disability living allowance;
- guardian's allowance;
- housing benefit;
- industrial injuries benefit;
- job grant;
- pensioner's Christmas bonus;
- payments out of the social fund;
- severe disablement allowance;
- statutory maternity allowance;
- state pension credit;
- winter fuel payment; and
- working tax credit.

New Deal and Flexible New Deal arrangements

4.45 Where an employer takes someone on under the New Deal arrangements, the tax treatment depends on the method of payment to the participant. Where an employer or New Deal placement provider pays the New Deal participant a wage, the wage is included in taxable emoluments. This will apply where:

- an employer employs a New Deal participant in respect of whom a subsidy is received;
- a New Deal Environment Task Force Option placement provider offers wage-based placements; or
- a New Deal Voluntary Sector Option placement provider offers wage-based placements.

Where someone is taken on under a full-time education and training placement, or on an allowance based on environment task force or voluntary sector placement, the New Deal participant receives a training allowance from the Employment Service. No PAYE tax or National Insurance contributions are due on this allowance.

The schemes currently on offer under New Deal arrangements are as follows:

- New Deal for Lone Parents;
- New Deal for Partners;
- New Deal for Disabled people;
- New Deal for people aged 50-plus; and
- New Deal for musicians.

From October 2009, the current New Deal programme has been replaced with the Flexible New Deal in certain areas of the UK. For further information, see the government website at www.direct.gov.uk.

TAXABLE STATE BENEFITS

Taxable benefits

4.46 Social security income is in principle taxed in the same way as other sources of income, but the majority of state benefits are not in fact taxable.

The following benefits are taxable as social security income under the *Income Tax (Earnings and Pensions) Act 2003*, broadly on entitlement in the tax year:

- bereavement allowance;
- carer's allowance;
- incapacity benefit (excluding certain long-term incapacity benefit, and short-term incapacity benefit not payable at the higher rate);
- income support (if payable to one member of a married or unmarried couple involved in a trade dispute) up to a taxable maximum;
- jobseeker's allowance (excluding child maintenance bonus) up to a taxable maximum;
- statutory adoption pay;
- statutory maternity pay;
- statutory paternity pay; and
- statutory sick pay.

Additions to the above taxable benefits for child dependency are not taxable.

Sickness, maternity, paternity, adoption and disability payments

4.47 Sickness or disability payments paid to employees, where such payments have been arranged by the employer, are taxed as employment income (regardless of whether they are paid to the employee or to members of their family or household) (*ITEPA 2003, ss 221, 660*).

Statutory maternity pay (SMP), statutory paternity pay (SPP), statutory adoption pay (SAP) and statutory sick pay (SSP) paid by the employer are also taxable under these charging provisions.

A lump sum received under a life, accident or sickness insurance policy is not normally regarded as income for tax purposes. From 6 April 1996, continuing benefits from certain policies are also exempt; otherwise, there is a standard 12-month period for exemption of benefits received in respect of a fall in earnings caused by ill-health or disability.

Agency workers

4.48 In the case of *Commissioners for HMRC v Thorn Baker Limited and others*, the Court of Appeal upheld the decision of the High Court and dismissed HMRC's appeal concerning the payment of Statutory Sick Pay (SSP) to agency workers. The case confirms that SSP is not payable to agency workers whose contract with the agency is for a specified period of three months or less. However, in response to the court's decision HMRC published a reminder for agencies who should note that their workers can become entitled to SSP if in a single contract:

- they work longer than the original period specified and the total period actually worked exceeds three months; or
- the contract is extended for more than three months.

Agency workers whose contracts are for three months or less can also become entitled to SSP if two or more such contracts with the same agency are separated by eight weeks or less (56 days) and:

- the total length of the contracts is more than 13 weeks;
- the total period actually worked becomes more than 13 weeks; or
- the contracts are extended so that together they can run for more than 13 weeks.

The Court of Appeal ruling applies to agency workers only. Other short-term contract workers are unaffected and remain entitled to SSP.

Incapacity benefit

4.49 Incapacity benefits are treated as income for tax purposes (*ITEPA 2003, s 660, Table A*), with the following exceptions:

- benefit payable for an 'initial period of incapacity'; and
- any increase in benefit which is in respect of a child (*ITEPA 2003, s 676*).

An 'initial period of incapacity' is the period for which short-term incapacity benefit is payable otherwise than at the higher rate.

Incapacity benefit is not treated as chargeable income where a person's period of incapacity for work started before 13 April 1995 and for part of the period prior to that date, the person was entitled to invalidity benefit.

Tax is charged on the amount of benefit accruing in the year of assessment (*ITEPA 2003, s 661*).

Employment and Support Allowance (ESA) was introduced on 27 October 2008 and replaced Incapacity Benefit and Income Support, paid because of an illness or disability, for new claimants only. Individuals already receiving Incapacity Benefit continue to receive it, but it is intended that recipients move to the new benefit between 2009 and 2013.

Employment and Support Allowance

4.50 Employment and Support Allowance (ESA) replaced Incapacity Benefit and Income Support from 27 October 2008. ESA is a benefit for people who cannot work because of illness or disability. It involves a new medical assessment called the Work Capability Assessment, which is designed to ascertain what people can do, rather than what they cannot.

ESA consists of two phases:

- the assessment phase rate is paid for the first 13 weeks of a claim while a decision is made on the claimant's capability for work through the Work Capability Assessment;
- the main phase starts from week 14 of a claim, if the Work Capability Assessment shows that illness or disability does limit the claimant's ability to work.

There are two groups within the main phase:

- Work Related Activity Group – where claimants are expected to take part in work-focused interviews with a personal adviser.
- Support Group – in which claimants are placed because their illness or disability has a severe effect on their ability to work. Claimants will not be expected to take part in any work but they can do so on a voluntary basis if they wish. Claimants will receive a support component in addition to the basic rate of ESA.

Income support

4.51 Employment and Support Allowance (ESA) replaced Incapacity Benefit and Income Support, paid because of an illness or disability, for new claimants only from October 2008. Individuals already receiving Income Support continue to receive it, but it is intended that recipients move to the new benefit between 2009 and 2013.

Income support is taxable if the claimant's right to the benefit is subject to a condition that he shall be registered for employment, or he is one of a married or unmarried couple and he is disqualified from receiving unemployment benefit because he is involved in a trade dispute (*ITEPA 2003, s 665*). This means that any income support which the striker receives in respect of his partner's needs is taxable.

Where income support is taxable, any sum paid in excess of the 'taxable maximum' is not taxable. The taxable maximum is:

- the weekly rate of unemployment benefit if the recipient is an individual;
- the weekly rate of unemployment benefit plus the adult dependent supplement where the recipient is one of a married or unmarried couple and the recipient is not involved in a trade dispute; or
- one-half of the amount which would otherwise be payable where the recipient is one of a married or unmarried couple and he is involved in a trade dispute.

The taxable maximum in respect of part of a week is calculated as follows (*ITEPA 2003, s 668(3)*):

$$\frac{N}{7} \times \text{TMW}$$

N = the number of days in the part of the week for which the claimant is actually paid income support; and

TMW = the taxable maximum for the whole week as calculated above.

No liability on income tax arises on payments of income support which are attributable to child maintenance bonus (*ITEPA 2003, s 666*).

Jobseeker's allowance

4.52 Payments of jobseeker's allowance are generally taxable as social security income (*ITEPA 2003, s 660*). However, where jobseeker's allowance paid in respect of a week or part of a week exceeds the taxable maximum, the excess is not taxable.

The taxable maximum varies according to whether the payment is of income-based or contribution-based jobseeker's allowance, and whether it is paid to one of a married or unmarried couple, or to a single person. The amount in each case is fixed by regulations under *Jobseekers Act 1995, s 4.*

Retirement pensions

4.53 The state retirement pension (categories A to D) is payable under *Social Security Contributions and Benefits Act 1992, ss 43–55* and the equivalent Northern Ireland provisions, and is accordingly taxable under *ITEPA 2003, s 577.*

From April 2005, people who choose to take their state pension late may receive a one-off payment of over £30,000 after five years. The government's Five-Year Strategy sets out details of what a person could expect to receive if they deferred a weekly state pension of £105 for any time over one year:

- £5,646 for one year;
- £11,673 for two years;
- £32,306 for five years; or
- £77,090 for ten years.

4.54 To receive additional state pension, the individual has to defer claiming for at least five weeks.

Extra state pension is earned at the rate of 1% of the normal weekly state pension rate for every five weeks the claimant defers (this is equivalent to about 10.4% extra for every year deferred).

Example 4.1

Anne decides to defer claiming her weekly state pension of £90. When she finally claims after two years, she chooses extra state pension. This will give her a total weekly state pension of £108.72 for life.

(This example assumes that the rate of weekly state pension remain at £90 throughout the period.)

4.55 To receive a lump sum payment, the individual has to defer claiming for at least 12 months (which cannot include any period before 6 April 2005). The lump sum is a one-off, taxable payment based on the amount of normal weekly state pension the claimant would have received, plus interest. They also receive their state pension paid at the normal rate from when they start claiming it.

The interest rate will always be 2% above the Bank of England's base rate (so, if the base rate was 4.5%, the rate of interest would be 6.5%). As the Bank of England base rate may change from time to time, the rate of interest used to calculate the lump sum can also change.

Example 4.2

Alan decides to defer claiming his weekly state pension of £105 for three years. When he finally claims, if he chooses a lump sum, he will get a lump sum of around £18,000 (before tax) as well as his normal weekly state pension entitlement.

(In this illustrative example, the lump sum is based on £105 state pension and interest of 6.5% for the whole period. In a real example, the amount will take account of changes in both the weekly state pension and the interest rate.)

Pension Credit

4.56 Pension Credit is an income-related benefit for people aged 60 or over living in Great Britain that provides, or contributes to, a guaranteed level of income of £132.60 per week for a single person (£202.40 for a couple). These amounts may be more for people who have caring responsibilities, are severely disabled or have certain housing costs.

People aged 65 and over can also be rewarded for some of their savings and income they have for their retirement. It gives pensioners a cash addition of 60p for every £1 of income they have above the level of basic state pension up to a maximum of £20.52 a week (£27.09 a week for couples).

After this, the maximum reward is reduced by 40p for every £1 of income above the income guarantee so that pensioners with incomes up to around £184 a week (£270 a week for couples) could still be entitled.

Pension Credit is a non-taxable state benefit.

Full details regarding applications for Pension Credit are available online at www.direct.gov.uk.

Statutory redundancy payments

4.57 Any redundancy payment, and the amount of any other employer's approved contractual payment, will be exempt from income tax under *ITEPA*

2003, s 309. 'Redundancy payment' has the same meaning as in *Employment Rights Act 1996, Pt XI* or *Contracts of Employment and Redundancy Payments Act (Northern Ireland) 1965, Pt XII*.

The reference to an 'approved contractual payment' is a reference to the amount of that employer's payment so far as not in excess of the amount of the relevant redundancy payment (and so that where, in consequence of *Employment Rights Act 1996, s 104(2)* or *40(2)* of the said Act of Northern Ireland, there is no relevant redundancy payment, the amount of the employer's approved contractual payment is nil). However, it should be noted that payments of over £30,000 on retirement or removal from office or employment are subject to tax.

Job Grant

4.58 Job Grant is a tax-free payment payable to those taking up full-time work of at least 16 hours per week. The amount of Job Grant payable depends on the claimant's circumstances, a lower rate applying for single people and couples without children, and a higher one for all lone parents and couples with children (currently £100 and £250 respectively). A Job Grant may also be payable if a partner is going into work at least 24 hours per week and, as a result, the claimant's entitlement to benefit ends.

In order to claim Job Grant, the claimant must be starting full-time work (at least 16 hours a week) and expect that work to last five weeks or more, and have been receiving Income Support, Jobseeker's Allowance, Incapacity Benefit, Severe Disablement Allowance, Employment and Support Allowance, Jobcentre Plus/New Deal Allowance payments where the allowance is based on Jobseeker's Allowance, Income Support, Incapacity Benefit, or Severe Disablement Allowance, or a combination of these benefits, for at least 26 weeks immediately before moving into full-time work.

Taxable benefits rates

4.59

	Weekly from 6 April 2010
Bereavement benefits	
Bereavement allowance – standard	97.65
Carer's allowance	
Each qualifying individual	53.90
Incapacity benefit	
Long-term	91.40

	Weekly from 6 April 2010
Short-term higher rate (weeks 29 to 52)	
under pension age	81.60
over pension age	91.40
Severe disablement allowance	
basic rate	57.45
age addition higher rate	15.65
middle rate	9.10
lower rate	5.35
Jobseeker's allowance	
Single: under 18	51.85
18 to 24	51.85
25 or over	65.45
Non-contributory retirement pension	
Single person (category C or D)	58.50
Age addition (over 80)	0.25
Retirement pensions	
Single person	97.65
Age addition (over 80) – each	0.25
Statutory adoption pay	
Rate	124.88
(Paid for maximum of 39 weeks)	
Statutory maternity pay	
For first 6 weeks – 90% of average weekly earnings with no upper limit	
Remaining 33 weeks – Standard rate or a rate equal to 90% of average weekly earnings, whichever is lower	
Standard rate	124.88
Statutory paternity pay	
Rate	124.88
(Paid for 2 weeks)	
Statutory sick pay	
(Above earnings threshold of £97)	79.15

Non-contributory benefits

4.60 National Insurance contributions (NICs) pay for only certain state benefits. Many benefits are based on need or circumstantial conditions, with no link to past contributions paid. Instead they are based on some other link to the system, such as residence, and they are often subject to income limits or means testing. These non-contributory benefits are funded from general taxation and include:

- attendance allowance;
- child benefit;
- constant attendance allowance;
- council tax benefit;
- disability living allowance;
- guardian's allowance;
- housing benefit (including council tax rebate);
- income-based jobseeker's allowance;
- income support;
- industrial injuries disablement benefit;
- invalid care allowance;
- reduced earnings allowance;
- category D retirement pension;
- one parent benefit;
- severe and exceptionally severe disablement allowances;
- social fund;
- statutory adoption pay;
- statutory maternity pay;
- statutory sick pay;
- statutory paternity pay;
- war disablement pension;
- war widow's pension; and
- workmen's compensation supplement.

Statutory sick pay, statutory maternity pay, statutory paternity pay and statutory adoption pay are linked with NICs in that entitlement is based on recent receipt of earnings subject to Class 1 NICs.

Contributory benefits

4.61 Eligibility for the remaining social security benefits depends on an individual satisfying certain requirements as to the level of contributions which have been made (ie contributory benefits), though in some cases certain circumstantial conditions also apply. Contributory benefits include:

- incapacity benefit;
- contribution-based jobseeker's allowance;
- maternity allowance;
- retirement pension (category A and B);
- widowed mother's allowance;
- widow's payment; and
- widow's pension.

The category A pension is payable on the basis of a person's own contributions, while the category B pension is payable to a woman by virtue of her husband's contributions or to a man by virtue of his late wife's contributions. The pension may consist only of the basic component or, if appropriate contributions have been paid, of basic and additional earnings-related components.

CLASS 3 NATIONAL INSURANCE CONTRIBUTIONS

Overview

4.62 Class 3 National Insurance contributions (NICs) are voluntary contributions. A person is never liable to pay Class 3 contributions, but he may be entitled to pay, to protect entitlement to widows' benefits and the basic retirement pension. In certain limited cases involving overseas employment, voluntary Class 2 contributions may be paid as an alternative to Class 3 in order to protect entitlement to incapacity benefit and maternity allowance on the employee's return to the UK.

Voluntary contributions count towards:

- basic state pension;
- widowed parent's allowance;
- bereavement payment;
- bereavement allowance; and
- child's special allowance.

They do not count towards:

- jobseeker's allowance;
- the earnings-related part of state pension;
- the earnings-related part of bereavement benefits;
- maternity allowance;
- incapacity benefit; or
- industrial injuries disablement benefit.

Further details on Class 3 NICs, including an application form, can be found in leaflet CA5603, available online at www.hmrc.gov.uk/nic/ca5603.pdf.

Eligibility

4.63 Class 3 contributions may be paid by anyone who is:

- over 16;
- not working;
- not liable to pay Class 1 and/or Class 2 contributions as an employed or self-employed person;
- been excepted from paying Class 2 contributions; or
- resident in the UK, living or working on secondment abroad. An individual may also pay either Class 2 contributions or voluntary contributions once the initial 52 weeks' Class 1 contributions liability period has ended.

Class 3 contributions cannot be paid if the person:

- is a married woman or widow who opted to pay reduced rate contributions during the whole tax year;
- is paying for the tax year in which they reach state pension age;
- is already entitled to a full basic state pension;
- does not have enough contributions to qualify for a minimum basic state pension unless he or she needs to pay voluntary contributions to qualify for the lump sum bereavement payment; and
- is paying for any week that he or she is entitled to National Insurance credits, including automatic credits, unless he or she needs to pay a voluntary contribution to satisfy the first qualifying condition for basic state pension or bereavement allowance.

Time limits

4.64 To count towards basic state pension and bereavement benefits, voluntary contributions must generally be paid before the end of the sixth tax year following the one in respect of which they are paid.

- If they are paid after the end of the second tax year in respect of which they are paid, they will normally have to be paid at a higher rate.

Making payment

Paying for earlier tax years

4.65 An individual who wishes to make payment of Class 3 NICs for earlier tax year(s) and is within the time limit for payment should contact:

HM Revenue & Customs
National Insurance Contributions Office
Contributor Caseworker
Benton Park View
Newcastle upon Tyne
NE98 1ZZ

If payment is made before this deadline, the voluntary contributions will be due at the original rate.

Deciding to pay

4.66 Before deciding whether an individual needs or should pay voluntary contributions, he should consider getting a state pension forecast. The forecast will advise in today's money values:

- the amount of basic state pension earned to date;
- the amount of basic state pension that can be expected at state pension age based on what has been earned already and what might be earned before retirement; and
- if a payment of voluntary contributions will boost basic state pension and the amount that can be paid, at today's rates.

A pension forecast can be obtained online at the government information website (www.direct.gov.uk), or by filling in form *BR19 State Pension forecast application form* (which can be obtained from any Department for Work and Pensions office or HMRC Enquiry Centre).

4.67 On 25 May 2006 the government published a White Paper entitled *Security in retirement: towards a new pensions system*. One of the proposals in this White Paper was to reduce the number of qualifying years needed to receive a full basic state pension to 30 for those reaching state pension age on or after 6 April 2010. The number of qualifying years currently required is 44 years for a man and 39 years for a woman.

The government has confirmed that, where individuals have continued to make voluntary contributions since 25 May 2006, but would have chosen not to do so had they been aware of the government's intention to reduce the number of qualifying years required for a full basic state pension to 30, they may be entitled to a refund.

A person may now want to claim a refund of voluntary contributions they have made since 25 May 2006 if, for example, they retire after 6 April 2010 and would have had at least 30 qualifying years in their contribution histories even if they had never made any voluntary contributions. If the proposed change to the number of required qualifying years is enacted, then these individuals would be entitled to a full basic state pension without the extra qualifying years earned as a result of the voluntary contributions made.

No refunds will be offered for any NICs that were paid prior to 25 May 2006. These contributions were paid properly at the time in accordance with the law and in line with government policy.

In practice, some people may choose not to claim a refund, as it means they will be forgoing the accruals of entitlement to bereavement benefits that those contributions would have provided.

Chapter 5

Employment

EMPLOYMENT

Employed or self-employed?

5.1 Whether an individual is employed or self-employed is an important question for tax purposes, as there are many differences in the way in which they are taxed.

Employees are taxed under the PAYE system, with income tax and Class 1 NICs being deducted from payments made to them. Class 1 NICs are also payable by their employers (see **5.32**). In contrast, the self-employed pay income tax and Class 4 NICs direct to HMRC and are also liable to Class 2 NICs (see **6.92**).

Some important consequences are that:

- the NIC liability of a self-employed individual is much lower than that for an employee (especially when taking into account the employer's liability) (see *Athenaeum Club v R&C Commrs* [2010] TC 00325);
- the self-employed have a cash-flow advantage in the timing of tax payments under self-assessment, compared with employees taxed under the PAYE system;
- the rules allowing tax relief for expenses are generally more relaxed for the self-employed; and
- except in limited circumstances, an employer who incorrectly treats an employee as self-employed is liable for the income tax and National Insurance that should have been applied under PAYE (subject to a potential right of recovery from the employee). However, as a result of the *Demibourne* case referred to in **5.4**, new regulations (*SI 2008/782*) came into force from 6 April 2008. The regulations extend the limited circumstances where HMRC may make a direction to transfer an employer's PAYE liability to an employee who has received payments from which tax has been under-deducted.

Indicative factors

5.2 There is no legislation to distinguish between employment and self-employment, but numerous cases decided in the courts have provided guidance as to the indicating factors (see **5.4**). An HMRC fact sheet (ES/FS1) entitled 'Employed or self-employed for tax and National Insurance contributions' is available online at www.hmrc.gov.uk/leaflets/es-fs1.pdf. HMRC's Employment Status Manual is a further valuable source of information, which can be accessed via their website (www.hmrc.gov.uk/manuals/esmmanual).

The guidance given by HMRC in booklet CWG2 states:

> '… "employee" means anyone who is gainfully employed in the UK and is:
>
> - engaged under a "contract of service". Where you pay somebody to work for you, that arrangement will normally amount to either a contract of service (employment) or a contract for services (self-employment). Almost everyone who works for an employer will be employed under a contract of service, including full-time, part-time, casual or temporary employment. A contract need not be written, but can be a verbal or implied working agreement, or
> - an office holder with earnings chargeable to tax. An office holder is someone appointed to hold a titled office (including an elective office), for example a company director, or
> - engaged through an agency or some other third party …
>
> … In addition "employee" includes, for most PAYE purposes, many pensioners and others who get PAYE income (eg ex-employees). Similarly "employer" includes, for most PAYE purposes, agencies, pension-payers and others who make payments of PAYE income.'

The term 'office' is widely defined in the legislation (*ITEPA 2003, ss 5, 564*) as any position which has an existence, independent of the person who holds it, and may be filled by successive holders. The interpretation of office has historically relied on the element of permanence (*Great Western Rly Co v Bater* [1922] 2 AC 1, 8 TC 231), although the position does not need to be particularly long term. Common examples of office-holders include coroners, company secretaries, clergymen and company directors.

Personal services provided through intermediaries

5.3 Detailed anti-avoidance rules prevent individuals paying less tax and National Insurance through the use of personal service companies and other intermediaries (*ITEPA 2003, ss 48–61*). The rules broadly apply where, but for the intermediary, the income arising from an engagement would have been treated as employment income of the individual.

The intermediary will be responsible for applying PAYE and NIC to earnings received from any engagements caught by the rules. The income from the worker's relevant engagements in the tax year, less amounts provided as salary and benefits in kind and less allowable expenses, are deemed to be paid as salary on 5 April. Allowable expenses include normal employment income expenses, employers' NICs and pension contributions and 5% of earnings. Details of how to calculate the deemed payment are contained in HMRC's guidance *Intermediaries Legislation (IR35) – Working through an intermediary, such as a service company*, which is available online at www.hmrc.gov.uk/ir35/index.htm.

See **5.130** for further commentary on personal service companies.

Case law

5.4 The following is a list of case law (in alphabetical order) of the main cases relevant to employment status. Also provided is the HMRC Employment Status Manual paragraph number, where applicable, where a summary of each case can be found, and a brief outline of the point of issue in each case:

ESM Para Number	*Case Title*	*Case Reference*
ESM7060	***Airfix Footwear Ltd v Cope***	**[1978] ICR 1210**

Whether Mrs Cope was engaged under a 'contract of employment' and therefore entitled to claim unfair dismissal under the *Trade Union and Labour Relations Act 1974*.

ESM7150	***Andrews v King***	**64 TC 332**

The tax inspector had contended that Mr Andrews was a self-employed gangmaster and assessable under Schedule D and, further, that he was the employer of the gang members and so obliged to operate PAYE. Mr Andrews contended that he and the other gang members were employees.

ESM7170	***Barnett v Brabyn***	**69 TC 133**

There were two issues the court had to consider in this case. The preliminary issue was whether it was open to Mr Brabyn to challenge additional assessments under Case I Schedule D on the ground that he was never an independent contractor, even though the main assessments had been appealed and determined under *TMA 1970, s 54*. It was decided he could challenge the additional assessments. The second and substantive issue was the nature of his employment status.

	Cable & Wireless v Muscat	**[2006] EWCA Civ 220**

An implied contract of employment was found to exist between Cable & Wireless and Mr Muscat, on the basis that Muscat's contract for services with his agency, Abraxas, did not reflect the reality of his relationship with

ESM Para Number	*Case Title*	*Case Reference*

C&W. In previous cases in which contractors have claimed employment rights from end users, they have failed because no contractual nexus existed: that is, the contractor's company had a contractual relationship with the agency, but not with the end user. This case makes it clear that a contractual nexus in the traditional sense is not necessary and an implied employment contract can be considered to exist.

ESM7200	***Carmichael & Another v National Power plc***	**[1999] 1WLR 2042**

Whether Mrs Carmichael ('Mrs C') was an employee under a 'contract of employment' as defined in the *Employment Protection (Consolidation) Act 1978* and therefore entitled to written terms of the particulars of employment. Under this Act it was necessary to be engaged under a contract of employment for a minimum of 13 weeks to obtain this entitlement.

ESM7190	***Clark v Oxfordshire Health Authority***	**[1998] IRLR 125**

The Oxfordshire Health Authority administered a 'nurse bank' and supplied the services of bank nurses to a number of hospitals within its area. Mrs Clark joined the nurse bank as a staff nurse in January 1991. Her employment ended in January 1994 and she then claimed unfair dismissal and race discrimination. For her case to succeed she had to establish that she had been engaged under a contract of service.

ESM7190	***Dacas v Brook Street Bureau UK Ltd***	**[2004] EWCA Civ 217**

The agency (Brook Street Bureau) was not held to be the employer. However, the Court of Appeal gave a very strong indication that the end user in that case (Wandsworth Council) may have been an employer of the agency worker (Mrs Dacas) under an implied contract of employment.

ESM7020	***Davies v Braithwaite***	**18 TC 198**

Miss Braithwaite claimed that various contracts between her and theatrical producers were contracts of service. The Revenue contended that she was exercising her profession as an actress and was therefore correctly assessed under Case II of Schedule D.

ESM7020	***Demibourne Ltd v HMRC***	**SpC 486**

This case concerned the way in which tax paid by an individual in an employment status case was to be treated for the purpose of a PAYE settlement with the employer. The particular concern was the potential difficulty raised by the case in terms of whether or not it was possible to continue with long-standing arrangements that had often been applied whereby HMRC had allowed an offset of tax paid by an individual whilst they were treated as self-employed in arriving at the PAYE settlement due

ESM Para Number	*Case Title*	*Case Reference*

from the employer, and the method to be adopted. (See also **5.1** for details of new regulations, which apply from 6 April 2008, and have been published as a result of this case.)

ESM7080 ***Edwards v Clinch*** **56 TC 367**

The question for determination was whether fees paid to Mr Clinch were chargeable to tax under Schedule E as emoluments of an 'office' or chargeable under Schedule D.

ESM7210 ***Express & Echo Publications Ltd v Ernest Tanton*** **[1999] IRLR 367**

Whether a newspaper delivery driver was engaged under a contract of service or a contract for services.

ESM7055 ***Fall v Hitchen*** **49 TC 435**

Whether a professional dancer was engaged under a contract of service or whether he was exercising his profession and, therefore, engaged under a contract for services.

ESM7280 ***Future Online Ltd v Foulds*** **76 TC 590**

Whether the *Social Security Contributions (Intermediaries) Regulations 2000* and *FA 2000, Sch 12* applied to the provision of services by an IT consultant working through his own service company.

ESM7050 ***Global Plant Ltd v Secretary of State for Social Services*** **[1971] 1 QB 139**

Whether drivers of earth-moving equipment were engaged under contracts of service or contracts for services.

ESM7160 ***Hall v Lorimer*** **66 TC 349**

Whether a freelance vision mixer was engaged under a series of contracts of service or assessable under Schedule D as a person in business on his own account.

ESM7165 ***Lane v The Shire Roofing Company (Oxford) Ltd*** **[1995] TLR 104**

Whether Mr Lane was engaged under a contract of service or a contract for services.

ESM7140 ***Lee Ting Sang v Chung Chi-Keung*** **[1990] 2 AC 374**

During the course of his work at a construction site in Hong Kong, Lee Ting Sang was injured and he claimed compensation under the *Employees' Compensation Ordinance*. The courts had to determine as a preliminary issue whether he was working as an employee under a contract of service.

ESM Para Number	***Case Title***	***Case Reference***
ESM7220	***MacFarlane & Skivington v Glasgow City Council***	**EAT/1277/99**

Mrs MacFarlane ('Mrs F') and Mrs Skivington ('Mrs S') had previously worked as gymnastic instructors for Glasgow City Council (the 'Council') on a casual basis, when in 1992 the Council attempted to regularise the relationship by sending them a document setting out their terms of engagement. Both declined to sign the document. In 1998, Mrs M and Mrs S claimed unfair dismissal. The preliminary matter was whether they had been engaged under contracts of service or contracts for service.

ESM7180	***McMeechan v Secretary of State for Employment***	**[1997] IRLR 353**

Mr McMeechan was on the books of an employment agency, Noel Employment Ltd, as a temporary catering assistant for about a year. When the agency became insolvent, he sought to recover from the Redundancy Fund, under *Employment Protection (Consolidation) Act 1978, s 122*, the unpaid earnings due to him in respect of his last engagement. This had been with a client, Sutcliffe Catering, and he was claiming the sum of £105. The underlying matter to be decided was whether Mr McMeechan had been an employee of the agency during the course of this particular engagement.

ESM7040	***Market Investigations Ltd v Minister of Social Security***	**[1969] 2 QB 173**

Whether an interviewer, who was engaged on a casual basis, was employed under a series of contracts of service or under a series of contracts for services.

ESM7070	***Massey v Crown Life Insurance Company***	**[1978] 1 WLR 676**

This case involved a claim for unfair dismissal under the *Trade Union and Labour Relations Act 1974*. Mr Massey could only have succeeded if it was found that he was employed under a contract of service.

ESM7240	***Montgomery v Johnson Underwood Ltd***	**[2001] EWCA Civ 318**

Whether a person who was engaged by an employment agency to provide her services as a receptionist/telephonist to a third party was engaged by the employment agency under a contract of service or by the third party under a contract of service.

ESM7025	***Morren v Swinton and Pendlebury Council***	**[1965] 1 WLR 576**

Whether an engineer, who worked for a local authority, was engaged under a contract of service or a contract for services for the purposes of the *Local Government Superannuation Act 1937*.

ESM Para Number	***Case Title***	***Case Reference***
ESM7090	***Narich Pty Limited v The Commissioner of Payroll Tax***	**[1984] ICR 286**

This is an Australian case that was decided by the Judicial Committee of the Privy Council. Judgments of the Judicial Committee in Commonwealth cases have no value to UK law where the points at issue only concern interpretation of statute of the Commonwealth country. However, they are of relevance where general law principles are considered. The point at issue was whether lecturers engaged to conduct weight-watching classes were employees or not.

ESM7110	***Nethermere (St Neots) Ltd v Gardiner and Taverna***	**[1984] IRLR 240**

The Industrial Tribunal had to consider as a preliminary issue whether the applicants were 'employees' employed under contracts of service or whether they were self-employed under contracts for services.

ESM7100	***O'Kelly and Others v Trusthouse Forte plc***	**[1984] 1 QB 90**

Mr O'Kelly and some other casual catering staff were claiming that Trusthouse Forte had unfairly dismissed them for an inadmissible reason. The preliminary issue in the case was whether they were employees working under contracts of service or independent contractors working under contracts for services.

ESM7030	***Ready Mixed Concrete (South East) Ltd v Minister of Pensions and National Insurance***	**[1967] 2 QB 497**

Whether an owner-driver of a vehicle used exclusively for the delivery of a company's ready mixed concrete was engaged under a contract of service or a contract for services.

ESM7120	***Sidey v Phillips***	**59 TC 458**

The point at issue was whether Mr Sidey received part-time lecturing fees under contracts of service or contracts for services.

ESM7230	***St John's College School, Cambridge v Secretary of State for Social Security***	**[2001] ELR 103**

Whether visiting instrumental teachers ('VITs') were engaged under contracts of service or contracts for services.

ESM7260	***Synaptek Ltd v Young***	**75 TC 51**

Whether the *Social Security Contributions (Intermediaries) Regulations 2000* applied to the provision of services by an IT consultant working through his own service company.

ESM Para Number	*Case Title*	*Case Reference*
ESM7250	***Todd v Adams***	**[2002] EWCA Civ 509**

The appellants claimed damages under the *Fatal Accidents Act 1976* and the *Law Reform Act (Miscellaneous Provisions) 1934* from the vessel owners, the respondents. There were two preliminary issues under consideration but only the second issue need be considered here. Under *Merchant Shipping Act 1995, s 185*, liability for maritime claims can be limited in certain circumstances but not where the servants of the ship owners are engaged under contracts of service. The relevant point at issue was, therefore, whether members of the crew of a trawler were engaged under contracts of service.

ESM7270	***Usetech Ltd v Young***	**76 TC 811**

Whether the *Social Security Contributions (Intermediaries) Regulations 2000* and *FA 2000, Sch 12* applied to the provision of services by an IT consultant working through his own service company.

ESM7130	***Walls v Sinnett***	**60 TC 150**

Whether a lecturer was engaged under a contract of service or a contract for services.

Employed or self-employed – establishing the facts

5.5 No single fact will be decisive in deciding employment status. The facts set out in the following paragraphs are based on the guidance provided in HMRC leaflet ES/FS1: *Employed or self-employed for tax and National Insurance Contributions* (www.hmrc.gov.uk/leaflets/es-fs1.pdf), and may be of assistance in building the wider picture.

- First, establish the terms and conditions of the engagement – normally established from the contract between the worker and client/employer, whether written, oral or implied or a mixture of all three.
- Then consider any surrounding facts that may be relevant – eg whether the worker has other clients and a business organisation.

Deciding employment status

Factors indicating employment

5.6

- Having to carry out the work personally;
- being told what to do, when and how to do the work;
- payment by the hour, week or month and eligibility for overtime pay;

- working set hours, or a given number of hours per week or month;
- working at the other party's premises, or at a location of the other party's choice;
- being part and parcel of the organisation;
- right of dismissal;
- mutuality of obligations (to provide work on the one hand, and to carry out that work on the other);
- receipt of employee benefits such as holiday pay, sick pay or a company car;
- long periods working for one party.

Factors indicating self-employment

5.7

- The ability to exercise control over the work carried out;
- financial risk;
- responsibility for meeting losses as well as taking profits;
- provision of equipment needed to do the job (as opposed to the small tools that many employees provide for themselves);
- freedom to hire other people on the individual's own terms to do the work taken on (and payment out of own funds);
- the requirement to correct unsatisfactory work in the individual's own time and at his own expense;
- the opportunity to profit from sound management.

Overall picture

5.8 None of these factors are decisive in themselves. It is necessary to look at the circumstances as a whole. Where the evidence is evenly balanced, the intention of the parties may then decide the issue.

HMRC provide an online status tool on their website at www.hmrc.gov.uk/calcs/esi.htm. If used correctly, HMRC will recognise the decision given by the tool.

What is chargeable?

5.9 Employment income (*ITEPA 2003, s 7*) is assessable as earnings of an employment or office, whether as a payment or benefits in kind. Taxable income may include:

- wages and salaries, fees and overtime;
- holiday pay, sick pay, maternity pay and paternity pay;
- bonuses;
- commissions;
- tips and service charges;
- travelling time payments;
- redundancy payments (subject to possible relief of up to £30,000);
- inducement payments and some termination payments;
- reimbursement of expenses; and
- benefits in kind.

PAYE

Basis of charge

5.10 Employment income (plus pension and social security income) is charged to tax under the *Income Tax (Earnings and Pensions) Act 2003*.

'Employment income' includes earnings (eg salary or benefits), amounts treated as earnings (eg under the provisions for personal services provided by intermediaries) and any amounts counting as employment income (eg termination payments) (*ITEPA 2003, ss 9–13, 62*).

Employment earnings are treated as being paid on the earlier of the date on which (*ITEPA 2003, s 15*):

- the payment is actually made; and
- the employee becomes entitled to the payment.

In the case of directors, earnings are treated as being 'received' on the earlier of the above dates, or the date on which:

- sums on account of the director's remuneration are credited in the company's records;
- the period, during which the director's remuneration is determined, ends; or
- the director's remuneration is determined, if that is after the end of the period.

Exceptions

5.11 These rules do not apply to benefits in kind, which are treated as received in the tax year in which they are provided. Pension and social security benefits are taxable on the amount due in the tax year irrespective of the time of payment (*ITEPA 2003, ss 571, 661, 683, 686*).

Employment income – basis of assessment

5.12

Applies to	**Basis of assessment**
Earnings of an employee resident and ordinarily resident in the UK (but not emoluments of an employee not domiciled in the UK from a non-UK resident employer for duties performed wholly abroad)	Total earnings in the tax year wherever the duties are performed
Earnings of an employee not resident (or resident but not ordinarily resident) in the UK	Earnings on duties performed in the UK
Earnings of an employee who is resident and ordinarily resident but not domiciled in the UK, from a non-resident employer for duties performed wholly abroad; and Earnings of an employee resident but not ordinarily resident in the UK for duties performed abroad (whether from a resident or non-resident employer)	Earnings remitted to or received in the UK

PAYE

5.13 'Pay As You Earn' (PAYE) is the system for deducting income tax (and NICs) from PAYE employment income. The total amount deducted each tax month (ending on the 5th) including employer's NIC must be paid to HMRC within 14 days of the end of the tax month (ie by the 19th) unless the payment is made electronically, in which case the remittance is due within 17 days after the end of the tax month (ie by the 22nd). Employers whose average monthly liability is less than £1,500 can choose to pay quarterly rather than monthly by the 19th (or 22nd) of July, October, January and April (*ITEPA 2003, ss 682–702*; *FA 2002, ss 135–136*; *SI 2003/2682, regs 69, 97*; *SI 2003/2495*).

Who is included?

5.14 In addition to employees and directors, the PAYE system generally applies to the following workers (although special rules apply in some cases):

agency workers, part-time and casual workers, domestic workers and nannies, foreign workers, students and youths in training schemes.

When is PAYE operated?

5.15 As a general rule both NICs and PAYE are operated when a payment of earnings is made to an employee.

If the employee is not a director, PAYE should be operated on the earlier of:

- when the payment is actually made; or
- when the employee is entitled to be paid, even if the pay is not drawn until later.

If the employee is a director, PAYE should be operated on the earlier of:

- when the payment is actually made;
- when the director becomes entitled to be paid; or
- when the payment is credited in the company accounts or records, even if:
  - the director cannot draw the money straightaway because there is a block on the right to payment; or
  - the credit is not specifically in an account in the director's name;
- when the remuneration is fixed or determined:
  - if the amount for a particular accounting period is determined before the end of that period, take the date as being when the period ends;
  - if the amount is determined after the period ends, take the date as being when the amount is determined.

Employers have a legal obligation to operate PAYE on the payments made to employees if their earnings reach the National Insurance lower earnings limit (LEL). For 2010/11, this is £97 a week, £421 a month or £5,044 a year.

What is included?

5.16 The HMRC guide CWG2: *Employer Guide to PAYE and NICs* provides useful guidance and sets out examples of items that are included in gross pay for income tax and NIC purposes (see the HMRC website at www.hmrc.gov.uk/guidance/cwg2.htm).

PAYE codes

5.17 The tax liability of an employee depends not only on his earnings, but also on the amount of personal allowances and reliefs available to set off against those earnings. The PAYE code represents the total allowances and reliefs available. HMRC provides a set of tax tables for use in conjunction with the codes, to enable the employer to calculate the amount of tax to be deducted from each payment of wages or salary (*SI 2003/2682, regs 13–14*). The tables allow, as near as may be, for the correct time proportion of the employee's annual tax liability to be deducted. Dedicated payroll software is often used instead.

PAYE returns

5.18 Employers are required to keep records of pay and deductions (form P11) for at least three years following the end of the tax year to which they relate. At the end of each tax year, details must be provided to HMRC for all past and present employees during that year, using the following forms (*SI 2003/2682, reg 73*):

- P14 – after the end of the tax year for each employee in respect of whom tax and/or NIC was deducted during the year;
- P35 – showing the total tax and NIC for each employee;
- P11D – giving details of benefits and expenses payments provided in the tax year to directors, and to employees earning £8,500 per annum or more (including benefits in kind); and
- P9D – showing details of taxable benefits and expenses payments for those earning less than £8,500 per annum (including benefits in kind).

Where no deductions have been made during the year for certain employees, the employer must also complete and submit form P38A by 19 May following the end of the tax year (*SI 2003/2683, reg 74*). The employees concerned are those who:

- worked for the employer for more than a week;
- earned in excess of £100 in the tax year; or
- earned in excess of the PAYE threshold at any time.

Internet service for PAYE

5.19 HMRC internet service for PAYE allows employers, agents and payroll bureaux to send and receive forms and returns over the internet.

Almost all employers are now required to file their Employer Annual Return forms P14 and P35 online at the end of the tax year. In addition, employers with 50 or more employees must also file forms P45 and P46 online. Under government proposals, this requirement will extend to employers with fewer than 50 employees from April 2011. Penalty charges of between £600 and £3,000 may apply for failure to comply with online filing obligations.

Mandatory filing of certain in-year PAYE forms, such as forms P45 and P46, is also being phased in from the following dates:

- from April 2009 for employers with 50 or more employees; and
- from April 2011 for employers with fewer than 50 employees.

Special PAYE procedures cater for special circumstances and special types of employees, as follows (*ITEPA 2003, ss 682–712*; *SI 2003/2682*).

Employees who leave – P45

5.20 Where an employee ceases to work for an employer, the employer must provide him with a certificate on form P45, which shows the code and the cumulative pay and tax up to the date of leaving. The employee can then produce the form P45 to his next employer to enable him to continue the cumulative system of tax deduction. The employee will also retain a copy of the form which may be needed to complete his tax return (*SI 2003/2682, regs 40* and *42*).

New employees – P46

5.21 If a new employee does not have a form P45 (either because he had no previous employment, has lost the form, never received one or does not want the new employer to know his previous pay), the new employer must prepare form P46 (*SI 2003/2682, regs 46–50*). This form provides details of the employee to HMRC (unless that employee is paid below the PAYE tax and NIC threshold, in which case the form is retained by the employer) and includes a statement from the employee to the effect that:

- he is taking up employment for the first time after a period of full-time education and has not been in receipt of jobseekers allowance or income support due to unemployment; and/or
- the employment is his only or main employment; and/or
- he is in receipt of a pension.

Depending on which statement or statements are made, the employer will use either an emergency code (either on a cumulative or a Week 1 or Month 1 basis) to deduct tax allowing for a personal allowance, or code BR to deduct tax at the basic rate. This code will be used until HMRC issues the employer with the appropriate tax code.

If the employee subsequently produces form P45, the code indicated on that form should be used instead.

Coding for benefits – P46(Car)

5.22 In order to ensure the correct amount of tax is deducted from the employee's pay, the tax code takes into account any taxable benefits in kind made to the employee. The code will generally be based on benefits received by the employee in the previous tax year except in the case of company cars for which details must be provided by the employer on a quarterly basis (within 28 days of an income tax quarter) on form P46(Car). The income tax quarter ends are 5 January, 5 April, 5 July and 5 October. From 6 April 2009, employers do not need to complete a form P46(Car) for an employee when one car is replaced with another.

PAYE codes

5.23 The PAYE code is used to deduct more or less the right amount of tax from an employee's pay or an ex-employee's occupational pension (*SI 2003/2682, regs 13, 14*). The number is generally the tax-free income allowed with the last digit removed. The letters following the number are explained below.

L	basic personal allowance
P	higher personal allowance for those aged 65 to 74
Y	higher personal allowance for those aged 75 or over
T	used where none of the other code letters apply (eg an age-related personal allowance may be reduced because of income exceeding the income limit or the employee does not want the employer to know what tax allowances are received) does not mean a temporary code has been applied
K	(followed by a number) indicates that total allowances are less than total deductions (eg where benefits exceed personal allowances) and that tax must be deducted at more than the normal rate to take into account the tax due on untaxed income (the maximum rate at which tax may be deducted is 50%)
NT	no tax to be deducted
0T	all earnings to be taxed (ie no tax-free amounts available)
BR	tax collected at the basic rate of 20%
D0	(followed by a number) tax to be deducted at the higher rate of 40%

A Notice of Coding is usually issued in January or February for the following tax year, allowing employers to use this code from 6 April. An amended notice is then issued in the following May or June to correct any allowances for the tax year which have been announced in the Budget, usually in March or April. So, for 2010/11, an initial notice will have been issued in January or February 2010, followed by an updated notice in May 2010, following the Budget in March 2010. Further notices may be issued with any amendments made by the taxpayer or the employer (eg through form P46(Car)).

PAYE threshold for 2010/11

5.24

Weekly	£125.00
Monthly	£540.00

Note that, in most years, the PAYE threshold for National Insurance contributions (NICs) is aligned with the personal tax allowance. Exceptionally, in 2008/09, the personal allowance and the Class 1 NIC primary threshold were originally announced as £105.00 per week. However, the government subsequently increased the income tax personal allowance for 2008/09 to £116.00 per week, but the threshold of £105.00 remained for NIC purposes.

An employer is not required to operate PAYE in respect of an employee whose rate of pay does not exceed the PAYE threshold.

Interest on PAYE paid late

5.25 Interest is payable on certain late payments of PAYE (*Income Tax (Pay As You Earn) Regulations 2003 (SI 2003/2682), reg 82*).

Where an employer has not paid the net tax deductible by him to the collector within 14 days of the end of the tax year, the unpaid tax carries interest at the prescribed rate from the reckonable date until the date of payment. Certain repayments of tax also attract interest.

Year-end returns

5.26

Forms	Due Date	Offence	Penalty
P14 P35	19 May after end of tax year	Failure to submit return by due date	(a) first 12 months: penalty of £100 for each 50 employees (or part thereof) for each month the failure continues

Forms	**Due Date**	**Offence**	**Penalty**
			(b) failures exceeding 12 months: penalty up to the amount of the PAYE or NIC due and unpaid at 19 April following the tax year
		Fraudulently or negligently making an incorrect return	Penalty not exceeding the difference between the amount payable under the return and the amount which would have been payable had the return been correct
P9D P11D	6 July after end of tax year	Failure to submit return by due date	(a) penalty of up to £300 per form
			(b) continuing penalty of up to £60 for each day on which the failure continues after imposition of initial penalty
		Fraudulently or negligently making an incorrect return	Fine up to £3,000

P60 – (the employee's copy of P14) must be given to the employee by 31 May after the end of the tax year, but need not be given to employees who have left during the year.

P46(Car) – For 2010/11, forms P46(Car) should be submitted by 3 May 2010, 2 August 2010, 2 November 2010 and 2 February 2011.

Payments made 'free of tax and NICs'

5.27 If an employer enters into an arrangement with an employee that all of his or her earnings are to be paid 'free of tax', the employer should note that:

- it is his responsibility to make sure that the employee understands and agrees with the terms under which the payment is made free of tax;
- payments made free of tax can increase employer costs; and
- there are extra PAYE duties involved.

For example, the tax due is worked out by reference to the 'true gross pay', not the amount the employee is actually paid.

Where an employer has such an agreement with employees, he must contact his local HMRC office to obtain a package containing the following forms:

- forms P11 (FOT);
- special 'free of tax' (FOT) Tax Tables, Tables G;
- leaflet FOT1 which will help work out the 'true gross pay' figure.

If an employer enters into an agreement with an employee that only part of his or her earnings are to be paid 'free of tax', the figure to enter on form P11 (working sheet) to calculate the PAYE and NICs due is the total of:

- the 'true gross pay' of the 'free of tax' element of the earnings; and
- the actual gross pay not within the 'free-of-tax' agreement.

To work out the 'true gross pay' of the 'free-of-tax' element, the following formula is used:

$$\frac{\text{'Free of Tax' element of pay} \times 100}{(100 - \text{employee's tax rate figure})^{*}}$$

* The tax rate figure depends on which tax table is used for the employee:

- if Table SR is used, the figure is 10 – starting rate (for years up to and including 2007/08);
- if Table B is used, the figure is 22 for years up to and including 2007/08 and 20 for 2008/09 onwards – basic rate;
- if Table D is used, the figure is 40 – higher rate.

Example 5.1

In 2010/11 an employer enters into an agreement to pay an employee a wage of £150 and £20 'free of tax' towards travelling expenses. The employee is a Table B employee.

The figure to use to calculate the PAYE and NICs due is the total of the 'true gross pay' of the 'free of tax' element.

$\frac{£20 \times 100}{(100 - 20)}$	£25.00
The actual gross pay not within the 'free-of-tax' agreement	£150.00
Figure to be entered on form P11 to calculate PAYE and NICs	£175.00

Payroll giving

5.28 Under the payroll deduction scheme, an employee's donation to charity from via the payroll attracts tax relief. Relief is available where (*ITEPA 2003, s 713*):

- an employee suffers deduction of tax under PAYE;
- the employer operates an approved scheme for the deduction of charitable donations;
- the employee authorises the employer to make the deductions;
- the employer pays the deducted sums to an approved agent;
- the approved agent pays the deducted sums to a charity or charities; and
- the sums deducted constitute gifts from the employee to the charity and are not paid under a covenant.

There is no maximum limit for payroll giving. The deduction of a donation to charity under the scheme occurs before PAYE is applied, thus giving relief by means of a 'net pay' arrangement (*ITEPA 2003, s 713*).

There are regulations under which payroll deduction schemes are approved (*SI 1986/2211*).

Employers can get tax relief for the costs of administering the scheme. Agencies usually recover their costs by making a deduction from the donations they handle but, if the employer chooses to fund any of the agency's costs, or match your employees' donations, he can get relief for that as well.

Employers offering Payroll Giving should remember that employees are entitled only to tax relief, not relief from NICs. When completing form P11 therefore, the employer needs to deduct the amount of the authorised donation from the employee's gross pay for PAYE purposes.

The amount of the authorised donation is not deducted from the employee's gross pay for NICs purposes.

Farming

Free board and lodging

5.29 If the general rules for taxing income were to be applied, a tax liability would arise on the value of free board and lodging supplied to employees who, under the *Agricultural Wages Acts*, would be entitled to take a higher cash wage instead (*ITEPA 2003, s 99*). ESC A60, however, allows farmers to provide free board and lodging without any tax consequences for the employee if all the following conditions are satisfied:

- The employee is a manual farmworker (ie not a director, clerk, bookkeeper and so on).
- The farmworker does not earn at a rate of £8,500 or more in the year.
- The contract between the employer and the employee provides for a net cash wage with free board and lodgings.
- The board and lodgings are provided either:
  - in the farmhouse; or
  - by a third party whom the employer pays direct under a contract the third party has with the employer to provide the employee with board and lodging.

Harvest casuals

5.30 Special rules apply to casual employees only who are taken on for harvest work, who are not family members.

Normal PAYE procedures must be followed for any part-time or casual employees that are taken on for non-harvest work who are family members, regardless of the type of work they do. If earnings do not exceed the primary threshold (£110 per week for 2010/11), no National Insurance contributions are payable. If earnings reach or exceed the lower earnings threshold (£97 per week for 2010/11) but do not exceed the primary threshold, the employee is treated as having paid NICs when claiming benefit. If earnings exceed the primary threshold, Class 1 NICs are payable by the employee and employer.

The following table is an extract from HMRC booklet CWG2(2010) and sets out these rules.

Employees on the government's Seasonal Agricultural Workers Scheme (SAWS) are not eligible for the special PAYE and NIC concessions for harvest casuals (HMRC booklet CWG2, Chapter 4).

Circumstances	Action
For PAYE	
The person is a daily casual and: • is taken on for one day or less • paid off at the end of that period • with no contract for further employment.	Do not deduct tax. Keep a record of the employee's name, address and amounts paid. Enter these details on form P38A at the end of the tax year as requested on form P35.

Circumstances	**Action**
For PAYE	
The employee is taken on for no more than two weeks and has not been taken on previously by you since 6 April and paid above the PAYE threshold without PAYE being applied.	Do not deduct tax. Keep a record of the employee's name, address and amounts paid. Enter these details on form P38A at the end of the tax year as requested on form P35.
The employee is taken on for more than two weeks.	No special procedures apply and normal procedures must be followed. The procedures are detailed in the Employer Helpbook E13(2010) *Day-to-day payroll.*
For NICs	
The employee is employed as a regular casual, eg taken on for a specified period and paid at regular intervals.	No special NIC rules apply and normal procedures must be followed. The procedures are detailed in the Employer Helpbook E13(2010) *Day-to-day payroll.*
The employee is engaged on an irregular basis: • to work outdoors harvesting perishable crops • is paid off at the end of each engagement, eg at the end of the day • has no contract for further employment.	NICs will not be collected where it is impossible for the employer to identify individuals and record their earnings. If the identity details are known NICs are due when the earnings for each engagement exceed the ET: • work out the NICs due at the time the earnings are paid • complete form P11 etc as detailed in the Employer Helpbook E13 *Day-to-day payroll.*

National Insurance contributions

5.31 Significant changes were made to the NIC regime in April 1999, when the Contributions Agency merged with the Inland Revenue to become the National Insurance Contributions Office (NICO). Employers no longer face separate audits for PAYE and NIC, and the rules for each of these taxes are being increasingly aligned so that most payments and benefits which are subject to income tax are now also subject to NICs.

Class 1 contributions

5.32 Unless specifically exempted, all employees and employers must pay Class 1 contributions on employee earnings. 'Primary contributions' are payable by employees, and 'secondary contributions' by employers. For 2009/10 and 2010/11, employees pay NICs from the earnings threshold to the upper earnings limit at a rate of 11%, with earnings above that limit subject to an additional 1% charge. There is no upper earnings limit for employers.

For employees paid within a 'zero rate' band below the earnings threshold (known as the 'lower earnings limit'), the rate of NIC is 0%, but entitlement to benefit is maintained and earnings count for the purposes of calculating statutory sick pay and statutory maternity pay.

Contracting out

5.33 Contributions payable by the employee and employer are reduced by a rebate where the employee is 'contracted out' of the State Second Pension (S2P) (formerly known as the State Earnings Related Pension Scheme (SERPS)). The rebate is based on contributions from the lower earnings limit, so it is given on contributions (even though they are not paid) between the lower earnings limit and the earnings threshold.

Class 1A contributions

5.34 Class 1A NICs are payable on most benefits in kind liable to income tax (eg private medical insurance contracted by the employer, and certain beneficial loans). The Class 1A NIC charge is levied on the employer only, based on company car and fuel scale charges, and on the cash equivalent of other benefits as identified on the employee's form P11D. Class 1A NIC does not apply to the following:

- benefits exempt from income tax, covered by a dispensation or Extra-Statutory Concession, or included in a PAYE Settlement Agreement (see **5.86**);
- benefits reported on form P9D (ie relating to lower paid employees, ie those earning at a rate of less than £8,500 a year);
- benefits liable to Class 1 NIC instead (eg shopping vouchers);
- benefits provided for business use, but with insignificant private use; and
- benefits specifically exempt from Class 1 NIC (eg mobile phones) or Class 1A NIC (eg employer provided childcare).

The HMRC booklet CWG5 (2010) *Class 1A National Insurance Contributions on Benefits in Kind* provides a useful summary of the liability arising in respect of the provision of benefits in kind (see the HMRC website at www.hmrc.gov.uk/guidance/cwg5.htm).

Example 5.2

During the tax year 2009/10, an employer provides healthcare and company cars to 25 of his employees.

The Class 1A NICs percentage rate for the 2009/10 tax year is 12.8%.

The cash equivalent figures reported on each employee's P11D are £150 healthcare and £3,000 car benefit.

To calculate the Class 1A NICs due:

Step 1 Add the total cash equivalent figures together:

Healthcare:	£150 × 25 =	£3,750
Car benefit:	£3,000 × 25 =	£75,000
Total benefits provided:		£78,750

Step 2 Multiply the figure from Step 1 by the Class 1A percentage rate:

£78,750 × 12.8% = £10,080.00

Class 1A NICs due = £10,080.00

Class 1B contributions

5.35 PAYE settlement agreements (PSAs) (see **5.86**) allow employers to account for any tax liability in respect of their employees on payments that are minor or irregular, or that are shared benefits on which it would be impractical to determine individual liability, in one lump sum. From 6 April 1999, the principle was extended to NICs through a new contribution class: Class 1B. Where an employer has a PSA with HMRC, he will be liable to Class 1B contributions on the amount of the emoluments in the agreement that are chargeable to Class 1 or Class 1A contributions, together with the total amount of income tax payable under the agreement (*SSA 1998, s 53*; *Social Security Act 1998 (Commencement No 4) Regulations 1999 (SI 1999/526)*).

Class 2 and 4 contributions

5.36 Paid by the self-employed (see **6.92**).

Class 3 voluntary contributions

5.37 Paid by those who otherwise would not pay enough contributions to earn a full pension (see **Chapter 4**).

Maximum contributions

5.38 Where an employee has more than one employment (or is also self-employed), liability for Class 1 contributions at the main rate cannot exceed the equivalent of 53 primary Class 1 contributions at the maximum standard rate. The additional 1% rate applies above that limit.

Tax deductions

5.39 Employers' NICs are deductible from taxable profits, but income tax is calculated on employees' earnings before deduction of NICs.

National Insurance contributions from 6 April 2010

5.40

Lower earnings limit	£97 a week	Upper earnings limit	£844 a week
	£421 a month		£3,656 a month
	£5,044 a year		£43,875 a year
Earnings threshold	£110 a week		
	£476 a month		
	£5,715 a year		

Class 1 contributions – weekly amounts

Standard rate				
Employees		*Employers*		
First £110	Nil	First £110		Nil
£110.01 to £844	11%	Over £110		12.8%
Over £844	11%			
Contracted out				
Employees		*Employers*	*Salary related schemes*	*Money purchase schemes*
First £110	Nil	First £110	Nil	Nil
£110.01 to £844	9.4%	£110.01 to £844	9.1%	11.4%

Over £844	1%	Over £844	12.8%	12.8%
(Rebate £95–£110	1.6%)	(Rebate £95–£110	3.7%	1.4%)
Reduced rate for women (employees)				
First £110	Nil			
£110.01 to £844	4.85%			
Over £844	1%			

Employees' rates are nil for men over 65 and women over 60, but normal employers' contributions are still payable. No contributions are payable for children under 16.

Rebates – deductions from contributions payable are made for rebates that would have applied to NICs on earnings between £97 and £110 for employees and employers at the rates above. Where the rebate reduces the employee's contributions to nil, the balance is offset against the employer's contributions.

Class 1A and Class 1B contributions 12.8%.

Class 1A contributions are payable by employers by 19 July following the tax year. The liability is paid separately from the employer's PAYE and NIC liability.

Class 1B contributions are payable by employers by 19 October following the tax year on the value of any items included in a PAYE settlement agreement which would otherwise be earnings for Class 1 or Class 1A, including the amount of tax paid.

Class 2 contributions	
Flat rate	£2.40 a week
Small earnings exception	£5,075 a year
Class 3 voluntary contributions	£12.05 a week
Class 4 contributions	
Percentage rate	8% payable on profits between £5,715 and £43,875 a year
	1% on profits exceeding £43,875
Exempt if pensionable age reached at start of tax year	

TAXABLE AND TAX-FREE BENEFITS

Benefits and expenses

5.41 Some expenses payments and benefits are treated as taxable remuneration (*ITEPA 2003, s 63*). Special rules apply to most directors and to certain other employees. Some benefits and expenses payments are taxable on all employees, regardless of their level of earnings. However, some benefits are not taxable in 'lower-paid employments', in which an employee's rate of earnings is less than £8,500 per annum (*ITEPA 2003, ss 216–220*).

Benefits taxable on all employees

5.42 All employees and directors are liable to tax on the provision of certain benefits irrespective of their level of earnings, including:

- living accommodation;
- non-exempt vouchers, eg travel season tickets, gift vouchers;
- loans written off;
- payments made on the employee's behalf and expenses payments other than those wholly for business purposes (eg travel between home and work);
- certain payments made by employer credit card;
- certain relocation expenses;
- assets transferred at below market value by the employer;
- gifts (if new, at cost or for 'lower paid' employees at second-hand value).

For employees earning at a rate of less than £8,500 per annum, these benefits must be reported on form P9D, where the total expenses payments and benefits exceed £25 in a tax year.

Benefits taxable on directors, and employees earning more than £8,500 per annum

5.43 Benefits provided to directors, and to employees who are not 'lower paid', ie those earning at a rate of £8,500 per annum or more (including family or household members) by reason of their employment, are taxed on the cash equivalent of that benefit. This applies whether the benefits and expenses payments are provided by the employer or by a third party.

The 'cash equivalent' of a benefit is generally the VAT-inclusive cost to the employer of providing it, less any amounts made good by the employee. However, there are special rules for valuing certain benefits (such as cheap loans, share options, company cars and fuel for private use, etc).

Where 'in-house' benefits (ie goods, services or facilities) are provided to the employee out of surplus capacity, the value for tax purposes is broadly the additional cost to the employer of providing the benefit.

In determining whether an employee earns more than £8,500 per annum, all expenses payments and the cash equivalent of all benefits must be included. Allowable expenses are not taken into account for these purposes, although certain deductions (eg employee contributions to the employer's pension scheme) may be taken into account.

Directors

5.44 The provisions apply to all 'directors', except for those who:

- earn at a rate of less than £8,500 per annum; and
- either alone, or together with associates and relatives, own not more than 5% of the company's ordinary share capital or right to assets; and
- work full-time; or
- work for a charitable or non-profit making body.

Benefits for directors and P11D employees

5.45 In addition to the benefits listed above for P9D employees, other benefits would also have to be reported on forms P11D for directors and employees earning at a rate of more than £8,500 per annum, including the following:

- cars made available by the employer for private use (see **5.53**);
- car fuel supplied for private motoring (see **5.51**);
- private medical insurance (unless for treatment whilst working abroad);
- interest-free or low interest loans (see **5.55**);
- goods or services supplied at less than their full cost;
- use of employer's assets (other than cars or vans);
- certain scholarships;
- taxable mileage allowances and passenger payments.

See also HMRC guidance CWG2 *Employer Further Guide to PAYE and NICs,* which provides useful advice on whether benefits and/or expenses are reportable for P9D or P11D purposes (see the HMRC website at www.hmrc.gov.uk/guidance/cwg2.htm).

Relocation expenses and benefits

5.46 The limit for qualifying expenses is £8,000.

Expenses must be incurred during the period from the date of the job change to the end of the next following tax year, although this period may be extended with the agreement of HMRC.

Qualifying expenses include (*ITEPA 2003, s 271*):

- *Disposal expenses and benefits* – legal and advertising expenses in connection with the disposal of an accommodation, penalty for redeeming a mortgage, auctioneers' and estate agents' fees, disconnection of public utilities, rent, maintenance and insurance costs while the property is unoccupied.
- *Acquisition benefits and expenses* – legal expenses in connection with the acquisition of a new main residence, loan fees and mortgage insurance costs, survey and land registry fees, stamp duty, connection of public utilities (abortive costs in connection with an acquisition that does not proceed are also allowed).
- *Transportation of domestic belongings* – including insurance costs.
- *Travelling and subsistence expenses and benefits* – for temporary visits to new residence before relocation, travel from old residence to new place of work or from new residence to old place of work where date of move and relocation of work do not coincide, travelling and subsistence costs for child under 19 relocating before or after parents for educational reasons, benefit of a car or van for use in connection with the relocation where it is not otherwise available for use.
- *Bridging loan expenses and beneficial bridging loans* – relief on any charge to interest at the official rate on a beneficial loan to the extent that the aggregate value of all other qualifying benefits and expenses falls short of £8,000.
- *Duplicate expenses and benefits in respect of the new residence* – replacement of domestic items (does not cover new school uniforms).

Living accommodation

5.47 There is an exemption to charge where (*ITEPA 2003, Pt 3, Ch 5*):

- it is necessary for the employee to reside in the accommodation, eg a caretaker;
- it is customary for the employee to be provided with accommodation; or
- the accommodation is provided by reason of security for the employee.

A director will not generally qualify for exemption unless the accommodation is occupied for security purposes.

The basic charge is:

- the higher of the annual value of the rent paid by the employer;
- less any rent paid by the employee.

An additional charge arises where the cost of providing accommodation exceeds £75,000 (unless the basic charge above is based on the full open market rent). The extra charge is calculated as follows:

- the excess cost (including cost of improvements) over £75,000 multiplied by the official rate of interest (4.75% for 2009/10; 6.10% for 2008/09);
- less the amount by which any rent paid by the employee exceeds the annual value.

The charges are proportionately reduced if the property is provided for only part of a year or if part of the property is used exclusively for business purposes.

Example 5.3

A senior executive is provided with a house by reason of his employment from his employer which cost the employer £175,000 in June 1999. The gross rating value of the property is £1,000 and the executive is required to pay his employer a rental of £1,500 per annum. Assuming that the executive occupied the property throughout the tax year and that the 'official rate' in force at 6 April (the beginning of the tax year) was 4.75%, the tax charges upon the employee for the year will be:

(a)	benefit under *ITEPA 2003, s 105:*		
	• (No charge arises because the rental of £1,500 payable by the employee is more than the gross rating value of £1,000)		NIL
(b)	the additional yearly rent ie:		
	• cost of providing accommodation	£175,000	
	Less	£75,000	
	Excess is	£100,000	
	• £100,000 × 4.75%		£4,750
(c)	Excess of rental payable over gross rating value:		
	• rental payable by employee	£1,500	
	Minus		
	gross rating value	£1,000	
	unused excess rent		(£500)
	The cash equivalent of the benefit is		£4,250

Homes owned abroad through a company

5.48 The living accommodation charge outlined above generally applies to overseas property as it does for property in the UK. A particular issue arises, however, where property is held through a company for legal reasons connected with the country in which the property is owned. *FA 2008, s 45* introduced legislation (by inserting new *ss 100A* and *100B* into *ITEPA 2003*) designed to ensure that individuals buying a home abroad through a company, typically for holiday use, will not face a benefit in kind charge in certain specified circumstances. The new rules are deemed always to have applied.

Subject to certain anti-avoidance rules, the exemption will apply if the following conditions are met:

- the living accommodation outside the UK is provided by a company for a director or other officer of the company ('D'), or a member of D's family or household;
- the company is wholly owned by D (alone or together with other individuals, but not as partnership property), and
- the company has been the 'holding company of the property' at all times since the 'relevant time'.

Although the legislation was contained in *FA 2008*, it is treated as always having had effect. This means that, where the provision of living accommodation outside the UK satisfies the statutory conditions, no liability to income tax in respect of the benefit of that provision arises for any tax year. Any individual who can show that they have paid income tax for any year before 2008/09 on the benefit of living accommodation which qualifies for exemption under *ITEPA 2003, s 100A* should write to:

Michael Robinson,
c/o Debbie Green,
HM Revenue & Customs,
CPPT Directors Office,
5th Floor, Trinity Bridge House,
2 Dearmans Place,
Salford,
Manchester,
M3 5DT.

Employees' additional household expenses

5.49 Payments by employers to cover reasonable additional household expenses incurred by employees in carrying out their regular employment duties at home are exempt from income tax (and NICs). Employers can pay up to £3 per week (£156 per year) without supporting evidence of the costs incurred. Above that level, the exemption is still available, but the employer must provide supporting evidence of the relevant additional household expenses incurred (*ITEPA 2003, s 316A*).

Child care and child care vouchers

5.50 A benefit-in-kind tax exemption applies to the provision of qualifying child care contracted by the employer, and on employer-provided child care vouchers from 6 April 2005. An employee can receive vouchers for registered or approved child care worth up to £55 per week/£243 per month, free of tax and National Insurance contributions, if certain conditions are met (*ITEPA 2003, ss 318 et seq*; *SI 2006/882*).

Car fuel rates

5.51 The car fuel charge operates on the same basis as the car benefit charge. The percentage arrived at under those rules is applied to a single set figure for all cars to arrive at the chargeable amount. The figure for 2010/11 is £18,000 (£16,900 for 2008/09 and 2009/10) (*ITEPA 2003, s 150*; *SI 2008/511*).

Fuel charges are reduced to nil if the employee is required to make good all fuel provided for private use, including journeys between home and the normal workplace. No taxable benefit arises if the employer only provides fuel for business travel (*ITEPA 2003, s 151*).

The charges are reduced pro rata where a car is not available for any part of the tax year (being at least 30 consecutive days). The charge is also reduced proportionately where an employee stops receiving fuel part way through the year (unless he again receives fuel in the same tax year, in which case the full charge will apply) (*ITEPA 2003, s 152*).

Fuel provided in respect of a private car for private motoring of a director or employee earning more than £8,500 per annum is assessed on the cost to the employer, less any contributions from the employee.

Employers pay Class 1A National Insurance contributions on the fuel charge.

Company vans

5.52 For 2006/07 and earlier years, there was a fixed taxable benefit of £500 per annum for the private use of a van not exceeding 3,500 kilograms, reduced to £350 if the van was four years old or more at the end of the tax year. For 2007/08 onwards, the taxable benefit is £3,000 regardless of the age of the van. For 2004/05 onwards, there is no benefit if private use is restricted to home-to-work travel. The benefit is proportionately reduced if the van is unavailable for part of the tax year (*ITEPA 2003, s 155*).

Where a van is shared between two or more employees, the fixed charge is split evenly between them, regardless of variations in private use, but the charge can be displaced by £5 for each day of private use where this produces a lower figure. For 2005/06 onwards, the rules for shared vans are simplified; each user is taxed on the fixed charge, reduced on a just and reasonable basis (*ITEPA 2003, s 156*).

The taxable amount is reduced by any payments made by the employee for private use.

Employer-provided fuel for private use of a van is subject to a taxable benefit charge of £550 per annum for 2010/11 (£500 for 2007/08 to 2009/10 inclusive) (*ITEPA 2003, ss 160 et seq*).

Employers pay Class 1A National Insurance contributions on the fuel charge.

Car benefit scale rates – 2010/11

5.53 Company car tax is graduated in relation to CO_2 (carbon dioxide) emissions and the list price of the car.

Car benefit charges for cars with an approved CO_2 emissions figure

5.54 The benefit is calculated on a percentage of the list price of the car appropriate to the level of the car's CO_2 emissions, as follows (*ITEPA 2003, s 139*):

- 15% of the list price of cars emitting up to 130g/km in 2010/11 (reducing to 125g/km for 2011/12);
- increased by 1% per 5g/km over the annual g/km limit;
- capped at 35% of the list price.

If the exact CO_2 emissions figure does not end in 0 or 5, it should be rounded down to the nearest 5g/km.

From 6 April 2012, there will be a new 10% band, and all CO_2 emissions thresholds will be moved down by 5g/km. This means that the 10% band will apply to company cars with emissions not exceeding 99g/km (*FA 2010, s 59*). This will be reduced to 5%, from 2012/13 to 2014/15 inclusive, for cars with emissions not exceeding 75g/km.

There is usually a 3% supplement on diesel cars (subject to 35% cap). For years to 5 April 2006, no supplement was applied to diesel cars that met the Euro IV emissions standard. From 6 April 2006, the diesel supplement applies to all diesel cars first registered from 1 January 2006 (as well as to older cars not meeting the standard). From 6 April 2011, the diesel loading will be applied to all diesel cars.

To provide a continuing incentive for employees and employers to choose environmentally friendly vehicles (referred to as qualifying low emissions cars (QUALECs)), a new 10% band was introduced from 2008/09 for petrol cars that emit 120g/km or less of CO_2 (*ITEPA 2003, s 139(3A)*). A reduced appropriate percentage of 5% applies, from 6 April 2010 for five years, for company cars with an approved CO_2 emissions figure not exceeding 75g/km (*FA 2010, s 59*).

Electric cars are specifically excluded from these measures as they continue to qualify for a 9% rate. Alternatively fuelled cars may be eligible for the 10% rate, but the existing discounts for LPG, bi-fuel (dual fuel) or hybrid cars only apply if the car is taxed at a rate above 10%.

With the 3% supplement (see above), the lowest charge for a diesel car will be 13%, unless it is approved for Euro IV standards and was first registered before 1 January 2006, when the rate will be 10%.

From 6 April 2008, a 2% discount from the appropriate percentage rate is given for cars that run on E85 fuel.

The reductions for alternative fuel cars given above are to be abolished from 6 April 2011, except that cars producing no CO_2 emissions when driven will continue to be taxed at zero per cent until 6 April 2015.

The following table provides the 'appropriate percentage' figures for calculating the taxable benefit of a company car, based on CO_2 emissions figures for petrol cars, for the 2010/11 tax year:

Carbon dioxide emissions in grams per kilometre	Percentage of list price chargeable as benefit (2010/11)	
	Petrol	Diesel
130 and below	15	18
135	16	19
140	17	20
145	18	21
150	19	22
155	20	23

Carbon dioxide emissions in grams per kilometre	Percentage of list price chargeable as benefit (2010/11)	
	Petrol	Diesel
160	21	24
165	22	25
170	23	26
175	24	27
180	25	28
185	26	29
190	27	30
195	28	31
200	29	32
205	30	33
210	31	34
215	32	35
220	33	35
225	34	35
230	35	35
235	35	35

Notes:

(a) The 'list price' (currently subject to an upper limit of £80,000 (see below)) is the price published by the manufacturer, importer or distributor (including delivery charges and taxes) at the time of registration. It includes any optional extras supplied with the car when first made available to the employee, together with any further accessory costing £100 or more. The list price is reduced by any capital contributions to the initial cost of the car, capped at £5,000.

(b) The £80,000 cap is to be withdrawn from 6 April 2011 (*FA 2009, Sch 28, para 2*).

(c) For all cars registered on or after 1 March 2001, the definitive carbon dioxide emissions figure is recorded on the vehicle registration document. For cars first registered between 1 January 1998 and 28 February 2001, the Vehicle Certification Agency will supply carbon dioxide and other relevant information on their website at www.vcacarfueldata.org.uk and in their free, twice-yearly edition of the New Car Fuel Consumption and Emissions Figures booklet. For cars registered after 31 December 1997 with no carbon dioxide emissions figure, the tax charge is 15% of the list price for engines up to 1,400cc, 25% for engines of 1,401cc to 2,000cc and 35% for engines above 2,000cc.

For cars registered before 1 January 1998, the tax charge is 15% of the list price for engines up to 1,400cc, 22% for engines of 1,401cc to 2,000cc and 32% for engines above 2,000cc. Older cars with no cylinder capacity are taxed on 32% of the list price (15% for electric cars).

(d) The value of the benefit is reduced proportionately if the car is not available for part of the year.

Beneficial loans

5.55 The taxable benefit on cheap or interest-free loans is the difference between any interest paid and the interest payable at the 'official rate' (*ITEPA 2003, s 175*).

For 2002/03 to 2006/07 inclusive, the official rate was 5%.

For 2007/08, the official rate was 6.25%.

For 2008/09, the official rate was 6.10%.

For 2009/10, the official rate is 4.75%.

There is no charge where:

- the loan has been made on commercial terms by employers who lend to the general public; or
- the total of all beneficial loans does not exceed £5,000 at any time in the tax year.

Tax is charged on the amount written off of any loans whether or not the recipient of the loan is still employed.

From 22 March 2006, cheap loans provided by employers to their employees which do not involve the payment of interest are taxed in the same way as conventional employee loans, ie on the difference between the interest (or its equivalent) payable by the employee and the amount of interest that would be payable at the official rate (*ITEPA 2003, Pt 7, Ch 3*, as amended by *FA 2006, s 97*). There are two ways of calculating the taxable benefit:

- the averaging method; and
- the alternative method.

The averaging method will apply unless the taxpayer elects for, or HMRC specifically requires, the use of the alternative method (*ITEPA 2003, s 183*). The time limit for an election is the first anniversary of the normal self-assessment filing date for the year in question.

Where the loan is not at the same level throughout the tax year, it may make a significant difference if one or other method is used.

The averaging method

5.56 The averaging method (*ITEPA 2003, s 182*) applies an average interest rate to an average loan balance. To calculate any tax charge using the normal method, the following steps need to be followed.

Step (1)

Find the balance of the loan outstanding on 5 April, ie the day before the start of the tax year. If the loan only came into existence during the year then the balance is taken on the day on which the loan was made.

Step (2)

Find the balance on 5 April at the end of the tax year. If the loan was fully repaid during the year then it is necessary to look at the balance on the day of repayment.

In both Steps (1) and (2) above, it is necessary to look at the maximum amount of the loan outstanding on each of the relevant days.

Two successive loans are treated as the same loan for the purposes of these first two steps.

Step (3)

Calculate the average of the two figures from Steps (1) and (2) above.

Step (4)

Calculate the average official rate of interest. (If the official rate of interest was unchanged for the whole year, or for the part of the year during which the loan was outstanding, this step can be ignored.) The legislation instructs that this should be done as follows:

(1) multiply the official rate of interest in force during each period by the number of days when it was in force;

(2) add together these products;

(3) divide the result by the number of days in the total period.

The result at this stage is a rough and ready average loan for the whole year.

Step (5)

It is now necessary to apply to this average loan figure the average 'official rate of interest' in force during the period for which the loan was outstanding during the year. This is done by using the formula:

$$A \times I \times \frac{M}{12}$$

A = the average loan as calculated above; and

I = the average interest rate as calculated above; and

M = the number of whole months during which the loan was outstanding in the year. For these purposes, a month begins on the sixth day of the calendar month. A loan taken out on 7 June and repaid on 4 September is therefore treated as outstanding for one month only.

Step (6)

Any interest paid by the employee in respect of that loan and for that year is deducted.

The result is the cash equivalent, or taxable value, of the loan in question for the tax year.

Example 5.4—Beneficial loan calculation – averaging method

Sophie's employer lends her £7,000 on 8 June for personal use. She repays £2,000 on 1 December. The remaining balance is still outstanding at the end of the tax year. The official rate of interest is 5% until 5 February when it is reduced to 4%.

The maximum outstanding at commencement of the loan was £7,000.

The maximum outstanding on 5 April at the end of the tax year was £5,000.

The average amount is, therefore, £6,000 ((£7,000 + £5,000)/2)

The number of whole months the loan is outstanding is nine. (Months run from 6th to 5th so the loan was not outstanding for the whole month 6 June to 5 July).

Period 8 June to 5 February = 243 days

Period 6 February to 5 April = 59 days.

Total number of days loan outstanding = 302

The average official rate of interest is, therefore, ((5 × 243) plus (4 × 59)) divided by 302. This is, therefore, 4.805%.

Interest payable is, therefore, £6,000 × 4.805% × 9/12 = £216.

If Sophie has paid no interest on the loan, her taxable benefit for the year will be £216.

Any interest that she does pay reduces the taxable benefit on a pound-for-pound basis.

The alternative method

5.57 Whereas the normal method uses a monthly basis, the precise method considers the amount of loan outstanding each day (*ITEPA 2003, s 183*). This is the process to be followed.

Step (1)

For each day in the tax year, multiply the maximum outstanding amount of the loan by the official rate of interest in force on that day.

Step (2)

Add together those daily amounts.

Step (3)

Divide the result by the number of days in the tax year.

Step (4)

Any interest paid by the employee in respect of that loan and for that year is deducted.

Example 5.5—Beneficial loan calculation – alternative method

The facts are identical to those in **Example 5.4** above.

	A	*B*	*C*	
Period	*No of Days*	*Loan balance*	*Interest rate*	*Cash equivalent*
		£	%	£
8 June to 1 Dec	177	7,000	5	169
2 Dec to 5 Feb	66	5,000	5	45
6 Feb to 5 April	59	5,000	4	32
Cash equivalent				246

Living expenses

5.58 No liability to income tax arises where an employer makes a payment to an employee in respect of reasonable additional household expenses which the employee incurs in carrying out duties of the employment at home under homeworking arrangements (*ITEPA 2003, s 316A*).

'Homeworking arrangements' are defined as arrangements between the employee and the employer under which the employee regularly performs some or all of the duties of the employment at home. There is no requirement for any part of the employee's home to be used exclusively for the purposes of the employment; if any part of the home is so used then part of the capital gains tax exemption on the disposal of the house may be lost.

'Household expenses' are defined as expenses connected with the day-to-day running of the employee's home (eg heating, lighting). Mortgage interest is unlikely to qualify for the exemption, unless and to the extent that it was an 'additional' household expense. In *Baird v Williams (HMIT)* (1997) SpC 122, the taxpayer failed to obtain a deduction for mortgage interest under what is now *ITEPA 2003, s 336*.

To minimise the need for record-keeping, HMRC have confirmed that employers can pay up to £3 per week (£156 per year) without supporting evidence of the costs the employee has incurred. If an employer pays more than that amount, the exemption will still be available but the employer must provide supporting evidence that the payment is wholly in respect of additional household expenses incurred by the employee in carrying out his duties at home (2003 Budget Day press release REV BN 3, paras 5 and 6) (*ITEPA 2003, ss 318 et seq*; *SI 2006/882*).

In *Tax Bulletin* number 68 (December 2003), HMRC stated that 'homeworking arrangements' do not cover 'employees who work at home informally and not by arrangement with the employer'. So, for example, the exemption will not apply to employees who simply take additional work home in the evenings.

Example 5.6

Sarah is an employee but works at home each Wednesday under the company's homeworking policy. Her employer pays her £3 per week towards the cost of additional household expenditure incurred as a result of working from home. This payment may be made tax free as the limit of £3 per week is not exceeded. There is no need to prove the additional household expenses in this case.

Example 5.7

Simon also works from home on a full-time basis under his company's homeworking policy. He keeps records of additional household expenses incurred, which total £284 for the tax year. His employer reimburses him with this amount. Although the payment exceeds £3 per week, it can be made tax free because the additional expenses can be substantiated.

Expenses not reimbursed

5.59 If the employer does not reimburse household expenses, the employee will only be entitled to a deduction for household expenses if the strict conditions of *ITEPA 2003, Pt 5* are met. If the employee uses his home as his base of operations and has no permanent office at his employer's base, HMRC will usually allow a proportion of the outgoings as expenses. Note, however, that it may be necessary to use a part of the home exclusively for work purposes to obtain the deduction, and that if the home is owned this may jeopardise part of the capital gains tax exemption. HMRC *Tax Bulletin*, issue 79 (October 2005), contains detailed coverage on this subject (www.hmrc.gov.uk/bulletins/tb79.htm).

Gifts, awards, prizes and tips

5.60 A gift received from an employer or third party by an employee may be taxable if it is received as a reward for services past, present or future (or simply, if it is provided by reason of the individual's employment by way of voucher or, in the case of an employee earning at a rate of £8,500 a year or more or a director) (*ITEPA 2003, ss 270* and *324*). Some factors of relevance in deciding whether a voluntary payment, benefit or perquisite may escape tax are as follows:

- Whether, from the recipient's standpoint, it accrues to him as a reward for services.
- If his contract of employment entitles him to receive the payment there is a strong ground for holding that it accrues by virtue of the employment and is therefore remuneration.
- The fact that a voluntary payment is of a periodic or recurrent character affords a further, though less cogent, ground for the same conclusion.
- If it is made in circumstances which show it is given by way of a present or testimonial on grounds personal to the recipient (eg a collection made for a vicar of a given parish because he is so poor, or a benefit for a professional cricketer in recognition of his long and successful career),

then the proper conclusion is likely to be that it is not a reward for services and is therefore not taxable.

Long-service awards

5.61 Not taxable provided the employee has had at least 20 years' service and the cost of the award to the employer does not exceed £50 for each year of service. No similar award must have been made in the previous ten years (*ITEPA 2003, s 323*).

Example 5.8

Arthur receives long service awards as follows:

For ten years' service	£250
For 20 years' service	£500
For 25 years' service	£750
For 30 years' service	£1,000
For 40 years' service	£2,500

The award of £250 for ten years' service is fully taxable, as he has not completed at least 20 years' service.

The 20-year award of £500 may be paid tax free, as all the conditions are met.

The 25-year award is taxed in full, as there has been an award within the previous ten years.

The 30-year award is also taxed in full, as there has been an award within the previous ten years, even though the earlier award was taxed.

£500 of the 40-year award is taxable, being the excess over £2,000 (40 years × £50 per year).

Taxed award schemes and staff suggestion schemes

5.62 Employers who provide non-cash incentive awards and prizes (eg cameras or holidays), and most of those who provide such prizes for employees of third parties, can operate HMRC's 'taxed award scheme'. Such schemes:

- allow the provider of the incentive to pay the tax due on the award, so that the incentive for the recipient is not blunted by having to pay tax on it; and
- provide an economical means of collecting the tax due (in bulk, instead of from individual recipients).

At commencement the provider enters into a contract with HMRC's Incentive Award Unit to pay the tax on the total value of the awards to be made. The provider can pay tax at different rates: there are separate contracts for different rate schemes.

The amount of the tax payable is worked out on the grossed-up value of the award to the recipient. Providers must give recipients details of the tax paid so that they can complete their tax returns, or claim repayment if appropriate. Providers give HMRC details of recipients so that any higher-rate tax can be collected.

Most awards under taxed award schemes are suitable for inclusion in a PAYE settlement agreement (see **5.86**) instead of a taxed award scheme. However, a third party who provides awards to the employees of another and who wishes to pay the employees' tax bill must use a taxed award scheme (*ITEPA 2003, s 703*).

Awards made under most staff suggestion schemes are tax free (*ITEPA 2003, ss 321* and *322*).

Christmas parties and gifts provided by third parties

5.63 Gifts made by a third party to any employee are not taxable provided the cost does not exceed £250 in any tax year. If the cost is, say, £251, all of the £251 is assessable. The same concession allows employers to provide one or more annual events at a cost of up to £150 per head without the employees incurring tax liability in respect of the benefit. The limit of £150 applies from 2003/04 onwards (*ITEPA 2003, s 264*).

Tips and service charges

5.64 Tips are generally part of an employee's taxable income in the same way as his other earnings (*ITEPA 2003, s 692; SI 2003/2682, reg 100*). However, not all employees return full details of the tips they receive. Therefore, HMRC may estimate the tips earned on the basis of the facts available to ensure that the correct amount of tax is paid. Before doing this, HMRC establish first who is in a position to receive them. Wherever possible they negotiate agreed figures with the employees concerned or with their representative where large numbers are employed at any one establishment.

Certain organised arrangements fall within the scope of the 'tronc' system which requires PAYE to be deducted by the 'tronc master'. If the tronc master fails to do this, the responsibility falls on the principal employer.

The following flow chart (extracted from HMRC booklet CWG2) provides useful assistance in deciding whether the 'tronc master' rules apply.

Tips, gratuities, voluntary service charges

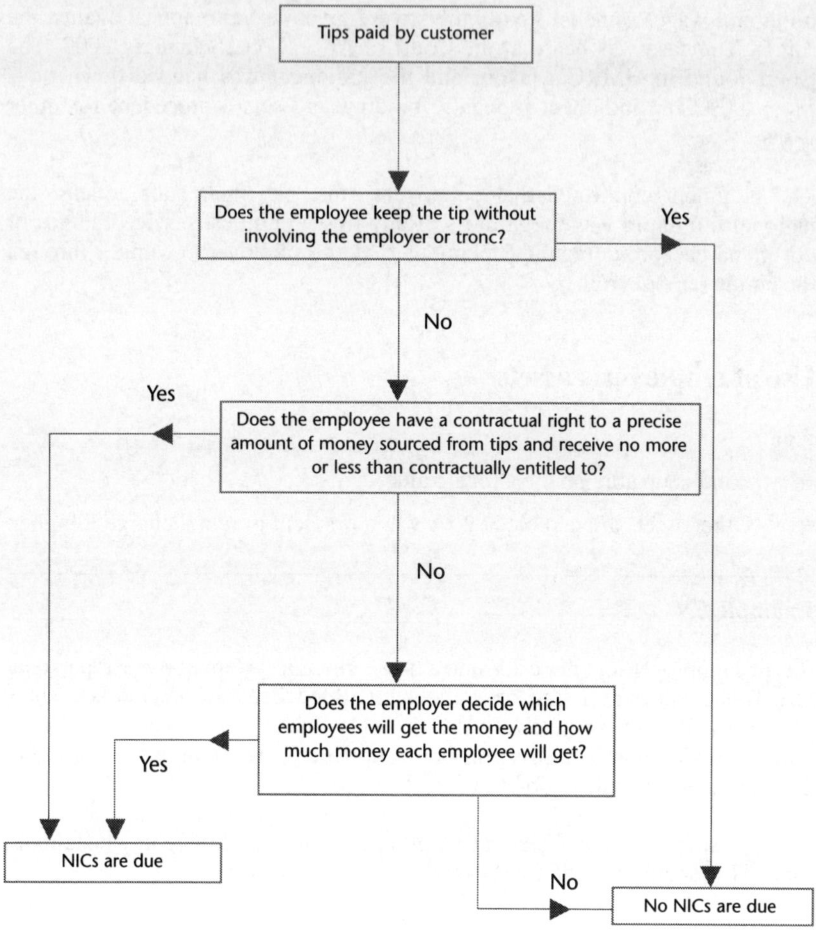

Tips and the national minimum wage

5.65 The Court of Appeal has ruled in HMRC's favour by upholding current national minimum wage (NMW) legislation relating to tips, gratuities and discretionary service charges in the case of Annabel's restaurant and night club and others. In June 2008, HMRC won an Employment Appeal Tribunal against Annabel's and others. The case involved the calculation of NMW pay where an independent tronc scheme was in operation. Troncs are a system of pooling and distributing service charges, tips and gratuities to staff in the service industries. Under specific circumstances, payments made as tips, gratuities, service charges and cover charges may count towards NMW pay. However, HMRC argued that tips, gratuities and voluntary service charges paid to workers by a tronc master via a tronc did not count towards national minimum wage. Annabel's and others were given leave to appeal against the ruling. The case was heard at the Court of Appeal on 15 January 2009. The Court found in HMRC's favour and the judgment was handed down on 7 May 2009. The judgment is legally binding and sets a precedent for other cases.

The judgment confirmed that employers must pay their staff at least the national minimum wage regardless of any tips, gratuities, service charges or cover charges, providing they are not paid by the employer to workers through the employer's payroll.

Use of employer's assets

5.66

- Land is taxable on the annual value.
- Other assets are taxable at 20% when first lent or rental charge if higher.

Example 5.9

Susan's employer lent her a TV and a home cinema system player for personal use. The assets were first made available in 2004 when they had market values of £400 and £600 respectively. In 2010/11, Susan's employer pays for an annual service contract covering both appliances. The contract costs £100. Susan makes no contribution towards the costs.

Susan's earnings are in excess of £8,500 per annum excluding any benefits in kind. The taxable benefit arising in 2010/11 is as follows:

	£	£
TV – higher of:		
• 20% market value when first made available (20% × £400)	80	
• annual hire/rent	Nil	
		80

	£	£
Cinema system – higher of:		
• 20% market value when first made available (20% × £600)	120	
• annual hire/rent	Nil	
		120
		200
Add: associated costs		100
		300
Less: amount made good by employee		(Nil)
Cash equivalent value		300

The charge arises where the asset is available for private use, even if no actual private use takes place.

Vouchers

5.67 Cash vouchers are treated as pay subject to PAYE. Non-cash vouchers are taxable as a benefit in kind except for:

- luncheon vouchers up to the value of 15p per day (*ITEPA 2003, s 89*); and
- vouchers exchangeable for non-taxable benefits such as parking facilities at or near work.

'Non-cash voucher' means (*ITEPA 2003, s 84*):

(a) a voucher, stamp or similar document or token which is capable of being exchanged for money, goods or services;

(b) a 'transport voucher' (as defined in *ITEPA 2003, s 84(3)*) (see below); or

(c) a 'cheque voucher'.

It does not include a cash voucher. A 'cheque voucher' is a cheque:

(a) provided for an employee; and

(b) intended for use by the employee wholly or mainly for payment for:

  (i) particular goods or services; or

  (ii) goods or services of one or more particular classes (*ITEPA 2003, s 84(4)*).

5.68 *ITEPA 2003, Pt 3, Ch 4* applies to a 'non-cash voucher' which is:

(a) provided for an employee by reason of the employee's employment; and

(b) received by the employee (*ITEPA 2003, s 82*).

If a non-cash voucher is within *ITEPA 2003, Pt 3, Ch 4*, the 'cash equivalent' of the benefit of the voucher is treated as earnings from the employment for the tax year in which the voucher is received (*ITEPA 2003, s 87(1)*). The cash equivalent is the difference between:

(a) the cost of provision; and

(b) any part of that cost made good by the employee to the person incurring it.

The cost of provision means the expense incurred by the employer in, or in connection with, the provision of the voucher and the money, goods or services for which it is capable of being exchanged. Money, goods or services actually obtained by the employee or any other person in exchange for the voucher will be disregarded (*ITEPA 2003, s 95*).

The Treasury may make regulations to remove from a tax charge a voucher or credit token used to provide an otherwise tax-exempt employee benefit (*ITEPA 2003, s 96A*).

Transport vouchers

5.69 The above provisions do not apply in relation to a 'transport voucher' provided for an employee of a 'passenger transport undertaking' under arrangements in operation on 25 March 1982, and intended to enable that employee, or a 'relation' of his, to obtain passenger transport services provided by:

- his employer;
- a subsidiary of his employer;
- a body corporate of which his employer is a subsidiary; or
- another passenger transport undertaking (*ITEPA 2003, s 86*).

For example, there will be no charge on a free train pass of a railway company's employee.

Mileage allowances

Cars and vans

5.70

2002/03–2010/11	Mileage allowance	
	First 10,000	Over 10,000
All cars	40p	25p
Each passenger making same business trip	5p	5p

(a) There is no charge to tax in respect of mileage allowance payments to employees in connection with business travel in a (non-company) car or van, to the extent that the payments are within the above limits.

(b) Where the employee receives no mileage allowance payments, or the payments are less than the statutory limits, he may claim a deduction from his emoluments equal to the statutory mileage allowance, or, where appropriate, equal to the excess over the payments received.

(c) Where an employee carries one or more other employees on a business journey, there is no charge to tax on passenger payments made to him within the above limit. This applies whether the car or van used is the employee's own or a company car or van. The employee cannot claim a deduction if no passenger payment is made to him.

(d) Employees cannot claim a deduction based on actual expenditure on a car or van. Neither are capital allowances or loan interest relief available.

(*ITEPA 2003, Pt 4, Ch 2*)

Other mileage allowances

5.71

Motorcycle allowance 2002/03–2010/11	24p
Cycling allowance 2002/03–2010/11	20p

Employers can pay employees up to the mileage allowance tax free for using their own cycles or motorcycles for business travel. Employees can claim tax relief on the mileage allowance if their employer pays no cycle or motorcycle allowance (or on the balance up to the mileage allowance if the employer pays less than this rate).

Advisory fuel rates for business use of company car

5.72

Rates 2007/08 to 2010/11			
From 1 February 2007			
Cylinder capacity	Petrol	Diesel	LPG
up to 1,400cc	9p	9p	6p
1,401–2,000cc	11p	9p	7p
Over 2,000cc	16p	12p	10p

From 1 August 2007			
Cylinder capacity	Petrol	Diesel	LPG
up to 1,400cc	10p	10p	6p
1,401–2,000cc	13p	10p	8p
Over 2,000cc	18p	13p	10p
From 1 January 2008			
Cylinder capacity	Petrol	Diesel	LPG
up to 1,400cc	11p	11p	7p
1,401–2,000cc	13p	11p	8p
Over 2,000cc	19p	14p	11p
From 1 July 2008			
Cylinder capacity	Petrol	Diesel	LPG
up to 1,400cc	12p	13p	7p
1,401–2,000cc	15p	13p	9p
Over 2,000cc	21p	17p	13p
From 1 January 2009			
Cylinder capacity	Petrol	Diesel	LPG
up to 1,400cc	10p	11p	7p
1,401–2,000cc	12p	11p	9p
Over 2,000cc	17p	14p	12p
From 1 July 2009			
Cylinder capacity	Petrol	Diesel	LPG
up to 1,400cc	10p	10p	7p
1,401–2,000cc	12p	10p	8p
Over 2,000cc	18p	13p	12p
From 1 December 2009			
Cylinder capacity	Petrol	Diesel	LPG
up to 1,400cc	11p	11p	7p
1,401–2,000cc	14p	11p	8p
Over 2,000cc	20p	14p	12p
From 1 June 2010			
Cylinder capacity	Petrol	Diesel	LPG
up to 1,400cc	12p	11p	8p
1,401–2,000cc	15p	11p	10p
Over 2,000cc	21p	16p	14p

Petrol hybrid cars are treated as petrol cars for this purpose.

HMRC accept that, where an employer reimburses an employee for the cost of fuel for business mileage in a company car at the above rates, no taxable benefit arises.

Restrictive covenants

5.73 A lump sum payment made in return for an undertaking by an employee to restrict his conduct or activities in some way is fully taxable as employment income. For example, the employee may agree not to set up in competition for a certain length of time or not to behave in any way detrimental to the ex-employer. A termination settlement may include an undertaking by an employee to reaffirm undertakings given as part of the original terms of the employment relating to the individual's conduct or activity after its termination. It may also include an agreement by the employee not to proceed with any legal action. Such undertakings are not considered to be restrictive covenants (*ITEPA 2003, ss 225–226*).

Lump sum payments

On taking up employment

5.74 Payments made to an individual as an incentive to take up an employment, often known as 'golden hellos' or 'golden handcuffs', are generally treated as advance pay for future services of employment and are therefore taxable as employment income. This is not the case where the payment is compensation for the loss or restriction of a right on taking up employment, but this is unusual and often difficult to prove.

In a case involving a football player, a sum paid by his old club when he had already joined his new club was still earnings, even though there was no link between the old club and his future services (*Shilton v Wilmshurst* 64 TC 78).

On termination of employment

5.75 Lump sum payments made on the termination of employment, often known as 'golden handshakes', are taxable under the normal employment income rules where they are paid for employment services rendered. Where the payments do not fall within those general rules they are taxable under special rules subject to an exemption for the first £30,000 (*ITEPA 2003, s 309*) (see **5.120**).

In general, a payment will be taxable under PAYE as earnings where the employee is contractually entitled to receive it (whether expressly written or implied by custom or practice) but will fall under the special rules where it is paid by way of compensation for breach of the employment contract.

Payments in lieu of notice and compensation for loss of office

5.76 If the contract obliges the employer to make a payment where due notice is not given, the payment arises under the contract and is taxable as an emolument in the normal way. Where the contract provides only for notice to be given, failure to give the notice is a breach of the contract. The payment is compensation for that breach rather than arising under the contract, and would therefore be taxable under the special rules provided that it is not the employer's normal practice to make such payments, and there is no understanding that the payment would be made (*ITEPA 2003, ss 401–416*).

Example 5.10

Gordon earns £60,000 per annum and his employment is to be terminated. His contract specifies a six-month notice period, with a discretionary PILON clause. Gordon works out three months of his notice period. His employer makes a payment of £40,000 at the end of this period. It is likely that the following treatment will apply:

- £20,000 will be taxed as a contractual payment in lieu of the three months' salary which Gordon would have received if he had worked out his notice period; and
- £20,000 will be treated as a termination payment.

Compensation payments for loss of office, or a variation of employment are usually treated as valid termination payments, and are therefore not treated as taxable earnings from the employment.

The concept of damages can apply to any contract, including an employment contract. Whenever one party to a contract acts contrary to its terms (ie breaches the contract), and by doing so inflicts a loss on the other party, the latter can sue for damages. So rules that apply to calculating damages generally also apply where an employer breaches an employment contract. Probably the most common breach is where an employer fails to give proper notice of termination. A payment of damages falls within *ITEPA 2003, s 401*.

When an employment tribunal, a court or parties to a termination settlement calculate damages they will often follow the *Gourley* principle. This principle is a rule of non-tax law that derives from *British Transport Commission v Gourley* (1955). The principle is that a person must not be placed in a better or worse position than if the contract had actually been carried out. The following example is slightly adapted from the guidance given in the HMRC Employment Income Manual (EIM13995):

Example 5.11

An employer fails to give proper notice of termination to an employee, and there is no contractual provision or expectation relating to payments in lieu of notice. The employer has breached the contract and the employee can claim damages.

The damages are first calculated by reference to the pay and benefits that the employee would have received during the notice period if proper notice had been given, for example gross pay of £2,000. Note that this is not, in fact, pay but is merely part of the calculation of the appropriate level of damages.

The payment of £2,000 would place the employee in a better position than if the contract had been carried out. If the employee had received pay during notice, it would have been taxed and liable to NICs, leaving (say) £1,500 in hand. As the damages payment itself is exempt from tax and not liable to NICs the employee would keep the whole £2,000. So, to satisfy the *Gourley* principle, the damages payment is adjusted to £1,500.

It is important to recognise that the £500 adjustment to the sum of damages in the above example is not a deduction of tax and must not be repaid as such. The actual payment made to the employee (£1,500) must be considered under the normal taxation rules for that termination payment.

See **5.126** et seq for further commentary on PILONs.

Gardening leave

5.77 If a payment is made where notice has been given but not worked, the employee continues to be employed until the end of the period and the payment is taxable as an emolument under the normal rules.

Redundancy payments

5.78 Genuine redundancy payments (ie where the job no longer exists) are taxable under the special rules, the first £30,000, including any statutory redundancy, being exempt from tax (*ITEPA 2003, s 309*).

Retirement

5.79 An ex-gratia lump sum payment made on an employee's retirement or death may be treated by HMRC as fully taxable employment income as a payment under an unapproved 'retirement benefit scheme'. This will not apply where the employer obtains tax approval for the payment to be treated as a relevant benefit under an approved scheme (*ITEPA 2003, ss 393–400*).

Exempt payments

5.80 Certain termination payments may be completely exempt (ie not just the first £30,000). These include payments on termination of employment by the death of the employee, or on account of injury or disability. Payments relating to employment which included an element of foreign service may be wholly or partly exempt, depending on the extent of that overseas work.

Expenses

5.81 Payments made to directors or employees to cover expenses, or to reimburse them for expenses they incur, are treated as employment earnings. This is irrespective of whether the payments are made by way of a round sum allowance or reimbursed on the submission of an expenses claim (*ITEPA 2003, ss 70–72*).

'Wholly, exclusively and necessarily'

5.82 Employees can generally claim relief for expenses incurred 'wholly, exclusively and necessarily' in the performance of their duties and for travel expenses necessarily incurred by employees in performing those duties. Alternatively, the employer can apply to HMRC for a 'dispensation' to avoid having to record these types of expenses on the form P11D so that the employees do not then have to claim the relief (*ITEPA 2003, ss 333–344*) (see below).

The 'wholly, exclusively and necessarily' test is a very broad one in comparison with expenses allowed as trading income which simply must be incurred 'wholly and exclusively' for business purposes. Numerous cases have decided that relief is not available for such expenses as:

- clothing worn for work which is suitable for use by the employee when not at work (thus failing the 'exclusively' test) (*Hillyer v Leeke* [1976] 51 TC 90);
- newspapers considered necessary reading for journalists (held as not being in the 'performance of their duties' but helping to carry out their duties more efficiently) (*Fitzpatrick v CIR* 66 TC 407);
- travel between home and work (not being in the performance of the employee's duties, if performance does not start until the employee reaches the place of work) (*Kirkwood v Evans* 74 TC 481); and
- rental of a telephone installed in an employee's home (this being a requirement for the particular employee who did not previously have a phone, but not a 'necessary' requirement for the office holder) (*Lucas v Cattell* (1972) 48 TC 353).

Employee expenses not reimbursed

5.83 Employees may also claim tax relief for allowable expenses they incur personally but which are not reimbursed by their employer such as fees and subscriptions to professional bodies, books (required by teachers and lecturers) and allowable training and travel expenditure.

A limited deduction ('flat rate expense allowance') is available for employees in various occupations, towards the upkeep of tools or special clothing necessary for work, although this does not prevent the employee claiming relief for the actual cost incurred, if higher.

For details of flat rate expenses, the structure of which is currently under review, see the HMRC Employment Income Manual at EIM32730a.

Benchmark rates

5.84 HMRC have introduced a set of benchmark scale rates that employers can use to make certain day subsistence payments free of tax and National Insurance contributions to employees who incur allowable business travel expenses. Employers do not have to use the benchmark rates. They can reimburse their employees' actual expenditure, or apply to HMRC to agree a scale rate appropriate for their business needs in a dispensation. The benchmark system operates from 6 April 2009. See HMRC *Brief* 24/09 online at www.hmrc.gov.uk/briefs/income-tax/brief2409.htm for further information. See also the HMRC Employment Income Manual at EIM05260.

Dispensations

5.85 All benefits and expenses are taxable, unless specifically exempt, and the employee or director is therefore normally required to claim tax relief for business items. However, the employer may apply to HMRC for a dispensation, to save having to report certain expense payments and benefits in kind provided to their employees, who would otherwise have to submit a matching claim for relief.

A dispensation is only applicable to an employee who is not 'lower paid'. It will generally be issued to an employer where (*ITEPA 2003, s 65*):

- HMRC is satisfied that no additional tax liability arises on the benefits or expenses (eg the employee is reimbursed expenses wholly, exclusively and necessarily incurred in the performance of his duties);
- expenses claims are independently checked, authorised and (where possible) vouched; and

- procedures are in place to fully account for any advances of expenses and to ensure any excess is repaid.

Despite the requirement that expenses claims be independently checked and authorised, HMRC will consider dispensations for controlling directors who decide their own expenses, if there is independent documentation to vouch for the expenditure.

Typical expenses payments and benefits covered by a dispensation include:

- travel and subsistence expenses (but not round sum allowances or business mileage payments);
- entertaining expenses (providing deduction from profits not claimed);
- professional fees and subscriptions; and
- business telephone calls (but not telephone rental).

PAYE settlement agreements

5.86 A PAYE settlement agreement (PSA) may be made with HMRC, under which the employer agrees to meet the income tax and Class 1B NIC liability on certain expenses and benefits given to employees. This means that the benefits or expenses covered do not need to be taxed under PAYE, or included on the employee's form P11D or P9D. The employer's tax liability under the PSA must be paid to HMRC by 19 October following the end of the tax year to which the payment relates (*ITEPA 2003, ss 703–707*; Statement of Practice 5/96; *SI 2003/2682, regs 105–117*).

The agreement generally covers:

- minor items such as taxi fares, personal incidental expenses in excess of the daily limit, presents for an employee in hospital and other small gifts;
- irregular items such as relocation expenses above £8,000 and one-off gifts which are not minor; and
- items where it is impracticable to apply PAYE, such as Christmas parties and similar entertainment not qualifying for relief.

Example 5.12

Client Co Ltd provides taxable benefits of £200 each to four higher rate employees during the year. The company agrees to meet the employees' tax liability under a PAYE settlement agreement. The tax due is calculated as follows:

Grossed-up value: $\frac{100}{(100-40)} \times 800 = £1{,}333.33$

Non-taxable benefits

5.87 Non-taxable payments and benefits include the following:

- free parking facilities;
- work buses with seating capacity of 12 or more (nine or more in the case of minibuses);
- mobile telephones (one per employee);
- free canteen meals (where provided to staff generally);
- child care facilities (where provided by employer);
- contributions by the employer to an approved occupational pension scheme or to an employee's personal pension scheme;
- luncheon vouchers worth up to 15p a day;
- personal expenses of an employee whilst working away from home of up to £5 a night (£10 if abroad);
- overseas medical insurance and treatment;
- sporting facilities provided in-house;
- bicycles or cycle safety equipment for travel to work;
- gifts not costing more than £250 per year from any one donor;
- qualifying removal expenses and benefits up to £8,000 per move;
- living accommodation provided in the performance of an employee's duties, or due to a threat to the employee's security;
- Christmas and other parties, dinners, etc, provided the total cost to the employer for each person attending is not more than £150 a year;
- long-service awards;
- certain other benefits (eg office supplies or services) provided for the employee's work, where any private use is not significant;
- assistance with home-to-work travel costs for disabled persons;
- retraining expenses and courses to help an employee find another job;
- emergency vehicles for employees required to take the vehicles home in order to respond quickly to emergencies when on call;
- vans provided by the employer for business travel, if any private use is insignificant
- from 14 August 2007, one health screening and one medical check-up per employee, per year (*SI 2007/2090*).

Subsidised meals

5.88 The provision by employers of meals in a canteen in which meals are provided for staff generally is exempted from the charge on directors and P11D employees. By concession, tax is not charged on such meals or on the use of any ticket or token to obtain such meals, if the meals are provided on a reasonable scale and either (*ITEPA 2003, ss 266, 317*):

- all employees may obtain free or subsidised meals on a reasonable scale, whether on the employer's premises or elsewhere; or
- the employer provides free or subsidised meal vouchers for staff for whom meals are not provided.

The concession does not apply, in the case of a hotel, catering or similar business, to free or subsidised meals provided for its employees in a restaurant or dining room at a time when meals are being served to the public, unless part of it is designated as being for the use of staff only.

The case of *Ansell v Brown* 73 TC 338, concerning a professional rugby player, confirmed that dietary supplements are not tax deductible, even where the need for extra nutrition arises from the nature of the duties performed.

From 6 April 2002, cyclists' breakfasts were exempted under the minor benefits provisions. No tax charge arose in respect of the first six such breakfasts provided to cyclists' in the tax year. If a cyclist was provided with more than six breakfasts, the excess over six was taxed. Further regulations came into force with effect from 25 June 2003, which completely remove this limit and consequently completely remove the charge on cyclists' breakfasts with effect from that date.

From 2005/06, the exemption for the tax charge on subsidised meals and recreational benefits is extended to persons other than employees who work on the premises of an employer who provides such benefits for their employees.

Income Tax (Exemption of Minor Benefits) (Amendment) Regulations 2004 (SI 2004/3087); *Income Tax (Exemption of Minor Benefits) (Amendment) Regulations 2003 (SI 2003/1434)*; *Income Tax (Exemption of Minor Benefits) Regulations 2002 (SI 2002/205).*

Mobile telephones

5.89 For 1999/2000 and subsequent tax years, an employer-provided mobile telephone (including one mounted in a car, van or heavier commercial vehicle) which is used for private calls is exempted from any income tax charge (but see below). A 'mobile telephone' is one not physically connected to a land line (including a car telephone), but not telepoint telephones or cordless extensions to domestic telephones (*ITEPA 2003, s 319*).

The exemption referred to above was revised from 6 April 2006. There was previously no limit to the number of mobile phones that could be loaned and no financial limit. *FA 2006, s 60* restricts the number of mobile phones employers can loan to employees for private use tax-free to one per employee, and does not extend to members of the employees' family or household. *ITEPA 2003, s 319* was also amended by *FA 2006* to ensure that, where an employee has been provided with a mobile phone for private use through a salary sacrifice arrangement, no charge arises under the general earnings charge of *ITEPA 2003, s 62(3)*, even if the employee has the right to surrender the phone for additional wages or salary.

Some employers have chosen to use vouchers as the mechanism for making available mobile phones to their employees for private use. In these circumstances a charge to tax and Class 1 NICs arises on the provision of the voucher. From 6 April 2006, the provision of a voucher is exempt from tax and NICs where it is used to facilitate the loan of a mobile phone to an employee for private use, but only where the benefit in kind arising on the loan of the mobile phone would have been exempt if a voucher had not been used. Effectively, this means that, from 6 April 2006, the method used by employers to loan mobile phones to employees will have no effect on the outcome for tax and NICs purposes.

Computer equipment

5.90 Prior to 6 April 2006 loans of computer equipment, up to the first £500 of benefit including related expenses (providing loans not restricted to directors or senior staff), were non-taxable. However, this exemption was severely restricted by *FA 2006* (*FA 2006, s 61*). The tax exemption is withdrawn totally from 6 April 2006, unless the computer was first made available to the employee, or a member of his family or household, before 6 April 2006. Transitional rules apply where the employer and employee had agreed in writing the terms on which the computer was made available before 6 April 2006 (*ITEPA 2003, s 320*). There is no benefit in kind where HMRC agree there is no significant use.

Works bus services

5.91 Any benefits attributable to an employee as a result of an employer either directly providing a works bus service or subsidising, in any way, a public transport bus service, are exempt from the general benefit-in-kind charge. Where such a benefit is made available through a ticket or voucher, any charge under the non-cash voucher rules is also exempted.

To qualify for this exemption for a works bus service, the buses used must have a seating capacity of 12 or more (a 'large' bus) and the facility must be available to employees generally. However, to make it easier for smaller employers to offer such a service, from 6 April 2002, the exemption is extended to allow the service to be provided by means of a minibus, which has a seating capacity of at least nine, but not more than 12 seats. To ensure that safety is not compromised by unscrupulous employers squeezing additional seats into vehicles, such as people carriers to bring them within the definition of 'minibus', the exemption will only apply to vehicles originally constructed to carry nine or more seats.

Where a subsidy is provided to a bus service operator, the fares paid by employees must not be lower than non-employee passengers' fares. The exemption only extends to bus services that convey employees on 'qualifying journeys'; these are trips between:

- an employee's home and workplace; or
- one workplace and another.

However, from 6 April 2002, employees may benefit from lower fares without a benefit arising, so long as the service is a local stopping service. From the same date, the definition of a qualifying journey is amended to accommodate the situation where the bus is used for only part of the journey to work (*ITEPA 2003, s 242*; *FA 1999, s 45*).

Bicycles and cycling safety equipment

5.92 The benefit of bicycles and cycling safety equipment provided by employers to employees for their commuting journey is exempt from the general benefit-in-kind charges.

From 6 April 2005, no tax charge arises where employees buy bicycles from their employer, provided that the bicycle has previously been loaned to them or to another employee, and that they pay market value (*FA 2005, ss 16* and *17*; *ITEPA 2003, s 244*; *FA 1999, s 50*).

Eye tests

5.93 From 6 April 2006 no tax or NIC charge arises when employers provide vouchers to employees for eye tests and corrective spectacles for VDU use. Vouchers used to provide equivalent benefits are also exempt (*ITEPA 2003, s 320A*; *FA 2006, s 62*).

SHARE SCHEMES

Introduction

5.94 When directors and employees acquire shares (and securities) in their company, income tax may be chargeable as employment income, for example where:

- the market value of the shares exceeds their cost price – the employee is liable to tax on the difference between cost and market value; or
- the employee has a right to acquire shares (an option) – the employee is liable to tax on the difference between the market value of the shares when the option is exercised and the cost of the shares (plus any amount paid for the option).

Legislation exists to counter avoidance schemes using employment-related securities to reward employees. Backdated to 5 December 2004, the legislation contained in *FA 2006, s 92* (amending *ITEPA 2003, s 420*), makes it clear that all options fall within the definition of securities. Options that are a right to acquire securities (call options) are not securities unless the main purpose of acquiring them is to avoid tax and National Insurance. *FA 2006, s 94* legislates for PAYE to be applied to employment-related options as a result of the retrospective changes introduced by *s 92* via the provisions in *ITEPA 2003, ss 222, 684* and *710* relating to notional payments.

Favourable tax treatment is, however, available to share incentive schemes approved by HMRC as detailed below.

Reportable events

5.95 There is an obligation for the 'responsible person' (normally the employer) to provide details of 'reportable events' to HMRC in respect of employment-related securities and options, eg certain acquisitions of shares by reason of employment, or chargeable events relating to restricted or convertible securities (*ITEPA 2003, s 421J*). HMRC must be provided with written details of the reportable event (normally on form 42 – www.hmrc.gov.uk/shareschemes/usf-form-42-2009.pdf) before 7 July following the end of the relevant tax year. HMRC may also issue a notice requiring the provision of reportable event information within not less than 30 days from the notice date.

Reportable events (*ITEPA 2003, s 421K*) are as follows:

- acquisition of securities or securities option;
- chargeable events affecting restricted securities;
- chargeable events affecting convertible securities;

- events where there is artificial enhancement of the value of securities;
- discharge of notional loan in relation to securities (partly-paid securities);
- disposal of securities for more than market value (stop loss);
- receipt of benefit arising from a security;
- assignment or release of securities option; and
- compensation or other benefit on securities option.

5.96 The legislation requires companies to disclose to HMRC details of company shares and unapproved share options issued to their directors and employees if this is by reason of a former, current or prospective employment. This must be done irrespective of whether the employees face an income tax and national insurance liability from the transaction. Failure to comply could prove to be very costly. If an individual, who has shares in a company, subsequently becomes a director or employee of that company, the acquisition of shares is reportable to HMRC. A £300 penalty applies to each reportable event.

HMRC have confirmed that a reportable event does not occur in relation to incorporation of a company where the company formation agent is the subscriber shareholder. However, if the subscriber shareholders are the prospective directors, this is likely to be a reportable event and, consequently, a return form 42 is required. Where an existing director or employee transfers shares to another director or employee (or prospective director or employee), a reportable event will arise and a form 42 must be submitted.

A reportable event may arise where shares are issued to someone who is not an employee or director at the time of the issue but becomes one at a future date. This will, however, depend on whether the shares are employment-related securities made available by reason of employment or prospective employment. The company will know why it is issuing shares to someone who is not an employee or director and the likelihood is that it relates to prospective employment and, therefore, reportable.

See the HMRC guidance on share schemes online at www.hmrc.gov.uk/shareschemes.

Enterprise Management Incentive scheme

5.97 The Enterprise Management Incentive (EMI) scheme allows certain independent trading companies to offer tax-favoured share options to employees.

The legislation governing EMIs is found at *ITEPA 2003, ss 417–421L, 527–541* and *Sch 5*.

From 6 April 2008 the company can grant EMI options worth up to £120,000 per employee (£100,000 prior to 6 April 2008), provided that the total value of unexercised EMI options does not exceed £3 million.

The company must satisfy certain conditions to qualify. For example, it must:

- be an independent company;
- carry on a qualifying trade wholly or mainly in the UK (note that the government intends to amend the 'wholly or mainly in the UK' condition so that the company granting EMI options is required to have a 'permanent establishment' in the UK. It is proposed to include the relevant legislation in the Finance Bill planned for Autumn 2010, with the effective date being the date of Royal Assent to that Bill); and
- have gross assets worth not more than £30 million.

The scheme is open to the employees of the EMI company or certain subsidiaries. The individual must be committed to working for at least 25 hours a week (or 75% of his working time, if less). Employees with a 'material interest' are excluded (ie where the individual and/or his associates control more than 30% of the company's ordinary share capital (or the assets on a winding up of a close company)).

Where all the conditions are satisfied, there will normally be no income tax for the employee to pay:

- when the option is granted; or
- on any increase in value between the grant and subsequent exercise of the share option (where the option can be exercised within ten years of its grant, and the employee pays not less than the market value of the shares when the option was granted).

For capital gains tax purposes, taper relief runs from the date when the options are granted, not from the date when they were exercised.

Share Incentive Plans

5.98 A company participating in a Share Incentive Plan (SIP) may give free shares to employees and employees of group companies without an income tax charge. Employees may also allocate part of their salary to purchasing tax-advantaged shares in their employer company, and receive tax relief for the cost of the shares (*FA 2000, s 47, Sch 8*; *FA 2001, Sch 13*; *ITEPA 2003, ss 488–515, Sch 2*; *FA 2003, Sch 21*).

A plan may offer the following types of shares:

- 'free shares' – a company can give an employee shares worth up to £3,000 per annum free of tax;
- 'partnership shares' – an employee may buy shares by deductions from salary, from a minimum contribution of £10 on any occasion up to a maximum of £1,500 per tax year (or 10% of salary, if less), these being allowable deductions for income tax and NICs; and
- 'matching shares' – the company may give an employee up to two free shares for each partnership share purchased.

The shares must normally be kept in the plan for three years. Employees who keep their shares in the plan for at least five years pay no income tax or NICs.

5.99 Income tax charges generally arise when free and matching shares are withdrawn from the plan, or when partnership shares are removed as below:

Shares held in plan	**Income tax charge**
0–2 years	Market value of shares withdrawn
3–4 years	Lower of initial value of shares and market value on withdrawal*
5 years and over	No tax (or NIC) charge

* For partnership shares, the market value of the shares removed, or the salary used to acquire the shares (if lower).

Other conditions and reliefs include:

- employees may reinvest dividends on plan shares up to £1,500 per year to acquire further ('dividend') shares in the company tax free (subject to a minimum holding period of five years beginning with the date of award of the plan shares in respect of which the dividend applied);
- the company may claim tax relief on the costs of setting up and running the plan, and for the market value of any free or matching shares used in the plan;
- the scheme must be open to all individuals on similar terms. However, directors and employees with a 'material interest' are excluded (ie where the individual and/or his associates control more than 25% of the company's ordinary share capital (or the assets on a winding up of a close company)).

Note: Share incentive plans were formerly known as employee share ownership plans (ESOPs).

5.100 Employees working for a group of companies could be prevented from benefiting from the plan where they have been moved around within the group. Changes in *FA 2001* ensure that an employee will satisfy a qualifying period of employment by having worked for any group company. When a group restructures, employees' participation in an SIP may be affected as prior to 10 July 2003 they could not participate in two SIPs run by connected companies in the same year. This unnecessary restriction was removed from 10 July 2003 for cases where a group restructures and an employee transfers to another company within the group.

The legislation specifies that the purpose of the plan must be to provide employees with shares in the company, which in turn, gives them a continuing stake in that company. The plan must not contain, and the operation of the plan must not involve, features which are neither essential nor reasonably incidental to that purpose. No conditions, apart from those required or authorised by the provisions of *ITEPA 2003, Sch 2, Pt 2* (ie those set out below), may be imposed on an employee's participation in an award of shares under the plan.

Although the scheme rules must require that all qualifying employees participate on the same terms, the rights of those participating in the scheme to obtain and exercise share options may vary according to level of remuneration, length of service, or any similar factors. There must not, however, be any preferential treatment for directors and senior employees.

The arrangements for the plan must not make any provision, or be associated in any way with any provision made, for loans to some or all of the employees of the company, or in the case of a group plan, of any constituent company. The operation of the plan must not be associated in any way with such loans (*ITEPA 2003, Sch 2*).

Approved save as you earn (SAYE) share option schemes

5.101 A company may obtain HMRC approval to operate a scheme for its directors and employees, under which options are granted to employees to acquire shares without an income tax charge arising on receipt of the option, or on any growth in value of the shares between the option being granted and exercised (*FA 2003, s 139, Sch 21*; *ITEPA 2003, Schs 3, 4*; *Finance Act 1995 (Contractual Savings Schemes) (Appointed Day) Order 1995 (SI 1995/1778)*).

There are a number of conditions to be fulfilled to obtain approval, including the following:

- the shares must be bought through a certified contractual savings scheme and any loans must not be payable before a date approved by HMRC except where the employee dies or leaves his job before that date;
- the price paid for the shares must not be less than 80% of their market value when purchased;

- all employees or directors must be able to participate in the scheme, except individuals who have held 5% of the share capital of a close company in the last 12 months;
- all those who have worked for a qualifying period must be permitted to participate in the scheme (the qualifying period must not exceed five years);
- the shares must be fully paid ordinary shares which are non-redeemable and they must be either quoted on a stock exchange or be shares in a subsidiary company.

5.102 It is possible to subject shares within savings-related share option schemes to restrictions connected with the termination of employment.

On a takeover of a company, scheme participants may exchange their rights of option in shares of the company taken over for equivalent rights in the acquiring company or another company. Scheme rules may be changed so that an exchange of rights is permissible and such a transaction will not give rise to a CGT charge.

The cost of the shares is funded by 'Save As You Earn' (SAYE) contracts taken out by the employee with a bank or building society. Interest and bonuses on scheme savings are exempt from tax.

The employee may save between £5 and £250 per month, usually as a deduction from pay (although tax relief is not given for SAYE contributions).

Options may be granted to acquire shares at their market value on that date subject to a maximum discount of up to 20%.

The options will normally be capable of being exercised after three, five or seven years, when the SAYE contract ends. The shares are purchased out of the employee's SAYE contract.

The scheme must be open to all directors and employees with at least five years' service, and on similar terms. Individuals with a 'material interest' in a close company are excluded.

Approved company share option plan (CSOP) schemes

5.103 Company share option plans (CSOPs) are HMRC-approved, tax advantageous share option plans. The schemes are discretionary, which means that the company is to select which directors and employees can participate in the scheme (*ITEPA 2003, Schs 3, 4*).

Under a CSOP, options are granted to the employee/director. No income tax is payable on grant. Normally, there is no income tax payable on the increase in value of the shares between grant and exercise provided that certain conditions have been met. For capital gains tax purposes, the cost of the shares is normally the price paid for them.

The value of shares for which a person may hold options under any approved scheme established by his employer or any associated company is limited to £30,000.

The share price must be specified at the time the option is granted and must not be manifestly less than their market value at that time.

The employee must not exercise his option less than three years or more than ten years after the date on which it was granted. *FA 2003, s 139, Sch 21*, removed the charge to income tax on a second option exercise within three years of a previous exercise.

The procedure for obtaining approval is substantially the same as that for approved savings-related share option schemes.

5.104 It is possible within limits to subject shares within an approved scheme to restrictions where the restriction is either attached to all shares of the same class or requires that the directors and employees sell all the shares upon cessation of employment and that shares be sold when acquired, if the acquisition of the shares occurs after cessation of employment.

Restrictions which are not permissible include those attaching to shares which limit the holder's freedom to dispose of the shares, or their proceeds of sale, or to exercise any right conferred by the shares; they do not include restrictions imposed by the Stock Exchange Model Rules for Securities Transactions by Directors, nor to any terms of a loan relating to repayment or security.

Only full-time directors and employees may participate in a scheme approved before 1 May 1995. The 'full-time' requirement is removed in respect of schemes approved on or after that date.

A company may include provisions in a scheme which permit options to be exercised by participators who, by the time of the exercise, may no longer be full-time employees. A provision may also be included allowing options to be exercised by the personal representatives of a deceased participator; in such cases, the exercise must take place within one year of the employee's death, but subject to the ten-year limit.

A person holding a 'material interest' in a close company is ineligible to participate in an approved share scheme involving that company. Broadly, a person has a 'material interest' for this purpose if he, alone or with any 'associate(s)', beneficially owns or is able to control more than 10% of the ordinary share capital of the company. A 'close company' for these purposes is, broadly, one which is controlled by five or fewer 'participators' or over half the assets of which could be distributed on its liquidation between five or fewer participators or director participators.

FOREIGN ASPECTS

Basis of assessment

5.105 The tax treatment of income derived from overseas sources, or of income arising in the UK to someone from abroad, often depends on whether the person liable to tax is resident, ordinarily resident or domiciled in the UK. These terms are explained in more detail in **Chapter 9**. Double tax relief might apply in cases of income having a foreign source and in cases of dual residence, where the UK and another jurisdiction both claim taxing rights under their domestic fiscal regimes.

The place of performance of duties is of major importance in determining how payments are treated for income tax purposes. Where duties are ordinarily performed in the UK, emoluments during any absence from employment are related to UK duties unless, but for that absence, they would have been emoluments for duties performed outside the UK. Thus, an airline pilot's rest days were not attributable to duties performed outside the UK. In order to bring himself within the exception, the taxpayer would have to show that had he worked on those days his actual duties would have been performed outside the UK and it did not matter that most of his time was spent on duties abroad.

Resident and ordinarily resident

5.106 Except in relation to such foreign emoluments as are mentioned above, any person who is resident and ordinarily resident in the UK, and UK domiciled, is liable to income tax on the whole of his earnings wherever earned and irrespective of whether they are remitted to the UK (*ITEPA 2003, s 15*). The taxpayer may be entitled to a special deduction where his duties are carried out wholly or partly outside the UK (see below) and, in many cases, double taxation relief will apply.

Resident but not ordinarily resident

5.107 An employee resident and domiciled, but not ordinarily resident, in the UK is liable to tax on earnings from duties performed in the UK, under *ITEPA*

2003, ss 25 and *26*. There was formerly a deduction for foreign emoluments (see below).

The relative levels of the emoluments received here and abroad may not reflect the relative duties performed here and abroad. The split may be made simply to suit the employee's convenience and there may be scope for tax planning in this area. He may, therefore, be remitting to the UK emoluments received abroad but attributable to the UK duties. Each case must be studied on its facts.

HMRC will accept that the total emoluments may be apportioned between UK and overseas duties on the basis of working days, unless there are special circumstances.

Not resident

5.108 An employee who is not resident in the UK is only liable to tax on earnings from duties performed in the UK, under *ITEPA 2003, s 27*.

Basis of charge

5.109 Emoluments are taxed in the year in which they are received, rather than earned. However, liability to the charge depends on residence and/or ordinary residence in the tax year in which the emoluments are earned.

Other deductions, in respect of expenses, etc are generally available in the same way irrespective of residence, ordinary residence or domicile.

Example 5.13

In 2009/10 Jim earns a bonus of £5,000. He is resident and ordinarily resident in the UK and is therefore chargeable to UK income tax. He will be assessed for 2010/11 when it is received even if, following a move abroad, Jim is not resident in the UK for 2010/11.

Example 5.14

Etienne lives in France but comes to work in the UK and is resident here in 2010/11. He is not chargeable on a bonus received in 2010/11 but earned in 2009/10 when he was not resident here.

The charge to income tax remains fundamentally the same, with the same available deductions (see below).

Foreign earnings deduction for seafarers

5.110 The 100% deduction in determining the foreign earnings which are brought into charge to income tax was withdrawn for all office holders, and for all employees except seafarers, with effect from 17 March 1998.

The definition of seafarers has been clarified to exclude explicitly those employed on offshore installations for oil or gas exploration or extraction. *FA 2004* included a measure to redefine 'offshore installation' to ensure that from 6 April 2004, foreign earnings deduction remains available only to the parts of the shipping sector for whom it was intended.

The deduction is calculated by reference to emoluments for the qualifying period after allowing such deductions as pension contributions, expenses and capital allowances.

To qualify for the 100% deduction, the duties of the employment must be:

- performed wholly or partly outside the UK; and
- performed in the course of a qualifying period consisting of at least 365 days, falling wholly or partly in any tax year.

For this purpose, seamen are generally treated as performing their duties abroad where the voyage, or any part of it, begins or ends outside the UK; this applies notwithstanding the provision which treats such duties as performed in the UK for most purposes. The days which a seafarer can spend in the UK as part of a qualifying period of absence are 183 days or one-half of the total days.

In the emergency Budget on 22 June 2010, it was announced that the seafarers' earnings deduction is to be extended to EU and EEA seafarers. The relevant legislation is expected to be included in the Finance Bill, planned for Autumn 2010, and will take effect from 6 April 2011.

5.111 Where duties of the employment are performed partly outside the UK, the earnings subject to the deduction are determined on a reasonable basis.

Where a period of leave immediately follows a qualifying period, the earnings attributable to that leave generally qualify for the 100% deduction (such period not being part of a qualifying period: see below).

A 'qualifying period' is a period of consecutive days which consists of days of absence from the UK. The qualifying period need not coincide with a complete tax year in order to take advantage of the deduction.

The date of departure from the UK counts as a day of absence (the test being whether an individual is present in the UK at midnight on a particular day); the date of arrival does not. Days spent abroad on holiday can be included towards the 365-day period.

For seafarers who have previously been resident in the UK and who return to the UK following a period of absence abroad during which they have not been resident or ordinarily resident in the UK, such absences are not taken into account when calculating the qualifying period (*FA 2004, s 136*; *ITEPA 2003, s 378*).

Incidental duties

5.112 Duties performed in the UK which are merely incidental to duties performed abroad are treated as if they were performed abroad (*ITEPA 2003, s 39*).

For the purpose of the 100% deduction for seafarers (see **5.110**), incidental duties performed abroad are treated as performed in the UK where the duties of the employment are in substance performed in the UK.

Whether duties performed in the UK are 'incidental duties' is a question of fact. It is the nature of the duties which is the most significant factor, but the time spent on such duties is also a factor to be taken into account (*ITEPA 2003, ss 341(6), (7), 376(4), (5)*).

HMRC guidance advises on whether certain items are regarded as incidental or not incidental to duties performed abroad:

Not incidental	Incidental
(1) Directors' meetings	(1) Overseas representative
A company director, usually working abroad, attends directors' meetings in the UK.	An overseas representative of a UK employer comes to the UK to report to the employer or receive fresh instructions.
(2) Three months or more	(2) Training
Duties performed for an aggregate period of three months or more.	An overseas employee visiting the UK for a training period not exceeding three months in a year and where no productive work is done by him in that time.

Travel expenses

5.113 Travelling expenses incurred by an employee necessarily in the performance of his duties are allowable in calculating chargeable income.

ITEPA 2003, s 370 allows a deduction for the employee's travel costs and expenses in certain cases where the employee's duties are performed abroad.

Expenses incurred in connection with certain overseas duties – either travel to take up a foreign employment with duties wholly overseas (and returning to the UK at the end of that employment), board and lodging while there or in travelling between an employment whose duties are at least partly overseas and any other employment – are eligible for relief if the employee is resident and ordinarily resident in the UK and the earnings are not foreign emoluments (*ITEPA 2003, ss 15, 21* and *22*).

Expenses are apportioned where travel is partly for another purpose.

Where an employer provides travel facilities or reimburses an employee the cost of travel, the employee is entitled to a deduction for the cost of the travel facilities or sum reimbursed. This rule applies to:

- travel between any place in the UK and the place of performance of any of those duties outside the UK (and any return journey) by the spouse/civil partner or any child of the employee;
- travel from any place in the UK to the place of performance of any of those duties (and any return journey) by an employee whose duties are performed partly outside the UK and can only be performed outside the UK; and
- travel from the place of performance of any duties of an office or employment outside the UK to any place in the UK (and any return journey) by an employee absent from the UK performing the duties of an office or employment which can only be performed outside the UK.

Similar provisions apply to the travel expenses of non-UK domiciled employees.

Before the travel expenses of the spouse or any child of the employee can attract the beneficial treatment, the following further conditions need to be met (*ITEPA 2003, s 371*).

Travel expenses of spouses, civil partners and children

5.114 The travelling expenses of the spouse, civil partner or any child of a resident and ordinarily resident employee from and to the UK are allowable for income tax purposes in certain cases, from the emoluments of the employee where the employee is absent from the UK for a continuous period of at least 60 days for the purpose of performing the duties of one or more employments and:

- the spouse, civil partner or any child of the employee accompanies him or her at the beginning of the period of absence; or
- visits him or her during that period.

Children must be aged under 18 at the beginning of the outward journey. Similar deductions are allowed where the employee visits his or her spouse, civil partner or any child of his or hers in the UK.

A maximum of two outward and two return journeys by the same person in any tax year are allowed.

Similar provisions apply to the travel expenses of the spouse, civil partner and any child of an employee not domiciled in the UK (*ITEPA 2003, s 371*).

Example 5.15

Ed is posted to the Hong Kong office of his employer. He has been absent from the UK for a continuous period of more than 90 days. Ed and his wife, Sarah, plan to visit Thailand when his wife visits him. Sarah flies from London to Hong Kong and the two of them fly on to Thailand. Ed's employer pays for Sarah's return trip to Hong Kong.

The cost of the return journey between London and Hong Kong is deductible from Ed's employment earnings. However, where Ed has to arrange for his wife to fly directly to Thailand, where he would meet her, the employer again bearing the cost, the cost of the return trip between London and Thailand would not be deductible, since Thailand is not the place of the performance of Ed's duties. The entire cost would, therefore, have been disallowed.

More than one job

5.115 Special provisions apply where the employee has two or more employments. These provisions are largely designed to prevent the 'loading' of earnings onto the overseas employment in order to avoid tax (*ITEPA 2003, ss 23(3), 24, 329(1), 331(2)*).

Where the duties of an employment and any associated employment (see below) are wholly performed abroad, the deductions referred to above will apply to all the earnings of the employment.

The 100% deduction for seafarers and the deduction relating to 'foreign emoluments' apply to only a proportion of the earnings from the employment abroad where the duties of the employment or any associated employment are not performed wholly outside the UK.

That proportion is one which is shown by the employee to be reasonable having regard to the nature of the duties and the time devoted to them within the UK and abroad and other relevant circumstances.

An employment is an 'associated employment' of another employment for these purposes if they are with the same person or with persons associated with each other. A company is associated with another if one of them has control of the other or both are under the control of the same person or persons. An individual or partnership is associated with another person (whether or not a company) if one of them has control of the other or both are under the control of the same person or persons.

'Golden handshakes'

5.116 Compensation payments made to employees for loss of office, etc are exempt from tax where the duties of the employment included 'foreign service'. Foreign service is a period of time during which the employee was not both resident and ordinarily resident in the UK or else the emoluments of the service qualify for the 100% deduction (*FA 1998, Sch 9*).

If the employee has been in foreign service, but this is insufficient to give full exemption from tax, part of the golden handshake may still be non-taxable. The amount which is not taxable will depend on the length of the foreign service in relation to the total length of service.

The foreign service, in general, must comprise one of the following:

- three-quarters of the whole period of service;
- the last ten years where the period of service exceeded ten years; or
- where the period of service exceeded 20 years, one-half of that period, including any ten of the last 20 years.

Personal reliefs for non-residents

5.117 Non-UK residents are generally not entitled to personal allowances and reliefs, unless the individual is (*ITA 2007, s 56*):

- a Commonwealth (including a British) citizen or citizen of the Republic of Ireland (or, from 1996/97, otherwise a European Economic Area (EEA) national);
- a person who is or has been a Crown servant;
- a widow (or, from 1990/91, a widower) of a Crown servant;
- a missionary;

- a person in the service of a British protectorate;
- a resident of the Isle of Man or Channel Islands; or
- a person who has been resident in the UK but is now resident abroad for the sake of his health or the health of a member of his family who resides with him.

In these cases, the non-resident is entitled to the personal reliefs to which residents are entitled.

To ensure compliance with certain aspects of the *Human Rights Act 1998*, legislation is contained in *FA 2009*, to withdraw the entitlement for non-resident individuals who currently qualify for UK personal tax allowances and reliefs *solely* by virtue of being a Commonwealth citizen. Whilst the vast majority of individuals affected will still benefit through other means such as double taxation treaties, citizens of Bahamas, Cameroon, Cook Islands, Dominica, Maldives, Mozambique, Nauru, Niue, St Lucia, St Vincent & the Grenadines, Samoa, Tanzania, Tonga and Vanuatu may be affected (*FA 2009, s 5* and *Sch 1*).

Remittance of income

5.118 Most income in the UK is charged on an 'arising basis'. However, in some situations, income is only charged to UK tax if received in the UK – the 'remittance basis'. The remittance basis may apply where the resident taxpayer is not domiciled in the UK or is a Commonwealth (including a British) citizen (or citizen of the Republic of Ireland) and is not ordinarily resident in the UK (*ITEPA 2003, s 33*).

Under the remittance basis, tax is charged on the amount received in the UK on a current-year basis.

Emoluments are treated as received in the UK if they are paid, used or enjoyed in the UK, or transmitted or brought to the UK; amounts treated as remitted which are not directly received are sometimes known as 'constructive remittances'. In the case of a person ordinarily resident in the UK, income applied outside the UK in satisfaction of any debt incurred in the UK (or overseas, if the money lent is brought into or received in the UK) is treated as received in the UK.

Income received in a tax year after the source of the income has ceased to exist is not taxable on the remittance basis so long as the remittance is not in the same tax year.

Income considered as remitted to the UK need not necessarily be paid to the taxpayer but income which is properly alienated abroad to another person is not regarded as remitted to the UK by the original owner if the new owner sends that money to the UK.

It is sometimes difficult to distinguish between income and capital, but, in general, the proceeds of investments purchased abroad with income that would be taxable if remitted are liable to tax as income if those proceeds are themselves remitted.

The fact that sums remitted are derived from a bank overdraft is not in itself sufficient to establish that the remittance is out of capital.

However, investments purchased out of income before taking up residence in the UK may be realised and the money remitted without liability.

Non-UK domiciled taxpayers

5.119 From 6 April 2008, a non-domiciled individual who has been resident in the UK for tax purposes for at least seven out of the previous ten years can only use the remittance basis for taxation of overseas income if they pay an annual tax charge of £30,000. If the individual elects not to pay the charge, he will be charged to UK tax as though he were resident, ordinarily resident and domiciled in the UK for that tax year.

In addition, from 6 April 2008, someone who is UK resident, but not domiciled or ordinarily resident, who claims the remittance basis for taxing overseas income, is only able to claim personal allowances, married couple's allowance and blind person's allowance against their taxable income if their unremitted foreign income is less than £2,000 a year (*FA 2008, s 25* and *Sch 7*).

Non-ordinarily resident employees

5.120 HMRC Statement of Practice 1/09 sets out how HMRC will treat transfers made from an offshore account which contains only the income relating to a single employment contract, and how earnings should be apportioned between UK and non-UK employment where an employee is taxed on the remittance basis.

Self-assessment

5.121 The obligation to file a self-assessment return on individuals with small amounts of income from overseas employment has been removed with effect from 6 April 2008 where the overseas income is less than £10,000, and overseas bank interest is less than £100 in any tax year, all of which is subject to a foreign tax (*FA 2009, s 51* and *Sch 27*).

Unremittable overseas income

5.122 Persons (including companies) who are liable to tax on their overseas income wherever it arises may be unable to remit the income to the UK. This income may be treated as income arising abroad and not chargeable to UK income tax where (*ITTOIA 2005, s 841*; *CTA 2009, s 1274*):

- a person is prevented from transferring to the UK, either by the laws of that territory or any executive action of its government or by the impossibility of obtaining foreign currency in that territory;
- the person has used reasonable endeavour to transfer; and
- that person has not realised in some other currency which he is not prevented from transferring to the UK.

Claims to this relief must be made not later than the first anniversary of the 31 January from the end of the tax year in which the income arises (*ITTOIA 2005, s 842*). The relief will be given only as long as the three conditions above continue to be satisfied, ie the tax liability is only postponed, not removed.

TERMINATION PAYMENTS

Taxable payments and benefits

5.123 Under the special rules, payments or benefits received on termination are taxable to the extent that they exceed £30,000. The cash equivalent of any non-cash benefits made on termination of employment (such as the provision of a company car) must be included when calculating the exempt amount. The payments and benefits are treated as income in the year in which cash is received or the benefits are enjoyed.

Example 5.16

AB ceased employment on 31 January 2009. His termination settlement included £20,000 payable immediately, with a further instalment of £10,000 payable in January 2010. He was also given use of a company car for 24 months. Suppose the cash equivalent of the car use was £2,000 in 2008/09, £8,000 in 2009/10 and £6,000 in 2010/11:

The payments and benefits for AB will be taxed as follows:

2008/09

£20,000 payable on 31 January 2009	
Car benefit £2,000	£22,000 within £30,000 exemption

2009/10	
£10,000 payable in January 2010	
Car benefit £8,000	£10,000 taxable (£18,000 – £8,000 exemption still outstanding)
2010/11	
Car benefit £6,000	£6,000 fully taxable

Tax payable

5.124 The amount of the lump sum received in excess of £30,000 is treated as the top slice of income (whereas, under the normal rules, savings income is treated as the top slice, dividend income being the highest part of that top slice).

Reporting requirements

5.125 If lump sum payments are made to employees before they leave, the excess over £30,000 is subject to deduction of tax under PAYE as under the normal rules. If the payments are made to employees after they leave, and after they have been given their forms P45, employers must deduct tax under PAYE at the basic rate. The employee then pays any higher rate tax under the self-assessment system, ie by 31 January after the end of the tax year in which the payment is received. Where a termination payment and benefits package exceeds £30,000, the employer must report details of the package to HMRC by 6 July following the tax year. The details must also be reported to the employee by that date to enable them to complete their tax return.

PILONs

5.126 Payment in lieu of notice and compensation for loss of office are looked at generally in **5.76**. In this section, PILONs are examined in further detail.

The phrase 'payment in lieu of notice' (PILON) is used to describe a range of payments made in a variety of legal situations. In considering the taxation of such payments, it is therefore important to establish the precise circumstances in which they are made.

In particular, it is necessary to distinguish between a PILON and a gardening leave situation (see **5.76**).

In the latter, an employee will typically be given proper notice of termination of employment but told not to attend work during the notice period. As proper notice is given, payment for the period to the termination date cannot properly be described as made in lieu of notice. The payment is simply the salary due for the period of notice and so taxable under *ITEPA 2003, s 62*, whether or not it is paid as a lump sum. In this case, the employment continues to the termination date, whether the employee works or not.

Where a PILON is given instead of notice, how it is taxed depends on whether it is contractual, customary or a payment of damages. In *SCA Packaging Ltd v R & C Commrs* [2007] EWHC 270 (Ch), the High Court upheld a decision of a special commissioner that sums paid to certain employees who were made redundant were emoluments from the relevant employees' employments so that the employer should have deducted and accounted for PAYE and National Insurance contributions (NICs).

Contractual payments

5.127 Where an employee receives a contractual PILON, it is chargeable under *ITEPA 2003, s 62* as earnings from the employment. A contractual PILON is one that has its source in the contractual arrangements between employer and employee. Such arrangements can take a variety of forms, including:

- the main contract document;
- a side letter to the main contract document;
- a staff handbook;
- a letter of appointment;
- a redundancy agreement; or
- an employer-union agreement.

Sometimes, arrangements give the employer a choice or discretion of giving notice or making a PILON. In *EMI Group Electronics v Caldicott* 71 TC 455, under the terms of the contract the employer had a reserved right to make a payment in lieu of notice. It was accepted that the right was exercised and the Court of Appeal held that such a payment is chargeable under *ITEPA 2003, s 62*.

An employer in this situation can choose not to give proper notice and also not to make a payment in lieu under the contract. If so, the terms of the contract are breached, and a payment for that breach falls within *ITEPA 2003, s 401*. It is dealt with as a damages payment. HMRC will examine such cases critically to ensure that there is evidence that the employer did in fact choose to breach the contract. *Richardson v Delaney* 74 TC 167 is an example of a case where the High Court rejected the employer's claim that such a breach had occurred.

Customary payments

5.128 As explained above, a payment made without legal obligation can be chargeable under *ITEPA 2003, s 62* if it is customary to make it. This is to be considered when there is no written reference in employment terms to PILONs.

For example, an employer may always make a payment for any notice period that is not worked, even though nothing is written down. This may be described as a custom or as an expectation, but the terminology used is less important than identifying the character of the payment. Provided that the payment is made as an automatic response, it is arguable that it is earnings within *ITEPA 2003, s 62*. That may be so even if an individual employee does not know about it; what is important is whether it is part of the employment relationship where the individual works.

The HMRC Employment Income Manual (EIM12977) states:

> 'The important point is less how long the expectation or custom has been in place than whether it is an automatic part of the employment. So where it is clear that an employer intends to follow a particular path in the future, a custom can come into being very quickly.
>
> A custom should not be argued to exist where there is a procedure for making a genuine critical assessment in the making of payments, so that they are not made automatically. For example, an employer makes PILONs instead of giving notice, but each payment is looked at under an internal written procedure that assesses what payment is to be made. The result is that some employees may be forced to sue for compensation, or some may receive less than the equivalent of gross salary (because, for example, they already have another job to go to). Such PILONs are likely to represent damages because an individual employee cannot be certain that a payment equal to salary due in the notice period will automatically be made.
>
> A custom may be industry-wide or confined to a small group of employees within a business or even a single employee. What is important is whether the payment is an automatic part of the employment relationship.'

Payments of damages

5.129 Where:

- there is no entitlement to or custom of making a PILON (see above); and
- the employer unilaterally dismisses the employee with less notice than the employee is entitled to; then

the employer has breached the contract.

In such circumstances, a PILON represents damages for breach of contract and is taxable under *ITEPA 2003, s 401*. The employment terminates with the employer's action.

It should be remembered that an employer would not normally breach a contract if it can be avoided due to the threat of legal action for damages. The working presumption to adopt is, therefore, that the employee will have been given proper notice. This presumption should be overturned only if there is evidence to support it.

IR35

Legislation

5.130 Anti-avoidance provisions to prevent individuals avoiding tax and NIC by providing services through an intermediary, such as a personal service company, came into effect from 6 April 2000. The legislation is widely referred to as the 'IR35 rules' after the number of the Budget press release in which they were first announced.

The rules were extended from 9 April 2003 so that income received by domestic workers, including nannies and butlers, in respect of services provided after this date via an intermediary, are also caught by the intermediaries legislation. This anti-avoidance measure means that workers who would otherwise be treated as employees, if they were engaged directly, can no longer avoid paying tax and NICs on any payments of salary by using a service company. Additional tax and NICs may have to be paid on the 'deemed payment' (see below).

The IR35 rules provide that (*ITEPA 2003, s 49*):

- where an individual ('the worker') personally performs, or has an obligation personally to perform, services for another person ('the client');
- the performance of those services by the worker is referable to arrangements involving a third party, rather than referable to a contract between the client and the worker; and
- the circumstances are such that, were the services to be performed by the worker under a contract between him and the client, he would be regarded as employed in the employed earner's employment by the client,

then the relevant payments and benefits are treated as emoluments paid to the worker in respect of his or her employment. These rules apply irrespective of whether the client is a person with whom the worker holds any office or employment. Under the rules, a deemed salary payment, subject to tax under

PAYE, may fall to be made to the worker on 5 April at the end of the tax year. The tax and NICs due on this deemed payment must be accounted for by 19 April.

The Conservative and Liberal Democrat coalition government pledged to review IR35 legislation and, according to the government, it is still on the agenda to be reviewed.

Factors determining employment status

5.131 Given that the issue of employment status has such far-reaching consequences, both for tax purposes and otherwise, it would be helpful to have a system that could determine the issue in any given circumstances. In most cases, it is clear whether a relationship is one of employment or of self-employment. There are however, many cases where it is unclear and there is currently no definitive guide providing absolute certainty. The basics of employment status are discussed at **5.1** et seq. With regard to personal service companies in particular, this is an area where judgment, experience and legal precedents all come into play. The point was highlighted in *Hall v Lorimer* 66 TC 349, as follows:

> 'In order to decide whether a person carries on business on his own account it is necessary to consider many different aspects of that person's work activity. This is not a mechanical exercise of running through items on a check list to see whether they are present in, or absent from, a given situation. The object of the exercise is to paint a picture from the accumulation of detail. The overall effect can only be appreciated by standing back from the detailed picture which has been painted, by viewing it from a distance and by making an informed, considered, qualitative appreciation of the whole. It is a matter of evaluation of the overall effect, which is not necessarily the same as the sum total of the individual details. Not all details are of equal weight or importance in any given situation. The details may also vary in importance from one situation to another. The process involves painting a picture in each individual case.'

In recent years, implied employment contracts have been examined in detail by the courts, with particular reference to personal service companies. In *Brook Street Bureau v Dacas* [2004] EWCA Civ 217, there was relief in the recruitment community that the agency (Brook Street) was not held to be the employer. However, the Court of Appeal gave a very strong indication that the end user in that case (Wandsworth Council) may have been an employer of the agency worker (Mrs Dacas) under an implied contract of employment.

Following on from the *Dacas* case, the Employment Appeal Tribunal (EAT) upheld a decision of an employment tribunal that an agency worker, operating through a personal services company, is the employee of the end user. In *Cable & Wireless v Muscat* [2006] EWCA Civ 220, an implied contract of employment was found to exist between Cable & Wireless and Mr Muscat, on the basis that Muscat's contract for services with his agency, Abraxas, did not reflect the reality of his relationship with C&W. In previous cases in which contractors have claimed employment rights from end users, they have failed because no contractual nexus existed: that is, the contractor's company had a contractual relationship with the agency, but not with the end user. This case makes it clear that a contractual nexus in the traditional sense is not necessary and an implied employment contract can be considered to exist.

More recently, in *Island Consultants Ltd v R&C Commrs* (2007) SpC 618, the special commissioners decided that, for the purposes of the IR35 legislation, a worker who had provided his services through a personal service company would have been regarded as an employee if he had contracted direct with the client.

Control and substitution

5.132 In September 2008, the High Court held that the IR35 legislation applied to the services of an IT consultant. The failure of the appeal against an earlier ruling of the Special Commissioners in December 2007 (*Dragonfly Consulting Ltd v R&C Commrs* (2007) SpC 655) represented a huge defeat for both Jon Bessell, the owner of Dragonfly Consulting, and the Professional Contractors Group (PCG) who supported him. In this case the provision of personal services and substitution was the main issue and, ultimately, the one on which Mr Bessell's case collapsed. In *Dragonfly Consulting Lt v HM Revenue & Customs* [2008] EWHC 2113 (Ch), four issues were argued before Mr Justice Henderson, namely: the relevance of the concept of 'worker'; intention; control; and substitution/personal service. HMRC will usually agree that a person who is an expert in their field is unlikely to be controlled as to 'how' he does the work. However, that does not preclude the possibility that the work provider could retain the right to control 'how' the work is done.

In the *Dragonfly* case, he Automobile Association (AA) wished to use Mr Bessell's services because he was an experienced expert who knew what he was doing. However, the contracts included terms that indicated that the AA could exert control and supervision rights. In addition, the team managers said they could monitor his work, could check it if there was a complaint, asking him to undertake certain tasks so they could check the quality of his work. The High Court approved the Special Commissioner's description of this as 'an on-going informal appraisal of the quality of the work'. This, they said, is unlike a self-employed person, where you would not expect to find such regular appraisal and monitoring.

As a separate issue of control, the court also looked at 'what' was done. The AA allocated tasks to Mr Bessell, and his progress was reviewed by a manager.

In his assessment of the facts, the Special Commissioner said that 'the engagement simply would not have worked if he did not do what was allocated to him' and he had to 'accept the AA's reasonable directions in relation to what he was doing (rather that how he did it)'.

Deemed salary calculation

5.133 To ascertain whether a deemed salary payment falls to be made, and the extent of any such payment, the following procedure is used:

Step (1)

The total amount of all payments and other benefits received by the intermediary during the tax year in respect of relevant engagements (*ITEPA 2003, s 55*) is reduced by 5%.

Step (2)

Add to the result of Step 1 the amount of any 'payments and benefits' received by the worker (or the worker's family: *ITEPA 2003, s 61(3)(b)*) in respect of 'relevant engagements' during the tax year, from any person other than the intermediary, where such amounts are not chargeable to income tax as employment income and would be so chargeable if the worker were employed by the client.

This rule ensures that any amounts paid directly to the worker as part of an arrangement to avoid the application of these provisions is caught.

Step (3)

Deduct from the total of Steps 1 and 2 the amount of any expenses met in the year by the intermediary, or (from 6 April 2002) met by the worker and reimbursed by the intermediary, that would have been deductible from the emoluments of the employment if the client had employed the worker and the expenses had been met by the worker out of those emoluments. For 2002/03 onwards, where the intermediary provides a vehicle for the worker, deduct any mileage allowance that would have been available had the worker been directly employed and provided their own vehicle (*ITEPA 2003, s 54(4)*).

If the result of applying Step 3, or at any later point, is nil or a negative amount, there is no deemed employment payment. Neither, by implication, is there a deductible deemed amount.

Step (4)

Deduct the amount of any capital allowances for expenditure incurred by the intermediary that could have been claimed by the worker had he been employed by the client and had incurred the expenditure (*CAA 2001, s 262*).

Step (5)

Deduct any contributions made in that year for the benefit of the worker by the intermediary to an approved retirement benefit scheme or personal pension plan that, if made by an employer for the benefit of an employee, would not be chargeable to income tax as income of the employee.

Step (6)

Deduct the amount of any employer's NIC (Class 1 or 1A: *ITEPA 2003, s 61(1)*) paid by the intermediary for the year in respect of the worker.

Step (7)

Deduct the amount of any payments or other benefits received in the year by the worker from the intermediary that are chargeable to income tax and do not represent items in respect of which a deduction was made at Step 3 above. From 6 April 2002, mileage allowance payments and passenger payments are deemed to be chargeable under the charge on employment income provisions and therefore included in the amount to be deducted.

If the result at this point is nil or a negative amount, there is no deemed charge on employment income.

Step (8)

Assume that the result of Step 7 represents an amount together with employer's National Insurance contributions on it, and deduct what (on that assumption) would be the amount of those contributions. The result of this 'netting down' is the deemed employment payment.

Deemed salary – example

5.134

Example 5.17

James and Matthew are directors of a service company – Techies Ltd – and they each own 50% of the shares. During 2009/10, they each undertake some engagements that are treated as relevant engagements under the IR35 rules. They also undertake some other engagements that are not relevant engagements.

During the year, Techies Ltd received income of £50,000 in respect of relevant engagements undertaken by James and a further £30,000 in respect of relevant engagements undertaken by Matthew. The company also has further income of £40,000, which is not derived from relevant engagements.

James and Matthew each draw a salary of £30,000. NICs of £3,108 are paid in respect of each salary payment ((£30,000 – £5,715) × 12.8%). The company also makes a contribution of £5,000 each to a registered employer's pension scheme.

James incurs travelling expenses of £2,500 in relation to the relevant engagements undertaken by him, and Matthew incurs travelling expenses of £1,000 in relation to the relevant engagements undertaken by him.

At the end of the tax year, the company must calculate whether a deemed payment falls to be made. This is calculated as follows:

	James	Matthew
	£	£
Income from relevant engagements	50,000	30,000
Less: travelling expenses	(2,500)	(1,000)
pension contributions	(5,000)	(5,000)
employer's NICs paid in year	(3,108)	(3,108)
5% deduction for expenses		
(£50,000/£30,000 × 5%)	(2,500)	(1,500)
	36,892	20,892
Less: salary paid in year	(30,000)	(30,000)
		(9,108)
Deemed payment and employer's NIC	6,892	
Less: employer's NIC		
$\frac{12.8}{112.8} \times$ £6,892	(782)	
Deemed salary payment	6,110	

No deemed salary payment falls to be made to Matthew, as the salary paid to him during the year exceeds the intermediary's income from relevant engagements that he undertook during the year after taking account of relevant expenses.

However, a deemed salary payment of £6,110 falls to be made to James on 5 April 2010.

Managed service companies

5.135 Legislation contained in *FA 2007, s 25* and *Sch 3* deems income to be employment income where individuals provide their services through managed service companies (MSCs) and their income is not already treated as employment income. This means that, from 6 April 2007, MSCs have to operate and account for PAYE on all payments that individuals receive for services provided through the MSC. If the MSC does not pay the tax and National Insurance contributions, HMRC can recover them from others, principally the MSC's director and the person who provided the company to the individual.

Broadly, MSCs are multi-person, personal service companies, often referred to as 'managed personal service companies' or 'composites'.

In a composite company scheme, several (typically ten to 20) otherwise unrelated workers are made worker-shareholders of the company. The size of the company is restricted to ensure that profits do not exceed the threshold for the small companies' rate of corporation tax. Each worker usually holds a different class of share in the company. This enables the company to pay different rates of dividend to each worker, and in practice the dividend received will be directly related to the company's income from the end client for work undertaken by that worker.

In a managed personal service company (MPSC) scheme, in contrast to a composite company, there is only one worker per company structure. The MSC scheme provider performs similar functions for MPSCs as for composite companies – it usually provides a director and exercises financial and management control of the company, typically performing this function for many MPSCs.

Broadly, the changes mean that HMRC no longer have to rely on the IR35 legislation to require the operation of PAYE and payment of NICs by the MSC.

New provisions also restrict tax relief for travel expenses paid to MSC workers.

Partnerships and companies

5.136 Since the introduction of the managed service company (MSC) legislation (*ITEPA 2003, Pt 2, Ch 9*) with effect from April 2007, HMRC have seen a growth in intermediary companies which are marketed to individuals for the provision of their services to clients. The companies claim that they are not MSCs, usually by virtue of the fact that the provider of the intermediary is an officer or partner of the intermediary and that consequently, as there is no separate MSC provider, the MSC legislation does not apply. HMRC have subsequently taken counsel's advice and have confirmed that they consider that companies and partnerships that otherwise fall within the MSC legislation (that is, fulfil the criteria of *ITEPA 2003, Pt 2, Ch 9*), but claim not to be MSCs because the provider is an officer or partner of the intermediary, *are* nevertheless MSCs.

HMRC will challenge and litigate in relevant cases. Where HMRC successfully challenge a company as being within the MSC legislation and that company is unable to pay the resultant PAYE and National Insurance debt, HMRC will invoke the transfer of debt provisions. For further information in this area, see the HMRC website at www.hmrc.gov.uk/news/cis-msc.htm.

SMALL FAMILY COMPANIES

Extracting profits

5.137 Given the rates of income tax and corporation tax currently in force, it is often considered to be advantageous for a family company director/shareholder to draw little or no salary or dividends, but to retain all profits within the company to be taxed only at the lower (small companies or normal) corporation tax rate. Of course, unless the director/shareholder has other sources of income, taking an income in one form or another from the company will be necessary to meet living expenses and other financial commitments.

The benefits of using corporation tax rates over income tax rates have reduced over recent years, following the increase in the small profits corporation tax rate from 19% to 20% from 1 April 2007 and from 20% to 21% from 1 April 2008 (note that this rate is set to be reduced again to 20% from 1 April 2011).

The decision as to whether to extract profits from the family company or retain them generally depends on what route will produce the most tax-effective overall benefit to the family. The most efficient tax planning strategy will normally be to pay out the company's income annually, by way of remuneration or dividends, rather than retaining it within the company, where it may become subject to the higher combined charges of corporation tax and capital gains tax.

Currently, the rate at which corporation tax is payable depends on the amount of a company's profits for the financial year in question. The full rate of corporation tax for the financial year 2010 (the year beginning on 1 April 2010) is 28%. The 'small profits rate' for the financial year 2010 is 21%. The lower and upper limits for the financial year for the purposes of the small profits rate are £300,000 and £1,500,000 respectively (*FA 2010, s 3*).

Remuneration versus dividends

5.138 The two main methods of extracting profits from a company are as remuneration and by way of dividend. Extraction of funds by way of a loan is not possible because of the company law restrictions and tax disadvantages (*CTA 2010, Pt 10, Ch 3* (loans to participators, etc)).

The tax effects of the two methods may be broadly contrasted as follows:

- Remuneration is deducted in arriving at the taxable profits of the company (provided the amount is justifiable (see *Copeman v William Flood & Sons Ltd* (1940) 24 TC 53), although HMRC rarely challenge the size of the directors' remuneration paid by trading companies where the directors are full-time working directors). The recipient is taxed on the remuneration through the PAYE system at the date of payment including a charge to NIC.
- Dividends are not deducted in arriving at the taxable profits.

Where the small profits rate of corporation tax applies, it will usually be more beneficial for the directors to receive remuneration by way of dividends. Where the full rate applies, then the payment of remuneration by way of salary will produce greater relief from corporation tax. The extraction of profits by way of salary will, however, give rise to a liability to NIC whereas a dividend does not.

5.139 A number of other factors must be taken into account:

- A reduction in salary may result in a decreased entitlement to certain earnings-related social security benefits. It is important to note that a full NIC contribution record must be maintained to ensure maximum social security benefits.
- The lack of a salary charge in the accounts may increase the value for CGT and IHT purposes of holdings valued on the basis of earnings. In addition, a higher dividend payment will increase the value of a holding calculated on a dividend yield basis, although it is unlikely to affect the valuation of a major interest.
- Dividends are payable rateably to shareholders in proportion to their holdings in the company, which may not necessarily correspond to the relative efforts of the directors in earning the profits. Dividend waivers may assist in these circumstances, but care must be taken.
- Dividends can only be paid out of distributable profits whereas, at least in theory, remuneration can be paid out regardless of the level of profits.
- In the longer term, there is a risk that, at some future date, the relative advantages might be reversed at a time when the flexibility to switch between the two methods is restricted.
- The national minimum wage legislation should be considered, as this applies equally to directors under contracts of employment as it does to employees.
- Overall, it will normally be best to extract profits using a mixture of salary, benefits and dividends, which can be varied according to individual circumstances.

Distribution policy

5.140 In deciding how profits are to be extracted, the following aspects should be considered:

- Individual shareholders are still subject to income tax on dividends which they receive; for 2010/11, this will be charged at 10% for lower or basic rate taxpayers, at 32.5% for those taxable at the higher rate, and at a new dividend additional rate of 42.5% for those liable to the additional rate of income tax of 50% (in each case covered by a 10% non-repayable tax credit) when the dividend is paid. The timing of the dividend may therefore affect the timing of shareholders' higher rate liabilities.
- Individual needs of shareholders may differ – some may require income, others may be more interested in capital appreciation. These conflicting interests may be met by the issue of separate classes of shares with differing distribution rights.
- Lower rates of corporation tax continue to apply where profits are retained or are distributed to other companies.

Family members

5.141 For income tax purposes, it is generally desirable to spread income around a family to fully utilise annual personal allowances and to take full advantage of nil and lower rate tax thresholds.

The term 'family' includes all individuals who depend on a particular individual (eg the owner of the family company) for their financial well-being. This may include not only the spouse, civil partner and children but also aged relatives, retired domestic employees, etc.

Distributions (usually dividends) from jointly owned shares in close companies are not automatically split 50/50 between husband and wife, but are taxed according to the actual proportions of ownership and entitlement to the income (*ITA 2007, s 836(3)*).

Possible methods of spreading income around the family include employing a spouse and/or children, waiving salary (to increase profits available as dividends) or dividends (to increase the amounts available to other shareholders), and transferring income-producing assets.

Some distributions of income to family members will not be beneficial for tax purposes, and to this effect, the following points should be borne in mind:

- a salary paid to spouse, civil partner children or other dependants is a tax deductible expense of the company only if it can be justified in relation to the duties performed;

- a salary paid to spouse, civil partner children or other dependants will attract a liability to NIC if it is above the lower earnings limit; and
- the investment income of an infant child (ie an unmarried child below the age of 18) is taxed on his parents, where it arises from a gift by them.

Income shifting

5.142 On 25 July 2007, the House of Lords gave its judgment in the landmark case of *Jones v Garnett* (also known as '*Arctic Systems Ltd*'). HMRC had previously lost this case in the Court of Appeal and, as a result, had appealed to the House of Lords. The case concerned dividends payments made by a company to Mrs Jones through which Mr Jones provided IT consultancy services. If the decision had gone against Mr and Mrs Jones, many married couples would have faced a very large tax and NIC cost, going back over the last six years.

In their judgment, their Lordships ruled that Mr and Mrs Jones were creating an arrangement in the nature of a settlement when they subscribed for one share each, and set up their company, Arctic Systems Ltd. However, the exemption for gifts between spouses also applied, and dividends paid to Mrs Jones were therefore not income arising under a settlement. The resulting decision meant that Mrs Jones (rather than Mr Jones) was assessable on the dividends she received from the family company, even though most of the profit was as a result of Mr Jones's efforts for the company.

Following the decision given in *Arctic Systems Ltd*, the government swiftly announced that it would effectively reverse the ruling by changing the law. A consultation was published in December 2007 with the intention of bringing in new legislation from 6 April 2008. The revised legislation focuses on 'income shifting arrangements that make use of companies or partnerships to gain a tax advantage'. While it was aimed at preventing the transfer of dividend income or partnership profits from a person who paid tax at 40% to an individual paying a lower rate of tax, the changes were widely drafted and caught situations in which a range of connected parties had invested capital in a business (eg businesses involving spouses, siblings and parents and children). The resulting outcry from the professional bodies and businesses subsequently prompted the government to announce its intention to delay indefinitely the introduction of the new legislation.

Disposal of shares

5.143 If a loss is made on the disposal of shares in the family company, the shareholder may in certain circumstances be able to obtain tax relief for it against income rather than against capital gains on other assets. This is only possible if the shares were acquired by subscription, not by purchasing them from an existing shareholder. For shares acquired on or after 6 April 1998 the company must be carrying on qualifying activities under the EIS provisions. The disposal must be the result of an arm's-length bargain, liquidation or of the shares becoming of negligible value.

For shares issued on or after 7 March 2001 the requirement that the company has to be unquoted both at the date of issue and at the date of disposal is replaced by one that it must be unquoted at the date of issue and that there must be no arrangements then in place for it to cease to be unquoted or for it to become a wholly-owned subsidiary of a new holding company which is to cease to be unquoted.

If the director/shareholder lends money to the family company for the purposes of its trade and the debt becomes irrecoverable, it may be possible to claim a CGT loss. If relief under *TCGA 1992 s 253* is not possible, a loss can only be claimed if the loan qualifies as a debt on a security under *TCGA 1992, s 251*. Unfortunately, there is no statutory definition of 'debt on a security': *s 251* refers the reader back to *TCGA 1992, s 132(3)(b)* which states that:

> '"security" includes any loan stock or similar security whether of the Government of the United Kingdom or of any other government, or of any public or local authority of the United Kingdom or elsewhere, or of any company, and whether secured or unsecured.'

This merely provides guidance as to the type of instrument that is considered to be a 'security' and it leaves undefined the meaning of 'loan stock or similar security'.

Following the various *dicta* in *WT Ramsay Ltd v IR Commrs* [1982] AC 300, HMRC, in their Capital Gains Tax Manual (CGTM53420–53436), have given their view of the characteristics which they consider need to be satisfied before a debt can qualify as a 'debt on a security'.

Chapter 6

Self-employment

STARTING A BUSINESS

Introduction

6.1 Broadly, there are three main vehicles through which a business may be conducted in the UK. These are as a sole trader, by a partnership, or through a company (either private or public).

Sole trader – this means that the trader is an individual who is self-employed. He will pay income tax through the self-assessment system, as well as Class 2 and Class 4 National Insurance (see **6.92**), and VAT if the registration threshold is reached (£70,000 from 1 April 2010.

Partnership – if there are two or more people in the business, they might want to consider a formal deed of partnership. Each partner pays income tax, through the self-assessment system, as well as Class 2 and Class 4 National Insurance (see **6.92**), and the business itself pays VAT once the registration threshold is reached. The concept of a limited liability partnership (LLP) was introduced from 6 April 2001 and broadly provides the organisational flexibility of a partnership, but with limited liability status for its members (see **6.98**).

Limited company – a company registration agent may be used to buy a company 'off the shelf' or a new one can be created and registered with Companies House. Limited companies should always display their full corporate name outside the business premises, and registration details must also appear on the stationery and, from 1 January 2007, on e-mail communications and websites. Company directors have certain obligations. They need to file statutory documents, such as accounts and annual returns. Companies are liable to corporation tax on company profits. Company directors are also employees of the company, so there are different National Insurance and PAYE obligations. Even though a company director is an employee, they still need to register for self-assessment. The same applies to each director in a limited company.

For further details on starting up in business, see the HMRC website at www.hmrc.gov.uk/businesses/tmastarting-up-in-business.shtml.

Choice of vehicle

6.2 If the particular trade involves a risk, isolating that risk within a company environment may seem favourable. Otherwise the choice of unincorporated or incorporated business vehicle often depends on whether trading losses are expected in the early years of trade. Most businesses that develop to a considerable size find the inconveniences of a sole trader or partnership structure too constraining. Thus, if growth is anticipated, the choice is effectively between sole trader or partnership status initially, followed by transfer of the business to a company, or trading through a company from the start.

If losses are anticipated in the early years, and the proprietors have other taxable income, earliest relief for the losses is obtained through an unincorporated business. Company losses are effectively locked into the company. A new company is unlikely to have other income against which to relieve the losses in the short term. Thus they must be carried forward for relief against trading profits when and if these materialise.

Anti-avoidance

6.3 Certain transactions designed to avoid tax on the sale of land by direct or indirect means are specifically brought into the charge to tax (*ITA 2007, Pt 13, Ch 3*).

Whilst the extent to which tax avoidance arrangements have diminished over recent years, due to the alignment of income tax and capital gains tax rates, the provisions are nevertheless very wide in scope and apply to all persons (which include companies and unincorporated bodies), whether or not resident in the UK. However, the land in question (or part of it) must be situated in the UK for the provisions to apply.

The anti-avoidance rules apply where (*ITA 2007, s 755*):

- land, or any property deriving its value from land (including shares in a land-owning company), is acquired with the sole or main object of realising a gain from disposing of the land;
- land is held as trading stock; or
- land is developed with the sole or main object of realising a gain from disposing of the land when developed;

and any gain of a capital nature is obtained from the disposal of the land, by the person acquiring, holding or developing the land, or by any 'connected person' or, where any arrangement or scheme is effected in respect of the land which enables a gain to be realised by any indirect method, or by any series of transactions, by any person who is a party to, or concerned in, the arrangement or scheme, and whether any such person obtains the gain for himself or for any other person (*ITA 2007, s 759*).

6.4 There are also supplementary provisions which ensure that the rules apply to many transactions whereby a person indirectly benefits, though where one person is assessed to tax in respect of consideration receivable by another person there is a right of recovery (*ITA 2007, s 761*).

However, the operation of the provisions is restricted where a company holds land as trading stock, or where a company owns 90% or more of the ordinary share capital (directly or indirectly) of another company which holds land as trading stock, and there is a disposal of shares in either the land trading company or the holding company, and all the land so held is disposed of in the normal course of trade by the company which held it, and all the opportunity of profit or gain in respect of the land arises to that company (*ITA 2007, s 766*).

It is worth noting that adjustments have been upheld in respect of:

- the grant by trustees of a lease of land to a developer, with a clause ensuring that the premium payable should be linked with the prices obtained from the sale of the underleases following the redevelopment of the land (*Page (HMIT) v Lowther* [1983] BTC 394); and
- the sale of properties through the medium of *Bahamian companies* (*Sugarwhite v Budd (HMIT*) [1988] BTC 189).

Trading indicators

6.5 There is no statutory definition which will absolutely define whether someone is trading. Case law provides the main pointers in this area. In statute the definition 'includes every trade, manufacture, adventure or concern in the nature of trade'. The most important aspect of the statutory definition is that it makes clear, by the use of the word 'adventure', that an activity does not need to become an established and successful one before the tax regime begins to take effect.

The indicators, pointers or 'badges of trade' are derived from case law and subject to gradual modification and extension. Whilst each pointer should be examined in isolation, the situation as a whole must also be considered. When applied to the facts of a new situation, some of them may point towards there being a trade and others toward the opposite conclusion. It is their cumulative effect that is decisive.

The badges of trade were reviewed in *Marson v Morton* (1986) 59 TC 381, [1986] STC 463, [1986] 1 WLR 1343. Eight points were made which expanded upon the badges of trade originally put forward by the *Royal Commission on the Taxation of Profits and Income* (1955).

The following introduces the tests developed by the courts.

Profit seeking motive

6.6 Generally, an intention by the taxpayer to make a profit is an indicator that he is trading, but it is not conclusive. In particular, two factors may lead to the opposite conclusion:

- the trader may be acquiring and realising capital investments rather than trading; and
- an intention to make a profit may be simply wishful thinking, if the facts are such that the individual is most unlikely to ever make a profit.

Equally, the fact that a taxpayer does not intend to make a profit or even positively wishes not to do so does not prevent a taxable profit arising if one is, in fact, made.

Type of asset

6.7 The type of asset, whether normally traded or not, will determine the initial presumption toward or away from trading. But this initial presumption may be overturned in the light of other factors.

Some assets, typically raw materials for manufacturing processes, tend to be acquired only for trading purposes. Their purchase and sale would indicate trading other than in the most exceptional circumstances. Other assets, however, may be acquired for personal pleasure (for instance, antiques), and as capital investments (for instance, shares).

Capital equipment that in most businesses is regarded as a fixed asset (for instance, heavy lorries) can also be traded.

If an asset produces income, such as rent, it is much more likely to be treated as an investment than an asset producing no income. This tendency is reduced, however, where the expenditure on maintaining the asset is such that the owner can make a return only by selling it at a profit.

In *CIR v Fraser*, CS 1942, 24 TC 498, three reasons were put forward for purchasing an article:

- own use or consumption;
- investment, possibly to yield income; and
- resale at profit, ie trading.

Repetition of transactions

6.8 Trades tend to be characterised by systematic buying and selling many transactions of an essentially similar character. Clearly, the more frequent and systematic the pattern of buying and selling, the more likely the activity will be regarded as trading.

An isolated transaction is not prevented from being 'an adventure' in the nature of trade, but other indicators would need to point in that direction. Sometimes a transaction, the first of what turns out to be a series, is not recognised as trading at the time. But the courts have agreed that later transactions may be taken into account in reaching a conclusion about the nature of the first one.

What was treated as a hobby may develop into a trade (*Hawes v Gardiner* (1957) 37 TC 671, [1957] TR 341).

Asset modification

6.9 Doing something to the purchased asset before sale is an indication that the person is engaged in trading. Typically, this may be of two kinds:

(1) an asset may require development, such as refitting (*IR Commrs v Livingston* (1926) 11 TC 538); or

(2) the owner may fulfil the role of a wholesaler, buying in bulk and dividing into smaller lots for retail sale – sometimes the owner may both develop the asset and divide it into smaller lots (*Cape Brandy Syndicate v IR Commrs* (1921) 12 TC 358).

See also **6.26**.

Circumstances of asset sale

6.10 Consideration should be given as to whether the sale is conducted in the usual way for dealings in that type of asset. If so, and particularly if that involved the person in establishing a sales office or sales team, there is a strong pointer that the activity amounted to trading. Disposal in an amateurish fashion, or to meet a clearly non-trading need, such as cash to make repayments on personal borrowings, points toward the opposite conclusion.

Time period between purchase and sale

6.11 Looking at the time interval between purchase and resale is one means of attempting to distinguish between a person who is trading and one who periodically changes investments.

Finance

6.12 The source of finance may be a neutral factor. When, however, a person borrows to finance a purchase in circumstances that make it necessary to resell promptly, it tends to indicate a trading intent. This argument was used in the *Wisdom* case where silver bullion was purchased using borrowings (*Wisdom v Chamberlain (HMIT)* (1968) 45 TC 92). The high interest rate indicated that a quick sale would be needed and this was what occurred.

Means of acquisition

6.13 Most assets are purchased rather than acquired by gift or inheritance. When the acquisition is other than by purchase it does present a strong indication that the person had no trading intention. Such a means of acquisition points toward non-trading at the start. That does not mean, however, that whatever the owner does subsequently with the asset, it can never be trading.

Trades and professions

6.14 Profits are charged to tax as trading income under *ITTOIA 2005*. The income tax charge applies to annual business profits, but can apply equally to occasional activities or even single transactions. The issue of what constitutes a trade, or whether a transaction is a trading receipt (or, for example, a capital receipt), may not be clear in every case (*ITTOIA 2005, Pt 5*).

It is important to establish whether an activity constitutes trading (or a profession) as different rules apply to the taxation of the income, the deductibility of expenses and, in particular, to the ways in which losses can be relieved. In the legislation, the word 'trade' is taken to include 'every trade, manufacture, adventure or concern in the nature of trade'. This definition has caused much difficulty in the past but has been adhered to nevertheless. The difficulty has been overcome to a large extent by decided cases.

It is equally important to consider whether income relates to professional or vocational work, or whether it amounts to casual income or profits taxable as miscellaneous income. For example, the royalties received by an established author would be taxable as professional or vocational work, but receipts for the occasional writing of articles would be taxable as miscellaneous income.

Case law has determined that the profits of an illegal trade will still be taxed (*Mann v Nash,* KB 1932, 16 TC 523, [1913] 1 KB 752; *Southern v AB,* KB 1933, 18 TC 59, [1933] 1 KB 713; and *IRC v Aken* [1988] STC 69).

What constitutes a trade?

6.15 The miscellaneous examples below are mainly based on decisions in court cases.

	Trading	*Not trading*
Betting	Professional bookmakers (even if unlawful)	Private betting (even if habitual)
Divers and diving supervisors	Emoluments of person employed in the UK to exploit the sea-bed	
Futures and options	Dealing in the course of a trade (ie by a bank or similar financial institution)	Dealing by pension schemes; relatively infrequent transactions; transactions to hedge specific investments; purely speculative transactions
Horse racing	Racing and selling the progeny of a brood mare; profits from stallion fees	Private horse racing and training
Illegal trading	Profits of a commercial business even if carried on unlawfully, eg bootlegging and prostitution	Crime, eg burglary
Liquidators and personal representatives	Where continuing the company's/deceased's trade	Where merely realising the assets
Miscellaneous	Profits from promoting a series of driving schools	The activities of the British Olympic Association
Property transactions	Established business of property development	Property held as an investment or residence; isolated transactions
Share dealing	Under the *Financial Services Act 1986* and also where transactions amount to trading	Prudent management of an investment portfolio

What is a profession?

6.16

	Trading	*Not trading*
Actors/artists	Normally trading even where based in UK with engagements abroad	Performers engaged for a regular salary, eg permanent members of some orchestras and of an opera, ballet or theatre company (taxable as employment income)
Authors	Regular newspaper articles; sale of authors' notebooks and memorabilia	Occasional writing or articles (taxable as Miscellaneous income under *ITTOIA 2005*)
Dramatist	A successful play after a series of failures	

Informing the authorities of a new business

6.17 In the UK, an individual starting in business on their own account does not generally need permission to do so. Exceptions to this general principle apply when entry to the sector concerned is regulated, either by government (such as the medical profession) or by professional institutes.

Any person starting up as self-employed must register with HMRC (*TMA 1970, s 7*). A self-employed person can use a single form, CWF1, to tell HMRC that they are self-employed for income tax and NICs. They can also notify on the same form that they need to register for VAT.

FA 2008, s 123 and *Sch 41* introduced a new penalties regime for failure to notify HMRC of a taxable activity under *TMA 1970, s 7*. The changes took effect from 1 April 2010 (*SI 2009/511, arts 2* and *3*). A penalty will only be charged if tax and NICs have been lost because of the failure to notify. When someone tells HMRC they should have registered a new taxable activity within a year of a penalty becoming due, any penalty can be reduced to nil. From 1 April 2010 the penalties which may be charged for failure to notify liability are as follows:

- 30% of tax unpaid for non-deliberate failure to notify;
- 70% of tax unpaid for a deliberate failure to notify; and
- 100% of tax unpaid for a deliberate failure with concealment.

Each penalty will be substantially reduced where the taxpayer makes a disclosure (takes active steps to put right the problem), and more so if this is unprompted.

For accounting periods beginning on or after 22 July 2004, companies are obliged to notify HMRC when the company first comes into the charge to corporation tax.

Basis of assessment

6.18 The profits of a trade, profession or vocation are taxed on the basis of the business accounts (*ITTOIA 2005, ss 196–225*). A business may choose the date to which accounts will be prepared. In general, income tax is charged on profits arising in the tax year, based on the 12-month accounting period ending in that tax year (ie a 'current year' basis). Capital allowances are treated as a trading expense of the accounting period, and balancing charges as a trading receipt (*CAA 2001, s 2*).

Special rules apply when a business commences or ceases, and where the business accounts are for a period longer or shorter than 12 months.

New businesses

6.19 On the commencement of a new business by an individual, the following rules apply.

First tax year – the new business is taxed on profits from the date of commencement to the end of the tax year (*ITTOIA 2005, s 199*).

Second tax year – the tax charge is based on the profits of the accounting period ended in the second tax year. However (*ITTOIA 2005, ss 200* and *201*):

- if the first accounts are made up to a date in the second tax year, but for a period of less than 12 months, the charge for the second tax year is based on the profits of the first 12 months;
- if the accounts are made up to a date in the second tax year, but for a period of more than 12 months, the charge for the second tax year is based on the profits of 12 months to the accounting date;
- if the first accounts are made up for more than 12 months and no account ends in the second tax year, the charge for that year is based on the profits of the tax year itself.

Third tax year – the tax charge is normally based on the accounts for the 12 months to the accounting date ending in the tax year.

Businesses ceasing

6.20 When a business ceases, it is usually taxed on profits from the end of the basis period for the previous tax year to the date of cessation (but see **6.33** for tax relief on 'overlap profits' upon cessation) (*ITTOIA 2005, s 202*).

Other points

6.21 *Overlap profits* – in the opening years of a new business, profits may be taxed more than once. This can also happen on a change of accounting date. The profit taxed in two successive tax years is called 'overlap profit'. Tax relief for overlap profits may be available on a change of accounting date, and can also be claimed on the cessation of business (see **6.32**) (*ITTOIA 2005, s 204*). Overlap profits are not indexed, so will diminish in value in real terms over several years.

Time-apportionment – in calculating business profits for a tax year, it may be necessary to time-apportion the profits for long accounting periods, or to combine the profits of two short accounting periods. Time-apportionment may be calculated in days, months or fractions of months, providing that the method is used consistently (*ITTOIA 2005, s 203*).

Example 6.1—Opening years

Arnold commences trade on 1 September 2008 and prepares accounts to 30 April, starting with an eight-month period of account to 30 April 2009. His profits (as adjusted for tax purposes and after capital allowances) for the first three accounting periods are as follows:

	£
8 months to 30 April 2009	24,000
Year to 30 April 2010	39,000
Year to 30 April 2011	40,000

His taxable profits for the first four tax years are as follows:

	Basic period		£	£
2008/09	1.9.08 to 5.4.09	£24,000 × 7/8		21,000
2009/10	1.9.08 to 31.8.09:			
	1.9.08 to 30.4.09		24,000	
	1.5.09 to 31.8.09	£39,000 × 4/12	13,000	37,000
2010/11	Y/e 30.4.10			39,000
2011/12	Y/e 30.4.11			40,000
Overlap relief accrued:				
1.9.08 to 5.4.09, 7 months				21,000
1.5.09 to 31.8.09, 4 months				13,000
Total overlap relief accrued				£34,000

Example 6.2—Closing year

Barbara commenced trading on 1 May 2007, preparing accounts to 30 April. She permanently ceases trading on 30 June 2010, preparing accounts for the two months to that date. Her profits (as adjusted for tax purposes and after capital allowances) are as follows:

	£
Year ended 30 April 2008	24,000
Year ended 30 April 2009	48,000
Year ended 30 April 2010	96,000
Two months ended 30 June 2010	5,000
	£173,000

Her taxable profits for the four tax years of trading are as follows:

	Basic period		£	£
2007/08	1.5.07 to 5.4.08	£24,000 × 11/12		22,000
2008/09	Y/e 30.4.08			24,000
2009/10	Y/e 30.4.09			48,000
2010/11	1.5.09 to 30.6.10:			
	1.5.09 to 30.4.10		96,000	
	1.5.10 to 30.6.10		5,000	
			101,000	
	Deduct overlap relief		22,000	79,000
				173,000

COMPUTING PROFITS

Profit and accounts

6.22 The profits in the accounts of the business are not always the same as taxable profits, and it is usually necessary to make adjustments to the accounts to arrive at the taxable profit for the accounting period. The business profits must generally be computed in accordance with 'generally accepted accounting practice', subject to any adjustment required or allowed by tax legislation or case law (*ITTOIA 2005, s 25*).

UITF 40

6.23 *FA 2006* implemented a one-off tax adjustment arising from accountancy changes brought about by Urgent Issues Task Force Abstract 40 (UITF 40) (*FA 2006, s 102* and *Sch 15*). This applies to trades, professions and vocations and to UK property and overseas property businesses.

Broadly, the tax adjustment, which is called adjustment income, that can be spread arises on a change of accounting policy where:

- in the first period of account ending on or after 22 June 2005 the trader follows GAAP and adopts the principles for revenue recognition of service contracts contained in UITF 40; and
- in the period before the trader followed GAAP but not UITF 40.

This means that spreading is only available for the adjustment income arising from following UITF 40 for the first time in the first period of account ending on or after 22 June 2005. If the trader adopted the accounting policy contained in UITF 40 in a period of account ending before 22 June 2005, they will not be able to spread any adjustment income arising from the earlier change in accounting policy.

No claim is necessary for spreading, but an election may be made for the adjustment to be taxed more quickly (see below).

Once the adjustment income attributable to UITF 40 has been calculated, it is spread according to the following rules.

In each of the first three tax years: the lower of:

- one third of the adjustment income; and
- one sixth of the profits of the business

is taxed.

'Profits' means the profits of the business calculated for income tax purposes leaving out any adjustment expenses (arising from any other change in accounting policy) or any capital allowances or balancing charges.

In the fourth and fifth years: if there is any adjustment income not yet taxed, the amount remaining untaxed will be taxed if it is the lowest amount.

In the sixth year: any remaining adjustment income is taxed.

Where the business has ceased, in the year of cessation the lower limit of one sixth still applies. In subsequent years, only the one-third alternative applies until the full adjustment has been charged.

Accelerating payment

6.24 Traders can make an election to pay the tax arising on the adjustment income more quickly. The election will mean that an extra amount of adjustment income is treated as arising in a particular tax year. The election must be made before the first anniversary of the normal self-assessment filing date for a tax year and must show how much extra adjustment income the traders wants to have taxed in that tax year. In future years, if there has been an election, the original adjustment income is treated as being reduced by the amount charged early.

Example 6.3

If there is adjustment income of £6,000 and an election has been made to charge an extra £1,000 in Year 1, when comparing one third of the adjustment income with one sixth of the profits, in the following year the amount of adjustment income for comparison is £5,000 not £6,000.

Partnerships

6.25 The legislation covers continuing, new and departing partners. It mirrors the legislation for partnerships on the withdrawal of the cash basis.

For partnerships, the adjustment is calculated from the figures in the partnership accounts in exactly the same way as a person who carries on business on their own account. It is charged each year on the individual partners.

For the first year, each instalment is apportioned among the partners in accordance with their profit-sharing entitlement in the 12 months ending immediately before the date on which UITF 40 was adopted.

For subsequent years, each instalment is allocated or apportioned according to the profit sharing arrangements for the 12 months immediately before the relevant anniversary of the date when UITF 40 was adopted (the date on which UITF 40 was adopted is the first day of the period of account when UITF 40 first applied). So the period of apportionment for any tax year is the 12-month period following the period of apportionment for the previous tax year.

This means that, as partners come and go, the individuals who are charged to tax will change, as will the amount on which they are charged as profit-sharing entitlements change. This also means that any election to pay more than the normal instalment for any year must be made by all the partners who are charged for that year.

There is nothing to prevent departing or joining partners from seeking an indemnity from the other partners to cover any charge.

Allowable trading expenses

6.26 Expenditure is generally allowable in computing profits for tax purposes, provided it is:

- wholly and exclusively for the purposes of the business; and
- not capital expenditure (although such expenditure may be eligible for capital allowances instead).

Appropriations of profit (eg proprietors' drawings and income tax) are not allowable business deductions, but should not normally appear as expense items in the accounts (*ITTOIA 2005, ss 32–55*).

The main work base needs to be identified to determine a claim for travelling expenses (*Horton v Young* (1971) 47 TC 60 and *Newson v Robertson* (1952) 33 TC 452, [1953] Ch 7, [1952] 2 All ER 728).

Note that repair works on a newly acquired asset will not generally be allowed for tax purposes if the repairs must be made to enable the asset to be brought in to business use (*Law Shipping Co Ltd v CIR,* CS 1923, 12 TC 621, but contrast *Odeon Theatres Ltd v Jones* (1971) 48 TC 257, [1973] Ch 288, [1971] 1 WLR 442, [1972] 1 All ER 681).

'Wholly and exclusively'

6.27 Apart from business expenses specifically allowed by tax law, expenditure cannot be claimed for tax purposes unless it is 'wholly and exclusively' for the purposes of the business.

An expense incurred for both business and private purposes cannot be deducted unless the business part of the mixed expense can be separately identified. The business element may then be claimed, provided it was incurred wholly and exclusively for business purposes (*ITTOIA 2005, s 34*).

Capital expenditure

6.28 It is important to distinguish between 'revenue' expenditure, which can be deducted from profits, and 'capital' expenditure, which cannot be deducted, although certain capital expenditure may qualify for capital allowances. Where capital expenditure does not qualify for capital allowances, it will generally form part of the allowable cost for capital gains tax purposes.

There is no definition of capital and revenue expenditure in the tax legislation, although their meaning has been considered in a number of court cases. Expenditure is commonly defined as capital if it brings about an 'enduring benefit of a trade'. In deciding whether an expense is capital or revenue it will generally be necessary to consider such factors as the type of asset on which the expenditure was incurred and the nature of the expenditure (eg repairs expenditure is normally allowable revenue expenditure, whereas improvement expenditure is not).

In *Strick v Regent Oil Co Ltd* (1965) 43 TC 1 at page 29 (see HMRC Business Income Manual BIM35560), Lord Reid described the difficulties in making sense of the large number of decisions on this topic:

> 'It may be possible to reconcile all the decisions, but it is certainly not possible to reconcile all the reasons given for them. I think that much of the difficulty has arisen from taking too literally general statements made in earlier cases and seeking to apply them to a different kind of case which their authors almost certainly did not have in mind – in seeking to treat expressions of judicial opinion as if they were words in an Act of Parliament.'

Non-trading income

6.29 Any non-trading income and capital profits included in the business accounts are not usually taxed as part of the business profits, but may be liable to tax under separate rules (eg rental income under (former) Schedule A, or capital profits assessed to capital gains tax).

Pre-trading expenditure

6.30 A deduction may be claimed for expenses incurred within seven years prior to the commencement of trading, where those expenses would have been allowed after trading commenced. The expenditure is treated as incurred on the first day of trading (*ITTOIA 2005, s 57*).

Disallowable expenses

6.31 Disallowable expenses include:

Bad debts (*ITTOIA 2005, s 35*)	general bad debts provision or debts relating to capital items, such as the sale of a fixed asset
Entertaining	entertaining expenses and hospitality except staff entertaining or advertising to the public generally
Gifts	except where carrying prominent advertising costing less than £50 per person per annum (but not food and drink)

Premises and plant*	costs of acquiring premises and fixed assets
Depreciation*	of fixed assets; profit or loss on sale (special rules apply to assets held on finance leases)
Legal and professional costs	relating to tax disputes; or purchasing of fixed assets (treated as part of the cost of the fixed asset)
Employee costs	wages, salary, drawings, benefits, pension payments, except relating to bona fide remuneration for employees
Car hire	where the retail price (P) of the car when new exceeds £12,000, the allowable rental is reduced by multiplying it by 12,000 + P/2P, unless the car is first registered after 16 April 2002 and is either electrically propelled or has CO_2 emissions not exceeding 120g/km
Personal	eg ordinary clothing, even if for business use; fines; fuel expenses for private use of vehicles; travel between home and business; non-business premises expenses
Repairs and renewals	general provisions for future repairs and renewals; alteration, improvements or replacement of fixed assets*
Interest and finance charges	on unpaid tax; otherwise generally allowable but not capital repayments or premiums on mortgage repayment
Annual payments	eg annuities, royalties, paid under deduction of tax at source – treated as 'charges on income'
Sundry	payments to political parties, some payments to charities

* See Capital allowances (**6.44**).

Allowable trading expenses – example

6.32

Example 6.4

A UK trader commences trading on 1 October 2009. His profit and loss account for the year to 30 September 2010 is:

	£	£
Sales		110,000
Deduct purchases	75,000	
Less: Stock and work in progress at 30.9.09	15,000	60,000
Gross profit		50,000

	£	£
Deduct:		
Salaries (all paid by 30.6.11)	15,600	
Rent and rates	2,400	
Telephone	500	
Heat and light	650	
Depreciation	1,000	
Motor expenses	2,700	
Entertainment	600	
Bank interest	900	
Hire-purchase interest	250	
Repairs and renewals	1,000	
Accountant's fee	500	
Bad debts	200	
Sundries	700	27,000
Net profit		23,000
Gain on sale of fixed asset		300
Rent received		500
Bank interest received (net)		150
Profit		£23,950

Further information

(i) Rent and rates. £200 of the rates bill is for the period from 1.6.09 to 30.9.09.

(ii) Telephone. Telephone bills for the trader's private telephone amount to £150. It is estimated that 40% of these calls are for business purposes.

(iii) Motor expenses. All the motor expenses are in respect of the proprietor's car. 40% of the annual mileage relates to private use and home to business use.

(iv) Entertainment. Includes entertainment of staff of £100 and of customers £500.

(v) Hire-purchase interest. This is in respect of the owner's car.

(vi) Repairs and renewals. There is an improvement element of 20% included.

(vii) Bad debts. This is a specific write-off.

(viii) Sundries. Includes £250 cost of obtaining business loan finance, £200 agent's fees to obtain a patent for trading purposes and a £50 'political donation' (in fact a bribe to a local council official).

(ix) Other. The proprietor obtained goods for his own use from the business costing £400 (retail value £500) without payment.

(x) Capital allowances for the year to 30 September 2010 amount to £1,520.

Trading income computation – Year to 30.9.10

		£	£
Profit per the accounts			23,950
Add:			
Repairs – improvement element		200	
Hire-purchase interest (40% private)		100	
Entertainment	note (e)	500	
Motor expenses (40% private)		1,080	
Depreciation		1,000	
Telephone (60% × £150)		90	
Goods for own use		500	
Illegal payment		50	
			3,520
			27,470
Deduct:			
Bank interest received – taxed income		150	
Rent received		500	
Gain on sale of fixed asset		300	
			950
			26,520
Less capital allowances	note (b)		1,520
Trading income profit			£25,000

Notes:

(a) Costs of obtaining loan finance are specifically allowable.

(b) Capital allowances are in all cases deductible as a trading expense (see **6.44**).

(c) The adjusted profit of £25,000 would be subject to the commencement provisions for assessment purposes.

(d) Pre-trading expenses are treated as incurred on the day on which trade is commenced if they are incurred within seven years of the commencement and would have been allowable if incurred after commencement.

(e) All entertainment expenses, other than staff entertaining, are non-deductible.

(f) Expenditure incurred in making a payment which itself constitutes the commission of a criminal offence (or would do if committed in the UK) is specifically disallowed. This includes payments which are contrary to the *Prevention of Corruption Acts*.

Profit adjustments

Overlap relief

6.33 The effect of the rules for taxing business profits using tax years often means that some profits are taxable more than once due to the profits in one accounting period overlapping two tax years. However, the rules for overlap profits ensure that the business is taxed over its life on the actual profits made by providing overlap relief.

Where accounting periods coincide with the tax year throughout the life of the business, overlaps will not occur. The tax year is the year ending 5 April. There are rules to avoid short overlap periods (*ITTOIA 2005, ss 208–210*). For example, if the first accounting date is 31 March, or 1, 2, 3 or 4 April, the accounts are treated as being to 5 April, unless an election is made to the contrary (*ITTOIA 2005, ss 204–207*).

Overlap profit

6.34 An 'overlap profit' is the amount of profit in an accounting period which is taxed in two successive tax years (*ITTOIA 2005, s 204*). Overlap profits can occur:

- as the result of transitional rules when pre-6 April 1994 businesses changed over from the 'preceding year basis' to the 'current year basis';
- due to the rules for taxing the profits of the opening years of a new business; or
- on a change in basis period for taxing the profits following a change of accounting date (*ITTOIA 2005, s 220*).

Overlap profits may arise more than once for different reasons. Where this occurs, those profits are combined to give a single figure.

A record needs to be kept of the amount of any overlap profits and of the overlap period as relief will be provided for these profits as set out below.

Overlap relief

6.35 Overlap relief reduces the profits of the tax year in which it is given. It may convert a profit into a loss, or increase a loss. The relief may be claimed:

- when the business ceases;
- if the business is sold; or
- if the basis period is longer than 12 months due to a change of accounting date.

Overlap losses

6.36 If a loss arises for the overlap period, so as to be included in the computations of two successive tax years, the amount in the second year is excluded from the computation. The loss will be subject to separate loss relief claims and is deemed to be 'nil' for overlap purposes.

Overlap relief – example

6.37

Example 6.5

Geraldine commences trade on 1 September 2007 and prepares accounts to 30 April starting with an eight-month period of account to 30 April 2008. She ceases trading on 31 October 2010, preparing accounts for the six months ending on that date. Her profits (as adjusted for tax purposes and after capital allowances) for the four accounting periods to cessation are as follows:

	£
8 months to 30 April 2008	24,000
Year to 30 April 2009	39,000
Year to 30 April 2010	40,000
6 months to 31 October 2010	22,000
	125,000

Her taxable profits for the four tax years 2007/08 to 2010/11 are as follows:

	Basis period		£	£
2007/08	1.9.07–5.4.08	£24,000 × 7/8		21,000
2008/09	1.9.07–31.8.08:			
	1.9.07–30.4.08		24,000	
	1.5.08–31.8.08	£39,000 × 4/12	13,000	
				37,000
2009/10	Y/e 30.4.09			39,000
2010/11	Y/e 30.4.10		40,000	
	1.5.10–31.10.10		22,000	
			62,000	
	Less overlap profit		34,000	
				28,000
				125,000
Overlap relief accrued				
1.9.07–5.4.08, 7 months				21,000
1.5.08–31.8.08, 4 months				13,000
Total overlap relief accrued				34,000

The business is taxed over its life on its total profits earned of £125,000.

Change of accounting date

6.38 Unless certain conditions are met, HMRC will not recognise a change of accounting date, in which case profits will continue to be taxed for 12-month periods ending on the original accounting date (*ITTOIA 2005, s 198*).

The conditions for a change of accounting date to apply are that:

- the change must be notified to HMRC normally by 31 January following the tax year of change;
- the first accounts to the new accounting date must not exceed 18 months; and
- there has been no change of accounting date in the last five tax years, or HMRC is satisfied that the change is for commercial reasons.

If these conditions are satisfied, or if the change takes place in the second or third tax years of the business, profits are taxed as follows (*ITTOIA 2005, s 200*).

Where the accounting period changes to an earlier date in the tax year

6.39 The basis period for the tax year is the 12 months ending with the new accounting date. The period to the new accounting date will be less than 12 months, so part of the profits in the previous accounting period will be taxed again in the subsequent tax year. These overlap profits should be recorded for a later relief claim (*ITTOIA 2005, s 216*).

Where the accounting period changes to a later date in the tax year

6.40 The basis period for the tax year will be a period of longer than 12 months ending with the new accounting date (*ITTOIA 2005, s 216*).

The profits chargeable will be subject to deduction of any overlap relief previously accrued. The length of the overlap period determines how much relief may be claimed.

The overlap relief deduction is calculated as follows using the following six-step process:

Step 1 – find total overlap profits for all overlap periods;

Step 2 – deduct any overlap relief previously claimed, to arrive at the remaining overlap profit;

Step 3 – find the total number of available overlap days (ie after any overlap days previously claimed);

Step 4 – divide the remaining overlap profit (Step 2) by the available overlap days (Step 3);

Step 5 – deduct the number of days in the tax year from the number of days in the period to the new accounting date; and

Step 6 – multiply the overlap profit in Step 4 by the number of days in Step 5.

Change of accounting date in second year of business

6.41 If the change occurs in the second tax year of a new business, the basis period for the tax year is the 12 months to the new accounting date. If the period from commencement to the new date is less than 12 months, the basis period is the first 12 months of the business (*ITTOIA 2005, ss 214–220*).

Change to an accounting date earlier in the tax year – example

6.42

Example 6.6

Harry has been trading for a number of years, preparing accounts to 31 August. In 2009 he changes his accounting date to 31 May, preparing accounts for the nine months to 31 May 2009. His taxable profits are as follows:

	£
Year ended 31 August 2008	21,500
9 months to 31 May 2009	17,000
Year ended 31 May 2010	23,000

Taxable profits for the years 2008/09 to 2010/11 are as follows:

	Basis period		£	£
2008/09	Y/e 31.8.08			21,500
2009/10	1.6.08–31.5.09:			
	1.6.08–31.8.08	£21,500 × 3/12	5,375	
	1.9.08–31.5.09		17,000	22,375
2010/11	Y/e 31.5.10			23,000
Overlap relief accrued 1.6.08–31.8.08: 3 months				5,375

Change to an accounting date later in the tax year – example

6.43

Example 6.7

Irene has been trading for a number of years, preparing accounts to 30 June. In 1998/99 on the change from the preceding-year to the current-year basis, overlap relief was accrued of £13,500 for an overlap period of nine months. In 2008, she changes her accounting date to 31 December, preparing accounts for the six months to 31 December 2008. Her taxable profits are as follows:

	£
Year ended 30 June 2007	21,500
Year ended 30 June 2008	23,000
6 months to 31 December 2008	12,000
Year ended 31 December 2009	27,000

Taxable profits for the years 2007/08 to 2009/10 are as follows:

	Basis period	£	£
2007/08	Y/e 30.6.07		21,500
2008/09	1.7.07–31.12.08:		
	1.7.07–30.6.08	23,000	
	1.7.08–31.12.08	12,000	
		35,000	
	Deduct overlap relief	9,000	26,000
2009/10	Y/e 31.12.09		27,000
Overlap relief carried forward £13,500 – £9,000			4,500

Utilisation of overlap relief in 2008/09

$$£13{,}500 \times \frac{18-12}{9} = £9000$$

CAPITAL ALLOWANCES

General

6.44 Business profits, after any adjustments for tax purposes (eg depreciation of fixed assets), are reduced by capital allowances to arrive at taxable profit (*CAA 2001, ss 2–6*).

Allowances may be claimed on certain capital expenditure, including (*CAA 2001, ss 393A–393W*):

- plant and machinery;
- industrial buildings (currently being phased out);
- hotels;
- mineral extraction;

- commercial buildings in enterprise zones (to be withdrawn from 6 April 2011);
- agricultural buildings (currently being phased out);
- patent rights and know-how;
- research and development;
- converting space above commercial property into flats for letting; and
- business premises renovation allowance (from 11 April 2007 for a period of five years).

Basis periods

6.45 Capital allowances are treated as a trading expense of the accounting period. This means that they can increase a loss, or turn a profit into a loss (*CAA 2001, s 2*).

Short and long accounting periods

6.46

- If the business accounts are shorter or longer than 12 months, the allowances are generally reduced or increased pro rata on a time basis.
- If the accounts are more than 18 months long, they are divided into separate periods, the first being 12 months long and the subsequent period(s) being 12 months or less to cover the remainder of the long accounting period. The total allowances of each period are then added together and deducted as a trading expense of the whole period.

Time expenditure incurred

6.47 Capital expenditure is generally treated as incurred when the obligation to pay becomes unconditional (eg the invoice or delivery date), whether or not the payment is in whole or part or is required at some later date. However, expenditure is treated as incurred on the date when payment is due where (*CAA 2001, s 5*):

- the credit period for that part of the expenditure exceeds four months;
- an obligation to pay becomes unconditional earlier than usual to bring forward a capital allowances claim.

Where payments for building work are made in stages, ownership may pass at an earlier date (on the issue of an architect's certificate) than the time when the obligation to pay becomes unconditional. In this case, where ownership has passed in one basis period, but the obligation becomes unconditional in the first month of the next period, the expenditure is treated as incurred in the earlier period.

Assets purchased under hire-purchase agreements

6.48 The expenditure is treated as incurred when the asset is brought into use (note that finance charges are not part of the purchase price but are deductible from profits) (*CAA 2001, s 67*).

Time limits, claims and elections

6.49 Claims for capital allowances must be made in the tax return, or amended return and are subject to the same time limits for the return, ie normally by the 31 January filing date following the tax year or, for amendments, normally by 12 months after that filing date (*CAA 2001, s 3*).

Planning point

6.50 There is no need to make a full claim for capital allowances where it is not tax efficient to do so, ie where better use could be made of other available reliefs and allowances. Where reduced claims are made for first-year or writing down allowances for machinery or plant, the allowances would be deferred to a future period. In the case of industrial buildings, the writing down period would be extended. Note, however, that unclaimed agricultural buildings allowances and research and development allowances will usually be lost.

Claim	***Time limit***
Amendment of claim where HMRC enquiries made into the tax return	30 days after settlement of enquiry (provided the original return was submitted by the filing date)
Further claims where assessment made by HMRC under powers of discovery	12 months from end of tax year in which assessment is made
Plant or machinery to be treated as a short-life asset	First anniversary of 31 January next following the tax year in which the chargeable period (in which the expenditure occurs) ends
Transfer of short-life asset to a connected person to be treated as taking place at tax written-down value	Two years from end of chargeable period in which disposal occurs

Claim	***Time limit***
Relief for excess capital allowances of a property income business to be set against other income of the same or following tax year	First anniversary of 31 January next following the tax year in which the chargeable period (in which the excess arises) ends
Plant or machinery which becomes a fixture subject to an equipment lease or energy services agreement to be treated as belonging to the lessor or energy services provider. Election to be made by both lessor/provider and lessee/ client (provided unconnected)	First anniversary of 31 January next following the tax year in which the chargeable period ends
Plant or machinery which becomes a fixture on land which is subsequently let to be treated as belonging to tenant. Election to be made by both lessor and lessee (provided unconnected)	Two years from date on which lease takes effect
Grant of long lease of building to be treated as sale of relevant interest by lessor. Election to be made by both lessor and lessee	Two years from date on which lease takes effect
Succession of trade between connected persons to be ignored in computing capital allowances	Two years from the date of succession
Disposal and acquisition of property between persons, one of which controls the other or both of which are under common control, to be treated as made at the lower of open market value and tax written-down value	Two years from the date of the disposal
Acquisition of relevant interest in capital expenditure on agricultural land and buildings to be treated as a balancing event	First anniversary of 31 January next following the tax year in which the chargeable period ends

Plant and machinery

First-year allowances 2008/09 onwards

6.51 Changes were made to first-year allowances (FYAs) from April 2008. Allowances at the rate of 100% are still available for the following types of expenditure incurred by a business of any size. If full FYAs arc not claimed, writing down allowance (WDA) is normally available at 20% on a reducing balance basis.

Expenditure	*Legislation (CAA 2001)*
Energy-saving plant or machinery	*ss 45A–45C*
Cars with very low CO_2 emissions	*s 45D*
Plant or machinery for certain refuelling stations	*s 45E*
Environmentally beneficial plant or machinery	*ss 45H–45J*

No first-year allowances are available, for a business of any size, for:

- expenditure incurred in the final chargeable period;
- cars (other than those with very low CO_2 emissions);
- certain ships and railway assets;
- long-life assets;
- plant or machinery for leasing;
- in certain anti-avoidance cases where the obtaining of a FYA is linked to a change in the nature or conduct of a trade;
- where an asset was initially acquired for purposes other than those of the qualifying activity;
- where an asset was acquired by way of a gift; and
- where plant or machinery that was provided for long funding leasing starts to be used for other purposes.

Temporary first-year allowances 2009/10

6.52 First-year allowances of 40% were given on a temporary basis for expenditure incurred in the year to 5 April 2010 (31 March 2010 for companies) (*FA 2009, s 24*).

Writing down allowances

6.53

Writing down allowances (WDAs) (CAA 2001, s 56) – 2010/11 rates	
Standard WDAs	20%
Long life assets	10%
Overseas leasing	10%
Integral features	10%
Cars	Main rate cars – those with emissions of up to 160g/km – 20% Cars with higher emissions – special rate pool – 10%

For 2008/09 onwards, WDAs of 20% per annum (25% prior to 2008/09) may be claimed on a reducing balance basis. The allowance is given on the amount of a 'pool' of unrelieved expenditure (or written-down value) brought forward from earlier periods after adding eligible expenditure during the period and deducting the proceeds on disposals (or original cost if lower) during the period.

A hybrid rate applies for chargeable periods straddling the date of change in rates from 25% to 20% (6 April 2008). So, for example, a business with a 31 December year end will have a hybrid rate of 21.25% for the year to 31 December 2008, calculated as three months at 25% and nine months at 20%.

Integral features

6.54 The following assets qualify as integral features:

- electrical systems (including lighting systems);
- cold water systems;
- space or water heating systems, powered systems of ventilation, air cooling or air purification, and any floor or ceiling comprised in such systems;
- lifts, escalators and moving walkways; and
- external solar shading.

Expenditure on thermal insulation and long-life assets is also allocated to the 'special rate' pool (see **6.60**).

Annual investment allowance (AIA)

6.55 An annual investment allowance was introduced for the first £50,000 of a business's expenditure on most plant and machinery where the expenditure was incurred on or after 6 April 2008. This limit was increased to £100,000 for expenditure incurred from 1 or 6 April 2010 (for corporation tax and income tax respectively) (*FA 2010, s 5(1)*). The AIA applies to businesses regardless of size and can be applied to expenditure on long-life assets and integral features as well as on general plant and machinery, but not on cars. Expenditure over the AIA limit will be dealt with within the normal capital allowances regime.

The term 'car' was specifically defined, until April 2009, to include a motorcycle, so no AIAs were given for expenditure on motorcycles. However, the definition was amended, broadly from April 2009, to exclude a motorcycle (*CAA 2001, s 268A*). It follows, therefore, that AIAs are available for expenditure on motorcycles from (broadly) 6 April 2009.

For a period of account more or less than six months, the AIA is proportionately increased or reduced.

Assets classified as plant and machinery

6.56 The terms 'plant' and 'machinery' are not defined in the legislation. 'Machinery' is therefore given its ordinary meaning (but includes such items as cars and ships). The uncertainty as to what constitutes 'plant' has resulted in a large number of court cases over the years. Broadly, it is necessary to distinguish between:

- assets used to carry on a business (which will generally be plant); and
- the setting in which that business is carried on (which usually will not).

When the business ceases

6.57 When the business ceases, no first-year or writing down allowances can be claimed in a period in which the business ceases.

Balancing adjustments

6.58

- A 'balancing allowance' is given if the sale proceeds are less than the balance of unrelieved expenditure (although, where assets are 'pooled' together, a balancing allowance only arises when the business ceases).
- A 'balancing charge' arises where disposal proceeds exceed the pool balance, so that capital allowances previously given are clawed back. However, if the proceeds exceed original cost, the excess is generally subject to capital gains tax rules. The charge is treated as an addition to profits (or a reduction in losses).

Assets pools

6.59 All qualifying expenditure on plant and machinery is included in a single 'main' pool, except in certain cases where separate pools must be maintained, including the following (*CAA 2001, ss 53–54*).

From 6 April 2008, businesses can claim a writing down allowance of up to £1,000 for each pool, where the balance of unrelieved expenditure in a general capital allowances pool, or the special rate pool (see below), has fallen below £1,000 (*FA 2008, s 81*, inserting *CAA 2001, s 56A*).

Special rate pool

6.60 Since 6 April 2008, a new special rate pool applies to certain plant and machinery. With effect from that date, expenditure on long-life assets, thermal insulation and integral features is allocated to the new special rate pool and the rate of WDA applicable to that pool is 10% per annum on a reducing balance basis (*FA 2008*, s *82* and *Sch 26*).

Cars

6.61 The tax rules granting relief for business expenditure on cars were changed quite significantly from April 2009. Formerly, the amount of relief claimable was based on the cost of the vehicle. From April 2009, the rate of relief is determined primarily by the level of engine emissions.

There is a new definition of a car for capital allowance purposes (*CAA 2001, s 268A*). Until April 2009, a car was specifically defined to include a motorcycle, so no AIAs were given for expenditure on motorcycles. However, this definition was amended (broadly from April 2009) to exclude a motorcycle.

6.62 The main features of the rules, which apply from April 2009, are as follows:

- The previous concept of 'expensive' cars is abolished, and the rate of tax relief is now based on the level of the vehicle's CO_2 emissions.
- Qualifying expenditure incurred from April 2009 is normally allocated to one of the two main pools for plant and machinery. Expenditure on 'main rate cars' (broadly, those with emissions of up to 160g/km) goes into the main plant and machinery pool, attracting allowances at 20%. Cars with higher emissions qualify for allowances at 10% in the 'special rate' pool.
- Cars with private use are kept in a single asset pool, but the rate at which allowances are given is still determined by reference to emissions.
- For cars purchased before April 2009, allowances are normally calculated according to principles applying up to that date, although complex transitional provisions exist.
- Car leases that began before 6 April 2009 generally continue to be subject to the former rules. For new leases of vehicles above the 160g/km threshold, a flat rate disallowance is made, calculated as 15% of 'relevant payments'. New cars with lower emissions will not be affected by the disallowance rules.
- Certain hire cars (eg taxis) that were formerly exempt from the restrictions for expensive cars are subject to the new rules from April

2009. Conversely, motorcycles were previously classified as cars for capital allowance purposes but are excluded from the definition from April 2009.

- The 100% first-year allowance for cars with very low emissions continues unchanged (see **6.63**).

Cars with very low CO_2 emissions

6.63 100% FYAs are available to all businesses that purchase new cars with CO_2 emissions not exceeding 110g/km (120g/km prior to 6 April 2008) driven. The scheme was due to end on 31 March 2008, but *FA 2008, s 77* extended the scheme for an additional five years until 31 March 2013.

Low emission cars are not subject to the former special rules for cars costing over £12,000 (which were abolished from 6 April 2009). *FA 2008* contained a transitional rule to ensure that lessees who entered into contracts to lease cars that qualified as low CO_2 emission cars before 6 April 2008 did not find mid-lease that, as a result of the change to the definition of a low CO_2 emissions car, their cars no longer qualified as such. The rule ensures that payments on leases in existence on 31 March 2008 for cars costing over £12,000 with CO_2 emissions above the new threshold, but below the previous threshold (ie between 110g/km and 120g/km), are not subject to the restriction for the period on and after 1 April 2008 until the expiry of the lease.

Areas designated as enterprise zones

6.64 Designations apply for ten years from the commencement date.

Construction expenditure will qualify for the special industrial buildings allowance (IBA) if it is qualifying expenditure on a site in an enterprise zone. It must be incurred within ten years of the designation of the zone, or within 20 years if it is incurred under a contract that was entered into within ten years of the designation.

Area	*Commencement date*
Dearne Valley	3 November 1995
East Midlands (North East Derbyshire)	3 November 1995
East Midlands (Bassetlaw)	16 November 1995
East Midlands (Ashfield)	21 November 1995
East Durham	29 November 1995
Tyne Riverside (North Tyneside)	19 February 1996
Tyne Riverside (North and South Tyneside)	21 October 1996

Enterprise zone allowances are to be withdrawn immediately from 6 April 2011.

Short-life assets (on election by the taxpayer)

6.65 'Short-life assets' are qualifying assets which are expected to be disposed of within five years. Where the asset is disposed of within four years from the end of the accounting period in which it was acquired, a balancing allowance can be obtained (or a balancing charge made). If the asset is still held at the end of that period, the tax written-down value is transferred to the main pool (*CAA 2001, ss 83–89*).

Long-life assets

6.66 'Long-life assets' are plant and machinery with an expected useful life of 25 years when new. Such assets normally only qualify for writing down allowances of 10% (6% prior to 2008/09), instead of the usual 20% (25% prior to 2008/09). The long-life asset rules do not generally apply where the total expenditure incurred during the period is less than £100,000. In addition, the provisions do not apply to certain types of asset including motor cars, or to plant and machinery in a dwelling house, retail shop, showroom, hotel or office (*CAA 2001, ss 90–104*).

Private use assets

6.67 There is a restriction in allowances if a sole trader or partner uses an asset partly for private use. Allowances are calculated and deducted from costs as normal, but only the business proportion of the allowances are allowed as a trading expense (*CAA 2001, ss 205–208*).

Assets leased to non-residents

6.68 Certain assets leased to non-residents who do not use them in a UK trade attract writing down allowances of only 10% and are subject to balancing charges and allowances (*CAA 2001, ss 107, 109*).

Connected persons

6.69 Where an asset is sold to a 'connected person' for use other than in a business, the sale proceeds are usually to be taken as the open market value. First-year allowances cannot be claimed on transactions between connected persons. A 'connected person' includes a spouse, certain close relatives, business partners, companies under common control, etc. On the succession of a business by a connected person (eg a business incorporation), an election can be made to substitute open market value with the asset's tax value if appropriate (*CAA 2001, ss 214, 217–218*).

Industrial buildings

6.70 Industrial buildings allowances (IBAs) are currently being phased out and will be abolished completely from April 2011 (*FA 2007, s 36*). To prepare the way for final abolition, most balancing adjustments, and the recalculation of writing down allowances on sale, were effectively withdrawn from 21 March 2007.

Industrial buildings are generally those used for the purposes of a qualifying trade (*CAA 2001, s 271*), such as:

- manufacture or processing of goods or materials;
- maintenance or repair of goods or materials used in the qualifying trade;
- storage of certain goods and materials, ie raw materials for manufacture or processing, or goods awaiting delivery to purchasers or storage on arrival in the UK from abroad; and
- undertakings concerned with water, sewerage, electricity, hydraulic power, tunnels, bridges, highways, mines, agricultural operations or fishing.

Dwelling houses, retail shops, showrooms, hotels, offices and buildings used for ancillary purposes are specifically excluded but hotels qualify for allowances under a separate heading. If an industrial building contains a non-industrial part (eg an office) allowances can only be claimed on the industrial part, unless the cost of the non-industrial part does not exceed 25%, in which case allowances are available on the whole building (*CAA 2001, ss 274, 277, 309–313*).

Qualifying expenditure on the construction of a building includes the cost of preparing, cutting, tunnelling or levelling land, but excludes the cost of the land itself (*CAA 2001, ss 292–297*).

New buildings and additional expenditure

6.71 Prior to 2008/09, where a building was new or bought from the builder, or where new capital expenditure was incurred on an existing building, writing down allowances were available at a flat rate of 4% per annum on cost commencing in the period the building was brought into use. From 2008/09 the rate is reduced to 3% and it will reduce by a further 1% each year, until the allowances are finally withdrawn from 6 April 2011.

Allowances may be claimed during periods of temporary disuse, but no allowances may be claimed if the building is in use for non-industrial purposes at the end of the period (*CAA 2001, ss 283–285*).

The allowance is increased or decreased for periods of more or less than a year.

Sale of the building

6.72 Prior to 21 March 2007, if the building was sold before the end of its 25-year tax life, a balancing adjustment arose on the difference between the sale proceeds and the unrelieved expenditure, any charge being restricted to the total allowances given. Where the building sold was not in industrial use throughout the ownership period and the proceeds were less than the capital expenditure, special rules restricted the balancing allowance for the period of non-industrial use. A balancing charge could result from applying this restriction.

Providing the building is used for a qualifying business, the purchaser can claim allowances on the lower of the cost of the building or the amount paid (providing there has been no period of non-industrial use), spread evenly over the remaining tax life of the building. If there has been a period of non-industrial use, the purchaser's allowance is generally based on the seller's residue of qualifying expenditure before the sale plus, prior to 21 March 2007, any balancing charge or less any balancing allowance (or the price paid for the building, if lower).

Balancing adjustments – from 21 March 2007

6.73 To prepare the way for the final abolition of industrial buildings allowance in 2011 (*FA 2007, s 36*), balancing adjustments and the recalculation of writing down allowances (WDAs) are withdrawn in respect of most balancing events occurring on or after 21 March 2007.

When a person ceases to have the relevant interest in an industrial (or agricultural) building (typically when the building is sold or a leasehold interest comes to an end), there is a balancing event. For the years up to and including 2007/08, this normally gives rise to a balancing adjustment based on any difference between the residue of qualifying expenditure ('RQE' – the cost less allowances claimed) and the proceeds from the event. Broadly, there will be a balancing allowance where the sale proceeds are less than RQE, and a balancing charge where the sales proceeds exceed RQE.

Prior to the date of change, the new owner on a purchase within 25 years of first use of an industrial building was entitled to a recalculated WDA. The recalculated WDA is based on the RQE after the sale, divided by the length of time between the date of sale and the end of the period of 25 years.

The *FA 2007* provisions withdraw balancing adjustments and the recalculation of writing down allowances in respect of balancing events occurring on or after 21 March 2007, unless:

- in pursuance of a relevant pre-commencement contract; or
- in respect of qualifying enterprise zone expenditure.

For the new holder of the relevant interest, the WDAs will be based on the previous owner's RQE.

Transitional provisions apply. A contract is a 'relevant pre-commencement contract' if it was:

- in writing and made before 21 March 2007;
- unconditional, or its conditions were satisfied before that date;
- no terms remained to be agreed on or after that date; and
- the contract was not varied in a significant way on or after that date.

Industrial building – example

6.74

Example 6.8

In December 1993, David bought a new building for his furniture-making business at the cost of £250,000 (including £50,000 for the land). In 1996 he had an extension built costing £150,000. This was to accommodate office space for administration and it virtually doubled the building's size. In October 2001 a new roof had to be built for the original part of the building at the cost of £20,000.

The building is sold in November 2006 for:

(a) £360,000 (including £60,000 for the land);

(b) £260,000 (including £60,000 for the land);

(c) £160,000 (including £60,000 for the land).

Allowances have been claimed to 2005/06 as follows:

	£
1993/94 to 2005/06, £200,000 @ 4% × 13 years	104,000
2001/02 to 2005/06, £20,000 @ 4% × 5 years	4,000
	108,000

The balancing adjustment in 2006/07 is as follows:

	(a)	(b)	(c)
	£	£	£
Sales proceeds (building)	300,000	200,000	100,000
Building cost	220,000	220,000	220,000
Cost of owning building		20,000	120,000
Allowances claimed	108,000	108,000	108,000
Balancing allowance/(charge)	(108,000)	(88,000)	12,000

The purchaser would get relief as follows:

	(a)	(b)	(c)
	£	£	£
Cost of building to purchaser	300,000	200,000	100,000
Restricted to original cost where lower than purchase price	220,000		
Annual allowance 1/12th*	18,333	16,667	8,333

**12 years remaining of a 25-year life, ignoring fractions of a year for purposes of illustration.*

The extension built in 1996 would not qualify for capital allowances as it relates to a non-industrial part of the building and exceeds 25% of the total cost. The size of the extension in this case is irrelevant. If the new building had originally included the administration offices, the size in terms of their area could have been used as a basis to calculate the proportion of the original costs allocated to them in the absence of a detailed breakdown of costs provided by the builders.

Flat conversion allowance

6.75 The introduction of a 'flat conversion allowance' (*FA 2001, s 67* and *Sch 19*) was part of a package of measures designed to encourage the regeneration of Britain's towns and cities and builds on recommendations made by the Urban Task Force in its report *Towards an Urban Renaissance*. In particular, it is intended to encourage expenditure on the conversion of disused business property for residential use.

The allowance applies in respect of expenditure incurred on or after 11 May 2001. Broadly, a 100% initial allowance will be available to certain property owners for the costs of converting redundant space over shops or offices into flats for letting (*CAA 2001, s 393A et seq*).

The scheme is very like the industrial buildings allowance (IBA) scheme (see **6.70**), in that flat conversion allowances (FCAs) can be claimed by the person that holds the relevant interest, and there is a balancing adjustment if the relevant interest is sold or the flat ceases to be held for letting out. There are, however, some differences:

- Where there is a transfer of the relevant interest, there is a recovery of allowances given, but the person to whom the relevant interest is transferred cannot claim FCAs.
- The allowances are not recovered if an event takes place more than seven years from the time the flat is suitable for letting.

Qualifying properties

6.76 In order to qualify, the property must have been built before 1980 and must not have more than five floors in total. An attic counts towards this total if it can be lived in. The ground floor must be for authorised business use and the storeys above must be primarily constructed as dwellings. In addition, it must appear that, when the property was constructed, the floors above the ground floor were primarily for residential use (*CAA 2001, s 393C*).

The upper floors must either be unoccupied or used for storage only in the year before conversion. Finally, at the time of conversion, the whole or greater part of the ground floor must be rated as follows:

- A1 retail shops;
- A2 financial and professional services;
- A3 food and drink;
- B1 other offices including R&D which can be carried out in residential areas; or
- D1 (A) medical, eg doctors' surgery or dental practice.

Qualifying flats

6.77 The conversion must take place within the existing boundaries of the building, except as is required to provide access to the new flats. Each flat must be self-contained with external access separate from the ground-floor premises. Each flat, which can be on more than one floor, must have no more than four rooms excluding kitchen, bathroom, cloakroom and hallways. It must be held for the purpose of short-term letting (not more than five years) and not let to a person connected with the person who incurs the expenditure on conversion.

The flat must not be a high-value flat, ie a flat that when completed and let furnished on a short-hold tenancy would expect to obtain a rent in excess of:

No of Rooms	Greater London	Elsewhere
1 or 2	£350 per week	£150 per week
3	£425 per week	£225 per week
4	£480 per week	£300 per week

Qualifying expenditure

6.78 Qualifying expenditure is capital expenditure incurred on, or in connection, with the conversion of part of a qualifying building into a qualifying flat, or the renovation of a flat in a qualifying building to create a qualifying flat, or repairs incidental to the conversion or renovation of a qualifying flat, or the provision of access to a qualifying flat. The part of the building on which the expenditure was incurred must have been unused or used only for storage for the year before the work begins (*CAA 2001, s 393B*).

Examples of qualifying expenditure are the costs of dividing a single property to create a number of separate flats, and the costs of building dividing walls or installing a new kitchen or bathroom. Capital repairs to the property incidental to the conversion or renovation may also qualify.

Expenditure on repairs may be treated as qualifying expenditure if it cannot be deducted in calculating business profits. Expenditure incurred in connection with the conversion or renovation of a flat may include costs outside the direct boundary of the new or renovated flat such as the creation of stairwells within the building or provision of extension, solely to provide access to the new flats. It may also include architect's and surveyor's fees. Examples of associated costs that may qualify are:

- inserting or removing walls, windows or doors;
- installing and upgrading plumbing, gas, electricity or central heating;
- re-roofing incidental to the conversion/renovation;
- providing access to the flat(s) separate from the commercial premises, including extensions to the building to contain this access, if required; and
- providing external fire escapes where regulations require.

Some expenditure does not qualify for FCAs. Expenditure does not qualify if it is incurred on or in connection with:

- the acquisition of land or rights in or over land;
- an extension to the building (unless it is required to give access to a qualifying flat);

- the development of land adjoining or adjacent to the building. This includes conversions forming part of a larger scheme of development; and
- the provision of furnishings or other chattels.

Allowances

6.79 The person incurring the qualifying expenditure is entitled to an initial allowance of up to 100% in the chargeable period in which the qualifying expenditure is incurred. The initial allowance will be withdrawn if the flat fails to qualify or is sold before first let (*CAA 2001, ss 393H, 393I*; *TCGA 1992, s 41*).

A balancing charge will arise if the flat is sold, a long lease is granted (a lease exceeding 50 years), the person who incurred the qualifying expenditure dies, the flat is demolished or destroyed, or the flat ceases to be a qualifying flat. No balancing adjustment is made if the balancing event occurs more than seven years after the time when the flat was first available for letting (*CAA 2001, ss 393J, 393K, 393L*).

On any amount not claimed as initial allowance there will be a writing down allowance of 25% per annum of the original qualifying expenditure. This again can be reduced to a specified amount.

Allowances will also be granted if the interest is acquired on the completion of the conversion, ie a person who incurs expenditure on conversion and is entitled to a relevant interest in the flat on completion of conversion is treated as having the same interest when the expenditure was incurred.

No capital allowances are available to the purchaser or assignee of a qualifying flat. Allowances can only be claimed by the person who incurred the qualifying expenditure.

The allowance will primarily be given against property business income of the period. If no property business income arises then it will be an allowance of a deemed property business source. If the result of the claim is a property business loss for an individual, then those losses can only be carried forward to set against later property business income only.

By contrast, if a company incurs a property business income loss it may be relieved against total profits of the same accounting period, surrendered by way of group relief, and any unrelieved balance carried forward to set against future total profits.

Business premises renovation allowance

6.80 From 11 April 2007, 100% business premises renovation allowances (BPRAs) will be available on qualifying expenditure incurred on the renovation of business properties that have been vacant for at least one year, in designated disadvantaged areas of the UK (*CAA 2001, Pt 3A*; *SI 2007/949*).

Since the scheme was first announced in *FA 2005* (*FA 2005, s 92* and *Sch 6*), two changes have been made (*SI 2007/945*). First, disadvantaged areas are now defined as Northern Ireland and the areas specified as development areas by the *Assisted Areas Order 2007*. Secondly, excluded from scheme are any premises that are refurbished by, or used by, businesses engaged in the following trades:

- fisheries and aquaculture;
- shipbuilding;
- the coal industry;
- the steel industry;
- synthetic fibres;
- the primary production of certain agricultural products; and
- the manufacture of products which imitate or substitute for milk or milk products.

There will be a clawback of relief if, within seven years of the premises being made available for letting, there is a sale, grant of a long lease or demolition or destruction of the premises. It is likely that this relief will only be available for a period of five years.

Anti-avoidance provisions apply in connection with sales where the control test is met, or the sale has been artificially arranged in order to obtain a tax advantage (*CAA 2001, s 568*); and sales where as part of a tax avoidance scheme, the proceeds are less than they would be on the open market (*CAA 2001, ss 325, 357, 570A*).

LOSSES

General

6.81 Business losses are generally calculated in the same way and using the same basis periods as business profits. Relief for trading losses may be obtained by (*ITA 2007, Pt 4*):

- set-off against other income in the same or preceding tax year (*s 64*), subject to a temporary extension to three years from 22 April 2009 (see **6.84**);

- carry-forward against subsequent profits of the same trade (*s 83*);
- carry-back in the early years of a trade (*s 72*);
- set-off against capital gains of the same or preceding tax year (*s 71*); or
- carry-back of a terminal loss (*s 89*).

Restrictions

6.82 From 12 March 2008, loss relief is restricted for individuals who carry on a trade but spend an average of less than ten hours a week on commercial activities. This measure is designed to counteract the use of contrived arrangements that generate trade losses which may be claimed as sideways relief or capital gains relief ('sideways loss relief'), by an individual, other than a partner, carrying on a trade in a non-active capacity.

Where a loss arises to an individual carrying on a trade in a non-active capacity as a result of tax avoidance arrangements made on or after 12 March 2008, no sideways loss relief will be available for that loss. Otherwise, there will be an annual limit of £25,000 on the total amount of sideways loss relief that an individual may claim from trades carried on in a non-active capacity (*FA 2008, s 60* and *Sch 21*).

Transitional rules will apply to the computation of losses subject to the annual limit where these arise for an individual's basis period which begins before 12 March 2008 and ends on or after that date.

Losses set against total income (s 64 relief)

6.83 Providing the trade is carried on with a view to making a profit on a commercial basis, a sole trader or partner may claim relief for the trading loss of a tax year (*ITA 2007, s 64*):

- against his total income of that tax year; and/or
- the preceding tax year (but see **6.84** regarding a temporary extension to this rule),

in any order.

Where a claim is made to relieve profits in one basis period by losses of both the same basis period and a subsequent period, the claim for the loss in the same period takes precedence.

Where basis periods overlap, and a loss would otherwise fall to be included in the computations for two successive tax years (eg in the opening years of a business), it is taken into account only in the first of those years.

Relief is not normally available for farming and market gardening losses, where losses were also incurred in the previous five years (calculated before capital allowances).

Temporary extension to carry-back rule

6.84 Originally announced in the 2008 Pre-Budget Report, the period for which companies and unincorporated business making trading losses (including losses from professions and vocations) can be carried back against earlier profits is extended from one year to three years, with losses being carried back against later years first. The extended carry-back period applies to trading losses incurred by unincorporated businesses in the tax years 2008/09 and 2009/10.

After losses have been carried back to the previous year, a maximum of £50,000 will be available to carry back to the earlier two years. A separate £50,000 limit applies to tax years within the duration of the extension. This means that a separate £50,000 cap applies to the extended carry back of losses incurred in each of the tax years 2008/09 and 2009/10 (*FA 2009, s 23* and *Sch 6*).

Losses set against gains (s 71 relief)

6.85 A claim for loss relief (under *s 64*) against total income of a tax year may be extended to capital gains, for the tax year of the loss and/or the previous year (*ITA 2007, s 71*).

- The trading loss must first be relieved against other income for the year of claim, and is also reduced by any other relief (eg under *s 72* – see below) already claimed in respect of the loss.
- The maximum capital gains available for relief is the amount of net gains (ie after deducting capital losses of the same year and losses brought forward from earlier years).
- The trading loss is treated as an allowable capital loss of the current year, and relief is therefore given against the capital gains available for relief, before capital losses brought forward.

From 2004/05 to 2007/08 (and for 2002/03 and 2003/04 by election), the maximum trading losses available for relief equal the gains before taper relief and the annual exemption (not after taper relief, as is otherwise the case) (*FA 2002, s 48*).

Losses carried forward (s 83 relief)

6.86 Any trading losses not otherwise relievable may be carried forward without time limit and set off against the first available profits of the same business carried on by the same owner in subsequent years.

Where a business is incorporated (ie transferred to a company), any unrelieved losses of the business may be carried forward and set off against the former sole trader's or partner's first available income derived from the company, first against earned income (director's salary, benefits, etc), then against investment income (dividends or interest from the company). The relief is available where the proceeds for the business consisted mainly of the issue of shares (more than 80% of which are retained), and provided the company continued the trade (*ITA 2007, s 83*; Business Income Manual BIM75500).

Losses in early years of trade (s 72 relief)

6.87 A loss incurred in any of the first four tax years of a new business may be carried back against the sole trader's or partner's total income of the three previous tax years, starting with the earliest year (*ITA 2007, s 72*). The relief must be set off to the maximum possible extent against all three tax years. It is not possible to restrict the claim to a particular year.

Relief is not available unless the trade is operated on a commercial basis, in such a way that a profit could be expected in that period within a reasonable time thereafter. In practice, this may be difficult to prove in the case of a new business and a viable business plan may be necessary to support a carry-back claim.

Terminal loss relief (s 89 relief)

6.88 Relief may be claimed for a loss incurred in the final 12 months of trading to be set against the trading income of the tax year in which the business permanently ceases and the three previous years, starting with the latest year. Capital allowances are treated as an expense in computing the loss (*ITA 2007, s 89*).

The terminal loss is calculated in two parts:

- the unrelieved trading loss of the tax year in which the business ceases (ie from 6 April to the date of cessation); and
- the unrelieved trading loss from a date 12 months before cessation, up to the following 5 April.

Profits must be taken into account in calculating the figures for each part but where the amount calculated in either part is a profit it is treated as nil.

The terminal loss may be increased by any unrelieved trade charges, and also by any available overlap relief (without restriction).

Losses in early years of trade – example

6.89

Example 6.9

Edna commences to trade on 1 December 2007, preparing accounts to 30 November. The first four years of trading produce losses of £12,000, £9,000, £2,000 and £1,000 respectively (after being adjusted for tax purposes and after taking account of capital allowances). For each of the four years of assessment 2004/05 to 2007/08, Edna had other income of £8,000.

The losses for tax purposes are as follows:

	£	£
2007/08 (1.12.07–5.4.08) (£12,000 × 4/12)		4,000
2008/09 (y/e 30.11.08)	12,000	
Less already allocated to 2007/08	4,000	
		8,000
2009/10 (y/e 30.11.09)		9,000
2010/11 (y/e 30.11.10)		2,000
2011/12 (y/e 30.11.11) note (b)		1,000

Loss relief for early losses is available as follows:

	2007/08	2008/09	2009/10	2010/11
	£	£	£	£
Losses available	4,000	8,000	9,000	2,000
Set against total income				
2004/05	4,000			
2005/06		8,000		
2006/07			8,000	
2007/08			1,000	2,000
	4,000	8,000	9,000	2,000

Revised total income is thus £4,000 for 2004/05, nil for 2005/06 and 2006/07, and £5,000 for 2007/08.

Notes:

(a) Where part of any loss would otherwise fall to be included in the computations for two successive tax years (as is the case for 2007/08 and 2008/09 in this example), that part is excluded from the computation for the second of those years.

(b) The loss for the year ended 30 November 2011 in this example is not available for relief for early year losses (*s 72* relief) as it does not fall into the first four tax years of the business even though it is incurred in the first four years of trading. It is of course available for the alternative reliefs, ie offset against total income of the same or preceding tax year (*s 64* relief) (depending on other income for 2010/11 and 2011/12) or carry-forward against profits of the same trade.

Terminal losses – example

6.90

Example 6.10

Frank, a trader with a 30 September year end, ceases to trade on 30 June 2010. Tax-adjusted results for his last two accounting periods are as follows:

	Profit/(loss)
	£
Year ended 30 September 2009	30,000
9 months to 30 June 2010	(9,000)

Frank has overlap reliefs brought forward of £2,000.

The terminal loss available is as follows:

			£	£
2010/11	(6.4.10 to 30.6.10)			
	(£9,000 + £2,000) × 3/9			3,667
2009/10	(1.7.09 to 5.4.10)			
	1.10.09 to 5.4.10	£11,000 × 6/9	7,333	
	1.7.09 to 30.9.09	(£30,000) × 3/12	(7,500)	
			(167)	—
Terminal loss				£3,667

In determining the part of a terminal loss arising in a part of the final 12 months (the terminal loss period) that falls into any one year of assessment, a profit made in that period must be netted off against a loss in that period. In this example, no net loss is incurred in that part of the terminal loss period falling in 2009/10. However, the two different years of assessment are looked at separately, so that the 'net profit' of £167 falling within 2009/10 does not have to be netted off against the 2010/11 loss and is instead treated as nil.

The £7,333 losses which cannot form part of the terminal loss claim may be claimed under the alternative *s 64* relief for offset against total income of the same or preceding tax year. In practice, where other income is sufficient, the whole of the £11,000 would in many cases be claimed under *s 64* relief in preference to terminal loss relief.

Time limits for claims

6.91

Claim	*Time limit*
Set-off against income or gains of the same or preceding tax year (*s 64*)	Anniversary from 31 January after end of tax year in which loss occurs
Set-off losses in early years of trade against three previous tax years (*s 72*)	Anniversary from 31 January after end of tax year in which loss occurs
Carry-forward against future profits of the same trade (*s 83*)	Five years from 31 January after end of tax year in which loss occurs
Carry-back of terminal losses (*s 89*)	Five years from 31 January after end of tax year in which loss occurs

NIC FOR THE SELF-EMPLOYED

National Insurance contributions

6.92 Self-employed earners (ie sole traders or partners) over the age of 16 and below state retirement age are liable to both Class 2 and Class 4 National Insurance contributions unless specifically excepted (*SSCBA 1992, ss 11, 15*; *SI 2001/1004, regs 45, 87, 94, 100*).

Class 2 contributions

6.93 Class 2 contributions are payable at a flat weekly rate (see **6.96**). Self-employed individuals with small earnings may apply for a certificate of exemption from paying Class 2 contributions if net earnings for the tax year are below a specified limit or if earnings for the previous tax year were below the limit for that year and there has been no material change in circumstances.

For these purposes, 'net earnings' are the profits of the business, as shown in the profit and loss account. If an individual has more than one self-employment, the profits (and losses) of each business are added together to arrive at earnings.

The newly self-employed must notify their liability to pay Class 2 contributions to HMRC. A new penalties regime applies for failure to notify chargeability from 1 April 2010 (see **6.17**).

Class 4 contributions

6.94 Class 4 contributions are payable on the profits of a trade, profession or vocation at a main percentage rate between a lower and upper profits limit, and at an additional rate on profits above that upper limit. The income tax and Class 4 contributions of a self-employed individual are collected together under self-assessment.

'Profits' for Class 4 purposes are generally calculated in the same way as for income tax. However, where trading losses have been relieved against other income or gains, they may nevertheless be carried forward and deducted from future profits for the purposes of computing the Class 4 liability.

If the taxpayer has more than one self-employment, the profits of each business are aggregated to calculate the Class 4 liability. Individual business partners are each liable to Class 4 contributions on their profit shares.

Maximum contributions at the main rate

6.95 An individual who is both self-employed and employed is liable to pay Class 1, 2 and 4 contributions. The overall maximum for contributions at the main rate is based on 53 times the maximum weekly Class 1 contributions at the main rate.

The liability for Class 4 contributions at the main rate cannot exceed a maximum based on 53 times the weekly Class 2 contributions plus the maximum Class 4 contributions paid at the main rate.

Class 4 contributions above that limit are payable at the additional rate. A claim for repayment of contributions may be made in appropriate circumstances, and additionally, where contributions are expected to exceed the maximum amount at the main rate, an application to defer payment of contributions can be made.

Rates and exemptions

6.96

	2008/09	2009/10	2010/11
Class 2 contributions			
Flat rate	£2.30 a week	£2.40 a week	£2.40 a week
Small earnings exception	£4,825 a year	£5,075 a year	£5,075 a year
Annual maximum payable	£119.60	£124.80	£124.80

Exempt for:

- men over 65 and women over 60;
- married women who elected before 12 May 1977 to pay reduced rate Class 1 or no Class 2 NICs (provided election not revoked by divorce or widowhood);
- someone not 'ordinarily self-employed' with small earnings from self-employment who does not therefore need to apply for a certificate of exemption;
- someone who is incapable of work, in legal custody or prison, or is receiving incapacity benefit or maternity allowance for a full week; and
- someone receiving invalid care allowance for any one day in a week.

	2008/09	2009/10	2010/11
Class 3 voluntary contributions	£8.10 a week	£12.05 a week	£12.05 a week

May be paid by those who would otherwise not have paid sufficient contributions to earn a full state pension.

	2008/09	2009/10	2010/11
Class 4 contributions			
Percentage rate up to upper annual limit	8%	8%	8%
Percentage rate above upper annual limit	1%	1%	1%
Lower annual limit	£5,435	£5,715	£5,715
Upper annual limit	£40,040	£43,875	£43,875

Exempt for:

- men over 65 and women over 60 at the start of the tax year;
- someone who is 16 at the start of the tax year and holds a certificate of exemption for that year;

- someone not 'ordinarily self-employed' with small earnings from self-employment who does not therefore need to apply for a certificate of exemption;
- someone not resident in the UK for income tax purposes;
- 'sleeping partners' who receive a share of profits but take no part in actively running the business;
- trustees and executors chargeable to income tax on income received on behalf of others (eg incapacitated persons); and
- divers and diving supervisors employed in the UK to exploit the sea-bed.

SOLE TRADER OR PARTNERSHIP?

Partnerships

6.97 Although, under the law of England and Wales, a partnership is not a separate legal person, it is treated as a separate entity for tax purposes (*ITTOIA 2005, ss 848–850*; *TMA 1970, s 42*). Within the partnership, entitlement to shares of profits and losses between the separate legal persons, the partners, is regulated by the partnership agreement. Their relationship with third parties is governed principally by the *Partnership Act 1890*. It makes partners responsible jointly for the debts and losses of the firm. Like sole traders, partners have no protection from creditors; their private assets are available to creditors for the payment of business debts. In Scotland a partnership is a separate legal person but this distinction is not important for tax purposes.

A partnership may be 'limited' (by the *Limited Partnerships Act 1907*). A limited partnership is one that has one or more limited partners. Limited partners are liable for the debts of the firm only up to the amount of the capital they have contributed. Both individuals and companies may be limited partners. Being a limited partner has implications for tax, particularly in restricting the amount of loss relief. Every partnership with limited partners must also contain at least one general partner, liable in full for the debts of the firm. Every limited partnership must register with the Registrar (who is the Registrar of Companies). Without registration a limited partnership becomes a general partnership.

In addition to full or general partners, who have unrestricted liability, and limited partners, there are two other types of partner, as follows:

(1) sleeping partners – a sleeping partner is one who plays no active role in the business; involvement is limited to an investment and a share of profits; and

(2) salaried partners – these may be full partners who choose to divide up the firm's profits first by reference to fixed amounts, described as 'salaries'; alternatively they may be individuals who are employees and are described as partners for prestige reasons only.

Limited liability partnerships

6.98 Limited liability partnerships (LLPs) were introduced from 6 April 2001. An LLP broadly provides the organisational flexibility of a partnership, but with limited liability status for its members. For tax purposes, an LLP carrying on a trade, profession or other business with a view to profit is generally treated as a partnership. The transfer of an existing partnership business to an LLP will not normally give rise to income tax or capital gains tax consequences. However, there is a potential restriction in loss relief for members of LLPs that carry on a trade. An LLP is taxed as a company during a liquidation of the business (*ITA 2007, Pt 4, Ch 3*).

Partnership tax return

6.99 Each partnership is required to submit a partnership tax return, showing business profits and the allocation of those profits between the partners. Each partnership must nominate a representative partner who is responsible for the submission of the partnership return. It is this partner who receives the notice from HMRC to complete a return and all other correspondence from HMRC concerning the partnership (*TMA 1970, s 12AA(1)–(3)*).

The partnership itself is not liable to tax on the profits allocated to each partner. Each partner is separately responsible for the tax on their own share of partnership income and gains, which is reported and assessed on their own individual self-assessment tax returns. Every partner is responsible for reporting his source of partnership income on his own tax return.

The trading profits, income and gains of the business are dealt with in a partnership tax return, made on behalf of all the partners each tax year. The return includes a partnership statement that may be a short or detailed (full) version. Most partnerships can adequately return details of the partnership profits on the short version, but if the partnership has particularly complex affairs the full version should be used.

A separate return is required for each accounting period ending in the tax year, based on the accounts of the period concerned. However, details of taxed income, trading charges on income and disposals of partnership assets are entered on those returns for the tax year in question. It is not strictly necessary to submit a copy of the partnership accounts and computations with the tax return unless the turnover exceeds £15 million. However, the Chartered Institute of Taxation recommends the submission of all accounts to give maximum protection in the event of an enquiry.

The partnership return must be submitted by 31 January following the end of the tax year to which it relates. However, if the return is not issued until after 31 October following the tax year, the filing date is extended to three months from the date the return is issued. Different filing dates apply to partnerships with corporate partners (*TMA 1970, s 12AA(4), (5)*).

Partnership tax returns are subject to largely the same amendment and HMRC enquiry procedures as for individual returns. An enquiry into a partnership return is automatically extended to include the partners' own tax returns, although this does not cover non-partnership aspects of an individual partner's return (*TMA 1970, ss 12AA–12AE*).

Penalties

6.100 Penalties for late partnership tax returns are not imposed on the partnership itself, but on the partners individually (*TMA 1970, ss 93A* and *95A*). No tax-related penalties are imposed for late partnership returns, as the partnership itself has no liability to tax. However, there is no reduction in the fixed penalties where the outstanding tax at the filing date is less than the amount of those penalties, as there is for individual taxpayer's returns.

A tax-related penalty may be imposed on the partners where a partnership return has been made fraudulently or negligently, up to a maximum of the additional liability properly payable by each partner. A penalty of up to £3,000 may be imposed for a failure to keep adequate records in support of a partnership tax return. There are also penalties for failing to provide HMRC with records and documents when required (*TMA 1970, s 12B*).

Calculating profits and losses

6.101 The rules for calculating partnership profits and losses are the same as for self-employed individuals (see **6.22**). However, all business expenses incurred by the partners individually must be deducted from partnership profits in arriving at taxable profits on the partnership tax return.

This also applies to capital allowances claimed on business assets provided by individual partners. Partners are not permitted to claim relief for such business expenses on their own individual tax returns.

If any of the partners is a company, the partnership profits are computed using corporation tax rules, but profits are allocated to individuals using income tax rules. Two separate computations are therefore required (*CTA 2009, s 1262*).

Capital gains

6.102 Partnership capital gains are assessed to capital gains tax on the partners themselves, not on the partnership (*TCGA 1992, s 59*).

Cash basis

6.103 Businesses are required to compute profits for tax purposes in accordance with generally accepted accountancy practice (subject to adjustments for tax law), being the accruals or earnings basis (see **6.22**). Certain professional partnerships, such as solicitors and chartered surveyors who traditionally used a 'cash' basis, were required to adopt an earnings basis to draw up accounts beginning after 6 April 1999. Partnerships which changed from the cash basis to the accruals basis needed to calculate a one-off catching-up charge which can be spread forward over ten years to reduce the effect on the taxable profits (*ITTOIA 2005, ss 25, 846–863*).

Allocating profits and losses

6.104 The taxable profits are allocated to each partner according to the profit-sharing arrangements for the accounting period. Partners' salaries, commissions and interest on capital accounts are not deducted in arriving at taxable profits; they are treated as a prior share of profits and are allocated to the partners concerned. The balance of profits is then allocated in accordance with the profit-sharing proportions in operation. This allocation cannot create or increase a loss for a partner. Any 'notional' loss calculated in this way must be reallocated to the other partners.

Each partner is treated as if his share of the partnership profit (or loss) had arisen from a separate trade carried on by that individual as a sole trader. The rules for taxing profits in the opening and closing years of a business therefore apply to each partner upon joining and leaving the firm. A change in the members of a partnership is not treated as a cessation of the business for tax purposes if at least one of the old partners continues after the change (*ITTOIA 2005, ss 846–863*).

Sideways losses

6.105 *FA 2005* brought in measures to restrict loss relief available to partners in certain circumstances (*FA 2005, s 74*). The rules are now contained in *ITA 2007, Pt 13, Ch 5.*

ITA, *2007, ss 64, 71* and *72* allow trading losses arising to an individual to be set against other income and capital gains. These reliefs may be claimed by individuals who carry on a trade in partnership – generally referred to as 'sideways loss reliefs'.

Currently, the amount of trading losses for a tax year for which a non-active partner can claim sideways loss relief is restricted broadly to the amount of capital that the partner has contributed to the partnership (*ITA 2007, Pt 4, Ch 3*). However, in March 2007 the government announced proposals to introduce new legislation to exclude certain capital contributions from this amount.

The capital contributions excluded are those paid by non-active partners on or after 2 March 2007 where the main purpose, or one of the main purposes, for contributing the capital to the partnership is for the partner to have access to losses for which sideways loss relief can be claimed.

An annual limit on the amount of trading losses for a tax year for which an individual who is a non-active partner in a partnership can claim sideways loss reliefs applies to trading losses sustained as a non-active partner on or after 2 March 2007. The limit for each tax year, for trading losses from all partnerships in which the individual was a non-active partner for that year, is the lower of:

- £25,000; or
- the amount of trading losses for the tax year for which the individual would otherwise be able to claim sideways loss reliefs.

A non-active partner for these purposes is a limited partner or any other partner who spends an average of less than ten hours a week personally engaged in carrying on the partnership's trading activities.

A trading loss for which sideways loss relief is not available can be carried forward and set against the individual's share of the partnership's trading profits for future tax years.

The limit does not apply to losses from carrying on a profession or a Lloyd's underwriting business.

Limited liability partnerships and members of LLPs are equally affected by these provisions.

Example of spreading the catching-up charge

6.106

Example 6.11

Frank and Drake traded as chartered surveyors up until 31 December 2004 when Frank left to trade in his own name. The firm had been very successful and had a catching-up charge of £200,000 arising in 2001/02. The firm's accounts were always drawn up to 31 December and the catching-up charge is assessed as follows:

Period ended 31 December	Tax year	Normal profits £	Catching-up charge spread £	Calculation of spread of catching up	Payable by
2001	2001/02	180,000	18,000	10% of profits	F and D
2002	2002/03	200,000	20,000	10% of profits	F and D
2003	2003/04	220,000	22,000	10% of profits	F and D
2004	2004/05	240,000	24,000	10% of profits	F and D
2005	2005/06	150,000	15,000	10% of profits	Drake only
2006	2006/07	130,000	13,000	10% of profits	Drake only
2007	2007/08	140,000	14,000	10% of profits	Drake only
2008	2008/09	130,000	13,000	10% of profits	Drake only
2009	2009/10	120,000	12,000	10% of profits	Drake only
2010	2010/11	110,000	55,000	balance	Drake only
			200,000		

Where profits are falling, or the partnership is shrinking, there is an incentive for partners to leave before the period to be assessed in 2010/11 to avoid the taxation of the balance of the catching-up charge.

Allocation of profits – example

6.107

Example 6.12

Andrew, Barry and Clarisa trade in partnership. Their profit and loss sharing ratios are 1:2:3. They are allocated salaries in the year to 31 March 2009 of £100,000, £60,000 and £10,000 respectively. Each is entitled to interest of £1,000 on capital per year. The partnership makes a taxable profit of £233,000 in the year to 31 March 2009. The profit allocation for tax purposes is:

	Total	Andrew	Barry	Clarisa
	£	£	£	£
Salary	170,000	100,000	60,000	10,000
Interest on capital	3,000	1,000	1,000	1,000
Balance of profits (in ratio 1:2:3)	60,000	10,000	20,000	30,000
Chargeable on partners for 2008/09	233,000	111,000	81,000	41,000

Allocation of notional loss – example

6.108

Example 6.13

The facts are as above but the partnership made a profit of only £149,000 in the year to 31 March 2009.

	Total	Andrew	Barry	Clarisa
	£	£	£	£
Salary	170,000	100,000	60,000	10,000
Interest on capital	3,000	1,000	1,000	1,000
Balance of profits (in ratio 1:2:3)	(24,000)	(4,000)	(8,000)	(12,000)
	149,000	97,000	53,000	(1,000)
Apportionment of Clarisa's loss		(667)	(333)	1,000
Chargeable on partners for 2008/09	149,000	96,333	52,667	—

Actual loss allocation – example

6.109

Example 6.14

Louise, Mary and Nicola are in partnership and prepare their accounts to 31 December each year. They have always shared profits and losses equally, but with effect from 1 July 2009 they change their agreement to the following:

	Louise	Mary	Nicola
Salaries		50,000	50,000
Interest	6,000	2,000	2,000
Balance of profits	3	1	1

For the year ended 31 December 2009, the partnership made a tax loss of £90,000. This loss is divided as follows:

	Total	Louise	Mary	Nicola
	£	£	£	£
To 30 June 2009	(45,000)	(15,000)	(15,000)	(15,000)
Salary to 31 December	50,000		25,000	25,000
Interest to 31 December	5,000	3,000	1,000	1,000
Balance of loss for six months	(100,000)	(60,000)	(20,000)	(20,000)
	(45,000)			
Losses of partners for tax year 2009/10	(90,000)	(72,000)	(9,000)	(9,000)

Non-trading income

6.110 The partnership non-trading income is also divided between the partners according to the sharing arrangements for the trade in that accounting period.

Taxed income

6.111 Income taxed at source is included in the partnership tax return as the income of the tax year itself, which will normally differ from the accounting period. This will either require an apportionment of income received in different accounting periods or, alternatively, details of taxed income actually received in the tax year.

Untaxed income

6.112 The partnership tax return should include details of untaxed income received in the partnership's accounting period. A partner's share of untaxed income is treated as arising from a separate business carried on by that individual. This income is therefore subject to similar opening and closing year rules as for trading income, and the rules for overlap relief may apply if untaxed income is taxed more than once in the early years of a business, or on a change in the partnership's accounting date. The 'separate business' rules start when an individual becomes a partner (or when the firm starts trading, if later) and end when he ceases to be a partner (or when the firm ceases trading, if earlier). The opening and closing year rules for untaxed interest are not applicable to changes in individual sources of untaxed income.

Partnership tax return

6.113 The partnership tax return must include the following details for every partner who was a member of the partnership at some time during the accounting period covered by the return:

- name;
- private address;
- personal tax reference;
- registered office; and
- National Insurance number.

Partnership statement

6.114 The partnership statement must contain the following for each period of account ending within the tax year of the return:

- the amounts of income or loss from each source;
- tax deducted or credited;
- partnership charges on income;
- proceeds from disposals of partnership assets; and
- each partner's share of each of the above, for the period covered by the return.

Example 6.15—Reporting of partnership income

Angela is admitted to a partnership on 1 January 2010. She needs to report her share of the partnership income to be assessed for the period 1 January to 5 April 2010, on her 2009/10 tax return by 31 January 2011. This income will be a proportion of her partnership profits for the accounting period to 31 December 2010, which are unlikely to be finalised by 31 January 2011.

The amount of partnership profits included in Angela's 2009/10 tax return will have to be a provisional figure. The relevant box should be ticked on the tax return so the HMRC computer can flag the return as containing provisional figures that are to be finalised later. Angela is obliged to report the final amount of her partnership profit for the year to HMRC as soon as the figure becomes available.

Use of provisional figures

6.115 HMRC set out a revised approach to dealing with provisional figures in tax returns in *Tax Bulletin* number 57 (January 2002). HMRC now accept that a taxpayer has made a return where a provisional or estimated figure is used, and will no longer send back a return as incomplete if it does not have an adequate explanation for the use of the figure, or if no date is given for the supply of the final figure. The use of a provisional or estimated figure may nevertheless make a return incorrect, in which case a penalty will be charged if there is negligence or fraud.

HMRC Helpsheets for the partnership tax return

6.116

Name	Title
SA850	Partnership Tax Return Guide
SA801(notes)	Notes on Partnership UK Property
SA802(notes)	Notes on Partnership Foreign
SA803(notes)	Notes on Partnership Disposal of Chargeable Assets
SA804(notes)	Notes on Partnership Savings, investments and other income
HS380	Partnerships: Foreign Aspects

FARMING AND MARKET GARDENING

Introduction

6.117 Farming or market gardening in the UK is treated for income tax purposes as the carrying on of a trade or part of a trade (whether or not the land is managed on a commercial basis and with a view to the realisation of profits) (*ITTOIA 2005, s 9*).

'Farming' means the occupation of land wholly or mainly for the purposes of husbandry, but does not include market gardening. Husbandry includes hop growing, and the breeding and rearing of horses and the grazing of horses in connection with those activities (*ITTOIA 2005, s 876*). 'Farming' has different meanings in different contexts for tax purposes. For example, for the purposes of restricting certain loss reliefs which would otherwise be available to farmers or market gardeners, 'farming' and 'market gardening' are interpreted as above, but with the difference that activities carried on outside the UK are included.

'Market gardening' means the occupation of land as a garden or nursery for the purpose of growing produce for sale (*ITTOIA 2005, s 876(5)*).

All farming (but not market gardening) carried on by one person (or partnership or body of persons) is treated as one trade.

Since 29 November 1994, 'short rotation coppice' is regarded for tax purposes as farming rather than forestry (*ITTOIA 2005, s 876(3)*). Consequently, the land on which it is undertaken is regarded as farmland or agricultural land and not commercial woodland. 'Short rotation coppice' means a perennial crop of tree species planted at high density, the stems of which are harvested above ground level at intervals of less than ten years.

'Farm land' excludes 'market garden land' (*ITTOIA 2005, s 876*). 'Market garden land' means 'land in the UK occupied as a nursery or garden for the sale of produce (other than land used for the growth of hops) and 'market gardening' is construed accordingly.'

Under strict interpretation of the law, anyone whose house has a garden attached may be a market gardener. However, in order to counter the use of a small garden as a mere device for tax avoidance, the rule which HMRC applies in practice is that only if commercial purposes predominate will the garden be regarded as a market garden. However, this rule is unlikely to be rigidly applied where the taxpayer sells fruit or vegetables as part of a wider business. For example, a farm shop on farm premises which sells farm produce is unlikely to be treated as a separate trade even if, in order to keep the shop worker busy, the taxpayer brings in goods from outside for resale.

Trading

6.118 All farming which is carried on by a sole trader, persons in partnership or body of persons is treated as one trade. Accordingly, profits derived from more than one farm must be aggregated into a single chargeable source of income where the taxpayer operates more than one farm at the same time, whether the farms are in the same or in different parts of the country.

Where the giving up of farming on one farm and the commencement of farming on another is treated as having taken place, the following consequences occur.

Trading losses from the farming operation which has ceased cannot be set off against profits generated from the new farm. The trading losses from the first farming operation could only be brought forward against trading profits from the second farming operation if the two sets of farming operations amounted, for income tax purposes, to a single continuing trade.

If the farmer is treated as having ceased to trade in respect of one farm, then any accumulated income tax losses at the date of such cessation are 'wiped out' and are not available for set-off or carry-forward (*ITA 2007, s 83*).

If a particular activity does not fall within the definition of 'farming' and 'market gardening', it may still be treated as being some other trade or part of some other trade within the ambit of *ITTOIA 2005*.

The taxpayer should take particular care to avoid the activity being regarded as casual or occasional. If the activity is treated as such, profits derived from it will be charged to income tax.

Share farming

6.119 'Share farming' is a method of farming where the owner or tenant of farmland (the landowner) enters into a contract with a working farmer (the share farmer). Typically:

- the landowner provides the farmland and buildings, fixed equipment and machinery, major maintenance of the buildings and his expertise;
- the share farmer provides labour, field and mobile machinery and his expertise;
- other costs such as seed, fertilisers and feed are shared. If there is a livestock enterprise then ownership of the animals is shared on the basis that each party owns a share in each animal;
- each party is rewarded by a share in the produce of the farm which he is free to sell as he likes; and
- each party produces his own accounts and is responsible for his own tax and VAT returns.

HMRC consider that both parties to a genuine share farming agreement are carrying on a 'farming' business for tax purposes.

Relief for fluctuating profits

6.120 Because personal reliefs which are unused in one tax year cannot be carried forward or backward to another tax year, and because of the progressive nature of income tax liability, a person who earns, say, £40,000 in one tax year and £10,000 in the next, pays more income tax than a similarly placed person who earns £25,000 in each of two succeeding tax years. Special relief is accordingly available to individuals and partnerships engaged in a farming or market gardening business to take account of fluctuating profits (*ITTOIA 2005, ss 221–225*).

Farming, for these purposes, includes the intensive rearing of livestock or fish on a commercial basis for the production of food for human consumption.

If, in two consecutive tax years, the profits assessable in one are 70% or less of those in the other, the profits of both years can be averaged.

A year in which a loss is incurred is, for the purposes of the relief, deemed to be a year of nil profit. Loss relief is, nevertheless, still available.

The introduction of self-assessment changed the method of dealing with capital allowances in the computation of profits, and consequently it also changes the measure of profits to be used in an averaging claim. The profits to be taken are the profits before any deduction for losses.

A claim for the relief must be made in writing within two years of the end of the second tax year to which the claim relates. Under self-assessment, the claim is to be related to the later year, with any necessary adjustments in respect of the earlier year being given in the later year.

The average profits for the second year can provide the basis for averaging the profits for years two and three.

Example 6.16

A farmer's profits for recent years are as follows:

Year 1 = £30,000; Year 2 = £10,000.

So, Year 2 profits are less than 70% of Year 1 profits. The farmer claims the relief.

His profits for each of Year 1 and Year 2 will be deemed to be:

$$\frac{£30,000 + £10,000}{2} = £20,000$$

The profits in Year 3 are £10,000. The farmer again claims relief. His profits for Years 2 and 3 will each be adjusted to:

$$\frac{£20,000 + £10,000}{2} = £15,000$$

There is a marginal relief where profits for one year are more than 70%, but less than 75%, of the profits of the other year.

A claim for relief cannot be made for a year of commencement or discontinuance.

Example 6.17

A farmer's profits were £16,000 in 2008/09 and £30,000 in 2009/10, and an averaging claim was made so that the profits of each year became £23,000. Assume the 2008/09 tax is increased by £1,680 (but the 2009/10 tax is reduced by £2,800, giving a significant reduction overall). The increase in the 2008/09 tax would be given effect by increasing the tax payable for 2009/10.

A claim was then made to average the previously averaged 2009/10 profits of £23,000 with those of 2010/11. The calculation of the effect on the tax position for 2009/10 would not treat the increase of £1,680 relating to 2008/09 as part of the tax payable for 2009/10.

Restriction of loss relief

6.121 In general, any loss incurred in farming or market gardening is unavailable for loss relief by offset against general income if, in each of the prior five years, a loss was incurred (disregarding capital allowances) in carrying on that trade, ie losses can only be relieved against general income for five years. The restriction also applies to capital allowances related to the loss (*ITA 2007, s 67(2)*).

Livestock, tillages and harvested crops

6.122 The treatment and valuation of stock-in-trade is a particular problem for farmers. This applies to livestock, tillages, harvested crops, etc. As a general rule, animals kept for farming are treated as trading stock; however, animals are not so treated where the farmer makes an election for 'the herd basis' (see below).

A number of long-standing practices were called into question by the Revenue, their views being set out in a business economic note (BEN 19) issued in April 1993. The Revenue later commented on their revised practice in ascertaining the cost of harvested crops (from 85% of market value to 75% thereof) and clarified further the areas in which they expected changes to valuation methods: full way-going valuations, dilapidations reserves, certificates under the 1942 NFU arrangement and production animals taken at cull value.

BEN 19 is reproduced in full in the HMRC Business Income Manual at BIM55410.

Herd basis

6.123 Where animals are treated as part of the trading stock, payments and receipts for animals bought and sold are dealt with in the accounts in the usual way. Trading stock will have to be revalued at the end of the period of account.

However, where an election for the herd basis is made, the initial cost of the herd, and of any animal added to the herd which is not a replacement animal, is not deducted in the accounts as an expense and the value of the herd is not brought into account (*ITTOIA 2005, s 111*).

Generally, where an animal is sold, or dies, and is replaced, the proceeds of sale are included as a trading receipt and the cost of the replacement animal is deductible as an expense. It is not always clear whether the acquisition of one animal is necessarily a 'replacement' for another.

HMRC have confirmed that they will accept that replacement treatment is applied where an animal is brought into the herd within 12 months of the corresponding disposal. If the interval is longer than 12 months, replacement treatment may be accepted if the facts of the case support it (HMRC Business Income Manual BIM55520).

Where at least 20% of the herd is sold within a 12-month period, and is not replaced within five years, any profit or loss is treated as a capital profit or loss. However, no chargeable gain will accrue on disposal as animals are wasting assets which are tangible moveable property.

An election for the herd basis can only be made in relation to 'production herds': ie herds of animals of the same species kept wholly or mainly for the sake of the products which they produce for the farmer to sell, eg dairy herds. An election must be made in writing and must specify the class of herds to which it relates. An election is irrevocable and must normally be made within two years of the end of the first chargeable period for which the farmer is chargeable under *ITTOIA 2005*, or is given relief for trading losses against general income. In commencement cases, the time-limit is extended to two years after the end of the first period of account if that is later.

The herd basis extends to cases where several farmers hold shares in one animal for the purposes of a herd, or in animals forming part of a herd.

Where there is a change in any of the persons carrying on the farming trade, HMRC's view is that the herd basis election made by the old 'farmer' ceases and the new 'farmer' can decide whether to make a fresh election.

Capital allowances cannot be claimed with regards to animals in respect of which the herd basis is used to compute profits.

INCORPORATION

When and how to incorporate

6.124 How and when to incorporate a business will ultimately be a matter of personal choice. However, the following factors may be considered in making this decision.

Personal risk

6.125 As a business grows, so do the risks associated with it. Many individuals become reluctant to bear personal liability for increasingly large trade creditors and other business commitments. Running their business through the medium of a company creates a barrier between creditors and their private assets.

External investment

6.126 Particularly if the owners are managing a strongly growing business, a company presents greater opportunities to attract external capital and motivate employees through tax-efficient shares schemes. Where the owners consider that their business will be floated on a stock exchange in the future, share option schemes need to be established well before the flotation, to allow the maximum growth in value.

Pension provision

6.127 A company provides much more flexible opportunities to provide pension provision, both for the owner-managers and employees. If the company is making significant profits a company pension scheme can prove to be an effective tax shelter as well as provision for a retirement income.

Tax efficient incorporation of a business

6.128 The difficulty faced by the owner wishing to transfer an unincorporated business to a company is that, without tax reliefs, capital gains tax is likely to be payable on the transfer of any chargeable assets. Since the business owner and the new company are connected persons for capital gains tax purposes, any transfer of the business to the company is treated as being at market value, whatever the actual purchase consideration. Two alternative incorporation routes seek to mitigate the consequences. The first, *TCGA 1992, s 162* is a form of rollover relief provided specifically for this purpose, but it has some drawbacks that can make it unattractive. The alternative is to use the provisions of *TCGA 1992, s 165* and make a gift of the business to the new company.

Rollover relief on transfer to a company

6.129 No claim is required, as this relief is automatic. However, there are circumstances in which it is disadvantageous to use it.

The relief is a form of rollover relief; that is to say the gains on the business' chargeable assets, that would otherwise be subject to tax, are deducted from the cost of acquisition of the shares in the new company.

There are three aspects to the conditions that must be met for the relief to apply. These are:

- a person who is not a company transfers to a company a business as a going concern;
- the transfer is of the whole assets of the business, or the whole of those assets other than cash; and
- the business is so transferred wholly or partly in exchange for shares issued by the company to the person transferring the business.

The transferor has to be a person who is not a company. This can include an individual, two (or more) individuals in partnership, trustees or personal representatives. Sometimes, partnerships include companies as partners. In these circumstances, no relief is given to the corporate partner, but relief is not precluded for individual partners.

The business must be transferred wholly or partly in exchange for shares issued by the company to the individuals transferring the business.

Relief

6.130 There are three stages in calculating the relief, as follows:

(1) calculate the gain or loss on each asset being transferred to the company;

(2) set off any losses against the total gains to produce a figure for aggregate gains; and

(3) split the aggregate gains between the amount attributable to consideration issued by the company in shares (including, by concession, assumption of trade liabilities) and the amount attributable to 'other consideration' (normally cash or debts).

Any gains attributable to non-share consideration are taxable immediately. Provided that the aggregate gains do not exceed the cost of the shares, the gains attributable to the share consideration are relieved in full (but otherwise will be restricted to the cost of the shares, with any excess being taxable immediately).

Incorporation using relief for gifts of business assets

6.131 As far as its application to business incorporation is concerned, the general scheme of *TCGA 1992, s 165* is uncomplicated. The first and overriding condition is that the relief applies to disposals 'otherwise than by way of bargains at arm's length'. Consequently, it applies both to outright gifts and sales which occur at a value less than market value. There are then three other types of condition, which are:

(1) the transfer must be made by an individual;

(2) the transfer must be made to a person who is resident in the UK; and

(3) the assets transferred must be used in a trade, profession or vocation carried on by the transferor.

In the first condition, the term 'individual' includes partners (other than corporate partners). In some circumstances, it also applies to trustees.

Except where there are restrictions because an asset has not always been used for trade purposes, if no payment is received for the disposal, the full amount of the gain may be held over that otherwise would have been chargeable. So, there is no chargeable gain at the time of the disposal, but the amount of the held-over gain is deducted from the transferee company's base cost. The held-over gain is therefore brought into the capital gains computation automatically on any subsequent disposal of the assets by the company.

Transfer to a company relief or gift of business assets relief?

6.132 The choice of methods will depend entirely on the circumstances of the case. The gifts of business assets route is currently used more widely and this is due principally to the perceived defect in *s 162* that all assets (other than cash) have to be transferred to the company. This can involve considerable amounts of stamp duty being payable. The increase in the top rate of stamp duty to 4% for assets worth more than £500,000 increases this cost; ie 4% applies to instruments executed after 27 March 2000.

Using the *s 162* route, a significant problem may arise where the business is of a type that requires large premises that appreciate in value. Insofar as it is commercially possible, it is good tax planning to keep such assets outside a company, to avoid the owner being exposed to a potential double capital gains charge (once when the company sells the premises) and again, indirectly, when the owner sells his or her shares in the company. Using the gifts of business assets rules selectively enables the business owner to keep such assets outside the company.

The taper relief rules (which apply up to 5 April 2008) contain problems for both types of transfer. In each case the gains are deferred, until either the assets or the shares in the company are sold. The taper relief rules do not (except in the context of reinvestment of gains on EIS shares) count the period of ownership of the asset before the deferral. Since, from 6 April 2002, the maximum taper relief for business assets accrues after two years, the owner will wish to consider whether the chargeable assets transferred, or the shares, are most likely to accrue the maximum taper relief before disposal.

SUBCONTRACTORS

Construction Industry Scheme (CIS)

6.133 All businesses in the construction industry (individuals, partnerships and companies) are subject to the construction industry scheme. This applies not only to construction work but also to work including installation (of most items from heating systems to shop fittings), repairs, decorating and demolition.

6.134 'Contractors' for these purposes include construction firms and any other business involved in construction work, although private householders and businesses spending less than £1 million per annum on construction work are excluded (*FA 2004, s 59*).

A 'subcontractor' is any business which has agreed to carry out construction operations for a contractor – whether by doing the operations itself, or by having them done by its own employees, or in any other way.

Reform of CIS

6.135 A consultation paper was published in the 2002 pre-Budget report, proposing major reform of the scheme and the resulting legislation is now contained in the *FA 2004* and the regulations (*SI 2005/2045*). The proposals included replacing existing documentation with a verification service run by HMRC, periodic returns and a new employment status declaration. It was originally planned that the new scheme would come into effect from April 2006, but this was subsequently delayed until 6 April 2007.

The following paragraphs relate to the CIS from 6 April 2007.

6.136 Key aspects of the CIS are as follows:

- Certificates, CIS cards or vouchers no longer exist.
- Contractors must check or verify' new subcontractors with HMRC.
- Subcontractors are paid either net or gross, depending on their own circumstances, but HMRC tell the contractor which treatment to use during verification.
- There is a higher rate tax deduction if a subcontractor cannot be 'matched' on the HMRC system. This rate applies until the subcontractor contacts HMRC and registers or sorts out any matching problem.
- There are no CIS annual returns.
- Contractors must make a return every month to HMRC, showing payments made to all subcontractors. Contractors must declare on their

return that none of the workers listed on the return are employees. This is called a Status declaration.

- Nil returns must be made when there are no payments in any month. These can be made over the telephone as well as via the Internet or on paper. There are financial penalties for failure to submit a return.

Employment status

6.137 Under the CIS, contractors must check or 'verify' new subcontractors with HMRC. Broadly, this means that HMRC will check that the subcontractor is properly registered for income tax and National Insurance contributions purposes.

A worker's employment status, that is whether they are employed or self-employed, is not a matter of choice. Whether someone is employed or self-employed depends upon the terms and conditions of the relevant engagement. The tax and National Insurance contributions (NICs) rules do, however, contain some special rules that apply to certain categories of worker in certain circumstances. A worker's employment status will determine the charge to tax on income from that employment or self-employment. It will also determine the class of NICs which are to be paid.

HMRC provide an 'Employment Status Indicator (ESI) Tool' on their website www.hmrc.gov.uk/calcs/esi.htm. Employers and contractors may use the tool to obtain an HMRC 'view' of the employment status of their workers. It should be noted that the tool will provide a general guide only which would not be binding on HMRC. To obtain a written 'opinion' of employment status in the construction industry, the contractor will need to telephone the CIS Helpline on 0845 366 7899.

Payments to subcontractors

6.138 There are a number of obligations that a contractor must comply with before payments can be made to subcontractors.

Verification

6.139 Verification is the process HMRC use to make sure that subcontractors have the correct rate of deduction applied to their payments under the CIS. There are three main steps to the process:

- the contractor contacts HMRC with details of the subcontractor;
- HMRC check that the subcontractor is registered with them;
- HMRC tell the contractor what rate of deduction to apply, if any.

Before a contractor can make a payment for construction work to a subcontractor, they must decide whether they need to verify the subcontractor.

The general rule is that a contractor does not have to verify a subcontractor if they last included that subcontractor on a return in the current or two previous tax years.

If a contractor does not have to verify a subcontractor, they must pay the subcontractor on the same basis as the last payment made to them. This means that, if the subcontractor was last paid under the standard rate of deduction, the current payment must also be made under the standard rate of deduction. If the last payment was made gross, because a deduction was not required, the current payment must also be made gross.

Verification reference number

6.140 Once HMRC have received the above information, they will check their records to see if the subcontractor is registered for tax and then tell the contractor to pay the subcontractor in one of the following ways:

- gross – ie without any deductions taken from the payment;
- net of a deduction at the standard rate (currently 20%);
- net of a deduction at the higher rate (currently 30%) because:
  - HMRC have no record of that subcontractor's registration, or
  - HMRC are unable to verify the details for any other reason.

(*SI 2007/46, reg 2*)

When HMRC verify a subcontractor, they will give the contractor a verification reference number. The verification reference number will be the same for each subcontractor that they have verified at the same time. If it is not possible to verify a subcontractor, HMRC will add one or two letters to the end of the number, so that it is unique to that subcontractor.

Payments under deduction

6.141 Deductions must only be made from that part of the payment that does not represent the cost of materials incurred by the subcontractor.

Any travelling expenses (including fuel costs) and subsistence paid to the subcontractor must be included in the gross amount of payment and the amount from which the deduction is made.

There are two steps that contractors must follow:

- Calculate the gross amount from which a deduction will be made by excluding:
  - VAT charged by the subcontractor if he is registered; and
  - any amount equal to the Construction Industry Training Board (CITB) levy.

  The contractor will need to keep a record of the gross payment amounts so that they can enter these on their monthly returns.
- Deduct from the gross payment the amount the subcontractor actually paid for the following items used in the construction operations, including VAT paid if the subcontractor is not registered for VAT:
  - materials

    The contractor can ask the subcontractor for evidence of the direct cost of materials. If the subcontractor fails to give this information, the contractor must make a fair estimate of the actual cost of materials. The contractor must always check, as far as possible, that the part of the payment for materials supplied is not overstated. If the materials element looks to be excessive, HMRC may ask the contractor to explain why;
  - consumable stores;
  - fuel (except fuel for travelling);
  - plant hire; and
  - the cost of manufacture or prefabrication of materials.

The contractor must provide a written statement to every subcontractor from whom a deduction has been made within 14 days of the end of each tax month. A tax month runs from the 6th of one month to the 5th of the next month so the statement must be provided by the 19th of the month.

Monthly returns

6.142 Each month, contractors must send HMRC a complete return of all payments made to all subcontractors within the CIS in the preceding tax month (*FA 2004, s 70*). This is regardless of whether the subcontractors were paid gross or net of either the standard or higher deduction. Monthly returns must reach HMRC within 14 days of the end of the tax month they are for. Returns may be made electronically or by post (*SI 2005/2045, reg 7*).

Penalties

6.143 HMRC will impose a penalty if £100 where a contractor fails to submit a monthly return on time.

If the contractor should have returned information about more than 50 subcontractors, the penalty will be a further £100 for each additional 50 subcontractors or part thereof. The penalty will be repeated for every month the return is outstanding.

If a contractor submits a monthly return that is incomplete or incorrect, HMRC may charge penalties where they believe the error or omission has been caused by negligence or intent on the part of the contractor.

Incomplete or incorrect returns include:

- persons or payments omitted from the return;
- persons or payments incorrectly entered onto the return;
- failing to make a declaration in respect of verification or employment status;
- incorrectly making a declaration in respect of verification or employment status.

If a contractor fails to produce records relating to payments made under the CIS when asked to do so, HMRC may charge penalties up to £3,000 (*FA 2004, s 72*). Penalties of up to £3,000 may be charged where a contractor:

- fails to give statements to subcontractors registered for payment under deduction recording their payments and deductions; or
- negligently or deliberately provide incorrect information in such statements.

Registration as a subcontractor

6.144 A subcontractor, starting working in the construction industry on a self-employed basis for the first time after 5 April 2007, should register for CIS if they do not want deductions at the higher rate made from their payments.

HMRC will only authorise a contractor to make gross payments to a subcontractor where the following conditions are satisfied.

The business test

6.145 To satisfy this condition, the subcontractor must provide evidence that he is carrying on a business in the UK which:

(a) consists of or includes the carrying out of construction operations or the furnishing or arranging for the furnishing of labour in carrying out construction operations; and

(b) is, to a substantial extent, carried on by means of an account with a bank.

Evidence prescribed to satisfy the business test is as follows (*SI 2005/2045, reg 27*):

- the business address;
- invoices, contracts or purchase orders for construction work carried out by the applicant;
- details of payments for construction work;
- the books and accounts of the business; and
- details of the business bank account, including bank statements.

The turnover test

6.146 The applicant must satisfy HMRC that, in the year following the making of the application:

- as an individual, his net business turnover from construction work (ie after the cost of any materials used to earn that income) is £30,000 a year or more (*SI 2005/2045, reg 28*); or
- as a partnership or company, the net business turnover from construction work (ie after deducting the cost of any materials) is £30,000 a year or more multiplied by the number of partners or directors.

In the case of 'close companies' (broadly, companies controlled by five or fewer individuals), the figure will be multiplied by the number of individuals who are directors and/or shareholders. For a husband and wife team, for instance, it would be £60,000.

An alternative test for partnerships and companies is that the business has an annual net turnover from construction work (after deducting the cost of materials) of £200,000 or more (*SI 2005/2045, reg 28*).

The compliance test

6.147 The subcontractor must have kept all his tax affairs up to date during the 'qualifying period' (the period of 12 months ending with the date of the application in question). This means he must have paid all tax liabilities, including any PAYE and subcontractor deductions, and submitted all tax returns on time. HMRC will not accept an application from a subcontractor who brings his tax affairs up to date just prior to submitting that application.

Subcontractor administration

6.148 Historically, some smaller subcontractors have often failed to keep the records of payments given to them by contractors. Moreover, contractors sometimes fail to give their subcontractors the required payment and deduction statements. Difficulties can subsequently arise because, when it comes to the completion of their annual tax return, the subcontractor concerned will not have a full record of his earnings and receipts. Subcontractors in this position usually contact HMRC at the end of the year and ask them to give back to them details of their payments and deductions, as reported on the returns of contractors for whom they have worked during the period, or year, in question. HMRC are often able to help out with this information where the subcontractor clearly has a genuine need for it. However, providing details of all payments and deductions reported on contractors' returns can cause problems. HMRC cannot know at all times which contractors a subcontractor may have worked for, nor can they ever be fully aware of what payments and deductions may have been made by any particular contractor. Although contractors are under a legal obligation to report this information to HMRC on a monthly basis, there have been occasions where a contractor's monthly return has not been accurate, complete or even received by HMRC in the first place. Subcontractors that rely on this information as a complete record in order to complete their own tax returns run the serious risk that they are making an incorrect or incomplete return and could be making themselves liable to a penalty for doing so.

HMRC say that this is a growing problem, with many subcontractors and some agents seeking to obtain this information from HMRC rather than keep their own records. One of the aims of the reformed CIS was to improve subcontractors' compliance with their tax obligations.

In order to stem the ever rising number of time- and resource-intensive, multiple and bulk requests for data that HMRC are receiving, the Department will no longer be able to provide this information on a bulk basis. Requests for missing details from individual subcontractors or their agents will continue to be provided when they can demonstrate that they have been back to the contractor concerned to request a duplicate or missing payment and deduction statement but have failed to obtain one. In cases where it is alleged that a contractor has refused to issue one or more original payment and deduction statements, HMRC will require the subcontractor or their agent to give details of the contractor so that further enquiries may be made.

Once HMRC are satisfied that a subcontractor has tried to obtain details of the missing payment and deduction statement, they will supply the missing information if they possibly can and, of course, where the information is currently held on the HMRC CIS system.

HMRC guidance on CIS

6.149 HMRC produce comprehensive guidance on the Construction Industry Scheme (see the HMRC website at www.hmrc.gov.uk/cis/index.htm.

For information regarding employment status, see www.hmrc.gov.uk/employment-status/index.htm. The HMRC employment status indicator tool can be accessed at www.hmrc.gov.uk/calcs/esi.htm.

Chapter 7

Property income

PROPERTY BUSINESS PROFITS AND LOSSES

General

7.1 The taxation of income from land and buildings changed radically for income tax purposes from 1995/96 onwards, and for corporation tax purposes from 1 April 1998.

Since 6 April 2005, income from property is taxed under *Income Tax (Trading and Other Income) Act 2005 (ITTOIA 2005), ss 260–262, 263–267, 268–275* and *859*. Prior to 2005/06, such income was taxed under former Schedule A.

Receipts, in relation to any land, include:

- any payment for a licence to occupy or otherwise to use any land or in respect of exercising any other right over the land; and
- rental charges, ground annuals and (in Scotland) feu duties, and any other annual payments reserved in respect of, or charged on or issuing out of, the land.

Excluded from the charge are profits:

- relating to farming and market gardening, mines, quarries and similar concerns, rents from mines, etc or rent from electric line wayleaves; and
- from letting tied premises, the rent from which is deemed to be a trading receipt.

Rents for 'caravans' confined to use at a single UK location and for permanently moored houseboats come within the property income charge. 'Caravan', for this purpose, broadly means any structure designed or adapted for human habitation which is capable of being moved. Sums payable, or valuable consideration provided, by a tenant or licensee for the use of furniture also come within the rules, unless they constitute receipts of a trade which consists in, or involves, the making available of furniture for use in premises (including caravans and houseboats) (*ITTOIA 2005, s 20*).

It is the person who is receiving or entitled to the income from the property who is charged to tax. It is important to note that beneficial entitlement may be unnecessary as far as, for example, an estate agent or other agent in receipt of such property is concerned (*ITTOIA 2005, s 271*).

The charge to income tax is computed on the full amount of the profits arising in the tax year.

Subject to any express contrary rules, property income profits are computed as if the trading income deductions rules were, in general, applicable. All businesses and transactions carried on or entered into by a person or partnership are treated as a single business for the purposes of calculating trading profits (*ITTOIA 2005, ss 264, 270*).

Example 7.1

John has a property business and makes his accounts up to 31 December each year. In recent years his profits have been as follows:

31 December 2008	£10,000
31 December 2009	£8,000
31 December 2010	£9,500

The profits will be taxable as follows:

2008/09		£	£
6 April 2008 to 31 December 2008 (270 days)	270/365 × £10,000	7,397	
1 January 2009 to 5 April 2009 (95 days)	95/365 × £8,000		2,082
			9,479
2009/10			
6 April 2009 to 31 December 2009 (270 days)	270/365 × £8,000	5,918	
1 January 2010 to 5 April 2010 (95 days)	95/365 × £9,500		2,473
			8,391

Partnerships are charged to tax on property income arising in the accounting period ending in the tax year in question, ie on the same basis as for trading income.

Property business profits

7.2 Rental business profits are computed on the same basis as the profits of a trade, using generally accepted accounting practice. Expenses are generally allowable if they are incurred wholly and exclusively for business purposes, and are revenue as opposed to capital in nature. Capital allowances are deducted as a business expense.

Legal and professional expenses in a letting business

7.3

Deductible from rental income	*Not deductible*
Insurance valuations	Purchasing or selling a property
Negotiation of rent reviews	Architect's and surveyor's fees, etc for improving a property
Evicting a tenant in order to relet the property	Planning applications (unless for permission to carry out repairs on a listed building)
Accountancy fees for preparing the letting business accounts	First letting or subletting of a property for more than one year
Renewing the lease for less than 50 years	
First letting or subletting of a property for one year or less	

Losses

7.4 The losses of a property business are computed in the same way as profits (see **6.81**). Rental business losses are generally carried forward and set off against future property business profits. Alternatively, it may be possible to set off losses against total income of the same year (or the next following year), to the extent that they relate to capital allowances or allowable agricultural expenses.

Example 7.2

Graham owns a house in Cyprus, which he only managed to let for seven weeks in 2010/11. As a result, he made a net loss from that property of £1,500. He also owns a flat in London which was let for the whole year and generated a net profit of £4,000 for 2010/11.

The loss from the Cyprus property of £1,500 cannot be set against the profit of £4,000 from the London flat, as it arose on an overseas property and must be kept separate. The Cyprus loss can be carried forward to set against future letting profits from overseas properties.

Allowances for capital expenditure

7.5 Expenditure on land and the structure of buildings is treated as part of the cost of the asset for capital gains tax purposes. Where appropriate, agricultural or industrial buildings allowances may be claimed (see **Chapter 6**), although it should be noted that these allowances are being gradually phased out over a four-year period from 2007/08. In addition, for expenditure incurred on or after 11 May 2001, 100% capital allowances can be claimed for the cost of renovating or converting certain space above commercial properties into flats for short-term letting. If the 100% allowance is not claimed in full, a writing down allowance of 20% a year (on cost) (25% prior to 2008/09) can be claimed until the expenditure is fully relieved. Stringent conditions apply, however, for expenditure to qualify.

From 11 April 2007 (for a period of five years), business premises renovation allowances (BPRAs) may be claimed for the costs of renovating or converting certain unused business property in any of the 2,000 or so areas of the UK that are designated as disadvantaged. The allowances offer 100% up-front tax relief and may be claimed by individuals or companies incurring capital expenditure on bringing qualifying business premises back into business use. The allowances are available both to landlords and to businesses occupying their own properties (*CAA 2001, s 360A*).

Plant and machinery allowances are available for expenditure on certain types of equipment used in the rental business. Such expenditure is 'pooled' together for capital allowances purposes.

Capital allowances are not available for expenditure on furniture and furnishings for use in dwelling houses (*CAA 2001, s 15(3)*). However, a deduction for wear and tear may be claimed, equal to 10% of the 'net rents' from furnished lettings (ie after deducting payments that would normally be borne by the tenant, such as water rates) (see **7.7**). In addition, a deduction may be claimed for replacing fixtures that are an integral part of a building (eg central heating systems), but excluding additional expenditure on 'improved' versions of those items. However, replacing single glazed windows with double glazed units is treated as allowable repairs and not disallowable improvements.

As an alternative to the 10% wear and tear allowance, a 'renewals basis' may be claimed. No relief is allowed for the original cost of an asset, but a deduction is given for the cost of replacing that asset (*CAA 2001, ss 35, 393A–393W*).

Wear and tear allowance

7.6 Where a taxpayer lets a residential property furnished, machinery and plant capital allowances cannot be claimed on furniture, furnishings or fixtures within the property. Instead a deduction can be claimed for either:

- a wear and tear allowance of 10% of the 'net rent' from the furnished letting to cover the depreciation of machinery and plant, such as furniture, fridges, etc supplied with the accommodation; or
- the net cost of replacing a particular item of furniture, etc but not the cost of the original purchase; this is called a 'renewals allowance' (ESC B47: see **7.11**).

A taxpayer may let both furnished and unfurnished property. If so, he must ensure that the 10% is calculated only on the net rent from the furnished lettings.

The 10% wear and tear allowance is only designed to provide a measure of relief for the depreciation of the machinery and plant within a residential property. It is not intended to cover:

- the capital cost of the residential property itself or the cost of improvements to the property (but a taxpayer may be able to claim relief for repairs);
- machinery and plant in other kinds of furnished accommodation, such as offices (where capital allowances may be claimed).

7.7 The wear and tear allowance is calculated by taking 10% of the net rent received for the furnished residential accommodation. To find the 'net rent' deduct charges and services that would normally be borne by a tenant but are, in fact, borne by the taxpayer (eg council tax, water and sewerage rates, etc).

The 10% deduction is given to cover the sort of machinery and plant assets that a tenant or owner-occupier would normally provide in unfurnished accommodation, including:

- movable furniture or furnishings, such as beds or suites;
- televisions;
- fridges and freezers;
- carpets and floor-coverings;
- curtains;
- linen;
- crockery or cutlery; and

- machinery and plant chattels of a type which, in unfurnished accommodation, a tenant would normally provide for himself (eg cookers, washing machines, dishwashers).

The relief is calculated simply on the net rents and not on the cost of particular items. But the deduction is only due if furnished accommodation is genuinely provided. A furnished property is one which is capable of normal occupation without the tenant having to provide their own beds, chairs, tables, sofas and other furnishings, cooker, etc. The provision of nominal furnishings will not meet this requirement. If the accommodation is not furnished, or only partly furnished, the 10% wear and tear allowance is not due.

The possible advantages of the 10% wear and tear allowance over the alternative (the renewals allowance) are that:

- it is simple to calculate; and
- the taxpayer gets a deduction from the outset; the renewals basis – outlined below – only gives relief when they replace the furnishings, etc.

If a taxpayer chooses to take the 10% wear and tear allowance, they cannot later claim for the cost of replacing the assets (but they can claim the cost of repairing them). Nor can they deal with some assets on one basis and some the other. If they take the 10% wear and tear allowance, that is the only relief they can have for the depreciation of machinery and plant (furniture, furnishings and fixtures, etc) of a type which, in unfurnished accommodation, a tenant would normally provide for himself (see the list above).

Renewals and 10% wear and tear allowance

7.8 However, in addition to the 10% allowance, a taxpayer can also deduct the net cost of renewing or repairing fixtures which are an integral part of the buildings. The net cost means the cost of the replacement less any amount received for the old item. See below for renewals of fixtures in unfurnished property.

Fixtures integral to the building are those which are not normally removed by either tenant or owner if the property is vacated or sold. For example, baths, washbasins, toilets, central heating installations. Expenditure on renewing such items is normally a revenue repair to the building. It is due even though the 10% wear and tear allowance has been deducted.

But a taxpayer cannot deduct:

- the original cost of installing these fixtures; or
- the extra cost of replacing a fixture with an improved version; for example, where a worn out but basic, cheap bathroom suite is replaced

with an expensive, high quality suite; they can only deduct the cost of replacing like with like.

The original cost of installation means either:

- the cost of installing the assets for the first time in a new property; or
- the cost of replacing worn out assets in an old property that has been bought to let; or
- which is being converted to let.

Renewals: furnished and unfurnished property

7.9 The cost of replacing machinery and plant supplied with the property can be claimed as an expense where neither the 10% wear and tear allowance nor machinery and plant capital allowances are claimed. This is called the 'renewals basis'. It is like the wear and tear allowance for furnished letting, in that:

- the renewals basis covers the same kind of assets; that is, free-standing movable machinery and plant assets like furniture, carpets, curtains, cookers, fridges, etc; and
- as a separate matter, revenue relief may also be due for replacing fixtures in the same way as in the wear and tear case (see above).

The renewals allowance is also available for unfurnished property. Here, HMRC will mainly be concerned with fixtures. However, the taxpayer may also provide some machinery and plant assets to the tenant (such as a heating boiler) although the let cannot be regarded as 'furnished'. The taxpayer can claim a renewals deduction in the same way, but they cannot claim the 10% wear and tear allowance because they do not come within the terms of ESC B47 (see below).

Whatever basis is chosen must be followed consistently each year.

Example 7.3

Malcolm replaces a washing machine in a flat he lets. He sells the old washing machine for £20 and buys a washer dryer costing £559 to replace it. The cost of buying a new washing machine like the old one would have been £399. Malcolm deducts from the £559 both the £20 received for the old machine and the £160 that represents the difference in cost between a washing machine and a washer dryer. His renewals deduction is therefore £379.

Sometimes, it is impossible to find the current cost of replacing an old asset with something identical. In this example, the old washing machine may be of a kind which is no longer made. Common sense has to be used to find the cost of a reasonable equivalent modern replacement.

Concessional allowances

7.10 Where a taxpayer claims that the 10% allowance is inadequate, HMRC may allow additional expenditure on a concessional basis. It is always open to the taxpayer at the outset to adopt the renewals basis instead. In other cases the 10% allowance may seem over generous, but HMRC should not seek to restrict the deduction for that reason.

HMRC Extra-Statutory Concession B47

7.11 This concession sets out the conditions under which a deduction for 10% of the net rents may be made for wear and tear on the furniture and furnishings in a let property. It also explains when the cost of renewing certain items which are fixed to the building, such as a bathroom suite, may be deducted, even though the 10% wear and tear allowance has been claimed.

The text of ESC B47 is as follows:

> **'Extra Statutory Concession B47**
>
> **Furnished lettings of dwelling houses – wear and tear of furniture**
>
> (1) *Section[s] 35(2), CAA 2001* specifically exclude[s] a claim for capital allowances on plant or machinery let for use in a dwelling house. Accordingly, capital allowances are not due on furniture and furnishings where the income from letting of furnished houses is assessable under *section 260, Income Tax (Trading and Other Income) Act 2005* (or Case VI, Schedule D for income tax cases up to 1994/95 and periods before 1 April 1988 for corporation tax) and is outside the scope of *section 503, ICTA 1988* (furnished holiday lettings) and *section 327, Income Tax (Trading and Other Income) Act 2005.*
>
> (2) In practice, an allowance for wear and tear may be made, where capital allowances are not due, by deducting 10% of the net rent received. For this purpose the rent is reduced by any part of the occupier's council tax and water rates which the landlord pays. If the rental includes payments for services which would normally be borne by a tenant and the amounts involved are material, these too should be subtracted before calculating the 10% deduction.
>
> (3) Where the 10% deduction is allowed, no further deduction is given for the cost of renewing furniture or furnishings, including suites, beds, carpets, curtains, linen, crockery, or cutlery. Nor is a further deduction allowed for chattels of a type which, in unfurnished accommodation, a tenant would normally provide for himself (for example, cookers, washing machines, dishwashers).

(4) However, in addition to the 10% allowance, the landlord can also claim the cost of renewing fixtures which are an integral part of the buildings, and which are revenue repairs to the fabric. These are fixtures which would not normally be removed by either tenant or owner if the property were vacated or sold (for example, baths, washbasins, toilets). Expenditure on renewing such items may be treated as expenditure on repairs even though the 10% allowance has been claimed.

(5) As an alternative to the 10% allowance, the actual cost of renewing furniture, furnishings and chattels may be claimed as a deduction. The amount to be allowed is the actual cost of the replacements excluding any additions or improvements, and after deducting the scrap value or sale price of the items replaced. The cost of the original items is not expenditure on renewals and is not allowable.

(6) Whichever basis a taxpayer chooses to adopt should be consistently applied to all furnished properties rented out.

(7) Before 1975/76, when the 10% basis started, there were several bases in common use. The Revenue will not disturb these so long as the let properties remain in the same ownership. Any properties acquired subsequently should be dealt with on one of the two bases described above.'

The tax charge

7.12 Unlike normal trading income, property business profits are taxable as investment income. This distinction is important because there are more reliefs available for trading income than non-trading income.

The profits of a property business are normally charged to tax based on the tax year itself (different rules apply to trading partnerships). Income from both furnished and unfurnished lettings is included as profits of the property business. Furnished holiday lettings income is also currently taxed as a property business, although it is effectively treated as trading income for most tax purposes. Note that the government intended to repeal the furnished holiday letting rules from 2010/11. Although the relevant legislation was included in the *Finance Bill 2010*, it was not subsequently enacted in *FA 2010*. Since the purpose of the repeal is to align UK and European law, it is likely that the legislation will be contained in a future Finance Act (see **7.27**).

Income tax on property business profits is usually collected as part of the self-assessment system of payments on account and balancing payments.

Special rules apply to the UK rental income of non-resident landlords.

Lease premiums

7.13 Premiums in respect of leases of more than 50 years' duration are charged to CGT. Grants, variations, surrenders and other lump sum payments in respect of leases which do not exceed 50 years are charged partly to CGT and partly to income tax under the property income provisions; such 'short leases' are also potentially subject to charges under *ITTOIA 2005* in the case of a sale with a right to reconveyance or leaseback or of a profit on sale. The duration of a lease is determined by reference to certain specific principles.

A 'lease' includes an agreement for a lease as well as any tenancy, but does not include a mortgage. A 'premium' includes:

> 'any like sum, whether payable to the immediate or a superior landlord or to a person connected [see below] with the immediate or a superior landlord.'

A person is 'connected' with an individual if that person is the individual's spouse or civil partner, or is a relative, or the spouse or civil partner of a relative, of the individual or of the individual's spouse or civil partner. 'Relative' means brother, sister, ancestor or lineal descendant (*ITA 2007, s 993*).

Duration of lease

7.14 There are rules for determining the duration of a 'lease', as follows (*ITTOIA 2005, s 303*):

- Rule 1 – Where the terms of the lease or any other circumstances render it unlikely that the lease will continue beyond a date falling before the expiry of the term of the lease and the premium was not substantially greater than it would have been (on certain specified assumptions) had the term been one expiring on that date, the duration of the lease is calculated to that earlier date.
- Rule 2 – Where there is provision for the extension of the lease beyond a given date by notice given by the tenant, account may be taken of any circumstances making it likely that the lease will be so extended.
- Rule 3 – Where the tenant, or a person connected with him, is, or may become, entitled to a further lease or the grant of a further lease (whenever commencing) on the same premises, or on premises including the whole or part of the same premises, the term of the lease may be treated as not expiring before the term of the further lease.
- Under this rule, the premium, or an appropriate part of it, payable on or in connection with either of the leases mentioned in the rule, may be treated as having been required under the other lease mentioned (*ITTOIA 2005, s 306(5)*).

The rules above are applied by reference to the facts known or ascertainable at the time of the grant of the lease or, in the case of a variation or waiver of a lease, the facts known or ascertainable at the time of the waiver etc (*ITTOIA 2005, s 304(1)*).

Example 7.4

Richard grants a lease of a property known as Sunnyside. The lease is expressed in the deed as being for a 51-year duration. Paul pays a premium of £3,000 in consideration of his being granted the lease. The normal rate that would be expected by way of premium for the grant of a ten-year lease of Sunnyside is £3,000. In addition, the terms of the lease specify that although the rent is £3,000 per year, after ten years the rent required under the lease will rise to £100,000 per year, which is a prohibitive amount for a property such as Sunnyside. This transaction will be caught by Rule 1, above. The lease would be treated as being a ten-year lease, and thus the premium would be regarded as one in respect of a lease of ten years' duration.

Example 7.5

Ruby grants a ten-year lease of Sunnyside to Thelma, at a full market rent. Under the terms of the lease, during the ninth year of its operation, Thelma has the option, in return for payment of £10,000, to choose that the lease be renewed for a further ten years, at a rent which is, considering the circumstances likely to exist at that time, less than market value. The £10,000 will be treated as a premium, and the lease will be regarded, by virtue of Rule 2 above, as being one for 20 years.

In this example, the situation would probably also be caught by Rule 3 and the premium could be allocated to either lease.

Tax treatment

7.15 The tax treatment of lease premiums paid to landlords depends on the length of a lease. If a lease is assigned, or granted for more than 50 years, it is treated as a whole or part disposal for capital gains tax purposes. If the duration of the lease is 50 years or less, part of the lease premium is treated as income in addition to actual rent. The income portion is normally calculated using the following formula:

$P \times (50 - Y/50)$, where

P = the premium; and

Y = the number of complete years of the lease, except the first.

The remainder of the premium is subject to the capital gains tax regime.

The income element of the premium is taxed on the landlord in the year the lease is granted.

The income element of the premium paid by a business tenant may be deducted as a business expense, but is spread evenly over the lease period (*ITTOIA 2005, ss 60–67, 276–307*).

Example 7.6

Bob grants Jean a lease for 21½ years for a premium of £10,000.

	£
Premium	10,000
Less: (21 – 1) × 2% × £10,000	(4,000)
Taxable amount	6,000

The part of the premium chargeable is taxable in full in the chargeable period in which the lease is granted.

7.16 In applying the above, it is assumed that all parties concerned act as they would act if they were at arm's length and that, where an unusual benefit is conferred by the lease, the benefit would not have been conferred had the lease been for a period ending on the likely date of determination, rather than on the actual date. The likely date of determination is in most cases the end of the period of the lease. An unusual benefit would be any benefit other than the right to enjoy the beneficial occupation of the premises or the right to receive a reasonable commercial rent in respect of them.

Where provision is made in the lease for the tenant to carry out work instead of paying a premium, the amount by which the landlord's estate has been increased in value by the provision requiring the work to be done is treated as a premium. However, if the work is of a type which, if the landlord and not the tenant were obliged to carry it out, would be deductible from the rent under general rules or as an expense of a property income business, the rule does not apply.

A complex form of relief may also be available (and continues to be available in the case of a property income business), if the premium arises on the grant of a sublease out of a head lease in respect of which a charge under these provisions has previously been made; also if a charge would have been made except for any exemption from tax; similarly, relief may be available if the previous charge arose as a result of the grant of a lease at undervalue.

Where it appears to an HMRC officer that the amount chargeable affects the tax liability of any other person, he may notify those other persons of the amount he proposes to charge. All parties may then object if they so wish and the amount will be determined by the commissioners as if it were an appeal.

The various payments under the present provisions are taxable in full in the chargeable period in which payment is received.

In general, the whole of a discounted premium is taxable in the relevant chargeable period. However, there is a relief where a premium is payable by instalments: originally, a taxpayer who satisfied HMRC that he would otherwise suffer undue hardship could elect to pay the tax chargeable by such instalments as HMRC might allow over a period not exceeding eight years. As this did not fit with self-assessment, the income or corporation tax payer now has the option to pay tax by instalments over the eight-year period.

Short leases: sale and leaseback income charges

7.17 In addition to the anti-avoidance provisions which deal with the duration of the lease and those which deal with the sale of land with the right to reconveyance, the legislation deals with ascertaining the charge to tax where land is sold and the agreement contains a provision for its lease back to the vendor or a person connected with him (rather than a reconveyance as such) (*ITTOIA 2005, s 285*).

The amount of the premium payable on the grant of the lease, plus the value at the date of sale of the right to purchase the reversion when the lease is granted, is taken to be the reconveyance price. The date of reconveyance is deemed to be the date of the grant of the lease.

Example 7.7

A landlord sells the property to the tenant for £30,000 but the agreement gives the landlord the right to take a 999-year lease for £15,000 after ten years.

If the value of the reversion was £500, the landlord would be charged as follows:

£30,000 – (£15,000 + £500) = £14,500 over ten years, discounted in accordance with the provisions treating only a portion of any premium as income.

This type of transaction is frequently used, not as a means of avoidance, but as a bona fide commercial method to finance the development of land; therefore, an express proviso excludes situations where the lease is granted and begins to run within one month after the sale.

The amount deemed to have been received is taken into account in computing profits in the period in which the estate or interest is 'sold'. The estate or interest is treated as 'sold' when any of the following occurs:

- an unconditional contract for its sale is entered into;
- a conditional contract for its sale becomes unconditional; or
- an option or right of pre-emption is exercised requiring the vendor to enter into an unconditional contract for its sale.

Where it appears to an inspector that the amount chargeable affects the tax liability of any other person, he may notify those other persons of the amount he proposes to charge; all parties may then object if they so wish and the amount will be determined by the commissioners as if it were an appeal.

Reverse premiums

7.18 Reverse premiums are the sums landlords pay to induce potential tenants to take a lease.

Reverse premiums received on or after 9 March 1998 are taxable as revenue receipts (*CTA 2009, s 98(1)*). However, the charge to tax does not apply to a premium to which the recipient was entitled immediately before that date, arrangements made on or after that date being ignored for this purpose.

Payments or other benefits made by a landlord to induce potential tenants are treated as taxable income of the tenant, except in certain specific circumstances. Benefits not involving an actual cash outlay by the landlord, such as the grant of rent-free periods of occupation, are not subject to tax (*ITTOIA 2005, ss 99–103*, BIM41050).

Inducements

7.19 The legislation taxes 'a payment or other benefit by way of inducement'. Such an inducement may take the form of a cash payment by the landlords, a period of rent-free occupation, a contribution to the tenant's costs or the assumption by the landlord of the tenant's liabilities. However, not all such inducements are caught by the rules. The following table summarises those inducements that are taxable under the reverse premium provision and those that are not.

Taxable	**Non-taxable**
Cash payments	The grant of a rent-free period of occupation
Contributions towards specified tenant's costs, eg relocation costs, start-up costs or fitting-out costs	The replacement by agreement of an existing rent with a lower rent because market conditions have made the original rent onerous
Sums paid to third parties to meet obligations of the tenant, eg rent to a landlord due under an old lease or a capital sum to terminate such a lease	A new lease by agreement without an onerous condition present in the former lease
An effective payment of cash by other means, eg the landlord writing off a sum owed by the tenant	

Broadly, inducements are caught if they involve the laying out of money. Benefits representing amounts foregone or deferred are not generally caught as they do not involve an outlay.

Tax treatment of receipts by way of reverse premiums

7.20 For tax purposes, a reverse premium is treated as a revenue receipt taxable under *ITTOIA 2005* (*CTA 2009, s 98(1)*).

The timing of the charge generally follows accepted principles of commercial accounting, the broad effect of which is to spread the reverse premium over the period of the lease, or to the first rent review, whichever is the shorter.

An anti-avoidance provision aims at preventing the exploitation of timing differences by the grant of a lease to a connected person on clearly uncommercial terms (eg a 25-year lease with no rent review clause).

The above provisions do not apply to a payment or benefit:

- if or to the extent that it is taken into account under the capital allowances provision relating to subsidies, contributions etc to reduce the recipient's expenditure qualifying for allowances;
- received in connection with a relevant transaction where the person entering into the transaction is an individual and the transaction relates to premises occupied or to be occupied as his only or main residence; or

- to the extent that it is consideration for the transfer of an estate or interest in land which constitutes the sale in a 'sale and leaseback transaction' as described in *ICTA 1988, s 779(1), (2)*.

RENT-A-ROOM RELIEF

Rent-a-room relief

7.21 The rent-a-room scheme is an optional exemption scheme that lets people receive a certain amount of tax-free 'gross' income (receipts before expenses) from renting furnished accommodation in your only or main home. The current annual exemption is £4,250 a year (£2,125 if letting jointly) (*ITTOIA 2005, Pt 7, Ch 1*).

Individuals can choose to take advantage of the scheme if they let furnished accommodation in their only or family home to a lodger. A lodger is someone who pays to live in the house, sometimes with meals provided, and who often shares the family rooms.

A lodger can occupy a single room or an entire floor of the house. However, the scheme does not apply if the house is converted into separate flats that are rented out. Nor does the scheme apply to let unfurnished accommodation in the individual's home.

An individual does not need to be a homeowner to take advantage of the scheme. Of course, those who are renting will need to check whether their lease allows them to take in a lodger.

If the lodger is charged for additional services, for example, cleaning and laundry, the individual will need to add the payments they receive to the rent, to work out the total receipts. If income exceeds £4,250 a year in total, a liability to tax will arise, even if the rent is less than that.

Rent-a-room scheme and running a business

7.22 The rent-a-room scheme can apply to taxpayers running bed and breakfast businesses or guest houses, or providing catering and cleaning services as part of a letting business. In such cases, the taxpayer must complete the relevant parts of the self-employment pages of their self-assessment tax return.

Example 7.8—Rent-a-room

Jo and Sinisha are single persons sharing a house as their main residence. They have for some years taken in lodgers to supplement their income. As Jo pays the greater share of the mortgage interest on the house, she and Sinisha have an agreement to share the rental income in the ratio 2:1, although expenses are shared equally.

Sinisha and Jo have elected for only the excess over the exemption amount to be taxed.

Sinisha has losses of £350 brought forward, which arose from this letting because he elected in one tax year for the exemption not to apply.

For 2009/10, the position is as follows:

	Jo	Sinisha
	£	£
Gross rents (y/e 5.4.10)	4,000	2,000
Allowable expenses	1,250	1,250
Net rents	2,750	750

Sinisha's share of gross rents is below his one-half share of the exempt amount (£2,125), so his election to tax only the excess is deemed to be withdrawn and his share is treated as nil. Jo's election to tax only the excess over the exemption continues to apply, so that her property income assessment will be £1,875 (£4,000 – £2,125).

For 2010/11, the position is as follows:

	Jo	Sinisha
	£	£
Gross rents (y/e 5.4.11)	5,400	2,700
Allowable expenses	2,250	2,250
Net rents	3,150	450

For both Jo and Sinisha, their share of gross rents exceeds their share of the exempt amount (£2,125 each). Since their share of the expenses also exceeds their share of the exempt amount, the election to tax only the excess will be unfavourable. It is therefore assumed that Jo withdraws her election (by 31 January 2013). They are both assessed on the basis of the normal property income computation, with Sinisha's £350 loss brought forward being set against his share.

Interpretation of rent-a-room relief and business use

7.23 HMRC have confirmed that rent-a-room relief is not available to exempt from tax income from the letting of part of a residence as an office or for other business purposes (HMRC Property Income Manual PIM4002). The relief only covers the circumstance where payments are made for the use of living accommodation. However, the relief is not denied where a lodger living in the home is provided with a desk, or the use of a room with a desk, which he or she uses for work or study.

Advantages and disadvantages of the scheme

7.24 There are advantages and disadvantages of the scheme – it is simply a matter of working out what is best for the individual concerned.

The principal point to bear in mind is that those using the rent-a-room scheme cannot claim any expenses relating to the letting (eg wear and tear, insurance, repairs, heating and lighting).

To work out whether it is preferable to join the scheme or declare all of the letting income and claiming expenses via a self-assessment tax return, the following methods of calculation need to be compared:

Method A: paying tax on the profit they make from letting worked out in the normal way for a rental business (ie rents received less expenses).

Method B: paying tax on the gross amount of their receipts (including receipts for any related services they provide) less the £4,250 (or £2,125) exemption limit.

Method A applies automatically unless the taxpayer tells their tax office within the time limit that they want method B – see below.

Once a taxpayer has elected for method B it continues to apply in the future until they tell their tax office they want method A. The taxpayer must tell their tax office within the time limit if they decide they no longer want method B to apply. They may want to do this where the taxable profit is less under method A, or where expenses are more than the rents (so there is a loss).

Example 7.9

A taxpayer may have gross receipts of £5,000 but their expenses are £6,000 so they have a loss of £1,000. Unless they opt out of method B, they will still be taxed on the excess of the gross receipts of £5,000 over the exemption limit of £4,250; that is, the taxable profit from letting in their own home will be £750.

Example 7.10—Where method B is better

Florence lets out a room in her own home for £100 a week. Nobody else lets a room in the house. Her gross receipts for the year are £5,200. She is not exempt from tax because her gross receipts exceed the exemption limit of £4,250. She has expenses of £1,000 so her profit is £4,200. The excess of her receipts over £4,250 is £950 (£5,200 less £4,250).

Using method A, she pays tax on her actual profit of £4,200.

Using method B, she pays tax on a profit of £950.

In Florence's case, method B is better and she elects for it. The profit of £950 is included in Florence's overall business computation if she has other rental business income from lettings outside her home. The profit of £950 will be the only rental business profit if Florence has no other letting income.

Example 7.11—Where method A is better

John lets out a room in his own home for a rent of £100 a week plus contributions to the heating and lighting. His total letting receipts for the year from letting the room are £5,200 rent plus £200 for lighting and heating = £5,400. He has expenses of £4,500 so his profit is £900. The excess of his gross receipts over £4,250 is £1,150 (£5,400 less £4,250).

John pays tax on his actual profit of £900 if he uses method A.

John pays tax on a profit of £1,150 if he uses method B.

In John's case, method A is better. Therefore, he either does not elect for method B or, if he has already done so, he tells his tax office that he no longer wants it to apply. The profit of £900 is included in John's overall business computation if he has other rental business income from lettings outside his home. The profit of £900 will be the only rental business profit if John has no other letting income.

Changing from method A to method B and vice versa

7.25 A taxpayer can change from method A to method B (or vice versa) from year to year. But each time they want to change, they must tell their tax office within the time limit (*ITTOIA 2005, s 801*).

Method B will automatically cease if the rent drops below the exemption limit of £4,250 (or £2,125). The taxpayer will then be automatically exempt from tax unless they ask within the time limit for their actual profit or loss to be taken into account. If, in the following year, their gross receipts go up and they want to use method B again, they must tell their tax office within the time limit. Otherwise, they are automatically taxed on the normal rental business basis (receipts less expenses) (HMRC Property Income Manual PIM4050).

Alternative method of calculation

7.26 The simplified method of calculation ('method B' above) is contained in *ITTOIA 2005, ss 795–798*, and elections for it are covered in *ITTOIA 2005, s 800*. An individual may elect for the alternative method of calculating profits given in *ss 796–798* to apply if:

(a) the individual qualifies for rent-a-room relief for a tax year, and

(b) the individual's total rent-a-room amount for the tax year exceeds the individual's limit for the tax year.

Any balancing charge is not counted in the total for this purpose. Under the alternative method of computation, tax is simply charged on gross receipts less the exemption limit, and no other expenses can be claimed, no capital allowances can be given, but any balancing charge is still taxable.

In practice, balancing charges in a continuing case are likely to be rare. This measure is to prevent exploitation of rent-a-room. It deals, for example, with the case where a taxpayer with a substantial boarding house business might otherwise elect for the alternative basis on a cessation of trading simply to avoid a large balancing charge.

The election must specify the tax year for which it is made, and has effect for that year and subsequent tax years (unless withdrawn by notice given by the individual).

An election or notice of withdrawal must be made or given to an officer of Revenue and Customs on or before the first anniversary of the normal self-assessment filing date for the tax year specified in the election or notice of withdrawal, or such later date as an officer of Revenue and Customs may, in a particular case, allow.

FURNISHED HOLIDAY LETTINGS

Trading income

7.27 The commercial letting of furnished holiday accommodation in the UK is currently treated as a trade for the income tax reliefs. The main advantage of this treatment is that any loss arising can currently be set against other income and is not restricted to rental profits. However, it is important that any such venture is carried out on a commercial basis with a view to making a profit within at least five years. Note that it was the UK government's intention to repeal the furnished holiday letting rules from 2010/11 but, in the event, this has yet to happen (see **7.32** for further details).The above treatment applies only where there is a 'commercial letting' of 'furnished holiday accommodation' which is situated in the UK.

'Commercial letting' requires that the property be let:

- on a commercial basis; and
- with a view to the realisation of 'profits'.

'Profits' here means the 'commercial', not the 'tax adjusted', profit. It should be noted that HMRC take the view that the required income profit motive may be displaced where the taxpayer's motive is the acquisition of a second, or retirement, home, or securing a long-term capital profit on disposing of the property. Claimants may also fail the above requirements where the size of the mortgage used to purchase the property is so large that the projected profitability is jeopardised or the commercial credibility of the scheme as a whole is, consequently, questionable even though individual lettings are on a commercial basis. In such cases, HMRC expect a written business plan to be prepared, with credible figures.

The separation of property income from trading income is a long-established principle in UK tax law. In *Salisbury House Estate Ltd v Fry* (1930) 15 TC 266, Lord Atkin said:

> '... the schedules are mutually exclusive; the specific income must be assessed under the specific schedule' (page 319).

and Lord MacMillan said:

> 'A landowner may conduct a trade on his premises, but he cannot be represented as carrying on a trade of owning land because he makes an income by letting it.' (page 330).

Lord MacMillan goes on to raise the possibility that a landowner may be providing services which are a separate trade.

The principle of *Salisbury House Estate Ltd v Fry* has often been applied by the courts subsequently.

In practice, it may sometimes be difficult to distinguish between a hotelier and a landlord of property which is let furnished. Generally, the essential distinction is taken to be the extensive degree of exclusive occupation of the accommodation that is granted in the course of a letting as opposed to the much more limited occupation rights of a guest in a hotel or lodging house. In *Griffiths v Jackson* (1982) 56 TC 583, Vinelott J said:

> 'The distinction between a hotelier or a lodging house keeper, on the one hand, and the owner of property who lets furnished rooms and provides services is no doubt in practice a narrow one, more particularly in these days of self-service hotels and motels, but the principle is clear and in the present case there can be no doubt on which side of the line the taxpayers' activities fall. It is quite clear from the terms of the tenancy agreements and the taxpayers' form of letter that they let rooms furnished to tenants, albeit with shared facilities and some services.'

Where the taxpayer seeks relief for losses in the early years of a trade, there is an additional, objective, condition that profits could reasonably be expected to be realised in the year of the loss or within a reasonable time thereafter. HMRC's view is that this test must be considered for each year for which relief is claimed and that it is necessary to look at the year of the loss and whatever, on the facts, is a reasonable time thereafter. And they dissent from a Special Commissioner's view that this relief is available so long as profits may be expected not later than a reasonable time after the end of the statutory four-year period (*Walls v Livesey (HMIT)* (1995) SpC 4).

7.28 'Holiday lettings' are defined as accommodation that satisfies conditions as to availability, letting and the pattern of occupation, as follows (*ITTOIA 2005, s 325*):

(a) available for commercial letting (ie with a view to the realisation of profits) to the public generally, as holiday accommodation, for a total period of at least 140 days in a 12-month period;

(b) so let for at least 70 such days; and

(c) periods for which the accommodation is let to the same person for more than 31 consecutive days does not amount to more than 155 days in the relevant period.

The appropriate 12-month period for which the conditions must be satisfied is in general the tax year or accounting period in question, except:

- where the accommodation in question was not let as furnished accommodation in the tax year or accounting period preceding the year in which it is so let, then, for the purposes of compliance with the tests for the current year, the 12 months beginning with the date on which the accommodation was so let in the current tax year or accounting period is relevant; and
- where the accommodation was let as furnished accommodation in the preceding tax year or accounting period, but is not so let in the following tax year or accounting period, then for the purposes of compliance with

the test for the current year reference is made to the 12 months ending on the date on which he ceased to let it in the current year.

Where the taxpayer has let out other furnished properties which satisfy all three of these conditions, except that the 70-day letting test is not met, then he may make a claim to 'average' the properties for this purpose. However, qualifying accommodation may not be specified in more than one claim for any one year or period.

In determining whether (b) above is satisfied, an average may be taken of all the taxpayer's holiday letting properties, upon making a claim (*ITTOIA 2005, ss 322–328*).

Losses

7.29 A person who makes a loss on all properties let as furnished holiday accommodation, taken together, can elect whether to set the loss against his general income for either the tax year in which the loss was made or the previous year in the same way as trading losses (see **6.84** regarding a temporary extension of the carry-back period from one to three years for 2008/09 and 2009/10). Any loss not claimed against general income must be set first against any other property business profits of the same year, any balance remaining being carried forward and set against the first available profits.

If the loss to any extent consists of capital allowances for plant and machinery, the whole loss can be set against any other property business losses of the same year or, where appropriate, carried forward against profits of the same business in later years.

Where a property business is made up solely of furnished holiday lettings, any losses can either be set against general income or carried forward.

However, a person whose property income business is made up partly of furnished holiday lettings and partly of other land and property can choose whether to set any loss from furnished holiday lettings against his general income. Any losses not claimed against general income must first be set against any other property income business profits in the same tax year, any balance being set against the first available profits of the same business in later tax years.

Example 7.12—Holiday lettings

Mrs Brown owns and lets out furnished holiday cottages. None is ever let to the same person for more than 31 days. Three cottages have been owned for many years, but Rose Cottage was acquired on 1 June 2010 and first let on that day. Rose Cottage was also let for 30 days between 6 April and 31 May 2011.

In 2010/11, days available for letting and days let are as follows:

	Days available	Days let
Honeysuckle Cottage	180	160
Primrose Cottage	130	100
Bluebell Cottage	150	60
Rose Cottage	150	90

Qualification as 'furnished holiday accommodation'

Honeysuckle Cottage qualifies as it meets both the 140-day availability test and the 70-day letting test.

Primrose Cottage does not qualify although it is let for more than 70 days as it fails to satisfy the 140-day test. Averaging (see below) is only possible where it is the 70-day test which is not satisfied.

Bluebell Cottage does not qualify by itself as it fails the 70-day test. However, it may be included in an averaging claim.

Rose Cottage qualifies as furnished holiday accommodation. It was acquired on 1 June 2010 so qualification in 2010/11 is determined by reference to the period of 12 months beginning on the day it was first let, in which it was let for a total of 90 days.

Averaging claim for 2010/11:

	Days let
Honeysuckle Cottage	160
Bluebell Cottage	60
Rose Cottage	90

$$\frac{160 + 60 + 90}{3} = 103.33 \text{ days}$$

All three cottages included in the averaging claim qualify as furnished holiday lettings, as each is deemed to be let for 103.33 days in 2010/11.

Reliefs for which furnished holiday lettings are treated as a trade

7.30 Reliefs for which furnished holiday lettings are treated as a trade include:

- retirement annuity relief and personal pensions;
- relief for losses;
- relief for pre-trading expenditure;
- treatment as earned income;
- Landlord's Energy Saving Allowance (LESA);
- rollover relief for capital gains tax;
- relief for gifts of business assets for capital gains tax;
- entrepreneurs' relief; and
- relief in respect of loans to traders for capital gains tax.

Benefits of furnished holiday lettings

7.31 Benefits for the taxpayer of treatment as a trader include the following:

- losses are not restricted to property business income, but can be set against general income or capital gains;
- capital allowances are available for expenditure on plant and machinery acquired for purposes of the letting;
- CGT rollover reliefs are available, where applicable and subject to the usual rules; likewise, relief for gifts of business assets and in respect of loans to traders;
- CGT entrepreneurs' relief may be due on the sale of property;
- the income attracts retirement annuity or personal pension relief.

It should nevertheless be noted that the 'rent-a room' exemption may prove more advantageous to the taxpayer.

Possible changes to the furnished holiday letting rules

7.32 Landlords with income from furnished holiday accommodation elsewhere in the European Economic Area (EEA) do not currently qualify for this treatment. They are treated, instead, in the same way as landlords of other types of overseas property, under the property income rules. Since this difference may not be compliant with European law, the UK government announced in the 2009 Budget that it should repeal the furnished holiday letting rules from 2010/11. The relevant legislation was included in the Finance Bill 2010 but was not enacted in *FA 2010*.

In the emergency Budget on 22 June 2010, the coalition government confirmed that the previous government's plans to repeal the furnished holiday lettings provisions have been scrapped. However, the new government is undertaking a consultation with a view to changing the existing tax treatment of furnished holiday lettings from April 2011. Changes expected include an increase in the number of days on which properties are either available for letting on a commercial basis or actually let. There may also be restrictions on the use of loss relief.

RENT FROM PROPERTY OUTSIDE THE UK

Overview

7.33 Rent and other receipts from properties outside the UK are taxed separately under *ITTOIA 2005, Pt 3, Ch 11* on an arising basis (*ITTOIA 2005, ss 270, 271, 357* and *831*).

The special rules for furnished holiday lettings (see **7.27**) do not apply to overseas properties.

Rental business basis periods

7.34 The current, fiscal year basis applies to income from properties that were first let on or after 6 April 1994. The basis period is, therefore, the year to 5 April.

Computing profit

7.35 The rules for computing the amount of rental profit or loss are the same as those used for UK property income businesses. Every property outside the UK has its profits computed using trading income principles for 1995/96 and later years, whatever basis periods are used.

The taxpayer computes the profit or loss for the rental business as a whole and not the result for individual properties. But they will need to make separate computations for tax credit relief purposes. This is to ensure that the overseas tax they pay on income from a property in one foreign country is only set against the UK tax on that property; they cannot set that foreign tax against UK tax due on income from a property in another country.

Travel

7.36 There are special rules for travel connected with overseas trades. These do not apply to rental income. However, deductions may be made for travel costs on the same basis as for UK property income businesses. That is, the taxpayer must be able to show that the travel was incurred wholly and exclusively for business purposes and not (wholly or partly) for some other purpose (such as a holiday).

Capital allowances

7.37 Capital allowances are available but normal capital allowances rules apply. For example, there is a rule which denies industrial buildings allowance for a building outside the UK unless it is used for the purposes of a trade which is taxable under *ITTOIA 2005* (*CAA 2001, ss 15, 282*).

Losses

7.38 All the overseas properties are treated as a single overseas letting business. Hence excess expenditure on one overseas property is automatically set against surplus receipts from other overseas properties. Any overall overseas rental business loss can be carried forward and set against future overseas rental business profits; but it cannot be set against UK rental business profits or against any other income.

Remittance basis

7.39 Overseas property income is taxed on the remittance basis where the rental income belongs to:

- a person domiciled outside the UK; or
- a Commonwealth citizen or a citizen of the Irish Republic who is not ordinarily resident in the UK.

No loss can ever arise on income taxed on the remittance basis.

Tax credit relief

7.40 Normally, the tax authorities of the country where the let property is situated will also charge tax on the letting profits. This means that a UK resident landlord will pay tax on the same profits both here and abroad. However, the double charge is relieved by deducting the overseas tax paid on the property income from the UK tax due on the same income. This is done either under the terms of a double taxation treaty with the overseas country or, where no treaty exists, under separate UK rules.

Foreign tax

7.41 If the overseas income has suffered foreign tax and a claim to tax credit relief is made, it will be necessary, for the purposes of the source by source rules, to identify the amount of UK tax attributable to income from each particular property. Where, therefore, tax credit relief is claimed, separate computations of profits and losses for each property will be required.

For the purposes of calculating tax credit relief, losses should be deducted in the order most favourable to the taxpayer's claim. Normally, this will mean that losses should be allocated first against the source that has suffered the lowest rate of foreign tax.

Example 7.13

A taxpayer has income assessable for 2009/10 from properties in the following countries:

	Country A	Country B	Country C	Total
Income	£6,000	£4,000	£6,000	
Expenses	£1,000	£6,000	£4,000	
Profit (loss)	£5,000	(£2,000)	£2,000	£5,000

The following amounts of foreign tax have been paid:

	Taxable	Rate of foreign tax	Tax deducted
Country A	£5,000	11%	£550
Country B	Nil		
Country C	£2,000	30%	£600
Total foreign tax			£1,150

Assuming that the overseas rental income is wholly chargeable at the basic rate of income tax (and that the basic rate of income tax is 20%), the income tax due will be £5,000 × 20% = £1,000.

Calculation of tax credit relief

Allocate losses to the income that has suffered the lowest rate of foreign tax (income from Country A):

Country A Profit	£5,000
Losses	£2,000
Net	£3,000 @ 20% = £600

All of the foreign tax paid of £550 relating to Country A is available for tax credit relief.

Country C Profit £2,000 @ 20% = £400

Although foreign tax of £600 has been paid, the amount available for tax credit relief is limited to the amount of UK tax charged on the same income (ie £400).

Summary

Income tax due	£600 + £400 =	£1,000
Tax credit relief	£550 + £400 =	(£950)
Net UK tax payable		£50

The balance of Country C's tax of £200 (£600 – £400) cannot be set off against the income tax attributable to the Country A income and cannot be repaid.

Note that, if all or part of the Country B loss of £2,000 had been set against income from Country C, the overall tax bill in the UK would be higher.

NON-RESIDENT LANDLORDS SCHEME

Overview

7.42 The Non-resident Landlords Scheme (NRLS) is a scheme for taxing the UK rental income of non-resident landlords.

The rules governing the scheme are contained in the *Taxation of Income from Land (Non-residents) Regulations 1995 (SI 1995/2902)*.

The HMRC website contains much useful information on the scheme at www.hmrc.gov.uk/cnr/nr_landlords.htm.

The scheme requires UK letting agents, referred to as 'non-resident landlord representatives' to deduct basic rate tax from any rent they collect for non-resident landlords. If non-resident landlords do not have UK letting agents acting for them, and the rent is more than £100 a week, their tenants must deduct the tax. When working out the amount to tax, the letting agent/tenant can take off deductible expenses.

Letting agents and/or tenants do not have to deduct tax if approval is obtained from HMRC. But, even though the rent may be paid with no tax deducted, it remains liable to UK tax. So, non-resident landlords must include it in any tax return HMRC sends them.

A 'non-resident landlord representative' is defined as (*ITA 2007, s 971(3)*):

'(a) a person by whom any sums are payable to the non-resident which are to be treated as receipts of a UK property business (within the meaning of *Chapter 2 of Part 3 of ITTOIA 2005* or *Chapter 2 of Part 4 of CTA 2009*), carried on by the non-resident, or

(b) a person who acts on behalf of the non-resident in connection with the management or administration of any such business.'

Applications for payments with no tax deducted

7.43 Non-resident landlords who are eligible can apply at any time for approval to receive their UK rental income with no tax deducted. This includes applying before they have left the UK or before the letting has started.

When approval has been given, HMRC sends a notice of approval to receive rent with no tax deducted to the non-resident landlord, and a separate notice to the letting agents or tenants named on the application form authorising them to pay rent to the non-resident landlord without deducting tax.

Authority to pay rent to a non-resident landlord with no tax deducted is generally backdated to the beginning of the quarter in which HMRC receives the non-resident landlord's application.

As the tax year for the NRLS starts on 1 April, the quarters are the three-month periods that end on 30 June, 30 September, 31 December and 31 March. So, if a non-resident landlord applies to HMRC on, say, 20 September, the authority they send to his letting agent/tenant will usually take effect from 1 July.

HMRC may refuse approval if they are not satisfied that the information in the application is correct, or the non-resident landlord will comply with their UK tax obligations.

HMRC may withdraw approval if:

- they are no longer satisfied that the information in the application is correct;
- they are no longer satisfied that the non-resident landlord will comply with their UK tax obligations; or
- the non-resident landlord fails to supply information requested by HMRC.

Where HMRC refuses, or withdraws, approval to receive rent with no tax deducted, the non-resident landlord can appeal to them within 90 days.

Where HMRC and the non-resident landlord cannot reach agreement, the appeal will be referred to the tax tribunal.

HMRC will tell an agent/tenant not to deduct tax if the non-resident landlord has successfully applied for approval to receive rents with no tax deducted. But rent paid with no tax deducted remains liable to UK tax. So, non-resident landlords must include it in any tax return HMRC sends them.

All non-resident landlords who receive rents with no tax deducted will have a tax district.

Some individuals who are not resident in the UK for tax purposes are not sent an annual tax return automatically, even though they have UK rental income. This is because many non-residents will have sufficient UK personal allowances to cover any liability.

Conditions for approval

7.44 Non-resident landlords can apply to receive their rent with no tax deducted on the basis that either:

- their UK tax affairs are up to date;
- they have not had any UK tax obligations before they applied;
- they do not expect to be liable to UK income tax for the year in which they apply; or
- they are not liable to pay UK tax because they are Sovereign Immunes (these are generally foreign Heads of State, governments or government departments).

'Usual place of abode'

7.45 Although HMRC refer to 'non-resident' landlords, it is usual place of abode and not non-residence that determines whether a landlord is within the scheme or not.

In the case of individuals, HMRC normally regard an absence from the UK of six months or more as meaning that a person has a usual place of abode outside the UK. It is therefore possible for a person to be resident in the UK yet, for the purposes of the scheme, have a usual place of abode outside the UK.

Letting agents

7.46 A letting agent is a person who:

- has a 'usual place of abode' (see **7.45**) in the UK;
- acts for a non-resident landlord in the running of their UK rental business;

- has the power to receive income of the non-resident landlord's rental business, or has control over the direction of that income; and
- is not an 'excluded person'.

An excluded person is someone whose activity on behalf of a non-resident landlord is confined to providing legal advice/services. However, solicitors who draw up a lease and collect the rent for the first period are not excluded persons.

The Centre for Non-Residents have produced a booklet called *Non-resident Landlords – Guidance Notes for Letting Agents and Tenants* that tells people what their responsibilities are under the scheme. The booklet can be found on the HMRC website at www.hmrc.gov.uk/cnr/nrl_guide_notes.pdf. In addition, there is a brief *Letting Agent's Guide to the NRL Scheme* which outlines the main features of the scheme. This guide can be found on the HMRC website at www.hmrc.gov.uk/cnr/nrl200.pdf.

Letting agents' obligations

7.47 Letting agents that have to operate the NRLS must:

- register with the Centre for Non-Residents;
- account quarterly for the tax due under the scheme by 5 July following the year ended 31 March;
- complete an annual information return; and
- where they have deducted tax, give the non-resident landlord a tax deduction certificate NRL6.

Tenants

7.48 Tenants of non-resident landlords have to operate the scheme if:

- the rent they pay is over £100 a week; and
- either:
  - they pay the rent direct to a non-resident landlord;
  - they pay the rent to a person outside the UK; or
- they pay the rent to a person who is not a letting agent in the UK.

The Centre for Non-Residents may sometimes instruct tenants to operate the scheme even where the rent paid is less than £100 a week.

Tenants' obligations

7.49 Tenants who have to operate the NRLS have to:

- account quarterly for any tax due under the scheme by 5 July following each year ended 31 March, give the non-resident landlord a tax deduction certificate NRL6; and
- complete an annual information return.

HM Armed Forces personnel and other Crown Servants

7.50 The NRLS applies to members of HM Armed Forces and other Crown Servants – for example, diplomats – if they have a 'usual place of abode' outside the UK. They are treated no differently from any other non-resident landlords, even though their employment duties overseas are treated as performed in the UK for the purpose of charging their salaries to tax. So if their absence from the UK is for more than six months, they are within the scheme.

Administration of the Scheme

7.51 The NRLS is administered by HMRC's Centre for Non-Residents:

HM Revenue & Customs
Centre for Non-Residents
Unit 364
St John's House
Merton Road
Bootle
Merseyside
L69 9BB
Telephone: 0151 210 2222

Expenses

7.52 Letting agents or tenants must generally tax the rental income they pay to non-resident landlords unless HMRC have told them not to. In calculating the amount to tax, they take into account any 'deductible expenses' they pay in a quarter. These are expenses that they can reasonably be satisfied will be allowable expenses for the non-resident landlords when the profits of their rental businesses are computed.

Allowable expenses of a rental business

7.53 Broadly, in calculating the profits of a rental business, expenses are allowable where:

- they are incurred wholly and exclusively for the purposes of the rental business; and
- they are not of a 'capital' nature.

Expenses paid by letting agents and tenants which will normally be allowable expenses are:

- accountancy expenses for the rental business;
- advertising costs of attracting new tenants;
- cleaning;
- costs of rent collection;
- council tax while the property is vacant but available for letting;
- gardening;
- ground rent;
- insurance on buildings and contents;
- interest paid on loans to buy land or property;
- interest paid on loans to build or improve premises;
- legal and professional fees;
- maintenance charges made by freeholders, or superior leaseholders, of leasehold property;
- maintenance contracts (eg gas servicing);
- provision of services (eg gas, electricity, hot water);
- rates;
- repairs which are not significant improvements to the property, including:
  - mending broken windows, doors, furniture, cookers, lifts, etc,
  - painting and decorating,
  - replacing roof slates, flashing and gutters; and
- water rates.

Letting agents and tenants can deduct only those expenses which they pay or which are paid on their direction. This means they cannot deduct:

- expenses which the landlord pays, even if they have details of the expenses;

- expenses which have accrued in a quarter but which have not been paid in the quarter;
- capital allowances; and
- any personal allowances due to the landlord.

Calculating the tax due

7.54 In order to calculate the tax due, the letting agents/tenants should:

- add together the rent they actually receive in the quarter plus:
  - any rent that they had the power to receive, and
  - any rent paid away at their direction to another person,
- less:
  - any deductible expenses that they paid in the quarter; and
  - any deductible expenses that were paid away in the quarter at their direction by another person.

It is the date letting agents/tenants actually receive/pay the rents (or pay the deductible expenses) that determines when they calculate tax. The periods for which the rents (or expenses) are due are not relevant.

Example 7.14

Anytown Lettings Ltd is due to collect rental income of £5,000 a quarter for Mr Anderson, who is a non-resident landlord. In one quarter it collects only £2,500. It pays out £200 for gardening and cleaning.

The calculation is:

	£
Rental income received	2,500
Less deductible expenses paid	200
	2,300

Basic rate tax on £2,300 = £460

Example 7.15

Anytown Lettings Ltd is due to collect rental income of £3,000 a quarter for Mr Brown, a non-resident landlord. But Anytown Lettings Ltd authorises the tenant to pay £1,000 to a third party in settlement of a loan (this is not a deductible expense).

The calculation is:

	£
Rental income received	2,000
Plus rental income paid away at Anytown Lettings Ltd's direction	1,000
	3,000

Basic rate tax on £3,000 = £600

Example 7.16

If, in Example 7.15, Anytown Lettings Ltd had authorised the tenant to pay £1,000 to a builder to repair a leaking roof, instead of the payment to a third party to repay a loan, the £1,000 would be a deductible expense. The calculation would then be:

	£
Rental income received	2,000
Plus rental income paid away at Anytown Lettings Ltd's direction	1,000
Less deductible expenses	(1,000)
	2,000

Basic rate tax on £2,000 = £400

Tenant-finders

7.55 Some people enter into arrangements with non-resident landlords whereby they find a tenant for the landlord's property. The tenant-finder then collects rent for a period from which he or she recovers the fee. The tenant subsequently pays rental income directly to the landlord. In such circumstances the tenant-finder does not have to operate the NRLS in respect of the landlord, provided:

- the period for which rent is collected is no more than three months; and
- the tax which would be payable would be no more than £100.

Example 7.17

Mr Jones finds a tenant for a non-resident landlord in respect of a property rented at £500 per month. Mr Jones collects two months' rent in order to recover his fee of £700. The tenant pays the rent direct to the landlord from the third month.

If Mr Jones were required to operate the scheme, his tax calculation would be:

	£
Rental income received	1,000
Less deductible expenses	700
	300

Basic rate tax on £300 = £60

As the tax is less than £100, Mr Jones does not have to operate the scheme.

Example 7.18

Mrs McGregor finds a tenant for a non-resident landlord in respect of a property rented at £2,000 a year. Mrs McGregor collects six months' rent in advance, from which she recovers her fee of £500. She also pays insurance and repairs of £400.

Mrs McGregor's tax calculation is:

	£
Rental income received	1,000
Less deductible expenses	900
	100

Basic rate tax on £100 = £20

The tax is only £20 but, because Mrs McGregor collects more than three months' rent, she must operate the scheme. She should deduct the tax of £20 and pay it with her quarterly return.

Where tenant-finders collect a period's rent and do not have to operate the scheme, the non-resident landlord will receive rental income with no tax deducted for that period. Subsequently, tenants will pay rent direct to the landlord and may have to operate the scheme. In these circumstances, it would be helpful if tenant-finders notify the tenant of his or her obligations under the NRLS.

Record-keeping requirements and penalties

7.56 Letting agents and tenants must keep adequate records to satisfy HMRC auditors that they have complied with their obligations under the scheme. In particular, for each non-resident landlord, letting agents and tenants should keep separately:

- a record of rental income received by the letting agent or paid by the tenant (showing the date and amount of each receipt or payment);
- copies of any correspondence with the landlord regarding their usual place of abode;
- unless the letting agent is authorised to pay rental income with no tax deducted, a record of expenses paid (showing the date and amount of each payment and a brief description of the expense); and
- invoices and receipts (or copies) to provide evidence of expenses paid.

Letting agents and tenants should retain records for six years after the end of the year to 31 March to which they relate.

Penalties may be charged under *TMA 1970, s 98* for failure to make a return or for making an incorrect return.

Chapter 8

Trusts and estates

TRUSTS AND SETTLEMENTS

Trust or settlement

8.1 A 'settlement' is sometimes referred to as a trust, implying that they share the same meaning. However, a settlement can include any disposition, trust, covenant, agreement, arrangement or transfer of assets.

From 6 April 2006, settled property is redefined as any property held in trust other than property held as nominee, bare trustee for a person absolutely entitled, an infant or disabled person (*Taxation of Chargeable Gains Act 1992 (TCGA 1992), s 60*). References in the legislation to a settlement are construed as references to settled property and the meaning of settlement is determined by case law. This measure effectively aligns what is treated as a settlement for the general purposes of income tax and tax on chargeable gains (*FA 2006, ss 88* and *89, Schs 12* and *13*).

The effect is that income tax will be charged on income arising to the trustees of a 'settlement' with the definition of settlement being derived from existing trust law and case law, and 'settled property' being defined in the tax legislation.

The existing definition of settlement in *Income Tax (Trading and Other Income) Act 2005 (ITTOIA 2005), s 620* still applies for the purposes of the settlements anti-avoidance legislation.

Since 6 April 2006, the trustees of a settlement have been treated as a single person for income tax and *TCGA* purposes.

The settlements legislation can apply if an individual enters into an arrangement to divert income to someone else, resulting in a tax saving. If those arrangements are bounteous, or uncommercial, or not at arm's length, or (for gifts between spouses or civil partners) wholly or substantially a right to income, the settlements rules can apply to cancel the income tax advantage.

Trust documentation

8.2 Under self-assessment, HMRC generally rely on information shown by trustees, settlors and beneficiaries in their annual tax returns or repayment claims. They do not usually request a copy of a new family trust document (HMRC Trusts, Settlements and Estates Manual TSEM1705). When a new trust is created, trustees are sent a form which asks them to give some basic factual information about the identities of the trustees and settlor and whether the trustees can accumulate income or distribute it at their discretion.

Trust income

8.3 A trust broadly arises when assets are transferred to trustees, who hold them on behalf of one or more beneficiaries. A trust is usually created by a written document, possibly during an individual's lifetime or perhaps by a will upon death.

For the purpose of determining liability for income tax, the liability of trustees to tax on income of a trust fund must not be confused with the liability of a beneficiary to tax on distributions from a trust fund.

The rate of tax borne by trustees depends largely on whether the trust is a discretionary trust, or whether a beneficiary is absolutely entitled to the trust income.

Trust income may be treated as the settlor's for income tax purposes where (*ITTOIA 2005, ss 619–648*):

- the settlor (or spouse or civil partner) retains an interest in the settled property (for example, as trust beneficiaries);
- an unmarried child of the settlor who is under the age of 18 receives settlement income (to the extent that the income exceeds £100 for a particular child); or
- capital sums (eg loans) are paid by the trustees to the settlor (or spouse/civil partner). Such amounts may be treated as the settlor's income for the year, within certain limits.

Settlor

8.4 *Income Tax Act 2007 (ITA 2007), s 467* defines a settlor for income tax purposes. This is based on the wider definition in the settlements anti-avoidance legislation. The measure took effect from 6 April 2006 and affects settlements whenever created.

A person is a settlor in relation to a settlement if it was made (or treated as made) by that person directly or indirectly, or if it arose on his or her death. A settlor of property means that which is settled or derived from settled property and a person is treated as having made a settlement if he or she has provided (or undertaken to do so) property directly or indirectly for the settlement. If A enters into a settlement where there are reciprocal arrangements with B, B is treated as the settlor for these purposes.

With effect from 6 April 2006 in relation to settlements whenever created, *ITA 2007, s 470* identifies the settlor where there is a transfer of property between settlements made for no consideration or less than full consideration. Where property is disposed of from settlement 1 and acquired by settlement 2 (even if in a different form), the settlor(s) of settlement 1 will be treated as the settlor(s) of settlement 2, unless the transfer occurs because of a will variation.

8.5 *ITA 2007, s 472* identifies the settlor in relation to will and intestacy variations occurring on or after 6 April 2006 regardless of the deceased's date of death. The measure applies where there is a variation in accordance with *TCGA 1992, s 62(6)* and property which was not settled property under the will becomes settled. In this case, a person mentioned in the group below is treated as having made the settlement and providing the property for it:

- a person who immediately before the variation was entitled to the property, or to property from which it derives, absolutely as legatee (as defined);
- a person who would have become entitled to the property, or to property from which it derives, absolutely as legatee but for the variation;
- a person who immediately before the variation would have been entitled to the property, or to property from which it derives, absolutely as legatee but for being an infant or other person under a disability; and
- a person who would, but for the variation, have become entitled to the property, or to property from which it derives, absolutely as legatee if he had not been an infant or other person under a disability.

If property would have been comprised in a settlement as a result of the deceased's will but the effect of the variation is that it becomes comprised in another settlement, the deceased will be treated as the settlor. He or she will also be the settlor if an existing settlement of which the deceased was settlor becomes comprised in another settlement. In both cases, the deceased is treated as having made the settlement immediately before his or her death unless the settlement arose on the person's death.

Trustees' income tax position

8.6 Trustees are liable to tax on trust income (whether by deduction or direct assessment) at the basic rate, or (before 6 April 2008) in relation to savings income, at the lower rate. Prior to 2004/05, they were not liable to higher rate tax in respect of that income, though they may have been liable to a special rate above basic rate or, in certain circumstances, for higher rate tax unpaid by beneficiaries of discretionary trusts. From 6 April 2004, the special rate of tax applicable to trusts was increased from 34% to 40%, ie the same as the higher rate of income tax. From 2010/11, the trust rate has been increased again and is now 50% (*FA 2009, s 6*).

From 6 April 2005, a basic rate band applies to the first slice of income of all discretionary trusts and accumulation trusts liable at the 'rate applicable to trusts'. This rate band was initially £500, but was increased to £1,000 from 6 April 2006. Anti-avoidance measures prevent multiple standard rate bands from being obtained where a settlor has made more than one settlement (*ITA 2007, s 492*). This restricts the band to the lesser of £200, or £1,000 divided by the number of settlements made by the same settlor.

Any one or more of several trustees is assessable and chargeable in respect of the trust income. However, trustees are regarded as representing the beneficiaries and are not treated as individuals for tax purposes, ie their personal circumstances are disregarded. Thus, trustees cannot set their own entitlement to personal reliefs against trust income. Further, resident trustees are not liable to tax on foreign income paid directly to a non-UK domiciled beneficiary, though a UK-resident beneficiary may be liable to tax on income arising to non-resident trustees under certain anti-avoidance provisions (see **8.25**).

From 6 April 2006, the trustees of a settlement are treated as a single person for both income tax and *TCGA* purposes.

Trust income is assessed under the provisions appropriate to its source: eg income from a trade is assessed under *ITTOIA 2005* and the trustees are entitled to claim any relief applying to that source of income (eg loss relief).

Employee share schemes

8.7 Trustees of employee share schemes are exempt from income tax in respect of interest received from such individuals to the extent that it is matched by interest paid to the company (*ITTOIA 2005, s 752(1), (2)*).

Trustees' management expenses

8.8 Trustees' management expenses (TMEs) are paid out of taxed income and cannot, therefore, be relieved against trust income for the purposes of basic or lower rate tax (prior to 6 April 2008) (*ITA 2007, Pt 9, Ch 8*). However, TMEs are deductible in computing the rate applicable to trusts (with discretionary powers) in full or in part.

To be an allowable TME, an item must at least be an expense. Not all payments out of the trust can be categorised as expenses. Some are distributions.

A distribution is a payment out of the trust that is either itself a gift made directly to the beneficiary, or is payment to a third party that procures a benefit for a beneficiary (as distinct from a benefit to the trust funds). Examples of distributions are:

- payment of cash or a grant to a beneficiary;
- the costs of procuring a benefit in kind for a beneficiary, such as the payment of a beneficiary's utility bills;
- the cost of providing gifts, medical treatment, support or entertainment to beneficiaries.

Distributions are not expenses, and so are never allowable TMEs.

TMEs are not like any other expenses for tax purposes.

There is a common misconception that they are on a par with tax deductions for trading. Where a trust carries on a trade, the normal trading income rules apply to the computation of the profit/loss of that trade. In contrast, TMEs are expenses incurred in the capacity of trustee, not in any other capacity such as a trader. They are not related to the expenses or deductions of a trade or rental business. Even if a large trust is run like a business, for TMEs' purposes the rules for allowable trading deductions are not in point. A separate set of principles, legislation and case law apply.

TMEs are the expenses of managing the trust, not the expenses taken into account in computing the profit/loss of a trade. The more common tax notions of 'capital' and 'income', eg construction of a new building versus repairs, do not apply. What is relevant is 'capital' and 'income' in trust law.

The allowance of TMEs for tax purposes is based, to a large extent, on trust law.

8.9 In managing a trust, the trustees may incur expenses in the course of exercising their duties and powers. These are to be distinguished from payments made to beneficiaries (distributions).

Expenses may be referred to as 'capital' or 'income' expenses, depending on which fund they are to be paid out of. For an expense to be properly chargeable to income in trust law the trustees must have authority to put the final burden of that expense on the income fund.

The administrative powers of trustees derive from four sources, any one or more of which might apply:

(1) an order of the court in a specific case;

(2) the provisions of the trust deed;

(3) trust statute; and

(4) general law in the field of trusts and equity (including principles to be discerned from case law).

In order to decide whether expenses are to be paid out of capital or income, trust law looks at the four sources in the above order. So, for example, for trust law purposes, a court order has priority over the provisions of the trust deed, and the provisions of the trust deed have priority over general trust law.

The main case on trust management expenses is *Carver v Duncan* [1985] AC 1082. The more recent case of *Trustees of the Peter Clay Discretionary Trust v Revenue and Customs Comrs* (2007) SpC 595 offers some further guidance in this area. In that case, the trustees claimed certain expenses (ie trustees' fees, investment management fees, bank charges, custodian fees and professional fees for accountancy services), some of which contained elements of both income and capital. The Special Commissioners held that, in principle, a proportion of all the expenses, apart from the investment management fees, was attributable to income and properly chargeable to income for the purposes of *Income and Corporation Taxes Act 1988 (ICTA 1988), s 686(2AA)* (now *ITA 2007, s 484*). In addition, the Commissioners held that the accruals basis was a proper way of allocating trust management expenses to particular tax years, as opposed to when such expenses were incurred and paid.

Whilst the decision will clearly be welcomed by most trustees and professional advisers, in appropriate cases they will be required to apply their judgment in apportioning trust management expenses between income and capital. This could be the 'trigger' for enquiries by HMRC and possible disagreements over the correct proportions to be used. Full disclosure of the expenses apportioned and the basis of apportionment will be necessary in such cases, to reduce the possibility of a subsequent 'discovery' by HMRC outside the normal enquiry window.

Trustees acting for incapacitated persons

8.10 The trustee, guardian, tutor, etc of any incapacitated person is chargeable to income tax to the extent that the incapacitated person would be charged and assessed. This is so where the trustee, etc has the direction, control or management of the property of the incapacitated person, whether or not that person resides in the UK.

A new tax regime for certain trusts with vulnerable beneficiaries took effect from 6 April 2004 (*FA 2005, s 23*). Certain trusts and beneficiaries can elect into the regime and, where a claim for special tax treatment is made for a tax year, no more tax will be payable in respect of the relevant income and gains of the trust for that year than would be paid had the income and gains accrued directly to the beneficiary.

A 'vulnerable beneficiary' is defined as (*FA 2005, ss 38–39*):

- a disabled person, including cases where a person is receiving kidney treatment or is living in certain prescribed accommodation; or
- a child under the age of 18 when at least one of his parents have died (subsequent remarriage by the surviving parent is disregarded).

Income and gains arising from the property held on qualifying trusts for the benefit of a vulnerable person will be eligible for the special tax treatment. This treatment does not apply in cases where the settlor is regarded as having an interest in the property from which the qualifying trusts income arose (*FA 2005, s 24*).

Broadly, the amount of income tax relief under the new regime is the difference between two amounts. The first of those amounts is what (were it not for the new rules) the income tax liability of the trustees would be in respect of the qualifying trusts income for the tax year. The second amount is the amount of extra tax to which the vulnerable person would be liable if the qualifying trusts income were that person's own income (see **8.24** for further details) (*FA 2005, ss 26–29*).

Example 8.1

Charles qualifies as a vulnerable beneficiary of a discretionary trust. The trustees make an election and claim in relation to rental income of £10,000 received by the trust in 2009/10. Charles's gross income in 2009/10 is £9,000 bank interest.

The trustee's income tax liability for the year is as follows:

	Gross		Tax
	£		£
Bank interest	9,000		1,800
Rental income	10,000		
	19,000		1,800
Less:			
Personal allowance		(6,475)	
Taxable income			12,525

	Gross		Tax
	£		£
Tax:			
12,525 × 20%		2,505	
Total		2,505	
Less: tax deducted at source		(1,800)	
Tax relating to rental income		705	

If a claim had not been made, the trustees' income tax liability would have been as follows:

	£	£
Rental income		10,000
Tax due:		
Basic rate band £1,000 × 20%	200	
(10,000 – 1,000) × 40%	3,600	
	3,800	

The election must be made jointly by the trustees and the beneficiary, and specify the commencement date. It must be made by 31 January following the tax year in which the commencement date falls (*FA 2005, s 37*). The election will be effective until the trust terminates, the trust ceases to be a qualifying trust, or the beneficiary ceases to be a vulnerable beneficiary.

Beneficiaries' income

8.11 To determine whether trust income is treated as the income of the beneficiary as it arises, or only on distribution to him, depends on whether the beneficiary has a vested or contingent interest in the income of the trust fund. If a beneficiary would have an interest in possession had a trust had effect under English law, he is so treated if it has effect under Scots law and the trustees are UK-resident (*ITA 2007, s 464*).

The following possibilities may arise.

(i) Adult beneficiary with a vested interest in income

The income is regarded as the beneficiary's income as it arises, even though it may not be paid over to him.

Example 8.2

The settlor of a trust directs the trustees to accumulate the income of the trust fund and to hold it along with the income for James upon his attaining 18 years of age. James becomes 18 but directs the trustees to receive the income from the trust fund and to continue to invest and accumulate it. Until James reaches his 18th birthday, he cannot demand the income be paid to him. Once he is 18, both the capital and income become his and the trustees continue to accumulate only at James' sufferance.

(ii) Infant beneficiary with a vested interest in income

If the beneficiary has an indefeasible vested interest, the income is treated as the beneficiary's as it arises. If there is a power of accumulation (eg the statutory power of maintenance and accumulation in *Trustee Act 1925, s 31*), the beneficiary is treated as having a contingent interest.

Example 8.3

Matthew, currently a minor, becomes entitled to a vested interest in certain estates. The trustees accumulate income, in accordance with *Trustee Act 1925, s 31*, until Matthew is 18. During his minority, Matthew is in the same position as if his interest was a contingent one and the income does not become his until he reaches 18.

(iii) Beneficiary with a contingent interest

Trust income is not regarded as the beneficiary's unless it is paid to him, eg under a discretionary power. A beneficiary with a contingent interest in the capital of a trust fund is, nevertheless, entitled to the income of the trust fund arising after he attains 18 years of age if *Trustee Act 1925, s 31* (above) applies.

Income applied for beneficiary's benefit

8.12 Income used at the discretion of trustees for the maintenance, education or benefit of a beneficiary is treated as the beneficiary's income in the year of receipt. The beneficiary is treated as having received the grossed-up amount. However, in some cases the income is treated as that of the settlor and not of the beneficiary, for example, where the beneficiary is an infant child of the settlor.

Payments out of capital

8.13 Whether or not a payment is treated as having been made out of trust income or capital is usually of significance only if the beneficiary is entitled absolutely to both income and capital of the trust fund. In such cases, payments to the beneficiary out of income retain their income character whilst payments to the beneficiary out of capital retain their character as capital. In other cases, it is the character of the payments in the hands of the beneficiary which is important.

Example 8.4

Trevor, the testator, directs trustees to pay his widow £6,000 out of income of the trust fund and, where the income is not sufficient to meet this obligation, the trustees are to raise and pay the balance out of capital. The payments out of capital are annual payments chargeable to income tax as part of the widow's total income.

Treatment of trust beneficiary's income

8.14 A beneficiary's share (as grossed-up) of the income of a trust fund forms part of his total income in the tax year in which it arises. The income is from the trust and not from the underlying property; hence, except in relation to discretionary trusts, the grossing-up process is at the basic rate by virtue of the deduction at source being under the normal rules for payments out of profits chargeable to income tax, etc in the hands of the trustees.

Example 8.5

In 2009/10, David has £4,000 of trading income, and trust income of £2,500 (received under deduction of basic rate income tax). His total income is thus £7,125 (ie £4,000 + (£2,500 × 100/80)) and his tax liability should be £130 (ie 20% × (£7,125 – £6,475)). As David has already suffered £625 by deduction, he can reclaim the balance of £495 from HMRC.

TYPES OF TRUST

Bare trusts

8.15 A bare trustee holds the trust property as its legal owner, but the beneficiary is absolutely entitled to the trust property, including any income or gains arising. The beneficiary is, therefore, taxable on the trust income, notwithstanding that the trustees may retain that income (eg in the case of a bare trust for a minor, until the age of 18).

However, where a parent creates a bare trust for an unmarried minor child, the trust income is treated as the parent's, subject to the £100 limit mentioned above. This applies to settlements made, or property added to existing settlements, after 8 March 1999 (otherwise, if the income is accumulated within the settlement while the child is unmarried and under 18, the normal bare trust treatment applies).

In addition, where settlement income has previously been accumulated (and treated as income of the settlor's child), if it is subsequently paid whilst the child is still unmarried and under 18, the income is treated as the settlor's for tax purposes, subject to the normal threshold of £100 (per parent, if appropriate).

Examples

8.16 The following examples, taken from the HMRC Trusts, Settlements and Estates Manual, illustrate whether or not a trust is a bare trust.

Example 8.6

Mrs A left the residue of her estate to such of her grandchildren as were alive at the date of her death.

She directed that the funds should not be paid to the grandchildren until they respectively attain age 21 years.

All of the grandchildren who were alive when Mrs A died are entitled to an equal share in the residue of the estate. There are no other conditions that they must fulfil before they become entitled. The direction about payment does not affect this basic position.

The beneficiaries have a vested interest and the trust is a bare trust.

Example 8.7

Mr B left the residue of his estate to 'such of my grandchildren as survive me and attain age 21 years'. If any grandchild dies before age 21, his/her prospective share goes to the other grandchildren who do attain that age.

Here there are two conditions to be met before the grandchildren become entitled to their shares in the estate:

(1) they must survive Mr B; and

(2) they must attain age 21 years.

Here the grandchildren did not take immediate vested interests at the death of the testator.

This is not a bare trust and the trustees must make a tax return.

Example 8.8

The trustees of a pension scheme decide under their discretionary powers to grant the sum of £20,000 to the child of a deceased member of the pension scheme. Because the child is only nine-years old they decide to appoint trustees to administer the fund and protect the child's interests until she attains age 18 years. The terms of the appointment from the pension scheme were in favour of the child absolutely.

This is a bare trust. The income ought to be returned as the child's own income and not that of the trustees.

Interest in possession trusts

8.17 An 'interest in possession' trust exists when a beneficiary has an immediate right to the trust income. The trustees are liable to income tax in a representative capacity where a beneficiary is entitled to the trust income, generally in accordance with the nature of that income.

The trustees receive no tax relief for expenses of managing the trust. The expenses are generally treated as being paid first out of the trust's dividend income, then savings income and finally other income. The net income of the trust (ie after expenses, etc) is paid to beneficiaries including a tax credit at rates applicable to the income source.

Rates of income tax for interest in possession trusts

8.18 Income from property and savings is charged to tax at the basic rate of 20%. UK dividends are charged at the 10% ordinary dividend rate.

Order of set-off of trust expenses against income

8.19

(1) dividend income (liable to tax at 10%)

(2) savings income (liable to tax at 20%)

(3) other income (liable to tax at 20%)

Income from an interest in possession trust – example

8.20

Example 8.9

In 2009/10, the Attree Trust has income and expenses of:

	£	£
Property income		500
Taxed savings income (tax deducted at source £300)		1,500
Dividends	900	
Add tax credits	100	
		1,000
		3,000
Expenses chargeable to revenue		400

The tax assessable on the trustees will be £100 (£500 at 20%). The expenses are not deductible in arriving at the tax payable by the trustees.

Arthur is sole life-tenant of the Attree Trust and as such is absolutely entitled to receive the whole trust income. His income for 2009/10 will include the following:

	£	£	£
Trust dividend income (gross)	1,000		
Trust interest income		1,500	
Other trust income			500
Deduct investment income ordinary rate tax (10%)	(100)		
Basic rate tax (20%)		(300)	(100)
	900	1,200	400
Deduct expenses (note (b))	(400)		
Net income entitlement	500	1,200	400
Grossed-up amounts:			
£500 × 100/90	556		
£1,200 × 100/80		1,500	
£400 × 100/80			500

Notes:

(a) This income falls to be included in Arthur's return even if it is not actually paid to him, as he is absolutely entitled to it. He will receive a tax certificate (form R185E) from the trust agents, showing three figures for gross income:

Trust income	Gross income	Tax deducted	Net income
	£	£	£
Income taxed at investment income ordinary rate	556	56	500
Income taxed at basic rate	1,500	300	1,200
Income liable at basic rate	500	100	400

(b) The trust expenses are deducted from savings income falling in priority to other income, first against dividend and similar income and then against other savings income.

(c) That part of Arthur's trust income which is represented by dividend and other savings income (£500 and £1,200 net) is treated as if it were received directly by Arthur. It is chargeable at the investment income ordinary rate and basic rate only, the liability being satisfied by the 10% and 20% tax credit respectively, except to the extent, if any, that it exceeds his basic rate limit.

Discretionary trusts

8.21 The trustees have discretionary powers to pay income at their discretion, or to accumulate it. Such trusts were liable to tax on income at 40% from 2004/05, except for dividend income, which was taxed at a rate of 32.5% from 2004/05. From 2010/11, the dividend trust rate has increased to 42.5% and the trust rate has increased to 50%.

From 6 April 2005, a basic rate band of £500 was introduced so that the above rates do not apply to the first £500 of trust income, which is instead taxed at the basic, lower or dividend ordinary rate, depending on the type of income. The basic rate band was increased to £1,000 from 6 April 2006 (*ITA 2007, s 491*).

The trustees may claim tax relief on certain expenses. The order of set-off for trust expenses is the same as for interest in possession trusts. Income paid to the beneficiaries is grossed up for income tax at the current rate of 50% (for 2010/11 onwards). The beneficiary will receive a tax certificate from the trustees, and the gross trust income forms part of the beneficiary's total income for the tax year of payment. The tax credit is set off against the beneficiary's income tax liability (*ITA 2007, Pt 9, Ch 7*).

Example 8.10—Distribution of dividend income by discretionary trust

The net dividend for a beneficiary of a discretionary trust for 2009/10 is calculated as follows:

		£
Dividend received		800
Tax credit	1/9	89
Gross dividend		889
Trust rates on dividends	32.5%	289
Net dividend for beneficiary		600

If the net dividend is distributed by the discretionary trust to a beneficiary, the tax position of the trust is:

		Full Dividend	Part dividend (60%)
		£	£
Net dividend		600	480
Grossed-up at 40%		1,000	800
Giving tax credit for beneficiary		400	320
Trustees must account for:		400	320
Less tax paid by them	289		
Less tax credit	89	200	200
Additional tax to be found by trustees		200	120

The optimum position for the trust would be to pay £480 of the dividend only. This way, the additional tax liability of £120 would be covered by the remainder of the dividend retained.

Comparison of net cash from a dividend of £1,000

8.22

	Via discretionary Trust	Direct to taxpayer
	£	£
Grossed-up distribution/dividend	1,000	1,111
Non-taxpayer		
Net distribution/dividend	600	1,000
Tax refund	400	0
	1,000	1,000
Basic rate taxpayer		
Net distribution/dividend	600	1,000
Tax refund (400 less 1,000 at 20%)	200	0
	800	1,000
Higher-rate taxpayer		
Net distribution/dividend	600	1,000
Tax due (1,000 at 40% less 400)	0	
(1,111 at 32.5% less 111)		250
	600	750

Both basic rate and higher rate taxpayers are 20% worse off where dividend income is received via a discretionary trust as compared with the receipt of the income directly.

Accumulation and maintenance trusts

8.23 An accumulation and maintenance trust is a particular type of discretionary trust, which is commonly used by parents and grandparents to provide funds for the benefit of children. The tax provisions treating the parent as liable to tax on trust income from funds settled on his unmarried minor children do not apply to such trusts, except to the extent that income is paid to or for the benefit of the child.

Following changes made to the inheritance tax (IHT) treatment of trusts in *FA 2006* (*FA 2006, ss 71A–71H* and *156*, *Sch 20*), new trusts created on or after 22 March 2006 cannot qualify as accumulation and maintenance trusts. New concepts of 'trust for a bereaved minor' and 'age 18 to 25' trust have been introduced, but these are defined differently from the accumulation and maintenance trust.

Accumulation and maintenance trusts already in existence before 22 March 2006 continued to be treated under the old rules (see below) until 6 April 2008 unless, before then, the interest in possession vested or the trust was restructured so as to accelerate interest.

The trustees are liable to tax at 42.5% (32.5% prior to 2010/11) on dividend income and 50% (40% prior to 2010/11) on non-dividend income, except for the first £1,000 of income taxable (£500 for 2005/06) at the appropriate basic, lower or dividend ordinary rate, as for other discretionary trusts (*ITA 2007, Pt 9, Ch 3*).

From 6 April 2008, existing accumulation and maintenance trusts must conform to new rules that require beneficiaries to take the trust assets absolutely on or before the age of 18 to continue to be taxed under the old regime. Existing accumulation and maintenance trusts, where the beneficiary will take the trust assets absolutely no later than 25, are taxed under the 'age 18 to 25' trust rules from 6 April 2008.

Example 8.11—Accumulation and maintenance trust

An accumulation and maintenance trust set up by Walter for his grandchildren in 1981 now comprises quoted investments and an industrial property. The property is let to an engineering company. Charges for rates, electricity, etc are paid by the trust and recharged yearly in arrears to the tenant. As a result of the delay in recovering the service costs, the settlement incurs overdraft interest.

The relevant figures for the year ended 5 April 2010 are as follows:

	£
Property rents	40,000
UK dividends (including tax credits of £500)	5,000
Taxed interest (tax deducted at source £700)	3,500
Total tax borne	48,500
Trust administration expenses – proportion chargeable to revenue	1,350
Overdraft interest	1,050
	2,400

The tax liability of the trust for 2009/10 is as follows:

	£	£
Property income £40,000 at 40%		16,000
Gross interest £3,500 at 20% (40 – 20)		700
Net dividends	4,500	
Deduct expenses	(2,400)	
	2,100	
£2,100 grossed at 100/90 = £2,333 @ 22.5% (32.5 – 10)		525

	£
Tax payable by self-assessment	17,225
Add: Tax deducted at source	700
Tax credits	500
Total tax borne	18,425

Notes:

(a) Expenses (including, in this example, the overdraft interest) are set first against the investment income and then against the other savings income, before other income. The effect is that the expenses, grossed-up at 10%, save tax at 22.5% (the difference between the 10% rate applicable to dividend income and the investment income trust rate of 32.5%).

(b) The net revenue available for distribution to the beneficiaries, will be:

	£
Gross trust income	48,500
Less tax borne	(18,425)
Less trust expenses	(2,400)
Available for distribution	27,675

(c) Of the tax borne, only £17,925 goes into the tax pool. Tax credits on dividends cannot enter the pool, unless there is sufficient balance brought forward from earlier years. The effect is that if the whole of the distributable income is in fact distributed, there will be insufficient tax in the pool to frank the distribution (£27,675 × 40/60 = £18,450), and the trustees will have a further liability which they may not have the funds to settle.

Trusts for the vulnerable

8.24 A separate tax regime applies for certain trusts with 'vulnerable' beneficiaries (ie disabled persons or relevant minors, as defined), from 6 April

2004. If a claim for special tax treatment is made, tax on trust income (and gains) is restricted to the tax that would be paid had the income and gains accrued directly to the beneficiary. The claim must be made by the first anniversary of 31 January following the end of the tax year in which it is to have effect, or longer if HMRC allows (*FA 2005, ss 23–29, 34–39, Sch 1*). (See also **8.10** regarding trustees acting for incapacitated persons.)

RESIDENT AND NON-RESIDENT TRUSTS

Residence rules for trustees

8.25 There are two sets of rules for deciding trustees' residence status: one for income tax, and the other for capital gains. The residence status for income tax purposes can be different from that for capital gains. The rules for capital gains are outside the scope of this publication.

Until 6 April 2007, the following rules applied to the residence of trusts:

- If all trustees are resident in the UK, the trustees are resident in the UK for income tax purposes.
- If all trustees are resident outside the UK, the trustees are not resident in the UK for income tax purposes.
- Where trustees who are all resident in the UK change to trustees who are all not resident, the trustees are resident in the UK for income tax for the part of the year that resident trustees were in office. They are not resident for income tax for the rest of the year.
- Where trustees who are all not resident in the UK change to trustees who are all resident, the trustees are not resident in the UK for income tax for the part of the year that non-resident trustees were in office. They are resident for income tax for the rest of the year.
- If there is a mixture of resident and non-resident trustees acting at the same time, the trustees are resident in the UK unless the settlor was:
  - not resident in the UK;
  - not ordinarily resident in the UK; and
  - not domiciled in the UK
- when the settlement was set up and when any later funds were added.

If the settlor meets all the conditions, the trustees are not resident in the UK for income tax.

8.26 These rules were simplified from 6 April 2007. From that date, common rules determine the residence of trustees. Trustees are now treated as if they were a single person, and the deemed person is treated as resident and ordinarily resident in the UK when: all of the trustees are resident; or at least one trustee is resident and at least one is not and the settlor is ordinarily resident or domiciled in the UK when the settlement was created (*ITA 2007, ss 474–476*).

Trustees may be resident in the UK and another country at the same time (dual residence). The HMRC Centre for Non-Residents checks in detail any claim for dual residence. If there is a double taxation agreement with another country, it may have a 'tie-breaker' provision. A 'tie-breaker' makes the trustees a resident of one of the countries, but this is only for the purposes of applying the provisions of the double taxation agreement (*TCGA 1992, s 69*).

Information needed for trusts

8.27 When setting up records for a trust, the Centre for Non-Residents requires:

- a completed form 41G(Trust); and
- the following information asked for on form INT25.

Changes in trusteeship

If there have been any changes in trusteeship since the trust was first set up, provide:

(1) the names and addresses of all the original trustees; and

(2) full details of all subsequent changes in trusteeship, including the names and addresses of all trustees involved, and the dates of the changes.

Settled property

(3) Where the original settled capital was cash, how has this been invested?

If there have been any additions to the original settled fund, state:

(4) the names and addresses of the donors;

(5) the nature and date of each addition;

(6) how the trustees have invested any cash additions.

If any loan has been advanced to the trustees, the following information for each loan:

(7) the date and amount;

(8) the name and address of the lender;

(9) the rate % of interest;

(10) how the loan has been invested;

(11) the period of the loan; and

(12) when the loan is repayable, and in what circumstances.

Share ownership

(13) Do the trustees (in connection with this settlement) have any interest, either direct or indirect, in the shares of an unquoted company?

If so, the following information (to the extent that it has not already been supplied when replying to an earlier question):

(14) the nature and amount;

(15) the names and addresses of the companies; and

(16) details of acquisitions and disposals. Include the relevant dates.

Settlor

(17) Has any interest in the capital or income been retained by:

- (a) the original settlor or that person's spouse or civil partner; or
- (b) any settlor of additional assets or that person's spouse or civil partner?

Beneficiaries

(18) State the full name of each existing beneficiary who can or may benefit from the income and/or capital of the trust. Give each beneficiary's HMRC Office and reference in that Office or their National Insurance number.

Law governing the trust

(19) Where the trust is not governed by the laws of England and Wales, state the law governing the trust.

Annual issue of return forms

(20) Are all the trustees not resident in the UK?

(21) If the answer to question 20 is 'yes':

- what untaxed UK income do they currently receive?
- have the trustees received, or are they likely to receive, other income from UK sources?

- can they currently pay income to beneficiaries at their discretion?
- can they currently accumulate income?

(22) If the answer to question 20 is 'yes', and the general administration of the trust is carried on outside the UK, who will be responsible for completing form 50(FS), which HMRC issue to monitor *TCGA 1992, ss 86, 98*?

Bare trusts

8.28 A bare trust, also known as a simple trust, is one in which each beneficiary has an immediate and absolute right to both capital and income. The beneficiaries of a bare trust have the right to take actual possession of trust property (see **8.15** for further details).

The property is held in the name of a trustee, but the trustee has no discretion over what income to pay the beneficiary. In effect, the trustee is a nominee in whose name the property is held and has no active duties to perform.

Bare trustees are not obliged to complete trust returns, but they can choose to make a return of trust income. They would then account for the UK income tax due.

The beneficiary gets credit for UK income tax that the bare trustee has paid.

The beneficiary of a bare trust returns the income on his personal Self-Assessment tax return.

The beneficiary enters it on the page for the particular income in question. There are instructions in SA107(Notes) under the heading 'Income from trusts and settlements'.

Income tax liability of non-resident trustees

Discretionary and accumulation and maintenance trusts

8.29 First, it is necessary to decide if the trust is within *ITA 2007, s 479*. This will be so if:

- the trustees have the power to accumulate income or make discretionary payments; and
- the trust income is not treated as that of the settlor.

Generally, discretionary and accumulation and maintenance trusts will fall into this category.

Tax is charged at the rate applicable to trusts. For 1999/2000 onwards, dividend-type income is charged at the dividend trust rate.

Foreign income is not chargeable to UK tax.

Interest from FOTRA (free of tax to residents abroad) securities remains chargeable to UK tax unless:

- the Centre for Non-Residents confirms that it is exempt; or
- the provisions of *ITA 2007, s 811* (limit on liability to income tax of non-UK residents) apply. Briefly, if no beneficiaries are ordinarily resident in the UK, the trustees do not pay tax on interest they receive gross.

With regard to other income received gross, if no beneficiaries are ordinarily resident in the UK, the trustees do not pay tax on interest they receive gross (*ITA 2007, s 811*). If *ITA 2007, s 811* does not apply, the trustees are chargeable to tax.

Subject to the possible effects of *ITA 2007, s 811*, other UK income remains chargeable to UK tax.

Interest in possession trusts

8.30 A non-resident trust, which is not within *ITA 2007, s 479*, is called an 'interest in possession trust' (see **8.17**).

Foreign income is not chargeable to UK tax.

ITA 2007, s 811 applies to interest from FOTRA securities. Briefly, if no beneficiaries are ordinarily resident in the UK, the trustees do not pay tax on interest they receive gross.

Subject to the possible effects of *ITA 2007, s 811*, other UK income remains chargeable to UK tax.

ADMINISTRATION OF TRUSTS

Self-assessment

8.31 Trustees and personal representatives are required to complete tax returns (form SA900), and are generally subject to the same self-assessment regime as individuals in terms of filing deadlines, payments on account of tax, interest and penalties, etc (*Taxes Management Act 1970 (TMA 1970), s 8A*).

The extent to which trustees are liable to tax depends upon their residence status and the type of trust (see **8.25** for further details concerning residence).

Notices are given, by an officer of the Board of Her Majesty's Revenue & Customs, for the purposes of establishing the amounts in which the following persons are chargeable to income tax and CGT, and the amount payable by them by way of income tax:

- the 'relevant trustees' (see below);
- the settlor or settlors; and
- the beneficiary or beneficiaries.

Notices may be given to any relevant trustee, or separate notices given to each relevant trustee, or to such of the relevant trustees as the officer thinks fit.

'Relevant trustees' are:

- for the purpose of trust income, any person who was a trustee at or after the time when the income arose;
- for the purpose of trust gains, any person who was a trustee during or after the tax year in which the gain accrued.

The relevant trustees are liable for any tax which falls due as a result of the self-assessment included in the return.

In the absence of a return, an officer of the Board may determine the amount of the relevant trustees' liability. Similarly, an assessment may be made on the relevant trustees where a loss of tax is discovered.

Bare trusts under self-assessment

8.32 Trustees of bare trusts (see **8.15**) are not expected to account for tax at the appropriate rate on income paid over to beneficiaries. Any income which is received gross by the trustees will be paid gross by them. In addition, trustees of bare trusts will not be required to complete self-assessment returns or make payments on account. (However, they are entitled, if they so wish, to make a self-assessment return of income (not capital gains) and to account for tax on it at the appropriate rate.) Beneficiaries must include income and gains from these trusts in their returns.

Penalties

8.33 There are three types of penalty for a failure to make a return. These are:

(1) fixed automatic penalty;

(2) daily penalty;

(3) tax-geared penalty.

Fixed automatic penalties

8.34 The fixed penalty applies if a return is not filed by the filing date (*TMA 1970, s 93*).

The filing date is normally 31 January after the end of the return year. This does not apply if HMRC issue the return after 31 October following the end of the return year. In these cases, the filing date is three months and seven days after the date HMRC issued the return provided there has not been a failure to notify.

The self-assessment system imposes the penalty automatically. It is only for the year of liability ended in the previous calendar year.

The first penalty is £100. There is a second penalty of £100, which applies if HMRC do not receive the return within six months of the filing date.

Trustees have 30 days to appeal against a fixed automatic penalty. The time starts from the date the penalty is imposed. The possible grounds of appeal are:

- they have a reasonable excuse for submitting the return late; or
- the penalty should be reduced (capped).

Trustees must make a separate appeal against each fixed automatic penalty.

If an appeal goes before the tribunal, the tribunal can:

- confirm the penalty; or
- set it aside.

The tribunal cannot reduce the amount.

Daily penalties

8.35 HMRC can ask the tribunal to impose a daily penalty (*TMA 1970, s 93(3)*). This cannot exceed £60 per day. This is only done in exceptional circumstances. For example:

- there are very large amounts of tax at risk;
- returns for several years are outstanding; or
- there are particularly pressing reasons for requiring the return.

A daily penalty is in addition to fixed automatic penalties.

Tax-geared penalties

8.36 In addition to the above penalties, where the failure to make a return extends beyond the anniversary of the filing date and there would have been a liability to tax shown in the return, the taxpayer is liable to a penalty up to the amount of tax which would have been shown (*TMA 1970, s 93(5)*).

It is based on the tax unpaid at the original filing date. HMRC cannot calculate the amount until they receive the return. They base the penalty on 100% of the tax unpaid at the filing date. It is subject to abatement.

HMRC Helpsheets for the Trusts and Estates tax return

8.37

Number	**Title**
HS390	Trusts and estates of deceased persons: foreign tax credit relief for capital gains
SA901(Notes)	Notes on Trust and Estate Trade pages
SA901L(Notes)	Notes on Trusts and Estate Lloyd's Underwriters pages
SA902(Notes)	Notes on Trust and Estate Partnership pages
SA903(Notes)	Notes on Trust and Estate UK Property pages
SA904(Notes)	Notes on Trust and Estate Foreign pages
SA905(Notes)	Notes on Trust and Estate Capital Gains pages
SA906(Notes)	Notes on Trust and Estate Non-residence pages
SA907(Notes)	Notes on Trust and Estate Charities pages
SA950	Trust and Estate tax return guide

TAXATION OF ESTATES

Death

8.38 On death, the property of a person passes to their personal representatives.

Personal representatives can be either executors of a will of a deceased person or administrators of the estate if there is no will. The roles of trustees and executors are quite different. The executors have a duty to gather in the assets, pay the liabilities and then to distribute the surplus according to the will. If any surplus is to be held on trust, the trustees then take over in respect of that part of the estate. The date at which this is deemed to happen is important for some tax purposes, but in general the trustees are deemed to inherit at the end of administration by the personal representatives (*TMA 1970, s 74*).

The personal representatives of a deceased individual are responsible for discharging the liabilities and obligations of the deceased, as part of the administration of an estate. This includes unpaid tax liabilities for periods up to the deceased's death, and also tax on income of the estate during administration (*TMA 1970, s 40*).

A personal representative is defined for income tax purposes as someone who is responsible for administering the death estate, whether in the UK or elsewhere (*ITA 2007, s 989*).

Income during the administration period

8.39 Income arising from the deceased's estate from the date of death to the completion of the administration of the estate is taxable on the personal representatives. When the income is distributed to the estate beneficiaries it then forms part of their taxable income.

Personal representatives do not receive personal allowances, but their liability to tax, for 2008/09 onwards, on estate income is limited to 10% on dividend income and 20% on savings and other income. There is no liability to higher rate tax.

Example 8.12

Graham dies unmarried on 25 July 2010. His executors are entitled to set off his full personal allowance of £6,475 for 2010/11 against his income tax liability for that year.

Expenses of administering the estate are not allowable deductions for income tax purposes, although relief for interest on a loan taken out to pay IHT is available for up to one year from the making of the loan (*ITA 2007, s 403*).

Estate income is paid to beneficiaries according to whether they are entitled to the estate assets (ie an 'absolute interest'), or whether they are entitled to income from an estate asset only (ie a 'limited interest'). See **8.44** onwards for further details on the treatment of estate income.

Broadly, a beneficiary entitled to an income-producing asset is generally taxable on income arising from the asset since the date of death. Any sums payable by the personal representatives to a residuary beneficiary during the administration of the estate are treated as the beneficiary's income for the tax year of payment. The payments are treated as net income, after deduction of tax at rates applicable to the types of income out of which they are paid (ie 10% for dividends and 20% for savings and other income). The beneficiary is taxable on the gross equivalent of the estate income. Estate distributions are treated as paid first out of basic rate taxed income, followed by savings income and then dividend income (*ITTOIA 2005, ss 649–682*).

End of the administration period

8.40 Upon completion of the administration period, the overall amount of income due to each beneficiary is compared with the payments already made. Where an amount remains payable to a beneficiary, the gross equivalent is treated as income of the tax year in which the administration period ends (or the tax year in which a beneficiary's interest ends, if earlier) regardless of when it was actually paid over to the beneficiary.

UK and foreign estates

8.41 A 'UK estate' is defined as an estate, the income of which comprises only income which either (*ITTOIA 2005, s 651*):

- has borne UK income tax by deduction; or
- is directly assessable to UK income tax on the personal representatives.

To be a UK estate, the personal representatives must not be entitled to claim exemption from UK income tax (in respect of any part of the income of the estate) by reason of their residence or ordinary residence outside the UK.

The amount of tax credit attaching to distributions by UK companies was reduced from 20% to 10% from 1999/2000. In addition, substantially all entitlement to payment of tax credits was also removed from that time, other than tax credits payable under double taxation agreements.

Payments funded from dividend income are now treated as made under deduction of non-repayable tax at the rate of 10%. The effect is to ensure that beneficiaries are taxed as if they had received the distribution direct (*ITTOIA 2005, s 680*).

If all the trustees are resident in the UK during the whole tax year, they are liable to income tax on UK and overseas trust income. If the trustees were only resident for part of the tax year, they will generally only be liable to income tax on overseas income for that part of the tax year in which they were UK resident (Extra-statutory Concession (ESC) A11).

In the case of mixed (resident and non-resident) trustees, their income tax liability depends upon the domicile and residence status of the settlor. The trustees are jointly treated as UK resident if the settlor was UK resident, ordinarily resident or domiciled when funds were provided to the settlement (or at the time of the settlor's death). Alternatively, the trustees are jointly regarded as non-UK resident if the settlor was not resident, ordinarily resident or domiciled in the UK at those times.

Income of person with limited interest in residue

8.42 Special provisions apply to persons with limited interests in the residue of the whole or part of an estate during the administration period (or part of it) (*ITTOIA 2005, s 678*).

A person is deemed to have a limited interest if he does not have an absolute interest and the income of the residue (or part of it) would be properly payable to him, or directly or indirectly paid for his benefit, if the residue had been ascertained at the commencement of the administration period. A life interest is a limited interest.

Any sum paid during the administration period in respect of a limited interest is, subject to adjustment on the completion of administration (or its Scottish equivalent), deemed to have been paid as income in the tax year in which the sum was paid. Where the sum is paid in respect of a limited interest which has ceased during the administration, the sum paid after the interest has ceased is deemed to have been paid in the last tax year in which the interest subsisted. Personal representatives may be treated as residuary beneficiaries in such a way that the deemed income forms part of the estate of a second deceased person. The legislation also caters for discretionary payments.

In the case of a 'UK estate' (see **8.41**) the personal representatives will have paid tax of 10% and any sum paid to a beneficiary is treated as a net amount after the application of the 10% rate. Payments are made first out of payments bearing tax at the 10% rate and there are provisions for effecting a reasonable apportionment of amounts between persons with different interests.

In the case of a 'foreign estate' (ie an estate that is not a 'UK estate'), the sum paid is treated as gross income chargeable under *ITTOIA 2005, Pt 5, Ch 6* with a possible proportionate reduction on proof of tax deduction in respect of the aggregate income of the estate.

From April 2008, provided certain conditions are met, dividends from non-UK companies will be given the same notional tax credit that is currently afforded to dividends paid by UK companies.

8.43 In respect of discretionary payments out of income, beneficiaries are treated as receiving income on which tax has been paid at the basic rate or, in the case of payments routed through trustees, at the rate applicable to trusts.

A residuary beneficiary who is neither resident nor ordinarily resident in the UK may claim to have his income from an estate in the course of administration treated as if it had arisen directly to him, so that he will not be liable to tax on, for example, foreign source income of the estate.

On the completion, after 5 April 1995, of the administration of an estate, where an amount remains payable in respect of a limited interest, the amount is deemed to have been paid as income of the tax year in which the administration period ends; if the sum is deemed to be paid in respect of an interest which ceased before the end of the administration period, then it is deemed to have been paid in respect of the last tax year in which that interest subsisted.

In many cases, therefore, adjustments will have to be made to assessments already made on the beneficiary during the administration period. The adjustments may be made within three years of 31 January following the end of the tax year in which administration of that estate was completed. This treatment is given in HMRC Extra-statutory Concession (ESC) A14, the full text of which is as follows:

'Extra Statutory Concession A14

Deceased person's estate: residuary income received during the administration period

A beneficiary who for a year of assessment is not resident or not ordinarily resident in the United Kingdom, and is deemed *under sections 657, 658(2) and 830(1), (2), Income Tax (Trading and Other Income) Act 2005 ('ITTOIA')* to have received income from a UK estate in that year, may claim to have their tax liability on that income from the estate adjusted to what it would be if such income had arisen to them directly and as a result they:

- could claim relief under *section 278, ICTA 1988* (claim to personal reliefs by certain non residents); or
- could claim entitlement to exemption in respect of FOTRA Securities issued in accordance with *section 714, ITTOIA*; or
- could claim relief under the terms of a double taxation agreement; or
- would not have been chargeable to income tax.

Relief or exemption, as appropriate, will be granted to the beneficiary only if the personal representatives of the estate:

- have made estate returns for each and every year for which they are required, and
- have paid all tax due and any interest, surcharges and penalties arising, and
- keep available for inspection any relevant tax certificates, together with copies of the estate accounts for all years of the period of administration showing details of all sources of estate income and payments made to beneficiaries.

Relief or exemption, as appropriate, will be granted to the beneficiary on a claim made within five years and ten months of the end of the year of assessment in which the beneficiary is deemed to have received the income.

No tax will be repayable to the beneficiary in respect of income they are deemed to have received where the basic amount of estate income, if received by a UK resident beneficiary of an estate, is paid sums within *sections 657(3), (4)* and *680(3), (4), ITTOIA*.'

Income of person with absolute interest in residue

8.44 Special provisions apply to persons who, during the administration period (or part of it), have an absolute interest in the whole or part of the residue of the estate of the deceased. A person is deemed to have an absolute interest if and so long as the capital of the residue (or of the relevant part) would, if the residue had been ascertained, be properly payable to him or, directly or indirectly, payable for his benefit (*ITTOIA 2005, ss 660* and *665*).

A person entitled to an absolute interest may receive payments during the administration period made out of either income or capital and these have to be distinguished. This is done by first calculating the residuary income during such part of the administration period in which the beneficiary had an absolute interest.

The 'residuary income' is ascertained by deducting from the income of the estate for that year (*ITTOIA 2005, s 666*):

- annual interest, annuities or other annual payments for that year which are a charge on residue (see below), except for any interest, etc which is allowable in computing the income of the estate;
- management expenses (unless allowable in computing the aggregate income of the estate) which, in the absence of any express provision in a will, are properly chargeable to income; and
- the income of the estate to which any person is specifically entitled as a devisee or legatee.

There is also a reduction in residuary income by way of relief for higher rate tax purposes ('excess liability'), where accrued income has also been included in the value of the estate for IHT purposes; the reduction is the grossed-up value of IHT attributable to the accrued income net of accrued liabilities.

8.45 The importance of calculating the residuary income lies in the fact that any sum paid during the administration period in respect of the absolute interest is deemed to have been paid as income to the extent that it does not exceed the residuary income for that year (less basic rate tax for that year in the case of a UK estate). Personal representatives may be treated as residuary beneficiaries in such a way that the deemed income forms part of the estate of a second deceased person. The legislation caters for successive absolute interests and discretionary payments.

Where any deductions exceed the amount of residuary income, the excess may be carried forward and treated as an amount to be deducted from the aggregate income of the estate for the following year. This replaces an earlier concession which stated that where the allowable deductions exceeded the gross income, the residuary income was nil and the excess could be carried backwards or forwards to other years for higher rate tax purposes.

In the case of a 'UK estate' (see **8.41**), the sum deemed to have been paid as income includes the amount by which the aggregated income entitlement of the person for the tax year exceeds the aggregate of all the sums which have been paid (as income) to that person in respect of that absolute interest. It is, therefore, grossed-up at the basic or lower rate in force for the year of payment; payments are made first out of payments bearing tax at basic rate and there are provisions for effecting a reasonable apportioning of amounts between persons with different interests. Where the lower rate applies (for years up to and including 2007/08), the income is then taxable in the hands of the beneficiary (or intermediate trustees) at that rate as the top slice of income.

In the case of a 'foreign estate', the amount paid is treated as gross income with a possible proportionate reduction on proof of tax deduction in respect of the aggregate income of the estate.

A residuary beneficiary who is neither resident nor ordinarily resident in the UK may claim to have his income from an estate in the course of administration treated as if it had arisen directly to him, so that he will not be liable to tax on, for example, foreign source income of the estate.

On the completion of administration certain adjustments may be necessary, giving rise to additional assessments or a claim for relief. Any further or adjusted assessment or claim for relief may be made within three years beginning with 31 January following the tax year in which the administration of the estate is completed.

Charges on residue

8.46 'Charges' on residue means the following liabilities (to the extent that the liabilities fall ultimately on residue) properly payable out of the estate and interest payable in respect of those liabilities:

- funeral, testamentary and administration expenses and debts;
- general legacies, demonstrative legacies, annuities and any sum payable out of residue under an intestacy;
- any other liabilities of the personal representatives; and
- (relating to Scotland only) any sums required to meet claims in respect of legal rights by the surviving spouse or children.

Thus, for example, interest payable in respect of a general legacy is a charge on residue and is not taken into account in calculating residuary income. In Scotland, sums required to meet certain claims by a surviving spouse or child are also charges on residue (*ITTOIA 2005, Pt 5, Ch 6*).

Income of legatees and annuitants

8.47 In the case of a specific legacy, the legatee is entitled to the income (subject to a contrary provision in the will) from the relevant property from the date of the testator's death. The income from the property, therefore, forms part of the legatee's total income as it arises, notwithstanding the general charge on the personal representatives.

In the case of a general legacy, the legatee is entitled to interest at 5%. If the legacy is an immediate one, the interest is generally payable (subject to a contrary provision in the will) only after the end of the executor's year. Such interest is charged to tax under *ITTOIA 2005* as part of the legatee's total income. However, a legatee may refuse to accept payment of the interest and in such instances the interest is only treated as his income if there is identifiable income which he can claim, eg from a fund set aside to meet the legacy.

In general, an annuitant is not entitled to the capital value of his annuity, though he is entitled to have a fund set aside to secure the annuity. The first instalment of the annuity is payable only at the end of the executor's year, but (subject to a contrary intention) the annuity runs from the testator's death and forms part of the annuitant's total income from that date.

In some cases, and in particular where the estate is insufficient to provide an annuity fund and also to pay the pecuniary legacies in full, the annuitant is entitled to the actuarial value of his annuity (duly abated, if necessary). This is regarded as a capital payment and is not included in the annuitant's total income. Thus, payments made in respect of an annuity are regarded as capital payments where the payments are made before it is discovered that the income of the estate is insufficient to pay the annuity in full.

References in a will or codicil to payments by reference to the former 'surtax' and 'standard rate' are treated as if they were to higher rate(s) and basic rate.

Estate in administration – example

8.48

Example 8.13

Sam died in March 2009. Ann is the residual beneficiary of his estate and she has an absolute interest. In the year to 5 April 2010 the personal representatives received the following income:

UK dividends (net)	10,000
Interest on deposit monies	4,000
Rental income	6,000

In January 2010, shares in M&S Plc valued at £5,000 were transferred to Ann, and in March 2010 she was paid £4,000 in cash. Expenses charged to income are £500.

The transfer of shares and the cash payment create the following taxable income of £9,000 net for Ann in 2009/10, which is calculated as follows:

		Gross	Tax	Net
	£	£	£	£
Property income less income tax at 20%	6,000	6,000	1,200	4,800
Interest		4,000	800	3,200
Dividends		1,244	124	1,120
		11,244	2,124	9,120

The balance of the UK dividends is calculated as:

	£
Gross dividends	10,000
Expenses	500
Distributed in 2008/09	1,120
Balance held	8,380

This amount will be carried forward to be treated as income of the beneficiary when it is paid in succeeding years, or on completion of the administration of the estate.

Early settlement of a deceased taxpayer's tax affairs

8.49 HMRC will, if requested, issue a tax return for a deceased person before the end of the tax year in which the individual dies.

This will allow the personal representatives to deal with the deceased's tax affairs without delay.

HMRC will also give early written confirmation if they do not intend to enquire into that return.

This will enable the deceased's personal representatives to finalise the estate.

PRE-OWNED ASSETS

Introduction

8.50 *FA 2004, s 84* and *Sch 15* introduced an income tax charge on benefits received by the former owners of property, referred to as pre-owned assets. Broadly, it applies to individuals (the chargeable person) who continue to receive benefits from certain types of property they once owned after 17 March 1986, but have since disposed of. The rules have effect for 2005/06 onwards.

The property within the scope of the charge can be grouped into three headings:

(1) land;

(2) chattels; and

(3) intangible property.

If the chargeable person has either disposed of any property within these headings by way of gift or, in some circumstances, sale, or contributed towards the purchase of the property in question and they continue to receive some benefit from the property, they are potentially liable to the charge. The benefit may be occupation of the land, use of the chattel or the ability to receive income or capital from a settlement holding intangible property.

There are several types of transactions relating to land and chattels that are excluded from the scope of the charge (see **8.55**). There are also provisions exempting the relevant property from the charge where the property is subject to a charge to IHT or where specific protection from IHT is given by legislation.

If the income tax charge applies, *FA 2004, Sch 15* contains provisions enabling the taxable benefit to be calculated. In the case of the occupation or use of land and chattels, the calculation of the taxable benefit will be determined to a large extent by the proportion which the value of the chargeable person's original interest in, or contribution to the purchase, bears to the current value of the property.

The conditions required for the charge to apply are virtually identical where the property in question is land or chattels, but they differ slightly in respect of intangible property.

Land and chattels

8.51 The charge applies where the chargeable person occupies any land or uses or possesses any chattels, either alone or with other persons, and either the 'disposal condition' or the 'contribution condition' is met.

Disposal condition

8.52 The disposal condition will apply if the chargeable person, at any time after 17 March 1986, owned relevant land or chattels, or other property whose disposal proceeds were directly or indirectly applied by another person towards the acquisition of the relevant land or chattels, and then disposed of all or part of their interest in the relevant land or chattels (or other property). If the disposal was an excluded transaction (see **8.55**), the disposal condition will not apply.

Note that the disposal condition will apply to the chargeable person's occupation or use of property even if that property was never actually owned by them. If they gave away other property (apart from cash) to another person who sold such property and used these proceeds to purchase the relevant land or chattel, the disposal condition is satisfied, unless it qualifies as an excluded transaction.

A disposition that creates a new interest in land or in a chattel out of an existing interest is taken to be a disposal of part of the existing interest.

Contribution condition

8.53 The contribution condition will apply if the chargeable person, at any time after 17 March 1986, provided any of the consideration given by another person for the acquisition of an interest in the relevant land or chattel, or for the acquisition of any other property the proceeds of the disposal of which were directly or indirectly applied by another person towards an acquisition of an interest in the relevant land or chattel. As with the disposal condition, if the provision of the consideration qualifies as an excluded transaction, this condition will not apply.

It can be seen that the contribution condition can apply not only where the contribution provided by the chargeable person is directly used to purchase the relevant land or chattel but where the contribution is indirect, too. If they provided all or part of the consideration (eg a cash gift) for the purchase of property by another person, who then sold the property and used the proceeds to purchase the land occupied, or the chattel used, by the chargeable person, the contribution condition is satisfied, unless it qualifies as an excluded transaction.

HMRC do not regard the contribution condition set out in *FA 2004, Sch 15, para 3(3)* as being met where a lender resides in property purchased by another with money loaned to him by the lender. Their view is that since the outstanding debt will form part of his estate for IHT purposes, it would not be reasonable to consider that the loan falls within the contribution condition (and, therefore, not reasonably attributable to the consideration (*Sch 15, para 4(2)(c)*), even where the loan was interest free. It follows that the 'lender', in such an arrangement, would not be caught by a charge under *Sch 15*.

Intangible property

8.54 The charge applies where the chargeable person settles intangible property or adds intangible property to a settlement after 17 March 1986 on terms that any income arising from the settled property would be treated under *ITTOIA 2005, s 624* (income arising under a settlement where the settlor retains an interest) as income of the chargeable person as settlor and any such income would be so treated even if *sub-section (2)* of that section did not include any reference to the spouse of the settlor. The settlor in this case is, of course, the chargeable person.

In this context, 'settlement' has the same meaning as it does for IHT purposes (*Inheritance Tax Act 1984 (IHTA 1984), s 43(2)*).

Intangible property means assets such as stocks and securities, insurance policies and bank and building society accounts. The provisions of this paragraph do not apply to land and chattels included in a settlement.

Excluded transactions

8.55 There are a number of situations where a charge to tax will not arise. Certain transactions are excluded from the charge, and there are also exemptions from the charge where certain conditions are met (*FA 2004, Sch 15, para 10*).

The concept of excluded transactions has no application to intangible property. They only serve to exclude from the income tax charge certain transactions relating to land and chattels.

Excluded transactions – disposal condition

8.56 For the purposes of the disposal conditions relating to land and chattels, the disposal of any property is an excluded transaction in relation to the chargeable person if:

- it was a disposal of their whole interest in the property, except for any right expressly reserved by them over the property, either:
  - by a transaction made at arm's length with a person not connected with them; or
  - by a transaction such as might be expected to be made at arm's length between persons not connected with each other.

  The exclusion clearly only applies to sales of the entire interest in the property at full market value, although the words 'except for any right expressly reserved' would envisage the sale of a freehold reversion subject to a lease, but only if it was on arm's-length terms.

  Concern was expressed that sales of a part share of property to commercial providers of equity release schemes would not qualify as an excluded transaction and an individual would be subject to the charge if he remained in occupation of the land. This concern was recognised in the rules governing the charge which specifically exempted from the charge disposals of part of an interest in any property by a transaction made at arm's length with a person not connected with the chargeable person. Furthermore, the exemption is extended to disposals of a part share to anyone, provided that they were made on arm's-length terms and either took place before 7 March 2005, or took place on or after that date for a consideration not in the form of money or assets readily convertible into money.
- The property was transferred to their spouse or civil partner, or former spouse or civil partner where the transfer has been ordered by a court.
- The disposal was by way of gift (or in accordance with a court order for the benefit of a former spouse or civil partner) by virtue of which the property became settled property in which his spouse or civil partner or former spouse or civil partner is beneficially entitled to an interest in possession. The spouse or civil partner must take an interest in possession from the outset. It is not an excluded transaction, however, if the interest in possession of the spouse or civil partner or former spouse or civil partner has come to an end other than on their death unless the spouse

or civil partner or former spouse or civil partner has become absolutely entitled to the property, in which case HMRC would accept that the benefit of the exclusion is not lost.

- The disposal was a disposition falling within *IHTA 1984, s 11* (disposition for maintenance of family).
- The disposal is an outright gift to an individual and is wholly exempted from IHT by either of the following sections of *IHTA 1984*:
  - *s 19* (£3,000 annual exemption); or
  - *s 20* (£250 small gifts exemption).

Excluded transactions – contribution condition

8.57 For the purposes of the contribution conditions relating to land and chattels, the provision by the chargeable person of consideration for another's acquisition of any property is an excluded transaction in relation to the chargeable person if:

- The other person was their spouse or civil partner, or former spouse or civil partner where the transfer has been ordered by a court.
- On its acquisition the property became settled property in which their spouse or civil partner or former spouse or civil partner is beneficially entitled to an interest in possession. The spouse or civil partner must take an interest in possession from the outset. It is not an excluded transaction, however, if the interest in possession of the spouse or civil partner or former spouse or civil partner has come to an end otherwise than on their death, unless the spouse or civil partner or former spouse or civil partner has become absolutely entitled to the property.
- The provision of the consideration constituted an outright gift of cash by the chargeable person to the other person and was made at least seven years before the earliest date on which the chargeable person occupied the land or had possession or use of the chattel.
- The provision of the consideration is a disposition falling within *IHTA 1984, s 11* (maintenance of family).
- The provision of the consideration is an outright gift to an individual and is, for the purposes of *IHTA 1984*, a transfer of value that is wholly exempt by virtue of *s 19* (£3,000 annual exemption) or *s 20* (£250 small gifts exemption).

Property in the estate

8.58 The charging provisions relating to land, chattels and intangible property do not apply to a person at a time when their estate for the purposes of

IHTA 1984 includes the relevant property, or other property which (*FA 2004, Sch 15, para 11(1)*):

- derives its value from the relevant property; and
- whose value so far as attributable to the relevant property, is not substantially less than the value of the relevant property.

Where their estate includes property which derives its value from the relevant property and whose value, so far as attributable to the relevant property, is substantially less than the value of the relevant property:

- the appropriate rental value of the relevant land;
- the appropriate amount in respect of the chattel; or
- the chargeable amount in relation to the relevant intangible property;

must be reduced by such proportion as is reasonable to take account of the inclusion of the property in their estate.

Example 8.14

If Mr Big transfers his house to a company wholly owned by him, then provided there are no loans to the company one can say that the value attributable to the company is not less than the value of the house. But if Mr Big gave the house to a company which was owned 25% by his wife, then the value of the 75% shares he holds would be substantially less than the value of the house. If he has lent money to the company and the company holds the house, we take the view that the company's value is less than the house unless (possibly) the loan is charged on the house.

Gifts with reservation

8.59 The charging provisions also do not apply to a person at a time when, for IHT purposes, the relevant property or property deriving its value from relevant property falls within the 'gifts with reservation' provisions set out in *FA 1986* (*FA 2004, Sch 15, para 11(3)*).

In addition, the legislation does not apply if the property:

- would fall to be treated as subject to a reservation but for any of *FA 1986, s 102(5)(d)–(i)* (certain cases where disposal by way of gift is an exempt transfer for purposes of IHT). But, where *s 102(5)(h)* is in point, *Sch 15* is disapplied only when the property remains subject to trusts complying with the requirements of *IHTA 1984, Sch 4, para 3(1)* (maintenance funds);

- would fall to be treated as subject to a reservation but for *FA 1986, s 102B(4)* (gifts with reservation: share of interest in land), or would have fallen to be so treated if the disposal by way of gift of an undivided share of an interest in land had been made on or after 9 March 1999. This refers to situations where the chargeable person transfers a share (usually 50%) of their property to the donee, and both the donee and the chargeable person continue to occupy the property, paying their share of household expenses; or
- would fall to be treated as subject to a reservation but for *FA 1986, s 102C(3)* and *Sch 20, para 6* (exclusion of benefit). This refers to situations where the chargeable person continues to use or occupy the property but pays full consideration in money or money's worth, or where they leave the property but have to move back at a later date due to an unforeseen change in their circumstances and are unable to look after themselves because of age or infirmity.

Where the contribution condition relating to land or chattels applies, *Sch 20, para 2(2)(b)* (which excludes gifts of money from the provisions that apply where property is substituted for the original gift) should be disregarded. For example, if A gives cash to his son and they buy a home jointly and live together, then, while they live together, the pre-owned assets tax charge will not apply.

Schedule 15 also contains provisions for the chargeable person to elect that the relevant property that would otherwise be subject to the charge be treated as property subject to a reservation for the purposes of *IHTA 1984*. If the election is made, no charge under the Schedule will apply.

Excluded liability

8.60 Where at any time the value of a person's estate for the purposes of *IHTA 1984* is reduced by an 'excluded liability' affecting any property, only the excess of the value of the property over the amount of the excluded liability can be treated as comprised in their estate for the purposes of this schedule.

A liability is an excluded liability if:

- the creation of the liability; and
- any transaction by virtue of which the person's estate came to include the relevant property or property which derives its value from the relevant property or by virtue of which the value of the property in their estate came to be derived from the relevant property,

were associated operations, as defined in *IHTA 1984, s 268*.

The 'amount' of the excluded liability will be the face value of the debt, including any rolled-up interest or accrued indexation where this has been allowed for under the terms of the agreement. For the purposes of computing the charge under this Schedule, it will be sufficient for the debt to be revalued taking into account outstanding interest, or accrued indexation, at the five-yearly valuation dates. Any reduction of the debt resulting from a repayment can be taken into account as it occurred, and may be reflected in a revised computation of the tax in the relevant year and subsequently.

Residence or domicile outside the UK

8.61 There is no charge to tax where an individual is not resident in the UK during the year of assessment in question.

If the individual is resident, but not domiciled, in the UK in any year of assessment, the legislation only applies to land, chattels or intangible property situated in the UK.

In applying the rules to a person who was at any time domiciled outside the UK, no regard should be had to any property which is excluded for IHT purposes under *IHTA 1984, s 48(3)(a)*.

An individual will be treated as domiciled in the UK at any time if they would be treated as so for inheritance tax purposes. This means that the 'deemed domicile' rules for inheritance tax will apply for the purposes of this income tax charge.

De minimis exemption

8.62 An exemption from charge applies where in relation to any person in a year of assessment, the aggregate of the amounts specified below in respect of that year do not exceed £5,000 (*FA 2004, Sch 15, para 13*).

Calculating the tax

8.63 The approach to valuing property for the purpose of the pre-owned assets rules is generally the same as for IHT purposes (*IHTA 1984, s 160*). In other words, it is the price that the property might reasonably be expected to fetch if sold in the open market at that time, without any scope for a reduction on the ground that the whole property is to be placed on the market at one and the same time.

The valuation date for property subject to the charge is 6 April in the relevant year of assessment or, if later, the first day of the taxable period.

When valuing relevant land or a chattel it is not necessary to make an annual revaluation of the property. The property should rather be valued on a five-year cycle. Before the first five-year anniversary, the valuation of the property will be that set at the first valuation date. Thereafter, the valuation at the latest five-year anniversary will apply.

Example 8.15

Andrew is first chargeable on 6 April 2007. A valuation is obtained then. He becomes non-UK resident for three years from 6 April 2008 to 6 April 2011. The charge does not apply during this period. He returns to the UK on 7 April 2011. A new valuation is made then and this is the start of the next five-year anniversary.

Land

8.64 The chargeable amount in relation to the relevant land is the appropriate rental value, less the amount of any payments which the chargeable person is legally obliged to make during the period to the owner of the relevant land in respect of their occupation.

The appropriate rental value is:

$$\frac{R \times DV}{V}$$

R is the rental value of the relevant land for the taxable period.

DV is:

- where the chargeable person owned an interest in the relevant land, the value as at the valuation date of the interest in the relevant land that was disposed of by the chargeable person or, where the disposal was a non-exempt sale, the 'appropriate portion' of that value;
- where the chargeable person owned an interest in other property, the proceeds of which were used to acquire an interest in relevant land, such part of the value of the relevant land at the valuation date as can reasonably be attributed to the property originally disposed of by the chargeable person or, where the original disposal was a non-exempt sale, to the appropriate portion of that property;
- if the contribution condition applies, such part of the value of the relevant land at the valuation date as can reasonably be attributed to the consideration provided by the chargeable person.

V is the value of the relevant land at the valuation date.

The 'rental value' of the land for the taxable period is the rent which would have been payable for the period if the property had been let to the chargeable person at an annual rent equal to the annual value. The annual value is the rent that might reasonably be expected to be obtained on a letting from year to year if:

- the tenant undertook to pay all taxes, rates and charges usually paid by a tenant; and
- the landlord undertook to bear the costs of the repairs and insurance and the other expenses, if any, necessary for maintaining the property in a state to command that rent.

8.65 The rent is calculated on the basis that the only amounts that may be deducted in respect of the services provided by the landlord are amounts in respect of the cost to the landlord of providing any relevant services. 'Relevant service' means a service other than the repair, insurance or maintenance of the premises. In other words, if the landlord provides other relevant services that are reflected in the rent, for example the maintenance of the common parts in a block of flats, then the cost of providing those services may be deducted from the rent.

The regulations do not specify the sources from which the required valuations should be obtained. However, HMRC would expect the chargeable person to take all reasonable steps to ascertain the valuations, as they would do if, for example, they were looking to let a property on the open market.

FA 2004, Sch 15, para 4(4) introduces the concept of a 'non-exempt sale' for a disposal which is a sale of the chargeable person's whole interest in the property for cash, but which is not an excluded transaction as defined in *para 10*. The 'appropriate proportion', which is relevant for ascertaining the appropriate rental value, is calculated as follows:

$$\frac{MV - P}{MV}$$

Where MV is the value of the interest in land at the time of the sale and P is the amount paid.

Example 8.16

Andrew sells his house to his daughter for £100,000. It is worth £300,000. He lives in the house. In these circumstances we would say that only two-thirds of the value of the house is potentially within the charge to pre-owned asset tax (POAT). However, since he made a gift of that two-thirds, HMRC would accept that he is protected under *FA 2004, Sch 15, para 11(5)* reservation of benefit from a charge on that two-thirds. Note that if he sold part of his house to his daughter at an undervalue then the non-exempt sale provisions would not apply. So, in Example 8.15 above, if he sold half his house to his daughter for £100,000 and that half share was in fact worth £300,000, although he would have reserved a benefit in two-thirds of that half share, the £100,000 cash would be subject to POAT.

Chattels

8.66 The chargeable amount in relation to any chattel is the appropriate amount, less the amount of any payments that the chargeable person is legally obliged to make during the period to the owner of the chattel for the possession or use of the chattel by the chargeable person.

The appropriate amount is:

$$\frac{N \times DV}{V}$$

N is the amount of the interest that would be payable for the taxable period if interest were payable at the prescribed rate on an amount equal to the value of the chattel at the valuation date. The prescribed rate is the official rate of interest at the valuation date.

Example 8.17

In 2008/09, Andrew was caught by *Sch 15* in respect of an earlier disposal of chattels. The chattels were worth £1,000,000 at the relevant valuation date on 6 April 2008. He will be treated as receiving a taxable benefit of 6.10% (official rate of interest in 2008/09) × £1 million = £61,000.

Note that the charge is computed differently from land and, while any rental payments made to the owner will reduce the amount on which he is chargeable, the fact that he pays a market rent for their use does not prevent an income tax charge arising. Hence, if he pays £10,000 rent, he will still be taxable on a £51,000 benefit. Tax is due on 31 January 2010 unless Andrew elects.

Intangible property

8.67 The chargeable amount in relation to the relevant property is N minus T.

N is the amount of the interest that would be payable for the taxable period if interest were payable at the prescribed rate on an amount equal to the value of the relevant property at the valuation date. The prescribed rate is the official rate of interest at the valuation date.

T is the amount of any income tax or CGT payable by the chargeable person in respect of the taxable period by virtue of any of the following provisions:

- *ICTA 1988, s 547, ITA 2007, Pt 13, Ch 2* or *ITTOIA 2005, s 624*;
- *TCGA 1992, s 77* or *86*;

so far as the tax is attributable to the relevant property.

Example 8.18

Mr A is the UK resident and domiciled settlor of a non-resident settlor-interested settlement. (You should assume that Mr A has not reserved a benefit in the settled property nor has an interest in possession in the trust and is, therefore, subject to the POAT charge.)

The settlement comprises 'intangible' property of cash and shares with a value of £1,250,000 at the valuation date. In the tax year 2008/09 the trustees receive income of £60,000 which is chargeable to income tax on Mr A under *ITTOIA 2005, s 624*. A further £350,000 capital gains are realised which are deemed to be Mr A's gains by virtue of *TCGA 1992, s 86*. In these circumstances, £24,000 income tax is payable on the £60,000 and £63,000 in CGT on the £350,000. The tax allowance (T) against the potential *Sch 15* charge is, therefore, £87,000. The chargeable amount (N) under *Sch 15* is 6.10% of £1,250,000 = £76,250. Since the tax allowance is greater than the chargeable amount, a charge under *Sch 15* will not arise.

Avoidance of double charge to income tax

8.68 There may be situations where:

- a chattel or land is caught by the rules applying to chattels or land; and
- there is also a charge in respect of intangible property which derives its value from the chattel or land.

In such situations, only one charge arises on the chattel or land and this will be the one which gives the largest chargeable amount. If this amount does not exceed the £5,000 *de minimis* limit no tax will be payable – the lower amount is disregarded completely.

Where the occupation, possession or use of any land or chattel is taxed as a benefit in kind in *Income Tax (Earnings and Pensions) Act 2003 (ITEPA 2003), Pt 3*, that Act takes precedence. However, if the chargeable amount under the pre-owned assets legislation exceeds the benefit in kind then the excess is charged under the pre-owned assets legislation (*FA 2004, Sch 15, para 18*).

The IHT election

8.69 The provisions of the pre-owned assets legislation are optional. The reason for this is that the provisions are simply a device to prevent the avoidance of IHT by exploiting gaps in the gifts with reservation legislation. The legislation has therefore provided taxpayers with the opportunity to opt back into the IHT rules. Such an option has to be made by the taxpayer in the form of an election. Owing to a defect in subsidiary legislation, HMRC have indicated that late elections will be accepted (Budget 2007, BN28), but it is unclear as to what extent. *FA 2007, s 66,* substituting *FA 2004, Sch 15, para 23(3),* states:

> 'The election must be made on or before:
>
> (a) the relevant filing date, or
>
> (b) such later date as an officer of Revenue and Customs may, in a particular case, allow.'

This may provide a let-out for those who have faced hefty income tax charges.

See also the HMRC website at www.hmrc.gov.uk/poa/poa_guidance3.htm#34 for further guidance.

Consideration should be given to making an election if the ultimate IHT charge is low. This might be the case if the estate will be quite small and, therefore, the nil rate band will not be used entirely or will only be slightly exceeded.

Chapter 9

Non-residents

RESIDENCE STATUS

Residence of individuals

9.1 The meaning of 'residence' for tax purposes is the same as its everyday English meaning. In The Oxford English Dictionary, the word 'reside' is defined as:

> 'To dwell permanently or for a considerable time, to have one's settled or usual abode, to live in or at a particular place.'

The tax tribunal will ultimately decide whether a taxpayer is resident or not in the UK in any tax year. Since this is a matter of fact rather than law, the courts will not interfere in such decisions unless no tribunal acting reasonably could have come to that decision on the evidence available. HMRC Claims Branch deal with the application of the residency rules.

To be resident in the UK in any year, an individual must, generally, be physically present in the UK during some part of the year of assessment. Where a person is present for any period whereby he is regarded as resident for that time, he is strictly also regarded as resident for the whole of the tax year. There is no statutory provision for splitting a tax year in relation to residence (but there are extra-statutory concessions in this area (see **9.2**)).

A Commonwealth citizen (or citizen of the Republic of Ireland) who is ordinarily resident in the UK is regarded as resident in the UK where he has left the country for only occasional residence abroad. 'Occasional residence' is not defined, but a person who for a number of years spent the major part of each year living abroad in hotels was held to have left the UK for only occasional residence abroad.

In deciding if an individual is resident or not in the UK, the following factors should be considered. Where there is no standard pattern of working hours (35–40 being considered as a typical UK working week), HMRC will look to determine full-time employment in the cases below on the basis of the nature of the job and local conditions or practices; it might include several concurrent part-time jobs.

Physical presence

9.2 Any person who spends six months or longer in the UK in the tax year in question will be regarded as resident in the UK for that year. In calculating the six-month period, days and hours are taken into consideration. Any day in which an individual is present in the UK at midnight will count as a day's presence. Days spent in transit, even involving changes between methods of transport, will not count as a day's residence, unless the individual carries out activities that are substantially unrelated to the transit process (eg a business meeting) (*FA 2008, s 24*).

One is still resident in the UK if one's residence abroad is temporary. It is possible to be resident in more than one country at any one time (*ITA 2007, s 829*).

Once there has been a finding that a taxpayer is resident in the UK, then he is treated as resident for the whole of that tax year. HMRC, however, by concession will allow a tax year to be split so that a taxpayer will be treated as resident in the UK for only part of that tax year in four situations (ESC A11: see **9.3**):

- where an individual comes to the UK to take up permanent residence or to stay for at least three years;
- where an individual comes to the UK to take up employment which is expected to last for a period of at least two years;
- where an individual ceases to reside in the UK if he has left for permanent residence abroad; or
- where an individual leaves the UK to take up full-time employment abroad, and:
  - he is absent from the UK for a complete tax year; and
  - his visits to the UK do not exceed six months in the tax year in question and do not average three months per year.

Split tax year concession

9.3 As mentioned in **9.2**, by concession, HMRC will allow a tax year to be split so that a taxpayer will be treated as resident in the UK for only part of that tax year. The full text of Extra-statutory Concession (ESC) A11 is as follows:

'Residence in the United Kingdom: year of commencement or cessation of residence

The *Income and Corporation Taxes Acts* make no provision for splitting a tax year in relation to residence and an individual who is resident in the United Kingdom for any year of assessment is chargeable on the basis that he is resident for the whole year.

But where an individual:

(a) comes to the United Kingdom to take up permanent residence or to stay for at least two years; or

(b) ceases to reside in the United Kingdom if he has left for permanent residence abroad;

liability to United Kingdom tax which is affected by residence is computed by reference to the period of his residence here during the year. It is a condition that the individual should satisfy the Board of Inland Revenue that prior to his arrival he was, or on his departure is, not ordinarily resident in the United Kingdom. The concession would not apply, for example, where an individual who had been ordinarily resident in the United Kingdom left for intended permanent residence abroad but returned to reside here before the end of the tax year following the tax year of departure.

This concession is extended to the years of departure and return where, subject to certain conditions, an individual goes abroad for full time service under a contract of employment. These conditions are:

- the individual's absence from the United Kingdom and the employment itself both extend over a period covering a complete tax year; and
- any interim visits to the United Kingdom during the period do not amount to:
  - (i) 183 days or more in any tax year; or
  - (ii) an average of 91 days or more in a tax year (the average is taken over the period of absence up to a maximum of four years); and
- for years up to and including 1992/93, all the duties of the employment are performed abroad or any duties the individual performs in the United Kingdom are incidental to duties abroad.

Where the concession applies and the tax year is split, *section 128, FA 1995* (limit on income chargeable on non-residents: income tax) does not apply for the period for which an individual is treated as not resident. That section only applies to complete years of non-residence.'

Accompanying spouses and civil partners

9.4 By concession, HMRC allow an accompanying spouse or civil partner to benefit, *inter alia*, from the concessionary treatment for the years of departure and return which is available to a person taking up full-time employment abroad.

The full text of Extra-statutory Concession (ESC) A78 is as follows:

> **'Residence in the United Kingdom: accompanying spouse**
>
> (1) The residence and ordinary residence status of a husband and wife is determined independently but the circumstances of one spouse may, in certain situations, be taken into account when determining the residence status of the other. This can apply when one spouse goes abroad for full-time employment, or to work full-time in a trade, profession or vocation, and is regarded as not resident and not ordinarily resident from the day following departure to the day before return. The following concession applies where an individual in this position is accompanied, or later joined, by his or her spouse who is not in full-time employment (or working full-time in a trade, profession or vocation) abroad.
>
> (2) Where the accompanying spouse is abroad for a complete tax year and interim visits to this country do not amount to:
>
> - 183 days or more in any tax year; or
> - an average of 91 days or more in a tax year (the average is taken over the period of absence up to a maximum of 4 years);
>
> then the accompanying spouse's liability to UK tax which is affected by residence, for the years of departure and return at the beginning and end of the period spent abroad, will be determined by reference to the period of his or her residence here during the year.
>
> (3) For years up to and including 1992/93 a further condition applied. If accommodation in the UK was available for the accompanying spouse's use, the tax treatment set out in paragraph 2 above would apply where no visits were made to the UK between the date of departure and the following 5 April or, for the year of return, between 6 April and the date of return.
>
> (4) In addition, for years up to and including 1992/93, the accompanying spouse who had available accommodation in the UK would be regarded as not ordinarily resident from the day after leaving the UK to the day before the date of return, provided that the absence was for three years or more and visits here averaged less than 91 days a tax year. If the absence abroad was expected to be for three years or more

but was cut short because the period of the spouse's employment was terminated unexpectedly, the shorter absence might qualify for this treatment provided that it included a complete tax year and any visits to the UK averaged less than 91 days a tax year.'

Example 9.1

Marco is Italian and comes to the UK to live for a period of four years. He will be treated as UK resident for income tax purposes from the date he arrives.

Hank is an American citizen and travels to London for the first time to visit relatives. He stays for 180 days during the tax year. He will not be treated as UK resident for income tax purposes for that year.

Ordinary residence

9.5 Where a person has been ordinarily resident in the previous tax year but goes abroad for an occasional residence, he will be treated as remaining resident in the UK.

Occasional residence must mean a period in excess of six months abroad each year, otherwise his presence in the UK for more than six months in a particular tax year would mean a finding of residence under the six-month rule.

Any day in which an individual is present in the UK at midnight will count as a day's presence (*FA 2008, s 24*).

The period of six months after which an individual is treated as resident in the UK is taken to be 182 days. The 182 days must fall within a tax year. It is possible, therefore, to spend a continuous period in excess of 182 days in the UK and still not be resident there. The last 181 days before 6 April and the first 181 days after 5 April could be spent in the UK without there being an automatic finding of residency. However, it does not follow that, because one spends less than six months in the UK in a particular tax year, one will not be resident in that year.

EMPLOYMENT MATTERS

UK visits and temporary residence

9.6 If an individual spends six months or more of any tax year in the UK he will be resident there for tax purposes. If he spends less than six months in the UK he may or may not be resident depending upon whether the visits are frequent and substantial: HMRC consider the regularity of the visits and the reason for them (see *Levene v CIR* (1928) 13 TC 486 and *Reid v CIR* (1926) 10 TC 673). It is more likely that a taxpayer will be resident in the UK if his visits are regular and form part of his way of life. If the nights spent in the UK on average amount to more than three months per tax year for four years, then the taxpayer will be resident from the first year. HMRC regard visits as sufficiently regular if they are on average for periods of three months or more per tax year. In applying the three-month rule any day in which an individual is present in the UK at midnight will count as a day's presence (*ITA 2007, ss 831, 832*; *FA 2008, s 24*).

For further information on arrival in the UK, see the HMRC website at www.hmrc.gov.uk/incometax/tax-arrive-uk.htm.

Employment income and benefits

9.7 Emoluments from an employment, including benefits in kind, are calculated under the normal tax rules. Apart from the travelling expense rules, expenses are deductible only according to the normal test of being wholly, exclusively and necessarily incurred in the performance of the duty of the employment.

Many international employers operate tax equalisation schemes, also known as tax protected pay or net pay. It is an arrangement that ensures that an employee has the same take home pay wherever employed. Payments under these schemes are taxable. Golden handshakes are also taxable but, in addition to the general £30,000 allowance, substantial foreign service may give a full or further partial exemption.

Stock options or share acquisition schemes may give rise to taxable income. Gains on the grant of an option escape tax if the individual is not resident and not ordinarily resident and his emoluments are foreign emoluments for duties wholly performed outside the UK. Gains on the exercise of an option will not necessarily escape tax if the individual is then non-resident. Gains arising in relation to share acquisition schemes are chargeable in the normal way, unless the employee is non-resident at the time the gain arises.

Form P85 (form P85(S) in repayment cases) is for completion by employees when they subsequently leave the UK. These are voluntary, rather than statutory, forms. Since self-assessment, these forms are still required to be completed but, in addition, any individual who receives a tax return form is required to complete the 'Non-residence' supplementary pages. It should be noted that since the introduction of self-assessment, HMRC have ceased to give residency rulings.

Liability to tax

9.8 The tax treatment of employment income of individuals domiciled outside the UK depends on whether:

- the employee is resident in the UK or not, and, if so, whether also ordinarily resident;
- the duties are performed wholly abroad or wholly or partly in the UK;
- remuneration is foreign emoluments.

Foreign emoluments are amounts paid by a non-resident employer (which includes a branch of a non-resident company or partnership) to a non-domiciled employee. An employer resident in the Republic of Ireland, or in the UK and abroad, cannot pay foreign emoluments.

The main points to note are:

- a non-resident is liable on emoluments for duties in the UK;
- a resident who is not ordinarily resident is liable on the same basis but, in addition, is liable on the remittance basis on emoluments for non-UK duties of that or other employments; and
- a resident who is also ordinarily resident is taxed on all emoluments for duties within and outside the UK; if the remuneration consists of foreign emoluments, the liability will be on the remittance basis if the duties are performed wholly abroad.

Where there is a difference in treatment between UK earnings and overseas earnings two separate contracts, one for UK and the other for foreign duties, are desirable. The contracts must be with separate employers as it is not possible to have two contracts of employment with the same employer. The use of two contracts allows the employer to specify that the foreign duties attract a higher rate of remuneration, although they will be treated as one employment for tax purposes.

Travel costs and expenses of non-domiciled employees

9.9 Non-UK domiciled employees can claim a deduction for expenses from an employment for duties performed in the UK (*ITEPA 2003, s 373*). The deduction is given for the amount included in respect of (a) the provision of travel facilities for a journey made by the employee, or (b) the reimbursement of expenses incurred by the employee on such a journey. Two conditions must both be met.

The first condition is that the journey ends on, or during the period of five years beginning with, a date that is a 'qualifying arrival date' in relation to the employee.

The second condition is that the journey is made:

- from the country outside the UK in which the employee normally lives to a place in the UK in order to perform duties of the employment; or
- to that country from a place in the UK in order to return to that country after performing such duties.

If the journey has a dual purpose, the deduction is given for so much of the amount included in earnings as is properly attributable to the work purpose.

Employee's spouse's, civil partner's, or child's travel

9.10 A deduction may be claimed for the travelling expenses in respect of (a) the provision of travel facilities for a journey made by the spouse, civil partner (*SI 2005/3229, reg 148(3)*), or child of the non-UK domiciled employee, or (b) the reimbursement of expenses incurred by the employee on such a journey. The following conditions must be met (*ITEPA 2003, s 374*):

Condition 1 – journey

The journey must:

- be made between the country outside the UK in which the employee normally lives and a place in the UK; and
- end on, or during the period of five years beginning with, a date that is a 'qualifying arrival date' in relation to the employee.

Condition 2 – employee's presence in the UK

The employee must be in the UK for a continuous period of at least 60 days for the purpose of performing the duties of one or more employments from which the employee receives earnings for duties performed in the UK.

Condition 3 – spouse, civil partner or child

The spouse, civil partner or child must be:

- accompanying the employee at the beginning of the 60-day period;
- visiting the employee during that period; or
- returning to the country outside the UK in which the employee normally lives, after so accompanying or visiting the employee.

'Child' includes a stepchild and an illegitimate child, but does not include any child who is aged 18 or over at the beginning of the outward journey.

The journey by a member of the employee's immediate family must be between the country outside the UK in which the employee normally lives and the place of performance of his duties in the UK.

Example 9.2

Marcus, who is domiciled in Italy, divorces his wife. She has custody of their two children and takes them to live in her native New York. A journey made by the children to visit their father in the UK would not qualify under this provision if it was direct from New York (not the taxpayer's usual place of abode). Equally, a return journey could not qualify, as to do so it must follow a qualifying journey.

Only two return journeys may be claimed by the same individual in a single tax year (*ITEPA 2003, s 374(8)*).

If the journey has a dual purpose, the deduction is given for so much of the amount included in earnings as is properly attributable to the work purpose.

Qualifying arrival date

9.11 A 'qualifying arrival date' is defined as the date on which a person arrives in the UK to perform duties of an employment from which he or she receives earnings for duties performed in the UK and which meets either of two conditions (*ITEPA 2003, s 375*):

(1) the person has not been in the UK for any purpose during the period of two years ending with the day before the date.

(2) the person was not resident in the UK in either of the two tax years preceding the tax year in which the date falls. If this condition is met and there are two or more dates in the tax year on which the person arrives in the UK to perform duties of an employment from which the person receives earnings for duties performed in the UK, the qualifying arrival date is the earliest of them.

For further information on arrival in the UK, see the HMRC website at www.hmrc.gov.uk/incometax/tax-arrive-uk.htm.

Example 9.3

Franco is domiciled in Italy and comes to the UK in June 2004 to work as a freelance IT consultant. He makes a home here, although he regularly returns to Italy for about six months a year. In January 2008, he gets a job in Italy in a UK company. He remains in Italy during his tenure of that employment. He returns to the UK in July 2010 to take up another post with the same company. Throughout this period, he maintains a house in the UK available for his use. He has a wife and family in Italy.

Franco satisfies the conditions because:

- (1)he is non-resident in the two tax years before that in which he returns to the UK (being physically absent for the duration) and it does not matter that he might nevertheless be regarded as ordinarily resident; and
- (2)he does not return to the UK at any time between July 2008 and July 2010.

If he returns to the UK for any purpose in this latter period (eg for holiday or interview), then he fails condition (2).

Travel within a foreign country

9.12 Although travel may commence or end at any place in the UK, the travel to or from the country outside the UK in which the employee normally lives can, on a strict reading, only qualify if it is to or from the point of arrival or, as the case may be, departure in that country.

Example 9.4

Jack is domiciled in France and has lived for many years in Paris. He travels to take up a post with the London branch of a French manufacturing business. Rather than take a direct flight to London, he travels via Amsterdam, stopping over for one night between flights. His point of departure is Amsterdam. The flight from Paris to Amsterdam is not from the country outside the UK in which Jack normally lives, rather it is within it.

However, HMRC have confirmed that they will normally interpret the phrase 'usual place of abode' pragmatically, so that bona fide cases will qualify for relief.

Meaning of 'a continuous period of at least 60 days'

9.13 HMRC accept that, for the purposes of *ITEPA 2003, s 374(4)* only, employees satisfy the 60-day rule where:

- they spend at least two-thirds of their working days in the UK over a period of 60 days or more; and
- they are present in the UK for the purpose of performing the duties of their employment both at the start and at the end of this period.

Foreign expenses

9.14 Expenses incurred in providing board and lodging to enable an employee to perform the duties of his overseas employment are deductible if either the board and lodging outside the UK is provided directly by the employer, or the employee incurs the expense and is reimbursed by the employer, and the following conditions are met (*ITEPA 2003, s 376*):

- the duties of the employment are performed wholly outside the UK;
- the employee is resident and ordinarily resident in the UK; and
- in a case where the employer is a 'foreign employer', the employee is domiciled in the UK (apart from this, the employee's domicile is irrelevant).

Where the board and lodging is provided partly for the performance of the duties and partly for another purpose, only the expenses attributable to the former are allowable as a deduction.

Example 9.5

Christopher is sent to Australia by his employer on business which takes one week to conclude. Whilst in Australia he decides to take a further fortnight's holiday. The hotel expenses of the three weeks are paid for by the employer.

In these circumstances, only the hotel expenses relating to the first week are allowable as a deduction.

Double tax treaties

9.15 Many double taxation treaties provide that a resident of a foreign country who can claim the protection of the treaty will not be liable to UK tax on emoluments for duties performed in the UK if:

- the individual is present in the UK for periods not exceeding in total 183 days in any tax year;
- the emoluments are paid by an employer who is not resident in the UK; and
- the cost of the emoluments is not borne by a permanent establishment or fixed base that the employer has in the UK.

Treaties often exclude public entertainers and sports people from the protection of such a provision, and their earnings are often paid under deduction of tax (see **9.67–9.69**).

PAYE MATTERS

UK presence

9.16 If an employer has a trading presence in the UK he will be required to deduct income tax and Class 1 NICs under PAYE from employees, regardless of whether he and/or the employee are non-resident. The remuneration will be charged to UK income tax.

Intermediaries

9.17 Primary legislation governs the PAYE liability of non-resident employers, and of those to whom employees are seconded in cases where the employer does not operate PAYE (*ITEPA 2003, ss 689* and *691*).

Employee of overseas employer

9.18 Where:

- an employee works for a person (the 'relevant person') other than his employer; but
- is still paid by his employer or an intermediary of his employer (see above) or of the relevant person;
- PAYE regulations do not apply to the payer or, if he makes the payment as an intermediary of the employer or of the relevant person, the employer; and
- PAYE is not deducted or accounted for in accordance with the regulations by the payer or, if he makes the payment as an intermediary of the employer or of the relevant person, the employer,

then the relevant person is required to account for PAYE on payments to the employee, grossed up if the payments are net of any income tax.

Where, under the 'notional payments' provisions (*ITEPA 2003, s 710*), an employer would be treated for the purposes of the PAYE regulations as paying an amount to an employee, he is also treated for *ITEPA 2003, s 689* purposes as making a payment of that amount. Where this happens, the amount of assessable income which the employee is treated as receiving is regarded as a gross amount.

In determining whether a payment is made by an intermediary of the person for whom the employee works, the same approach is taken as in *ITEPA 2003, s 687(4)*.

Mobile UK workforce

9.19 Where employees of a UK employer ('the contractor') work for another person, but continue to be paid by or on behalf of the contractor, and it is likely that PAYE will not be accounted for even though all parties are based in the UK, HMRC may give a direction that the person to whom the employees are seconded must deduct PAYE tax from any payments made by that person to the contractor in respect of the work done by the employees.

A direction must specify both the contractor and the person to whom the employees are seconded, must be given by notice to that person, and may be withdrawn at any time by notice to that person. HMRC must take 'such steps as are reasonably necessary' to ensure that the contractor is given a copy of any such notice as relates to him.

Payments to non-resident employees

9.20 Where an employee is not resident, or not ordinarily resident, in the UK, and works partly in the UK and partly overseas, only some of his income from employment will be taxable under the charge on employment income provisions (*ITEPA 2003, s 690*). In such cases, the employer, or a person designated by the employer, may apply for a direction that a particular proportion of any payment made to the employee in a tax year should be treated as liable to PAYE. If, however, there is no direction in force, the entirety of any payment made to the employee in the tax year will be liable to PAYE.

An application for a direction must give 'such information as is available and is relevant to the application' (*ITEPA 2003, s 690(4)*). The application itself must be given by notice to the employer or the person designated by the employer, and must specify the employee and the tax year. The direction may be withdrawn by notice to the employer or designated person from a specified date, which must be no less than 30 days from the giving of the notice (*ITEPA 2003, s 690(6)*).

Whether or not a direction is in force, the validity of any assessment of the employee's income, and any right to repayment of overpaid tax or obligation to pay tax underpaid, remain unaffected.

Relevant payments

9.21 PAYE is to be applied on the making of a 'relevant payment' (*SI 2003/2682, reg 21(1)*). With certain exceptions (see below), the term 'relevant payment' is defined to mean a payment 'of, or on account of, net PAYE income'. 'Net PAYE income' is then defined as PAYE income, less allowable pension contributions and allowable donations to charity (as further defined in each case). To complete the circle, 'PAYE income' is defined in accordance with *ITEPA 2003, s 683* (ie encompassing employment income, pension income and social security income).

The following are excluded from the definition of 'relevant payment':

- PAYE social security income, but subject to the exceptions in *Pt 8* of the *PAYE regulations*;
- UK social security pensions;
- excluded relocation expenses;
- excluded business expenses;
- excluded pecuniary liabilities; and
- excluded notional payments.

An employer who provides an employee with assessable income in the form of 'readily convertible assets' is treated as making a payment to the employee of an amount liable to PAYE. The PAYE net is similarly extended to remuneration by way of non-cash vouchers, credit tokens and cash vouchers. Payments of assessable income deemed to have been made under these provisions are called 'notional payments', and there are particular rules for accounting for tax on such payments.

Apart from statute, there is no obligation on an employer to operate PAYE in respect of a payment only part of which is assessable under the charge on employment income provisions.

An exception to this rule is provided by *ITEPA 2003, s 690*, which subjects to PAYE certain relevant payments to employees not resident, or not ordinarily resident, in the UK, who work partly overseas and partly in the UK.

UK domiciled individuals

9.22 A UK-domiciled individual coming to the UK will normally be treated as resident and ordinarily resident here from the date of his arrival, in which case he is liable to UK income tax on his worldwide income (*ITEPA 2003, Pt 2, Ch 4*) (see **9.36** for commentary on domicile). The following table shows the liability to tax on employment income according to the individual's residence status; and the place where the duties of the job are performed.

Duties performed	**In UK**	**Abroad**
R & OR	Liable	Liable
R but not OR	Liable	Liable if remitted to UK
Not R	Liable	Not liable

R = resident

OR = ordinarily resident

The following table shows the position with respect to investment income:

Source of income	**UK**	**Foreign**	**FOTRA**
R & OR	Liable	Liable	N/A*
R but not OR	Liable	Liable if remitted to UK	Not liable
Not R but OR	Liable	Not liable	Not liable
Not R and not OR	Liable	Not liable	Not liable

FOTRA = Free of tax to residents abroad

* UK government FOTRA securities are only for those people who are not resident or are not ordinarily resident in the UK. Taxpayers who are resident and ordinarily resident in the UK will be liable to UK tax on interest from FOTRAs, even if they are domiciled outside the UK.

The investment income table contains some oversimplifications. The liability of non-residents is restricted to tax deducted at source.

Non-domiciled individuals

9.23 The following table shows the income tax exposure on employment income paid by a non-resident employer (*ITEPA 2003, Pt 2, Ch 5*):

Duties performed	**In UK**	**Abroad**
R & OR	Liable	Liable
R but not OR	Liable	Liable if remitted to UK
Not R	Liable	Not liable

R = resident

OR = ordinarily resident

The following table sets out the position with respect to investment income:

Source of income	**UK**	**Foreign**	**FOTRA**
R & OR	Liable	Liable if remitted to UK	Liable if remitted*
R but not OR	Liable	Liable if remitted to UK	Not liable (remittance basis for British subjects)
Not R but OR	Liable	Not liable	Liable
Not R and not OR	Liable	Not liable	Not liable

FOTRA = Free of tax to residents abroad

* UK government FOTRA securities are only for those people who are not resident or are not ordinarily resident in the UK. Taxpayers who are resident and ordinarily resident in the UK will be liable to UK tax on interest from FOTRAs, even if they are domiciled outside the UK.

Departure

9.24 Broadly, an individual who is in the UK for 183 days or more in any tax year will be treated as resident for tax purposes for the whole of the tax year. In addition, where there is habitual residence over a period of several years, an individual will be treated as 'ordinarily resident' in the UK. By concession, HMRC will agree to split the tax year where an individual goes abroad under a contract of employment. The conditions are as follows:

- the individual must be absent from the UK for an entire tax year;
- the employment must extend over an entire tax year;
- the individual must not spend more than 182 days in the UK in any tax year; and
- he must not spend 91 days or more in a tax year in the UK on average, over a period up to four years (see below).

In these circumstances, the person is treated as neither resident nor ordinarily resident with effect from the date of his departure.

The taxation of the income of people who are domiciled in, but not resident in, the UK is as follows:

Employment income	
– Overseas duties	No liability
– UK duties	Liable in respect of UK duties
Rent from UK property	Taxable
UK source taxed investment income	No further liability
FOTRA securities	No further liability

On leaving the UK, employees should complete form P85. For further information on leaving the UK, see the HMRC website at www.hmrc.gov.uk/incometax/tax-leave-uk.htm.

It is possible to be resident in more than one country and in some cases there will be actual or potential double taxation of the same income. The UK has double taxation treaties with most countries and in most cases relief will be available; either the treaty will give one country the right to tax a particular type of income (eg rent from property located in that country), or it will provide for credit relief (ie one jurisdiction will permit the set-off of tax paid in the other country). For a list of countries with which the UK has a double tax agreement (DTA) in force, see the HMRC booklet HMRC6 (www.hmrc.gov.uk/cnr/hmrc6.pdf).

The split-year concession only applies to the self-employed if they are going abroad for at least three years and will be not ordinarily resident in the UK following their departure. They will remain liable to UK tax to the extent that any part of the business is carried on in the UK. If the overseas country has a significantly more favourable tax regime it may be worthwhile incorporating an offshore company with non-resident directors so that the exposure to UK tax is limited to the profits of the UK branch.

Where the partnership carries on business partly in the UK and partly abroad, the non-resident partner's taxable share in the UK is limited to his share of the profits of the trade carried on in the UK.

Leaving the UK

9.25 Where an individual who has been resident and ordinarily resident in the UK leaves the UK, he will be treated for UK tax purposes as follows:

- if the absence is for a short period only, he will remain resident and ordinarily resident in the UK (see HMRC6, para 8.1);
- if the individual goes abroad for full-time service under a contract of employment, the split-year tax treatment set out at **9.3** may apply.

In *Shepherd v R & C Commrs* (2005) SpC 484, the taxpayer was an airline pilot who, prior to his retirement, claimed to have set up a home in Cyprus. He rented a fully furnished apartment, and then went on to purchase a property there. From the time he first rented the apartment, he ensured that his visits to the UK were less than the 91-day limit. In the year that concerned the appeal (1999/2000), his visits totalled only 80 days. He claimed that he had separated from his wife but they continued to share the matrimonial home throughout the period involved. In addition, he had described himself on his tax return as married and not separated and, when making a will in Cyprus, he left the property to his 'dearest wife'. He also remained on the electoral register and had mail sent to him there. He claimed that, when staying over in the UK between flights to and from Cyprus, he normally stayed with his parents; however, the Special Commissioner found that he stayed mainly at the matrimonial home. The Commissioner held that he was resident in the UK for 1999/2000 because he had gone abroad only for occasional residence. His continued, albeit on a much reduced scale, occupation of the matrimonial home indicated that he had not severed his connection with the UK sufficiently to show that his residence in Cyprus was anything other than occasional. His appeal in the High Court ([2007] BTC 426) was subsequently dismissed.

9.26 In *Grace v R & C Commrs* (2008) SpC 663, the taxpayer was an airline pilot who had formerly lived in the UK but, in 1997, he set up home in South Africa (the country of his birth) and claimed to be non-UK resident. His former wife and children continued to live in the UK but he only saw them on rare occasions. He maintained a house in the UK but only stayed there to rest before or after his flights.

The Special Commissioner held that, although Mr Grace was resident in the UK before October 1997, in that year there was a distinct break and, since then, his settled mode of life was in South Africa and not in the UK. This decision was found applying the principle established in *IR Commrs v Combe* (1932) 17 TC 405 that, if a person resident in the UK left for another country, and if there was a 'distinct break', then even if he returned for lengthy visits, he need not be resident if he had a settled mode of life elsewhere. The Special Commissioner then considered whether the taxpayer was ordinarily resident in the UK. *ICTA 1988, s 334* (now *ITA 2007, s 829*) did not apply, as the taxpayer's presence abroad from October 1997 was not for the purpose only of occasional residence abroad but for the purposes of continuous and settled residence in his house in South Africa and he only returned to the UK for the purpose of his work.

The High Court subsequently overturned the Special Commissioner's decision and held that there had been several errors in arriving at that decision. The judge said that 'temporary' (in former *TA 1988, s 336(2)* (now *ITA 2007, s 832*)) was not descriptive of the taxpayer's presence but of the taxpayer's purpose. In turn, this meant that it was for the Special Commissioner to decide whether the reason for the taxpayer's presence in the UK was casual or transitory. The recurrent nature of his regular presence in the UK (*Shepherd v R & C Commrs* considered) led to the conclusion that his purpose for being in the UK was neither casual nor transitory. It was also found that the Special Commissioner was wrong in law to discount the reason for the taxpayer's regular presence in the UK in his own house as being attributable 'only' to his work. He said the Commissioner had overlooked the fact that someone may be here for the exigencies of work and still have his presence treated as voluntary.

Furthermore, the Commissioner was wrong in concluding that there had been a 'distinct break' in the taxpayer's life when he set up home in South Africa. That conclusion, the judge said, was inconsistent with the undisputed facts that the taxpayer had retained the house in the UK which remained furnished, continued the same employment, and continued to be present regularly in the UK for the purposes of that employment. All that happened after he set up home in South Africa was that he acquired another home there.

On appeal against the decision of the High Court, the Court of Appeal referred the case to the First-tier Tribunal (*Grace v R & C Commrs* [2009] BTC 704).

91-day test

9.27 The case of *Robert Gaines-Cooper v HMRC* (2006) SpC 568 attracted some attention from tax practitioners and their clients because there has been some suggestion that the decision changed the basis on which HMRC calculate the '91-day test' (see above). HMRC Brief 01/07 however, confirmed that this is incorrect.

The '91-day test' is set out in HMRC booklet HMRC6: Residents, Domicile and the Remittance Basis (www.hmrc.gov.uk/cnr/hmrc6.pdf). HMRC believe that this guidance is clear that the '91-day test' applies only to individuals who have either left the UK and live elsewhere or who visit the UK on a regular basis. Where an individual has lived in the UK, the question of whether he has left the UK has to be decided first. Individuals who have left the UK will continue to be regarded as UK resident if their visits to the UK average 91 days or more a tax year, taken over a maximum of up to four tax years.

HMRC's normal practice, as set out in booklet HMRC6, is to disregard days of arrival and departure in calculating days under the '91-day test'.

In considering the issues of residence, ordinary residence and domicile in the *Gaines-Cooper* case, the Commissioners needed to build up a full picture of Mr Gaines-Cooper's life. A very important element of the picture was the pattern of his presence in the UK compared to the pattern of his presence overseas. The Commissioners decided that, in looking at these patterns, it would be misleading wholly to disregard days of arrival and departure. They used Mr Gaines-Cooper's patterns of presence in the UK as part of the evidence of his lifestyle and habits during the years in question. Based on this, and a wide range of other evidence, the Commissioners found that he had been continuously resident in the UK. From HMRC's perspective, therefore, the '91-day test' was not relevant to the *Gaines-Cooper* case, since Mr Gaines-Cooper did not leave the UK.

HMRC now confirm that there has been no change to its practice in relation to residence and the '91-day test'. Accordingly, HMRC state in Brief (01/07) that they will continue to:

- follow the published guidance on residence issues, and apply this guidance fairly and consistently;
- treat an individual who has not left the UK as remaining resident here;
- consider all the relevant evidence, including the pattern of presence in the UK and elsewhere, in deciding whether or not an individual has left the UK; and
- apply the '91-day test' (where HMRC is satisfied that an individual has actually left the UK) as outlined in booklet HMRC6, normally disregarding days of arrival and departure in calculating days under this 'test'.

See also *R (on the application of Davies & Anor) v R & C Commrs; R (on the application of Gaines-Cooper) v R & C Commrs* [2010] EWCA Civ 83, in which the Court of Appeal, dismissing applications for judicial review, clarified the interpretation of HMRC's 1999 edition of booklet IR20 in relation to leaving the UK to work full-time abroad and leaving the UK permanently and definitely, and held that HMRC had not been shown to have made any unannounced alteration in their interpretation of the guidance. Mr Gaines-Cooper has now been granted leave to take the case to the Supreme Court.

Returning to the UK

9.28 Generally, individuals returning to the UK from overseas postings will be resident and ordinarily resident in the UK from the date of return (*ITEPA 2003, Pt 2, Ch 5*).

TRADING

Charge on foreign income from trade, profession or vocation

9.29 Income of a UK resident derived from a trade, profession or vocation which is carried on wholly abroad is liable to tax only if it was remitted to the UK where the trader is:

- not domiciled in the UK; or
- a Commonwealth (including a British) citizen or a citizen of the Republic of Ireland and is not 'ordinarily resident' in the UK.

In all other cases, the income of a resident is liable to tax whether or not the income is remitted. Income arising in the Republic of Ireland is treated as if it arose in the UK but is nevertheless entitled to the same deductions (and subject to the same limitation of reliefs) as apply to trades etc carried on abroad.

The income of a non-resident derived from a trade carried on wholly abroad is not liable to tax. However, a non-resident trading in the UK through a branch or agency is liable to tax on consequent profits.

Partnerships

9.30 A trade carried on in partnership is treated as resident in the place that the business is controlled and managed, ignoring the residence status of the individual partners concerned.

Where a non-resident partnership trades both in the UK and overseas, a UK resident partner will be taxable on both the UK profits and the overseas profits. A non-resident partner will not be liable to UK income tax and the overseas profits (*ITTOIA 2005, s 849*).

Where a partnership has an overseas trade, and a UK resident partner who is not domiciled in the UK, he will only be liable to UK tax on profits from the overseas trade on a remittance basis. The usual rules apply to profits from the UK trade.

If a partner's residence status changes during a tax year, and that partnership's business is partly carried on in the UK and partly abroad, he will be treated as ceasing to be a partner at the time of the change, and then immediately becoming a partner again after the date of change. This means that separate tax calculations may be made for a tax year.

Trading in the UK

9.31 A 'non-UK resident' trading in the UK is only liable to UK tax where he is trading through a branch or agency.

Whether a person is trading in the UK through a branch or agency is a question of fact, but the distinction has to be made between trading with the UK and trading in the UK: soliciting orders in the UK will not by itself constitute trading in the UK. An important factor is whether the contract for sale or supply of services was made abroad, but the contract may not be conclusive.

UK resident trading wholly abroad

9.32 An individual who is resident in the UK and carries on a trade, profession or vocation wholly abroad, either alone or in partnership, is liable to tax on all his income from such a trade. The income is assessed on a current-year basis. Losses etc can only be set off against the income of that or another overseas source, foreign emoluments, other overseas income and certain pensions.

However, a person who is not domiciled in the UK or else is a Commonwealth (including a British) citizen (or a citizen of the Republic of Ireland) who is not ordinarily resident in the UK is liable only on a remittance basis (*ITTOIA 2005, s 7*).

Expenses connected with foreign trades

9.33 Special rules apply to travel expenses and board and lodging expenses incurred by an individual taxpayer whose trade, profession or vocation is carried on wholly outside the UK, and who has failed to satisfy HMRC that he is not domiciled here or else, being a Commonwealth (including a British) citizen (or a citizen of the Republic of Ireland), is not ordinarily resident here.

Where the rules apply, the travel and board and lodging expenses are to be treated as deductible provided that the taxpayer's absence from the UK is wholly and exclusively for the purpose of performing the function of the foreign trade.

In certain conditions, travel expenses of the taxpayer's spouse and any child of his are deductible.

Travel between foreign trades is also deductible, subject to conditions (*ITTOIA 2005, ss 92–94*).

Non-resident entertainers and sportsmen

9.34 There is a system of withholding basic rate income tax from payments made to visiting, non-resident entertainers and sports personalities. Except where the activity in point is performed in the course of an office or employment, it is treated as if it were a trade, profession or vocation exercised in the UK and the income from it plus payments connected with it are chargeable to income tax on a current-year basis; it is stated that regulations dealing with the system generally can provide specifically for losses and reliefs (*ITA 2007, Pt 15, Ch 18 (ss 965–970)*).

Where a payment is made in respect of an appearance by a non-resident entertainer or sportsman in the UK, the payer must deduct tax at the basic rate. This rule does not apply if:

- the payment is below £1,000;
- the recipient has agreed a lower or nil rate of withholding tax with HMRC.

Tax is calculated on a current-year basis.

Non-residents trading through a branch or agency

9.35 Where non-residents carry on a trade in the UK through a permanent establishment, for the purposes of self-assessment, HMRC will, broadly, treat that permanent establishment as the non-resident's 'UK representative', and look to it for the performance of various tax obligations. Certain persons are excluded from being a UK representative.

The amount of income tax chargeable for any tax year on the total income of any person who is not resident in the UK is limited to the sum of (*ITA 2007, s 811*):

- tax deducted, or treated as deducted, at source (including tax credits) from income received under deduction of tax; and
- tax on the non-resident's total income computed without regard to (*ITA 2007, s 813*):
  - savings and investment income;
  - gains from disposals of certificates of deposit;
  - various social security benefits;
  - income arising from transactions carried out on the non-resident's behalf by brokers and investment managers who are not treated as the non-resident's UK representative (SP 1/01);

– income designated for this purpose by the Treasury in regulations;

– personal allowances;

– relief under any double tax treaty.

The limitation on charge does not apply to the income of non-resident trustees if any of the trust's beneficiaries is an individual ordinarily resident in the UK or a company resident in the UK (*ITA 2007, s 812*). 'Beneficiaries' are broadly defined to include both actual and potential beneficiaries who:

- are or ever might become entitled to receive income from the trust; or
- have income from the trust paid to them or applied for their benefit by legitimate exercise of the trustees' discretion,

and 'trust' income includes capital derived from accumulated income.

DOMICILE

Introduction

9.36 The charge to income tax and capital gains tax in the UK is largely founded on residence status. However, the domicile of an individual will also be of importance in determining his liability and the taxation of foreign emoluments under *ITEPA 2003*. This is particularly important following changes brought in by *FA 2008*, which apply from April 2008 (see **9.49**). Domicile is also important for the purposes of inheritance tax. The concept of domicile is one of general law and within the jurisdiction of the UK domicile is regarded as being the equivalent of a person's permanent home. Broadly, a person is domiciled in that country in which he makes his permanent home. An individual is not domiciled in the UK as such, but rather in one of the areas of jurisdiction that together constitute the UK, namely England and Wales, Scotland, and Northern Ireland.

There are three kinds of domicile:

- domicile of origin;
- domicile of choice; and
- domicile of dependency.

Domicile of origin

9.37 Every individual has a domicile which is acquired at birth and is known as a domicile of origin. In the case of a legitimate child this will be the domicile of his father, and in the instance of an illegitimate child that of his mother. There need be no connection between an individual's place of birth and his domicile of origin, eg a legitimate child born in England to a father of Scottish domicile would acquire a Scottish domicile of origin.

It is not possible to have more than one domicile. The domicile of origin subsists until it is displaced by a new domicile of either choice or dependency.

Domicile of origin is characterised by two factors, its permanence and the heavy burden of proof required to displace it. In *IR Commrs v Bullock* (1976) 51 TC 522, the taxpayer was born in Nova Scotia, Canada, in 1910 and his domicile of origin was there. He came to England in 1932 to join the Royal Air Force. He married an English wife and they visited Canada on a number of occasions. He hoped to persuade his wife that they should live there after his retirement. He retired in 1961. His wife did not wish to reside in Canada and the couple continued to live in England. In 1966, he executed a will appointing a Nova Scotia corporation as executor. The will contained a declaration that his domicile was in Nova Scotia, Canada, and that he intended to return to that country upon his wife's death. All his assets were in Canada. The Court of Appeal held that for the taxpayer to have acquired a domicile of choice in England he must have intended to make his home there until the end of his days unless and until something happens (which was not indefinite or vague). The possibility that the taxpayer would survive his wife was not unreal. He had not formed the intention necessary to acquire a domicile of choice in England and therefore his domicile of origin still subsisted.

In Bullock's case, 40 years of residence in England was insufficient to displace the taxpayer's domicile of origin. The domicile of origin can never be completely lost. Since a person cannot be without a domicile, English law automatically assumes a domicile of origin. Thus, if an individual abandons a domicile of choice without acquiring a new domicile of choice, his domicile will be one of origin ensuring that he is not without a domicile. In *Udny v Udny* (1869) LR 1 Sc & Div 441, Colonel Udny had a domicile of origin in Scotland. He acquired an English domicile of choice and resided in that country for some 32 years. He then left England and went to live in France where he resided for the following nine years. On these facts, the House of Lords held that upon his departure for France, Colonel Udny abandoned his English domicile of choice but did not acquire a French domicile of choice. In consequence, his Scottish domicile of origin revived.

Domicile of choice

9.38 A domicile of choice is that domicile which an individual of legal capacity, not being dependent for his domicile upon another person, may acquire by taking up residence in another country with the intention of permanently residing there. In order to establish a domicile of choice an individual must demonstrate both residence and intention.

In *Plummer v IR Commrs* [1987] BTC 543 the taxpayer's family moved to Guernsey, and it was her intention also to settle there. However, she remained in the UK to continue her education at school and, later, university. Her claim to have established a Guernsey domicile of choice failed, since Guernsey had not become her chief place of residence.

In *Executors of Moore deceased v IR Commrs* (2002) SpC 335, the taxpayer was a US citizen born in 1924, with a domicile of origin in the US. In 1942, he moved from Missouri to New York, where at some point he purchased an apartment which he sold in 1983. He then rented an apartment there. During the 1980s, the deceased and his partner spent time in England and the US. They purchased a holiday home in Ireland, which was sold in the early 1990s. In March 1991, the deceased was granted consent to enter the UK for the limited purposes of his employment as an artist. He purchased a flat in London. His leave to remain in the UK expired in March 1995, but he continued to live in London. There was no attempt to deport him. In October 1995, his partner died but the deceased continued to live in the UK. He renewed his US passport on which he travelled.

The deceased died in March 1997 in London, where his funeral took place. He had made US tax returns but no UK tax returns although, following his death, payment was made to the Revenue in respect of UK income tax and capital gains tax based upon his residency in the UK. He left two wills, one in US form dealing with his US assets and the other in English form disposing of the whole of his estate worldwide (apart from those assets in the US which were dealt with separately) to a wide range of beneficiaries and English charities. He also charged his UK estate with sole liability of all his just debts, funeral and testamentary expenses. The will was executed in London.

The Revenue issued a notice of determination that the deceased died domiciled in England and Wales. The US executors supported the notice but the UK executors appealed, contending that the deceased died domiciled outside England.

The Special Commissioner, in allowing the appeal, said that the issue was whether the deceased had acquired a domicile of choice in England. That required that he had a fixed and determined purpose to make England his permanent home. The intention did not have to be immutable, but an intention to make a home in a new country merely for a limited time or for some temporary or special purpose was insufficient. The true test was whether he intended to make his home in the new country until the end of his days unless and until something happened to make him change his mind. The burden of proof was on the Revenue to show on the balance of probabilities that the deceased acquired a domicile of choice in England (*IR Commrs v Bullock* (1976) 51 TC 522 applied).

On the evidence, it appeared that the deceased's living solely in London prior to his death was determined more by ill-health than by a desire to make England his permanent home. His nomadic existence just happened to end up in London, rather than being the result of his forming the intention to stay, as was illustrated by his short-term immigration status. He never really gave up his New York connections. There was no clear evidence that he really had the necessary intention to acquire a domicile in England and quite a lot of evidence that he kept up his connections with New York. Accordingly, he did not die domiciled in England and Wales.

9.39 In *Surveyor v IR Commrs* (2002) SpC 339, the taxpayer was born in England in 1958 and acquired from his father a domicile of origin in the UK. He went to work in Hong Kong in 1986 and, until 1991, he returned to the UK once or twice a year for holidays. He married a UK national who had been resident in Hong Kong since 1984. In 1991, the taxpayer became a partner in his firm and was given the option of returning to the UK. He refused on the basis that he saw Hong Kong as his home and had no intention of returning to the UK to live. By 1994, he had three children and he purchased an apartment in Hong Kong for use as his family home. It was sold in 1995, as it was too small to accommodate a family, but the taxpayer continued to live in rented accommodation in Hong Kong. After the early 1990s, the taxpayer rarely visited the UK, except on occasional business trips.

In 1997, when the handover of Hong Kong to China was imminent, the taxpayer and his wife applied for permanent resident status, as they desired to remain permanently in Hong Kong, even though it was not compulsory. In order to obtain that status, they had satisfied certain criteria, including seven years' continuous residence in Hong Kong and the possession of certain financial and academic or business qualifications. Thereafter, they were entitled to live and work in Hong Kong without needing a work permit and/or the sponsorship of an employer. The taxpayer could also travel in and out of Hong Kong using only his permanent resident's identity card and did not need a passport or visa. He would have been subject to restrictions if he had not acquired permanent resident status.

In 1999, the taxpayer built a holiday home in Thailand. From 2000 to 2002, he lived and worked in Singapore, because his employer relocated him there, although he returned to Hong Kong on a regular basis. In July 2002, the taxpayer left his job and returned to Hong Kong, where he purchased an apartment with the help of a Hong Kong-based mortgage.

In 1999 the taxpayer created a Jersey settlement which would have contained 'excluded property' for inheritance tax purposes if he was domiciled outside the UK at that time. The Revenue took the view that the taxpayer was domiciled in the UK but the taxpayer appealed to the Special Commissioners on the basis that he had established a domicile of choice in Hong Kong.

The Special Commissioner, in allowing the appeal, said that the intention to abandon a domicile had to be unequivocal and that the standard of proof was the balance of probabilities; however, so serious a matter as the acquisition of a domicile of choice was not to be lightly inferred from slight indications or casual words. There had to be 'convincing evidence' of a settled intention to reside in another place, otherwise the person remained domiciled in England. The test was whether the taxpayer intended to make his home in a new country until the end of his days unless and until something happened to make him change his mind.

Applying those principles to the present case, the evidence supported the conclusion that, at the date of the creation of the settlement in August 1999, the taxpayer had the intention to reside permanently in Hong Kong. At that time, his residence in Hong Kong was not for a limited period or for a particular purpose but was general and indefinite in its future contemplation. His intention was directed towards one country and that was Hong Kong. His family, social business and financial ties were all there.

The Revenue had argued that, when the taxpayer completed form DOM1 in 1999, he had stated that his intention for the future was to remain permanently in the Far East and that he was building a family residence in Thailand to meet those requirements. The Far East was not a territory and did not have a distinctive legal system, both of which were a requirement for domicile. However, the form also said that the taxpayer considered himself as domiciled in Hong Kong and the statements about the Thailand house had to be considered in that context. On the evidence, the existence of the house in Thailand did not alter the intention of the taxpayer to make Hong Kong his permanent home. It did not point to the conclusion that, in August 1999, it was the taxpayer's intention to reside permanently in more than one country; nor that he intended to settle in one of several countries. Moreover, the temporary move to Singapore did not affect the taxpayer's intention in August 1999 to reside permanently in Hong Kong.

Domicile and residence

9.40 Residence is a matter of fact. Alone, without the necessary intention, it will be insufficient to establish domicile. However, intention may be inferred from the fact of residence since an individual's residence in a particular country is generally regarded as being prima facie evidence that he is also domiciled in that country. Thus, whilst no particular length of residence is required to establish a domicile of choice, the greater the period of residence the more strongly an intention to permanently reside is to be inferred. In *IR Commrs v Duchess of Portland* [1982] BTC 65, Nourse J opined that: 'residence in a country for the purposes of the law of domicile is physical presence in that country as an inhabitant of it. If the necessary intention is also there, an existing domicile of choice can sometimes be abandoned and another domicile acquired or revived by a residence of short duration in a second country.'

However, in *IR Commrs v Bullock* (1976) 51 TC 522, a period of 40 years' residence in England was insufficient to displace the taxpayer's domicile of origin. In *Ramsay v Liverpool Royal Infirmary* [1930] AC 588, a man born in Scotland in 1845, and thus with a Scottish domicile of origin, left that country in 1892 and henceforth resided in the city of Liverpool, in England. Whilst this individual often stated that he was proud to be a Glasgow man, he expressed a determination never to return to Glasgow. He resided in Liverpool for the final 36 years of his life leaving England on only two occasions during that period, once to visit the USA and once to visit the Isle of Man. He arranged for his own burial in Liverpool. On these facts, a unanimous House of Lords held that he had died domiciled in Scotland.

In *Anderson (Executor of Muriel S Anderson) v IR Commrs* (1997) SpC 147, the deceased had lived in Scotland all his life until, in 1974, at the age of 64, he retired and sold his home in Scotland. He moved to a property which he acquired in Cornwall, where he died eight years later, and his ashes were scattered in Scotland. A Special Commissioner concluded that his domicile remained in Scotland.

These cases illustrate that, whilst residence is an essential element in establishing a domicile of choice, it is the intention of the individual that is the determining factor.

Intention

9.41 The intention which is required for the acquisition of a domicile of choice in a particular country is the intention to reside permanently or for an unlimited time in that country.

In *Re Furse (deceased); Furse v IR Commrs* [1980] 3 All ER 838, the testator had a domicile of origin in Rhode Island, USA. In 1923, at the age of 40, the testator and his family came to England, and the following year they purchased a farm in Sussex where the testator resided until his death in 1963. During his periods of residence in England the testator indicated that he would not return to the USA until such time as he was rendered incapable of leading an active life on his farm in England. Fox J held that in view of the fact that the testator's intention was to go on living his accustomed life on the farm in England and only to leave when he was no longer able to lead an active physical life there, it was clear that he had no intention, save on a vague and indefinite contingency, of leaving England. It followed that at the time of his death the testator had acquired a domicile of choice in England.

Although the merest possibility of a future contingency is probably insufficient to deny the acquisition of a domicile of choice, there is no doubt that a contingency which is both realistic and unambiguous (eg the end of a job) will have that effect. In practice, it will be rare to find a person who has consciously formed the requisite intention to acquire a domicile of choice; consequently, such an intention will normally have to be inferred from the individual's conduct. The courts will look for any instance which is evidence of a person's residence or of his intention to reside permanently in a country. As Scarman J observed in *In the Estate of Fuld (No 3)* [1968] P 675:

> 'Domicile cases require for their decision a detailed analysis and assessment of facts arising within that most subjective of all fields of legal inquiry – a man's mind.'

In the case of *Re Clore (dec'd)* [1982] Ch. 456 the testator had received professional advice to acquire a foreign domicile. He followed the advice received and started to make arrangements to sever his more important connections with the UK. He retired as company chairman, instructed the sale of his two residences, bought an apartment in Monaco to which he removed some furniture, and made a Monaco will. Despite these actions, it was held on the evidence that he had not formed a settled intention to reside permanently in Monaco, and thus had not lost his English domicile.

It is impossible to formulate a rule specifying the weight to be given to particular evidence. All that can be gathered from the case law in this respect is that more reliance is placed upon conduct than upon declarations of intention, especially if they are oral.

Abandonment of domicile of choice

9.42 A domicile of choice is less retentive, and therefore more easily abandoned, than a domicile of origin (*Qureshi v Qureshi* [1972] Fam 173 at 191). There is some dispute as to the required intention necessary to abandon a domicile of choice. In seeking to abandon a domicile of choice in a particular country an individual must clearly cease to reside there. The uncertainty concerns whether such cessation of residence must be accompanied by:

- a positive intention not to return; or
- mere absence of any intention to return.

It must also be remembered that where a domicile of choice is abandoned, the domicile of origin will stand in its place unless and until it is replaced by a new domicile of choice.

Married women

9.43 Formerly the domicile of a married woman was dependent upon her husband's domicile. If he acquired a new domicile of choice then she acquired it too. She retained this domicile not only as long as her husband was alive and she was legally married to him, but also during widowhood or following divorce unless and until it was changed by the acquisition of another domicile.

This former rule was abolished by *Domicile and Matrimonial Proceedings Act 1973, s 1* (operative from 1 January 1974) and a married woman can now acquire a separate domicile from her husband.

Where a woman married prior to 1974, and thus acquired her husband's domicile upon marriage, she is treated as retaining that domicile, as a domicile of choice, or domicile of origin if it be so, until it is changed by the acquisition of a new domicile of choice or revival of the domicile of origin on or after 1 January 1974 (*Domicile and Matrimonial Proceedings Act 1973, s 1(2)*).

It would appear that a woman, living in England with her husband, who was married before 1 January 1974 will only be able to change her (now) domicile of choice by choosing to leave her husband for permanent residence abroad.

American wives of UK-domiciled taxpayers

9.44 A unique situation is afforded to US wives of British tax residents where the marriage took place before 1 January 1974. Under art 4(4) of the US–UK double taxation Convention of 31 December 1975 (*SI 1980/568*), a pre-1974 marriage is regarded as having taken place on 1 January 1974, and thus the new law applies to the determination of the wife's domicile. The consequence is that a pre-1974 American wife has the best of both worlds. For income tax and capital gains tax purposes only, her domicile will be determined independently of her British husband's domicile, and she can claim to be domiciled in one of the states of the USA. If her claim is successful, her overseas income and capital gains will be assessed on the remittance basis. For capital transfer tax and inheritance tax purposes, a pre-1974 American wife will generally have her husband's UK domicile, and consequently enjoy the exemption for transfers between spouses. She will in any case have a deemed UK domicile for inheritance tax purposes after 17 out of 20 years of residence.

UK tax position of overseas voters

9.45 UK taxpayers resident abroad are required, if they wish to exercise their right to vote in the UK, to complete a declaration on their registration forms which states: 'I do not intend to reside permanently outside the United

Kingdom'. In a written answer in the House of Lords on 17 October 1986 (Hansard, vol 480, col 1018) the Secretary of State for Employment considered the effect of signing such a declaration on the signatory's domicile and UK tax position. He said that making such a declaration would not affect the UK tax position of voters who were temporarily non-resident and maintained their links with the UK. However, where an individual with a UK domicile goes abroad and it becomes necessary to determine whether he retains his UK domicile or acquires a foreign domicile, any expression of his intentions (such as the declaration) would be only one of a number of factors to be taken into account, and the question of where he was domiciled would ultimately be resolved by looking at the extent to which he had in fact severed his ties with the UK so as to make his permanent home abroad.

In order to determine, for inheritance tax, capital gains tax and income tax purposes, whether a person is domiciled in the UK on or after 6 April 1996, the following factors are to be ignored (*FA 1996, s 200(1), (2)*):

- where a person does anything with a view to, or in connection with, being registered as an overseas elector; or
- where a person, when registered as an overseas elector, votes in any election in which he is entitled to vote by virtue of being registered.

A person is registered as an overseas elector if he is registered in any register mentioned in *Representation of the People Act 1983, s 12(1)* on account of an entitlement to vote conferred on him by *Representation of the People Act 1985, s 1*, or is registered under *Representation of the People Act 1985, s 3* (*FA 1996, s 200(3)*).

Where a person's domicile is to be established for tax purposes, he may require that the above-mentioned factors should be taken into account (*FA 1996, s 200(4)*).

Domicile of dependency

9.46 The domicile of a dependent person is determined by the domicile of the person on whom he or she is dependent. Should the domicile of the latter change, then the domicile of the dependent person will change accordingly. A dependent person cannot alone change his domicile. There are two categories of dependent persons: children and mentally incapacitated persons.

Children

9.47 At birth, a child acquires a domicile of origin. This will normally be the domicile of the father, unless the child is either illegitimate or born after the father's death, in which case it will be the domicile of the mother. Between the time of his birth and attaining the age of 16, an unmarried child is incapable of acquiring a domicile of choice by his own act. He may, of course, acquire a new domicile of dependency if that person upon whom he is dependent does so (but note the decision in *Re Beaumont* [1893] 3 Ch 490 where the court took the child's welfare into account upon the remarriage of her mother). Once a child reaches 16 years of age, he becomes capable of acquiring a domicile of choice in his own right (*Domicile and Matrimonial Proceedings Act 1973, s 3*). However, until he acquires an independent domicile he will retain his domicile of dependency as a (now) domicile of choice (note the decision in *IR Commrs v Duchess of Portland* [1982] BTC 65: see **9.40**).

Domicile and Matrimonial Proceedings Act 1973, s 3 states that a married person under the age of 16 is capable of acquiring an independent domicile. Whilst English domiciled children are incapable of contracting marriage below this age, the provision will be important in relation to a child below that age whose foreign marriage is recognised here.

In Scotland, a minor with legal capacity, ie a girl of 12 years or over or a boy of 14 years or over, is capable of acquiring an independent domicile.

Mentally incapacitated persons

9.48 A mentally incapacitated person will be unable to acquire an independent domicile by his own act if he is incapable of forming the requisite intention. A mentally incapacitated child will, during infancy, continue to take his father's domicile as a domicile of dependency. Upon attaining majority such a person will probably continue to depend upon the domicile of his father. An adult who becomes mentally disordered probably retains the domicile he possessed prior to the disorder.

REMITTANCES

The remittance basis

9.49 The remittance basis of taxation has been in existence for some 200 years and has operated largely in its present form for about 90 years. However, significant changes were introduced in *FA 2008*, which mainly affect UK residents who are normally liable to UK tax on the whole of their worldwide income and gains arising in a tax year – the arising basis. The remittance basis is available to UK-resident individuals who are not domiciled in the UK, or not ordinarily resident in the UK. It provides for foreign-sourced income (and, in the case of non-domiciled individuals only, foreign sourced gains) to be charged to tax by reference to the extent to which they are remitted to, or received in, the UK.

Where the remittance basis applies, it allows the taxpayer to defer tax on foreign income or gains that have arisen until amounts in respect of those income or gains are received in the UK (if they ever are). It does, however, have to be shown that what is received in the UK is 'in respect' of that income or gain.

Broadly, the legislation covers three categories of tax charge, namely relevant foreign income, employment income and capital gains. Historically the remittance basis has applied automatically for both employment income and capital gains. With effect from 6 April 2008, the claims mechanism applies to all three categories of charge. It is therefore up to taxpayers who are UK resident but not domiciled or not ordinarily resident, to decide whether they wish to be taxed on the remittance basis for each tax year. Self-assessment returns allow those who are entitled to the remittance basis to make a claim if they so wish. Those eligible can choose from one tax year to the next whether they wish to be taxed on this basis.

HMRC will assume that taxpayers with unremitted foreign income and gains of less than £2,000 have used the remittance basis unless they are notified that the taxpayer wishes to be taxed under the arising basis. In addition, a claim to use the remittance basis will not be required where an individual has total UK income or gains of no more than £100 which has been taxed in the UK, provided they make no remittances to the UK in that tax year (*FA 2009, Sch 27, paras 3* and *4*).

The obligation to file a self-assessment return on individuals with small amounts of income from overseas employment was removed with effect from 6 April 2008 where the overseas income is less than £10,000, and overseas bank interest is less than £100 in any tax year, all of which is subject to a foreign tax (*FA 2009, s 52*).

9.50 The changes to the remittance basis rules from April 2008 do not apply to those non-UK domiciled individuals whose unremitted income and/or gains for a tax year are less than £2,000 (see **9.53**). They will automatically be taxed on the remittance basis for that year, without the need for a claim (*ITA 2007, s 809C*). In addition, individuals entitled to claim the remittance basis who have no UK income or gains, and who do not remit any foreign income or gains, will not have to claim the remittance basis in years they are not liable to the remittance basis charge (RBC). This avoids them having to complete a self-assessment return only so they can claim the remittance basis and then have no tax to pay.

Personal allowances

9.51 From 6 April 2008, those who make a claim under *ITA 2007, s 809B* to be taxed on the remittance basis will lose their entitlement to various personal tax allowances (*FA 2008, Sch 7*). *Section 809G* lists these as, for income tax purposes, personal allowance and blind person's allowance, tax reductions for married couples and civil partners, and payments for life insurance; and for capital gains tax (CGT), the annual exempt amount.

However, this does not apply to individuals who are eligible to use the remittance basis without a claim in a tax year (see **9.50**) because they meet the conditions set out in *s 809C* (because their unremitted income and gains for a tax year are less than £2,000). They retain their entitlement to all those various allowances and reliefs.

£30,000 annual charge

9.52 Eligible adults (ie individuals who are 18 in the relevant year) who choose to be taxed on the remittance basis and have been UK resident for longer than seven out of the past ten years will be required to pay an additional tax charge. This charge, the remittance basis charge (RBC), is set at £30,000 (*ITA 2007, s 809H*). This charge is in addition to the tax liability for the year in question on any income and gains remitted to the UK, and any UK income or gains taxed on the arising basis. The £30,000 will be paid on nominated income and gains not remitted to the UK in the year. (These income and gains are called 'nominated' income and gains because the taxpayer is free to nominate the income and gains not remitted to the UK in the year on which tax of £30,000 is payable. For example, this could be £75,000 of unremitted foreign deposit interest on which UK tax was due at 40%, so leading to an income tax charge of £30,000.) If, in subsequent years, that 'nominated' income or gains upon which the RBC has been paid is, in fact, remitted to the UK, then that income or gains will not be taxed again.

However, there are ordering rules to ensure that if 'nominated' income or gains is, in fact, remitted when other untaxed income and gains remain unremitted, then that unremitted income and gains is treated as being remitted before the 'nominated' income and gains (*ITA 2007, ss 809H* and *809I*).

The record keeping necessary for *ss 809H* and *809I* can be avoided if individuals ensure that 'nominated' income or gains upon which the RBC is paid are not remitted to the UK, or only remitted after the remittance of all other unremitted income and gains since the first year of residence from April 2008. If an individual is confident they will never need to remit that 'nominated' income or gains, paying the RBC will not involve any extra complexity or record keeping.

The £30,000 charge will have to be paid by someone who has been resident in the UK for longer than seven out of the last ten tax years up to and including the year in which a claim is made under *s 809B*. The period of residence might be continuous or broken.

£2,000 'de minimis' rule

9.53 The *FA 2008* changes referred to at **9.9** and **9.50** above will not apply for a particular tax year to those whose unremitted foreign income and gains for that year are less than £2,000. The remittance basis will apply automatically to their overseas income and gains without a claim, and they will not lose personal allowances or be required to pay the £30,000 tax charge (see **9.52**). In the Explanatory Notes to *Finance Bill 2008*, HMRC have shown the following two examples where the *de minimis* rule would be met for the year 2008/09:

Example 1:

Unremitted income and gains in 2008/09 = £1,500

Unremitted income and gains from previous years = £0

Example 2:

Unremitted income and gains in 2008/09 = £1,500

Unremitted income and gains from previous years = £4,000

Although the total of unremitted income and gains in Example 2 is £5,500, it is only the amount proper to the year of assessment which is considered for the *de minimis* rule.

Anti-avoidance measures

9.54 *FA 2008* introduced measures to close various loopholes and address certain flaws and anomalies in the way the rules previously operated. HMRC perceived that those eligible for the remittance basis could often arrange their affairs so that they received or enjoyed foreign income or gains in the UK without any liability to UK tax, even though they had in substance remitted the foreign income or gains to the UK. The general aim of the new measures is to ensure that income or gains to which the remittance basis applies are only excluded from charge to UK tax where they are genuinely kept offshore and not brought to the UK. Where they are in effect remitted to the UK in such a manner that the individual has the use or enjoyment of them in the UK, the individual will be liable to tax on them if he has effectively remitted them to the UK.

'Ceased sources'

9.55 Under a long-standing interpretation of the legislation and case law in respect of relevant foreign income, HMRC have accepted that no tax liability can apply if the source of the income benefiting from the remittance basis no longer exists in the year of remittance – the 'source doctrine'. This means that if an individual arranges for a bank account to be closed at the end of one tax year and remits the interest in the next year, there was likely to be no liability. *FA 2008, Sch 7* overturns the 'source doctrine', so that a charge can be imposed where relevant foreign income that has benefited from the remittance basis is remitted, whether or not the source exists in the year of remittance. (That is already the case with employment income and capital gains, where the legislation is cast in terms preventing this outcome.)

'Cash only'

9.56 Prior to *FA 2008*, on the basis of case law, the general view was that relevant foreign income could only be taxed if it was brought into the UK as cash. So, if a remittance basis taxpayer turned relevant foreign income into an asset outside the UK and then imported that asset, it was unlikely that any charge would arise on the income (unless and until the asset was sold in the UK and there were cash proceeds). *FA 2008, Sch 7* contains legislation to ensure that money, property and services derived from relevant foreign income brought into the UK will be treated as a remittance and taxed as such.

Any asset purchased out of untaxed relevant foreign income which an individual or another relevant person owned on 11 March 2008 will be exempt from a charge under the remittance basis, for so long as that person owns it, even if the asset is outside the UK at that date and later imported.

Any asset purchased out of untaxed relevant foreign income and in the UK on 5 April 2008 will also be exempt from a charge under the remittance basis, for so long as the present owner owns it, even if the asset is later exported and then re-imported.

For the future, the following exemptions will be available to assets brought to the UK, purchased out of untaxed relevant foreign income:

- the 'personal use rule', applying to clothes, shoes, jewellery and watches, for the use of the individual or members or their immediate family;
- the 'repair rule' for assets brought to the UK for repair and restoration;
- the 'temporary importation rule' where assets are in the UK for less than a total period of 275 days; and
- assets costing less than £1,000.

There is also a new 'public access rule', allowing exemption for works of art, collectors' items and antiques brought into the UK for public display.

If an asset is sold in the UK while any of these exemptions is in force, the exemption will cease at that point and the tax charge that arises under existing law will apply at that point.

If property meets the personal use rule, the repair rule or the public access rule then the time during which it meets any of those rules is taken into account in deciding whether it meets the temporary importation rule. So, for example, if an asset comes to the UK for repair, and that repair takes 75 days, then after the repair is complete it can be kept in the UK for a further 200 days under the temporary importation rule. Property to which the temporary importation rule applies remains exempt if, before the end of the 275-day period, it is then put on public display and meets the terms of the public access rule.

FA 2009 extended the scope of the exemptions that allow individuals using the remittance basis to bring property, which has been purchased out of overseas investments and savings, into the UK, to include property purchased out of foreign employment income and foreign chargeable gains, as well as relevant foreign income. The extension to the existing rules applies from 1 April 2008 (*FA 2009, Sch 27*).

Offshore mortgages

9.57 Previously, individuals paying tax on the remittance basis who borrowed money from a non-UK institution could repay the interest on that loan out of untaxed foreign income without giving rise to a tax charge on the remittance basis, even if the loan was advanced into the UK. Without special rules the effect of other changes to the legislation made by *FA 2008, Sch 7* would be that repayments on such loans advanced to the UK would be treated as a remittance on or after 6 April 2008. *Schedule 7, para 86* therefore provides 'grandfathering' provisions for certain loans made before 12 March 2008. Subject to conditions, interest payments out of untaxed relevant foreign income will not be treated as a remittance on or after 6 April 2008.

The loan must be made to the individual outside the UK before 12 March 2008. It must be for the sole purpose of enabling the individual to purchase a residential property in the UK. Before 6 April 2008 the money has to be received in the UK and used to acquire the property, and repayment of the debt has to be secured on that property.

These rules apply to interest payments for the remaining period of the loan, or until 5 April 2028 if sooner. If the terms of the loan are varied or any further advances made after 12 March 2008, the repayments will be treated as remittances from that point.

DOUBLE TAXATION RELIEF

Introduction

9.58 The UK has entered into numerous double tax treaties with other countries to mitigate the effect of double taxation of income and capital gains but far fewer in relation to gifts and inheritances.

Treaties are made with one country in each case, but members of the Organisation for Economic Co-operation and Development have subscribed to a model form and many treaties follow that form. Where a treaty applies, it explains when UK domestic tax law applies and where the overseas tax law applies. The treaty does not override UK tax law in that the treaty cannot impose a liability. It can say which authority has the taxing rights if they exist and there would, otherwise, be double taxation. Double taxation arises because different countries employ different criteria to found their tax jurisdiction. For example, a US citizen who is taxable in the UK as a resident or because of a UK source of income will remain liable to US tax on worldwide income and gains by virtue of US citizenship.

A UK resident may claim double tax relief even where no treaty is in force. This relief is called unilateral relief. Relief will be given by a credit equal to the lower of the UK tax or foreign tax on the overseas income or capital gains. If there is no UK tax on the income, such as where profits are covered by current year losses, the foreign tax can be deducted in calculating the income or gains for UK tax.

A treaty will normally go further than allowing credit by assigning exclusive taxing jurisdiction to one country or other by limiting withholding taxes (eg on dividends, interest and royalties). Treaties can apply to dual residents but usually require an individual to be treated as a resident of only one country, determined by criteria in order of priority (eg permanent home, centre of vital interests, and nationality). They usually permit a country to tax business profits only if derived from a local permanent establishment. The permanent establishment is usually a fixed place of business defined in some detail. However, a permanent establishment might be a temporary site office or mobile home or caravan. The terms of the specific treaty must be checked. It is possible for a person to be taxed in one country on one type of income or profit but in another country for another type of income.

Credit is also available for overseas tax similar to inheritance tax charged on the gift of an asset, in lifetime or on death. Few treaties have been negotiated and many do not adequately cover lifetime gifts, because they were negotiated when the former estate duty was in force. In addition to deductions and credit they also lay down useful criteria for determining and so resolving conflicts over the domicile of an individual and the location of assets.

Forms of double tax relief

9.59 Double tax relief may be given in several different forms. These can usefully be categorised as follows:

Treaty exemption – Income which has been taxed in one territory is specifically exempt by treaty from tax in another territory. This method does not generally prevent the second territory taking the amount of exempt income into account when computing the tax to be charged on the remaining taxable income.

Credit relief – Relief may be provided either by treaty or unilaterally. Income which has been taxed in one territory (usually the territory of source) is not exempt from tax in the second territory, but the tax paid in the first territory in respect of that income is deductible from the tax payable in the second territory in respect of that income.

Deduction – Income which has been taxed in one territory is reduced by the amount of that tax in determining the amount of income which is taxed in the second territory (*TIOPA 2010, Pt 2*).

Model treaty provisions

9.60 Two chief methods of relieving double taxation are adopted in 'tax treaties'. First, taxing rights over certain classes of income are reserved entirely to the country of residence of the person deriving the income. Secondly, all other income may be taxed (in some cases, only to a limited extent) by the country of origin of that income; if the country of residence of the recipient also taxes that income, it must grant a credit against its tax for the tax levied by the country of origin.

Many tax treaties are based on the 1977 or 1992 Model Convention published by the Organisation for Economic Co-operation and Development. They usually provide that a national from one territory should not be treated more harshly than a national from the other territory (a 'non-discrimination clause'); though the EC Treaty requires similar treatment within the EC, the matter in point must fall within the provision for the reliefs effected by arrangements agreed with foreign governments.

Some of the usual exemption provisions of treaties are noted below, but it is emphasised that each treaty must be looked at individually for its specific provisions.

Business profits

9.61 The profits of any business carried on by a resident of country A is taxable only in country A, unless the business is carried on in country B through a permanent establishment (a fixed place of business, eg a branch, office, factory or mine) in country B. Where this is the case, the profits of the business are taxable in country B, but only to the extent that those profits are attributable to the permanent establishment.

Shipping, inland waterways and air transport

9.62 Profits from the operation of ships, aircraft or inland waterways transport are taxable only in the country in which the place of effective management of the relevant enterprise is situated.

Interest, dividends, royalties, non-government pensions

9.63 Interest, dividends, patent and copyright royalties, and non-government pensions are often taxable only in the country of residence or are taxed at a reduced rate in the other country. Recipients of dividends are often entitled to a proportion of the tax credit to which a UK resident would have been entitled. Where a tax credit on a dividend is to be determined subject to a deduction based on the aggregate of the dividend plus the tax credit, the deduction is calculated on the gross amount of the dividend and the tax credit, without any allowance for the deduction itself.

From April 2008, provided certain conditions are met, dividends from non-UK companies will be given the same notional tax credit that is currently afforded for dividends paid by UK companies. This will mean that no additional tax liability will arise for basic rate taxpayers, and an additional 25% on the net dividend will arise for a higher rate taxpayer.

Professional services

9.64 The income of a person in respect of professional services is generally only taxable in the country in which he is resident, unless he has a fixed base regularly available to him in the other country for the purpose of providing his services. However, actors, musicians and athletes are generally liable to tax in both countries.

Salaries and wages

9.65 Most salaries and wages are generally taxable only in the country of residence unless the employment is exercised in the other country, in which case income derived from such employment is also taxable in the other country. However, usually the treaty will contain a provision that the salary etc is only taxable in the country of residence if:

- the taxpayer is present in the other country for an aggregate period not exceeding 183 days in the relevant tax year;
- the salary etc is paid by, or on behalf of, an employer who is not resident in the other country; and
- the payments are not borne by a permanent establishment which the employer has in the other country.

However, actors, musicians and athletes are generally liable to tax in the country in which they perform.

Government salaries and pensions

9.66 Government pensions, salaries etc are generally taxable only in the country responsible for paying the pensions, salaries etc. However, the income is only taxable in the other country if the services are rendered in that country and the taxpayer is resident in, or is a citizen of, that country.

Teachers and researchers

9.67
Under some DTAs, teachers or professors who come to the UK to teach in schools, colleges, universities or other educational establishments for a period of two years or less can be treated as exempt from UK tax on their earnings from the teaching post. Temporary absences from the UK during this period normally count as part of the two years.

Some DTAs also cover individuals who engage in research. In such cases, the rules are normally the same as for teachers.

Where an individual covered by the exemption stays for more than two years, the exemption does not apply and they will be liable to UK tax on the whole of their earnings from the date of arrival in the UK. Some agreements only allow exemptions to be given if the earnings are liable to tax in the individual's home country.

In addition, where exemption has been granted for a visit (or visits) of up to two years, some DTAs do not allow further exemption for visits made at a later date.

Students and apprentices

9.68 Most DTAs allow overseas students or apprentices visiting the UK solely for full-time education or training exemption from UK income tax on payments from sources outside the UK for maintenance, education or training. A number of DTAs also provide that students or apprentices visiting the UK will be exempt from UK tax on certain earnings from employment here. Individual agreements impose various restrictions on this relief, including, for example, monetary limits and conditions as to the type of employment.

Entertainers, sportsmen and sportswomen

9.69 Under most DTAs, if an individual who is not resident in the UK comes to the UK as an entertainer, sportsman or sportswoman, any payments received will be liable to UK tax. This includes actors and musicians performing on stage or screen and those participating in all kinds of sports.

Personal allowances and reliefs

9.70 Many double tax agreements provide that individuals who are resident in country A are entitled to the same personal allowances, reliefs, and deductions for the purposes of tax in country B as subjects of country B who are not resident in that country.

Often, the double taxation agreement will exclude entitlement to the personal allowances etc where the income consists solely of dividends, interest or royalties.

To ensure compliance with certain aspects of the *Human Rights Act 1998*, legislation is contained in *FA 2009*, effective from 6 April 2010, which withdraws the entitlement for non-resident individuals who currently qualify for UK personal tax allowances and reliefs solely by virtue of being a Commonwealth citizen (*FA 2009, Sch 1*). Whilst the vast majority of individuals affected will still benefit through other means such as double taxation treaties, citizens of Bahamas, Cameroon, Cook Islands, Dominica, Maldives, Mozambique, Nauru, Niue, St Lucia, St Vincent & the Grenadines, Samoa, Tanzania, Tonga, and Vanuatu may be affected.

Calculation of double tax credit relief available

9.71 In many cases, double tax agreements provide that where there is no deduction or exemption from UK tax, credit is to be given for any foreign tax which is paid and which corresponds to income tax whilst similar credit is given by 'unilateral relief'; this reduces the amount of UK tax chargeable except in certain cases where a non-resident company is connected with a state or province of a foreign territory which operates a 'unitary tax' regime. In general, a claim for relief by way of credit for foreign tax must be made within the period ending four years following the end of the tax year within which the income falls to be charged to tax (*TMA 1970, s 43*).

Taxpayers who have claimed relief for foreign tax must notify HMRC if there is an adjustment to the amount of foreign tax and the relief claimed has become excessive as a consequence. For trades, professions and vocations, there are special rules relating to the years of commencement and cessation.

An overseas dividend manufacturer may have his right to double tax relief restricted, in particular, in respect of tax credits on overseas dividends received when the tax credits have been offset against tax due on manufactured overseas dividends paid, or when the overseas dividends have been effectively paid on to a non-resident.

Where no credit is allowable, the foreign tax may be deducted. A person may elect that any treaty provision giving credit is ignored.

From April 2008, provided certain conditions are met, dividends from non-UK companies will be given the same notional tax credit that is currently afforded for dividends paid by UK companies. This will mean that no additional tax liability will arise for basic rate taxpayers, and an additional 25% on the net dividend will arise for a higher rate taxpayer.

TAX PLANNING – FOREIGN ASPECTS

Introduction

9.72 This section takes a brief look at planning issues for foreign nationals working in the UK and for British citizens going abroad.

For foreign nationals coming to the UK, it is assumed that the individuals are not domiciled in the UK and, in the case of employees, it is further assumed that they are employed by non-resident employers so that their earnings qualify as chargeable overseas earnings (*ITEPA 2003, s 23(2)*).

Large numbers of British citizens now go to live abroad for various periods of time and for various reasons. Since tax is territorial, there will inevitably be tax considerations and it is always best to plan well in advance of departure.

Residence

9.73 The key to most tax planning issues for income tax purposes will centre on residence status, so it is imperative to get this right from the outset of any transaction. It should be born in mind that any person who spends six months or longer in the UK in the tax year in question will be regarded as resident in the UK for that year and will subsequently be taxed under UK tax law. In calculating the six-month period, days and hours are taken into consideration. One is still resident in the UK if one's residence abroad is temporary. It is possible to be resident in more than one country at any one time.

Once there has been a finding that a taxpayer is resident in the UK, then he is treated as resident for the whole of that tax year. HMRC, however, by concession will allow a tax year to be split so that a taxpayer will be treated as resident in the UK for only part of that tax year in certain circumstances – see **9.2** above.

Working in the UK

9.74 Emoluments of foreign nationals working in the UK are calculated under the normal charging provisions of *ITEPA 2003* – this includes charges arising on benefits in kind. Apart from the travelling expense rules already mentioned, expenses are deductible only according to the normal test of being wholly, exclusively and necessarily incurred in the performance of the duty of the employment. Pension contributions to an approved scheme are deductible, but the pension will be taxed when received, and, being UK source income, will remain permanently liable to UK income tax. Pensions paid on behalf of a foreign employer are not liable to UK tax.

It used to be possible for a UK-resident individual to obtain a deduction of 100% against earnings from abroad if they related to a period of absence of 365 days, even if those days did not include one complete income tax year. The deduction has been abolished for all qualifying periods beginning after 17 March 1998 except for seafarers (see **5.110**). An individual who is abroad for one complete tax year will, of course, not be resident. There were detailed rules for calculating days of absence, which could include weekends and rest days and travelling time. Careful planning was required to attract the 100% deduction.

Many international employers operate tax equalisation schemes, also known as tax protected pay or net pay. It is an arrangement that ensures that an employee has the same take home pay wherever employed. Payments under these schemes are taxable. Golden handshakes are also taxable but, in addition to the general £30,000 allowance, substantial foreign service may give a full or further partial exemption.

Where there is a difference in treatment between UK earnings and overseas earnings two separate contracts, one for UK and the other for foreign duties, are desirable. The contracts must be with separate employers, as it is not possible to have two contracts of employment with the same employer. The use of two contracts allows the employer to specify that the foreign duties attract a higher rate of remuneration.

9.75 *Non-residents*

The following points may be considered by a foreign national taking up employment in the UK:

- Relief under a double tax treaty or exemption from UK tax may be obtained if the visitor is considered non-UK resident in any year and meets certain other treaty conditions.
- A claim for allowances on arrival in the UK may avoid the withholding of excessive PAYE deductions.
- The length of an employment arrangement is crucial in claiming non-ordinary residence status. A contract of employment or letter from a foreign employer specifying the intended length of assignment can assist greatly.

Working overseas

9.75 To achieve the most favourable tax treatment, it is essential to obtain detailed local advice on the tax system of the host country, and careful consideration of the double taxation agreement, where such an agreement exists. Many countries have more burdensome tax regimes than the UK. Historically, the traditional approach of UK tax advisers has been to try and minimise liability to UK taxes. However, while the UK's income tax rates remain some the lowest in Europe, advisers may wish to consider whether it might be better to maximise that proportion of their clients' income over which the UK has sole taxing rights.

For planning purposes, the following points may be worth consideration:

- Advance planning is essential – the tax considerations of any proposed transaction should be considered well in advance of departure from the UK.
- HMRC booklet HMRC6 is a useful reference guide.
- A detailed knowledge of the local tax system of host country is desirable.
- Consider timing and duration of visits to UK to avoid being classed as resident in a tax year if at all possible.
- The UK currently has comparably low income tax rates. In attempting to mitigate a liability to UK income tax, check that that same income is not liable to a higher rate in the host country.
- Aim to minimise pre-return income when returning to UK.
- Consider interaction of income tax and capital gains tax – conflicts may arise.

Guidance on residence

9.76 The HMRC website has much useful guidance on residence, ordinary residence, domicile and other aspects relating to international taxation. Readers may find the following links useful:

Residence and domicile issues	www.hmrc.gov.uk/cnr/residencedomicile.htm
HMRC6: Residence, domicile and the remittance basis	www.hmrc.gov.uk/cnr/hmrc6.pdf
Income tax when arriving in the UK	www.hmrc.gov.uk/cnr/faq-resdom.htm
Income tax when leaving the UK	www.hmrc.gov.uk/incometax/tax-leave-uk.htm
Tax on foreign savings and investment income	www.hmrc.gov.uk/taxon/foreign.htm
Frequently asked questions for non residents	www.hmrc.gov.uk/cnr/faqs_general.htm
Residence and domicile – guidance on the tax rules introduced by *FA 2009*	www.hmrc.gov.uk/cnr/faq-resdom.htm
Residence and domicile – guidance on the tax rules introduced by *FA 2008*	www.hmrc.gov.uk/cnr/res-dom-tax-amends.htm

Chapter 10

Income tax: planning considerations

INTRODUCTION

10.1 Proper tax and financial planning can lower and defer a liability to income tax, freeing up cash for investment, business or personal purposes. However, whilst the tax implications of any planned investments should play an important part in investment strategy, no transaction should be undertaken purely for tax reasons. The wider financial aspects must also be carefully considered, especially where its value represents a large part of the family fortunes or where it provides a livelihood for one or more members of the family.

The most basic form of year-end planning often involves pushing tax bills into the future by deferring income into the next year and accelerating deductions into the current year.

INDIVIDUALS

10.2 The following points may be considered by taxpayers before the end of each tax year to help minimise their annual liability to income tax:

- Ensure that personal allowances and basic rate bands are fully utilised. Using personal allowances and basic rate bands may seem an obvious point, but is surprisingly frequently missed. Unused allowances are not available to be carried forward, so it is important to ensure that they are utilised each year. Simple planning can be applied, such as changing ownership of assets or creating an employment. However, care is needed to escape the anti-avoidance legislation.
- Ensure that tax is being paid at the lowest rate on investment income. If a spouse, or civil partner, pays tax at a different rate, consider transferring income-producing assets to give the income to the person paying at the lower rate.
- Tax-efficient investments are covered in detail in **Chapter 3**. However, as a general point, a review of bank and building society accounts should

be made before the tax year end. Many people still have large sums of cash in ordinary accounts paying very little interest when they could be earning over 5% gross interest from specialist accounts. Make sure that ISA allowances have been fully utilised for all the family.

- For 2010/11, the ISA subscription limit is £10,200 for everyone, up to £5,100 of which can be saved in cash. The overall investment limits on ISAs mean that a couple could save a substantial amount in tax-efficient savings accounts (see **3.26** for further commentary on ISAs).

- Regular sums can be invested in National Savings (some products offer a tax-free return, which is particularly attractive to 40% and 50% taxpayers), banks and building societies (see **3.28**). Those willing to accept the possibility of greater risk perhaps equalling greater reward might consider the stock market, stock market-linked investments or buy-to-let property.

- Ensure that adequate pension contributions have been made. Paying pension contributions can currently give tax relief at the maximum income tax rate of up to 40%.

- Consider paying into pensions for family members. The introduction of stakeholder pensions allow contributions to be made for all UK residents, even children, as there is no requirement to have any earnings. Consider making payments of up to £3,600 for family members, as the fund will grow in a tax-free environment. The net cost is only £2,880 for 2008/09 onwards.

- Take advantage of tax exemptions. Everyone has a yearly capital gains exemption. In 2010/11 the exemption is £10,100, and gains up to this figure can be made without tax. Taxpayers should therefore consider realising gains from investments up to this figure. Gifts between spouses and civil partners are tax free, so it is possible to double the yearly exemptions available by giving shares or other investments to a spouse or civil partner.

- Realise losses. With regards to shares standing at a loss, consideration should be given to selling them so that the loss can be set against any gains made over and above the capital gains annual exemption. If the taxpayer wishes to retain the investment, it could be bought back by the spouse or partner, within an ISA. It will not be tax effective for the taxpayer to buy back the investment, unless he or she waits for 30 days before doing so. In addition, care must be taken not to fall foul of anti-avoidance legislation which prevents loss relief being claimed where certain arrangements exist, the main purpose, or one of the main purposes, of which is to secure a tax advantage (*FA 2007, s 27*).

- Capital gains tax may be deferred through the use of an Enterprise Investment Scheme investment (see **3.37**).

- Making charitable donations via the Gift Aid scheme is an effective way to reduce taxable income. If donations have been made, it is important that the taxpayer has ticked for Gift Aid so that the charity can benefit from the basic rate tax relief. Higher rate taxpayers should make the necessary claim on their tax return for further relief. If future donations are planned, the taxpayer may wish to bring these forward to before 5 April to ensure the tax relief is obtained at an earlier date.
- Employees should check that their PAYE tax code number for the following tax year is correct and ensure that any inaccuracies are amended.

MINIMISING THE ADDITIONAL RATE OF TAX – 2010/11 ONWARDS

10.3 From 2010/11, in addition to the 50% rate, the clawback of the personal allowance where income exceeds £100,000 means that there is an effective 60% marginal rate of tax on income between £100,000 and approximately £112,000. Furthermore, there is the prospect of a marginal 1% National Insurance charge, rising to 1.5% from April 2011, on employment and business income, leading to a maximum rate of 61.5% in some cases.

Many businesses will already be suffering the 50% tax rate on their profits, particularly if they have an accounting date early in the tax year. These businesses need to consider their future business structure carefully, and possibly use companies to run all of the business or be a partner. Given the current corporation tax marginal rate of 29.5%, consideration might also be given to changing the accounting date to get the best possible result.

Opportunities for careful planning of income and reliefs exist at the margins. For example, making a Gift Aid payment could drop taxable income below the £150,000 threshold and permit higher rate tax relief on pension contributions.

BUSINESSES

10.4 The following points may be considered by businesses before the end of each tax year to help minimise their annual liability to income tax:

- An annual investment allowance (AIA) applies from 2008/09. This was worth £50,000 for 2008/09 and 2009/2010 and has been increased to £100,000 for 2010/11. However, from 1 April 2012 the AIA is set to drop to £25,000. The allowance is available for expenditure on qualifying plant and machinery of small and medium-sized businesses (see **6.55**). This means that businesses will receive immediate relief for their qualifying expenditure. The timing of expenditure will be important to ensure that relief is received sooner rather than later, where appropriate.

- If it is usual practice for the company to pay bonuses to directors or dividends to shareholders, careful consideration should be given as to whether payment should be made before or after the end of the tax year. This will affect the payment date for any tax and may affect the rate at which it is payable. Remember that any bonuses must be paid within nine months of the company's year end to ensure tax relief for the company in that period.
- Where there are beneficial loans made to office-holders and employees, these should be reviewed prior to the end of the tax year and accounting year to minimise income tax, national insurance and corporation tax.
- Where remuneration can be justified, it may be beneficial to make payments to a spouse or other family members to reduce the overall tax and national insurance liability.
- Review timing of disposal and acquisition of business assets to minimise tax or obtain tax deferral.
- Deferment of Class 2 and 4 National Insurance contributions should be obtained if Class 1 contributions will be paid on employment income.
- Employers may consider making tax-free gifts to staff, including:
  - *Long service awards*. Broadly, there will be no tax charge so long as the employee has been employed for at least 20 years and the article given has a value not exceeding £50 for each year of service.
  - *Suggestion scheme awards*. Such awards must be made under a properly constituted suggestion scheme, based on a set percentage of the expected financial benefit to your business. The maximum award allowed is £5,000. There is also a concession for 'encouragement awards' of £25 or less to reflect meritorious effort on the part of the employee concerned.
  - *Staff functions*. Staff annual functions (eg a dinner dance or Christmas party) are tax free where the total cost per person attending is not more than £150 per year (including VAT).
  - *Promotional gifts*. Such items are normally purchased for advertising purposes and must display a 'conspicuous advertisement'. Staff may receive promotional gifts tax free provided that the overall cost of the articles involved does not exceed £50 per person per year. Gifts of food, drink, tobacco or vouchers are specifically excluded.
- If it is expected that profits from a business will be below the small earnings exception (£5,075 in 2009/10 and 2010/11), exception from payment of Class 2 contributions can be applied for.

- Employers should review dispensations for items normally declared on form P11D.
- Employers should check procedures for year-end payroll returns as deadlines will approach after 5 April.

NATIONAL INSURANCE CONTRIBUTIONS

10.5 The following points may be considered by employers wishing to mitigate NICs:

- Increases in the amount the employer contracts to contribute to company pension schemes.
- Share incentive plans (shares bought out of pre-tax and pre-NIC income).
- Small companies may consider disincorporation and instead operate as a sole trader or partnership.
- Reduction in salary and increase in bonus to reduce employee (not director) contributions.
- Payment of dividends instead of bonuses to owner-directors.
- Provision of childcare.

TRUSTS

10.6 Trusts will find that they will be paying 50% income tax from April 2010 on most of their income unless they are 'life interest' trusts. Even higher rates than 50% may apply if trusts receive dividend income that is fully distributed. Trustees need to consider their position, particularly with regard to future investment policy, and time the distribution of funds to beneficiaries carefully. In some cases, trustees might consider the winding up of trusts (or converting to life interest trusts) to use the lower rate tax bands of beneficiaries. Trusts still have their uses to protect family wealth and avoid capital taxation.

Discretionary trustees, who face the punitive 50% rate on virtually all their income, should seriously consider giving one or more beneficiaries an entitlement to receive the trust income (known as an 'interest in possession'), in which event the 50% will not apply at the trust level. Any such appointment may be revocable at any time, so that the trust can revert to discretionary nature if the trustees so decide at some future time.

Index

[All references are to paragraph number]

U

V